The Trouble with Ownership

MATERIAL TEXTS

A complete list of books in the series is available from the publisher.

The Trouble with Ownership

Literary Property and Authorial Liability in England, 1660–1730

Jody Greene

PENN

University of Pennsylvania Press
Philadelphia

Printed in the United States of America on acid-free paper

10 9 8 7 6 5 4 3 2 1

Published by
University of Pennsylvania Press
Philadelphia, Pennsylvania 19104-4112

Library of Congress Cataloging-in-Publication Data

Greene, Jody.
The trouble with ownership : literary property and authorial liability in England, 1660–1730 / Jody Greene.
p. cm. — (Material texts)
Includes bibliographical references and index.
ISBN 0-8122-3862-1 (cloth : alk. paper)
1. English literature—Early modern, 1500–1700—History and criticism. 2. Liability (Law)—Great Britain—History—17th century. 3. Liability (Law)—Great Britain—History—18th century. 4. English literature—18th century—History and criticism. 5. Copyright—England—History—17th century. 6. Copyright—England—History—18th century. 7. Authorship—History—17th century. 8. Authorship—History—18th century. I. Title. II. Series.

PR431.G69 2005
820.9'3554'09032—dc22

2004061224

For Carla

Contents

Je ne considère pas qu'il soit d'aucune façon légitime d'avoir écrit que les structures ne descendent pas dans la rue, parce que, s'il y a quelque chose que démontrent les événements de mai [1968], c'est précisément la descente dans la rue des structures. Le fait qu'on l'écrive à la place même où s'est opérée cette descente dans la rue ne prouve rien d'autre que, simplement, ce qui est très souvent, et même le plus souvent, interne à ce qu'on appelle l'acte, c'est qu'il se méconnait lui-même.

—Jacques Lacan, 1969, responding to Foucault's "Qu'est-ce qu'un auteur?"

Introduction

A new historical understanding of print is needed. What will it look like? One immediately evident feature will be its regard for the labors of those actually involved in printing, publishing, and reading. Another will be its respect for their own representations of printing, embracing both its prospects and dangers. The dangers in particular will loom larger and more substantial than they have hitherto. Historians tend to disregard such perils as accidental. Early modern readers and writers knew otherwise.

—*Adrian Johns,* The Nature of the Book

The story of modern, proprietary authorship is by now a familiar one. In the English context, it goes something like this: the period from 1660 to 1800 saw an explosion in new opportunities for authors unparalleled in the history of authorship. Increases in literacy, the growth of cities, falling paper prices, the influx of international commercial capital, the end of prepublication censorship, and above all, the newfound willingness of authors to make their work public transformed British literary culture from a courtly coterie into a thriving marketplace. In addition to these expanding material, commercial, and cultural opportunities, authors for the first time found themselves endowed with rights. A notion of literary property emerged in this period that transformed the relation between author and work, in the words of Mark Rose, into one of "proprietorship."[1] Authorial copyright, albeit in a most rudimentary fashion, was codified for the first time in the "Copyright Act" of 1710, in a move that established the author, in Rose's formulation, as "a legally empowered figure in the marketplace" (4).

The Act for the Encouragement of Learning, as the Copyright Act was formally known, has been described by recent commentators as a kind of historical accident, "an entirely contingent means," in the words of David Saunders and Iain Hunter, "of regulating the unstable technical, economic, and cultural capacities created by a new apparatus of literary production."[2] The act, they write, was only tangentially designed to address the needs and rights of authors, and offered little more than a "makeshift solution" to a whole range of commercial and legal problems confronting the print trade and the authorities who took it upon themselves to oversee that trade (485).

Nonetheless, the act had profound effects on the practice of authorship, in addition to its effect on the organization of the trade as a whole.[3] In the first place, the act was important because it conceived of an author's primary—even aboriginal—relation to his or her work as a matter of ownership. Although the nature of the proprietary relationship is never spelled out in the act, the phrase "Proprietor or Proprietors" stands in, after the opening lines, for the author, as well as for the printers, booksellers, and others whose interests might be covered under its provisions. Living authors were henceforth considered to have control over their property, in the form of an exclusive right to determine who was to copy the work. This right was alienable for a fixed term, no longer passing to the buyer in perpetuity.[4] Authors were permitted to retain the right to control the reproduction of their works as long as they could afford to publish without the aid of a third party to put forward the printing costs and act as an intermediary with the book trade. Should the author find it necessary to sell or otherwise part with this copyright, however, he or she could assign it to anyone—not only, as had previously been the case, to a member of the Stationers' Guild. This single change in the law may have had the greatest effect on the organization of the book trade, as Lyman Ray Patterson remarks in *Copyright in Historical Perspective.* "The radical change in the statute," he writes, "was not that it gave authors the right to acquire a Copyright—a prerogative until then limited to members of the Stationers' Company—but that it gave that right to all persons."[5] Henceforth the company's monopoly on the trade in printed materials would be broken, although company members continued to wield significant commercial weight throughout the eighteenth century. Moreover, although it remained the norm for most authors to sell their copyright, since most did not have access to the means of printing and publishing their own works, it was tempting for authors to try to eliminate the publisher's potentially lucrative role in this process, whether by keeping the copyright themselves or by attempting to reassign the right to a member of the trade willing to share the profits more equally than the traditional stationer. This, as later chapters show, was a favored strategy of that great authorial innovator Alexander Pope and also of his unlikely comrade-in-arms, John Gay.

Yet authors quickly found that the Copyright Act had consequences not only for authorial rights but also for authorial liability. The lapse of the Licensing Act in 1695 had left something of a vacuum in the enforcement of press regulation. Although the licensing system had been only haphazardly effective in its final decades, and although the law regarding postpublication crimes such as libel and sedition remained unchanged, the absence of prepublication oversight made illicit, antigovernment publishing easier than it had been under the watchful eye of the licenser.[6] In particular, it allowed for the rapid growth of periodical literature, including newspapers and weekly gazettes and reviews, the control of which preoccupied the government consistently from 1695 until the passage of a tax on periodicals in 1712.[7] Above all, the disappearance of a centralized regulatory authority threatened to let forth a flood of wholly anonymous works—works with no information whatsoever on their title pages—as well as those sporting false imprints misidentifying the author, printer, bookseller, place of publication, and/or date of release.[8] While all of these features could be falsified under the prior system, doing so was more difficult when a figure like Roger L'Estrange, with his own intimate knowledge of the ways of the trade, was at work surveying the press on a daily basis, as he was from 1663 until he was finally relieved of his duties in 1688.[9]

Until the lapse of the Licensing Act, the stationers—with the help of government appointees such as L'Estrange—had been responsible for both the commercial and the ideological regulation of the book business, in a systematic trade-off of rights and responsibilities that had been in effect since the charter of the Stationers' Company in 1557. After 1695, and especially after 1710, however, these two functions—call them *copyright* and *censorship*, though neither term is satisfactory for covering the range of proprietary and regulatory interests described in this volume—were now no longer carried out by one centralized body, but were instead, at least according to almost all recent commentators, split off from each other. Rose goes so far as to argue that "the passage of the Act marked the divorce of copyright from censorship" (48). In so doing, he joins a long line of those who have seen in the relationship between these two regulatory functions an unhappy family romance. Rose himself describes the relationship between "censorship and trade regulation" after 1557 as a "marriage" (13). During the seventeenth century, he continues, they began to effect a "separation" that was made complete only in the divorce of 1710 (16). Fredrick Seaton Siebert takes the familial metaphor further by noting that the putative split left "progeny"—children of divorce—in the form of the generations of copyright legislation extending into the present: "Henceforth the protection of property rights in printed matter was divorced completely from any attempts at control of the content or quality of such printed matter. The sire of the Act of 8 Anne was the Printing Act of 1662; its progeny, the series of copyright acts in England and the U.S."[10] Siebert's reproductive formulation at least has the benefit of making it possible to postulate, through a kind of genetic analogy, the persistence of ideological regulation in intellectual property law. If the Licensing Act of 1662 truly spawned the Act of Anne, then some resemblance between the "sire" and his offspring should be visible, some trace of copyright's roots in censorship still left for historians to follow.

Historians, however, have been resistant to recognizing the persistence of ideological regulation in authorship's new proprietary formation. Without exception, in fact, scholars of the book have declined to acknowledge what all early modern commentators on the topic, whatever their political stripe, took for granted: that "owning" one's book was synonymous with owning up to it, and that literary property was thus inseparable from regulation. In the words of Daniel Defoe, whose 1704 *Essay on the Regulation of the Press* makes an argument for authorial property rights that is grounded in assumptions about authorial liability, "'Twould be unaccountably severe to make a Man answerable for the Miscarriages of a thing which he shall not reap the Benefit of."[11] Authors, Defoe insists, in a battle he would ultimately lose, should be required to set their names to their works not only to put a stop to the "licentious Extravagance of Authors" (3) but also to record their "undoubted exclusive Right of Property" to their books (21). Even if compulsory authorial imprints remained undesirable to his contemporaries in the book trade, however, Defoe's recommendations concerning the compatibility of censorship and copyright would ultimately find their way into the Act of Anne, which continued the longstanding regulatory practice of balancing rights and responsibilities in matters related to the press.

To claim responsibility for a work after 1710 was not only to advance a proprietary claim, this book argues, but also to admit liability for its contents. Insofar as the Act of Anne constituted a method for keeping track of those responsible for literary works, it also put into effect a system of recording liability for them. Specifically, the act made a provision for continued oversight of the press, in its recommendation that all works should be entered in the Stationers' Register prior to publication, despite the fact that the stationers no longer held their traditional monopoly over the trade. Ostensibly, the Act of Anne was designed to put a stop to the piracy of literary works. In order to be able to combat such piracy, it was necessary to devise a means of recording who held copyright in a literary work, when that copyright was assigned, and for how long it was guaranteed. The drafters of the act turned to the Stationers' Register to fulfill this recording function: "The Register was to be the official record of copy ownership," John Feather writes, "and entry was, apparently, to be required as a precondition of claiming and defending rights."[12] Entry was not to be compulsory for all works, as it had been in the past;

rather, it was necessary for anyone who wanted to guard their proprietary interests against competitors. Entry, that is, seems to have been designed to protect rather than to regulate authors and other holders of copyright.

Yet almost by accident the statute succeeded in installing a form of press regulation, even if it did not address itself directly to the question of crimes and punishments. Authors, as Pope's case amply demonstrates, considered a claim to copyright to be a sure means of tracing responsibility for a literary work, especially a literary work that might by its very nature be deemed dangerous or legally actionable. In keeping with the provisions of the act, the authorities need only turn to the register to find a record of the transfer of "the Title" to any book published after the act went into effect. Included in this entry must be the "Consent of the Proprietor"—which is to say, in nearly all cases, of the author—for this transfer of title.[13] The requirement of authorial consent, ostensibly designed to combat piracy for all those in the book trade and to protect the proprietary rights of authors, thus acted equally effectively as a means of controlling authors. Claiming and defending rights required authors to assume obligations as well; owning one's book could just as easily be construed as a confession of responsibility. The new benefits attached to authorship did not come without a cost, then, as authors found themselves subject to liabilities that made their profession as hazardous as it was newly lucrative.

The experience of individual authors who tried to use the Act of Anne to their own advantage—authors such as Pope and Gay—also suggests that whether or not the act was intended to further the cause of press regulation, it succeeded in doing so. In fact, the provision concerning entry in the register remedied the greatest single problem that had faced would-be controllers of the English press for more than fifty years: the difficulty of finding and holding liable the authors of printed works, rather than their more easily located printers and distributors. These members of the book trade leave material traces of their participation, while authors, especially careful ones, do not. As L'Estrange attested in his 1663 tract, *Considerations and Proposals in Order to the Regulation of the Press,* "Touching the *Adviser, Author, Compiler, Writer,* and *Correcter,* their Practices are hard to be Retriev'd."[14] Or, in the words of Chief Justice Scroggs in the 1680 trial of Henry Carr, accused of writing and publishing a libelous pamphlet, "It is hard to find the Author, it is not hard to find the Printer: But *one Author* found, is better than *twenty Printers* found."[15] The Act of Anne made finding the author—retrieving his or her practices—not only possible but virtually infallible. It did so not by inventing new means of tracking down authors but instead by encouraging authors, in effect, to give themselves up voluntarily. By holding out the incentive of literary property and its attendant benefits, the Act of Anne succeeded—as 150 years of legislation and royal prerogative had not—in luring authors into owning their part in what was still, in 1710, a surprisingly risky business.

Authorship and the History of the Book

Readers familiar with the field of book history, as well as the history of authorship, will already have noted the degree to which the project of this book runs counter to current trends in both of these fields. Much of the work of the past two decades has been devoted to unseating the author from his place at the center of the history of the book—a liberal, masculinist, individualist history, these critiques contend, which, at least in its earliest formulations, failed to do justice both to the actual structure of the book trade in early modern England and to the contributions of the many individuals involved at all levels of that trade. In particular, as scholars like Paula McDowell and Marcus Nevitt have shown, a myopic attention to authors in the history of printed works has left the role of women in the early modern book and pamphlet trade almost entirely unwritten. At the same time, it has erased the contributions of working men and women to the early development of literate culture—a point most compellingly made by Adrian Johns in his revolutionary study, *The Nature of the Book.*[16] Through the work of scholars such as these, what might have remained a problem in the local history of the book thus becomes part of a larger problem in early modern social history, including both women's history and the history of the working classes. In these invaluable studies, the entire industry devoted to what is currently called *knowledge production* is reconceived as a collaborative, collective, frequently anonymous project.

In her influential reconstruction of the workings of the London book trade after 1680, *The Women of Grub Street,* McDowell insists that she is proposing nothing less than "a new model for the study of the literary marketplace as a whole" (12). In specifying what exactly is new about her model of print historiography, she singles out the author as the figure for everything that is wrong with the older model she hopes to displace:

> Authors who print their writings are not the only labourers involved in the production of their texts; nor can authors be understood in isolation from the publishing institutions within which they work. Twentieth-century literary critics' interest in

> bourgeois subjectivity and the rise of individualism has meant that dominant literary critical models emphasize individuals (especially authors). But traditional "man-and-his-work" approaches, with their post-Romantic emphasis on individual authors, are not the most useful models for the study of non-élite men's and women's involvement in the print marketplace. This is especially true of literature in politically tumultuous periods, when authors, publishers, and other printworkers often worked closely together. (12)

There is no question that McDowell is correct on all counts—correct about the near exclusive focus that early literary historians placed on authorial individualism; correct about the collective responsibility for printed works in all periods, but especially in "tumultuous" periods such as the one that followed the Restoration of Charles II; and correct about the way in which a focus on the author masks the participation of all sorts of historically invisible cultural laborers, not only in making books but also in making meaning in early modern England. If anything, McDowell here speaks in too limited terms of the stakes of her project, for it is surely not only those interested in "the study of non-élite men's and women's" roles in print culture who stand to benefit from the recognition that the author is not a singular individual with sole power to determine meaning through autonomous acts of literary creation. The author, as Nevitt notes in an influential article on women and early newspapers, is only one figure in the "collective enterprise" of early modern publishing, and to recognize him—or her—as such is to remake not only the history of the book trade but also cultural history as a whole (87).

As Nevitt goes on to specify, condensing the insights of McDowell's longer study, this collective characteristic of the book trade had notable consequences for questions of liability and accountability, especially in periods when dangerous books were being produced and circulated.[17] "Th[e] overlap between authorship, publishing, and printing," he writes, had both economic and legal consequences, since "whilst costs could be cut, it also made the job of a censor or licenser more difficult" (86). Rather than being able to determine a single agent liable for any dangerous work, or even to identify the possessor of what Nevitt calls the original "seditious intention" (86), the licenser or other "censoring" agent was presented with a whole range of figures to whom partial liability could be attributed.[18] This proliferation of suspects meant more individuals to prosecute, more sites to keep under surveillance, and more possible lightning rods for the mobilization of public sympathy—a lament taken up by L'Estrange in his *Considerations* and throughout his career. Wherever possible, government forces tried to be frugal with their labor by centering liability for a printed work in one figure—most frequently, in any person whose name could be positively linked to that work, regardless of "seditious intention." In most cases, this meant that the printer or publisher was subject to prosecution, rather than the author, since it was those agents whose names appeared on the title page of virtually every work that came off the presses in the early modern period. Nevitt thus concludes, after looking at a series of seventeenth-century seditious libel cases, "as it was the printer who affixed his/her name to frequently anonymous works, and was accordingly punished, it was printers who were frequently tarred with the brush of originative agency" (104 n.12).

Given my virtually complete agreement with the insights of McDowell, Nevitt, and critics like them committed to a better understanding of the workings of the early modern book trade in general, and the regulation of printed works in particular, it can only seem perverse to insist, nonetheless, that the figure of the author had not only a central place in the regulation of that trade but also a privileged one with relation to the trade's other members. The ability to make such a counterintuitive argument depends upon drawing a distinction between a set of material historical events—who actually produced printed works? Who faced indictments, prosecutions, and punishments as a result of those works?—and another kind of history, a history of the discourse surrounding responsibility for printed works, which tells a rather different tale both about attribution and about accountability. To study this alternative history is not in any way an attempt to resituate the author as the actual productive center of the history of the book; it is, instead, to offer a history of how the author came to be understood to occupy that cultural role in the first place.

As an initial step toward making clear what this alternative history might look like, it is instructive to return to the "new model" proposed by McDowell and elaborated by Nevitt. Nevitt identifies four features of the early modern book trade that made press regulation more complex than some later commentators have acknowledged. First, to recapitulate, rather than being attributable to a single individual, every work was a "collective enterprise." From this initial insight, the other three follow. Nevitt's second point is that collective agency made it more difficult to locate the possessor of the original "seditious intention." Third, anyone whose name could be directly associated with the work through an imprint—most often, the printer—was held liable for that work. Finally, in the most telling formulation of all, Nevitt concludes that whoever was punished for a printed work was "tarred with the brush of originative agency." Even as he demonstrates the failure of the law—as well as later historians—to do justice to the complexities of the print trade, Nevitt concisely articulates the presuppositions that grounded regulatory measures and subsequent histories, laying bare their circular logic. The person to whom responsibility for a printed work was attributed was an individual who could be linked to the work through the medium of a proper name, who could then be understood to be possessed of both an identifiable intention and an originative agency. We are accustomed to understanding these as the definitive attributes of the modern author. As Nevitt shows, however, before they were thus limited in their scope, these attributes could be applied to anyone in the book trade to whom responsibility for a printed work could be affixed and on whom punishment for that work could be exacted. As L'Estrange's *Considerations* puts it, "*let the* Person *in whose Posession* [an offending book] *is* found, *be Reputed, and Punish'd as the* Author *of the said Book, unless he* Produce *the Person, or Persons, from whom he receiv'd it*" (2). If signature, intention, origination, and now *possession* are the distinctive attributes of modern authorship, and if these attributes could be applied to anyone in the book trade, who would then be known by the name of "Author," then authorship comes to look more and more like a refinement in the mechanism for the regulation of printed books. As Rosemary Coombe puts it, "the figure of the author, or the role of the author-function, might be seen as that of an elite broker for the management of textuality."[19] In describing authorship in these terms, Coombe is making explicit the debt she shares with virtually all recent works on authorship, including this one: the debt to Michel Foucault's 1969 essay, "What Is an Author?," which for the first time attempted to bring together the theoretical notion of authorship as a proprietary relationship with that of authorship as a punitive regime.

Attribution, "Penal Appropriation," and the Consequences of Copyright

No work on the history of authorship has had more influence than Foucault's essay, which was originally given as a seminar at the Société française de Philosophie on 22 February 1969, and delivered the next year, in modified form, as a lecture in the United States.[20] Foucault's essay does not offer a "sociohistorical analysis" of authorship, although he does not dismiss the importance of such a project: "Certainly it would be worth examining how the author became individualized in a culture like ours, what status he has been given, at what moment studies of authenticity and attribution began, in what kind of system of valorization the author was involved, at what point we began to recount the lives of authors rather than of heroes, and how this fundamental category of 'the-man-and-his-work-criticism' began" (141). In some sense, this book attempts to offer one piece of such a sociohistorical analysis, with particular attention to the author's status and to his (or her) changing place in a system of "attribution," out of a conviction that through the process of attribution, the twin poles of modern authorship—ownership and liability—come together.

Yet Foucault's real innovation in the essay lies elsewhere, in his description of discourses as "objects of appropriation" (148). In attempting to describe why some forms of discourse have authors—why, that is, they are characterized by what Foucault calls an "author-function"—while others do not, he writes: "First of all, discourses are objects of appropriation. The form of ownership from which they spring is of a rather particular type, one that has been codified for many years. We should note that, historically, this type of ownership has always been subsequent to what one might call penal appropriation. Texts, books, and discourses, really began to have authors (other than mythical, 'sacralized,' and 'sacralizing' figures) to the extent that authors became subject to punishment, that is, to the extent that discourses could be transgressive" (148). At the outset, then, authorship for Foucault is a dangerous business, born of the need to find individuals responsible for "transgressive" cultural productions. In what might be seen as a paranoid theory of the etiology of authorship, Foucault emphasizes the historical priority of "penal appropriation" over the more recent forms of "ownership" that govern the relationships between authors and the "texts, books, and discourses" they produce. Anyone conducting the sort of sociohistorical study of authorship passed over by Foucault—exploring, for instance, as this book does, the rhetorics and regulations associated with printed works in early modern England—quickly finds that Foucault's chronology is quite persuasive. The author appears as a legal persona in English documents as the subject of regulation—and even of "penal appropriation"—long before that figure appears as the subject of a more positive form of "ownership" in 1710.

Where Foucault's discussion of the "author-function" produces some difficulty, however, is in assessing the relationship between chronology and causality. Foucault is clear that "penal appropriation" precedes the ownership of texts: the production of discourse, he writes, "was a gesture fraught with risks before becoming goods caught up in a circuit of ownership" (148). He is less explicit, however, about the exact relationship between these two dimensions of authorship after the advent of a notion of ownership of texts came into being. Indeed, rather than insisting that these two forms of "appropriation"—penal and proprietary—are coincident, or even related, he seems to suggest that the form of ownership that is codified in measures such as the Act of Anne *displaced* "penal appropriation," getting rid of the risks formerly associated with textual production. Evidence for this reading of Foucault's essay comes in a famous passage in which he singles out literature from other forms of discourse as the place where, in the new, more congenial world of literary property rights, authors can turn to regain some of the frisson they experienced under the earlier regime:

> Once a system of ownership for texts came into being . . . the possibility of transgression attached to the act of writing took on, more and more, the form of an imperative peculiar to literature. It is as if the author, beginning with the moment at which he was placed in the system of property that characterizes our society, compensated for the status that he thus acquired by rediscovering the old bipolar field of discourse, systematically practicing transgression and thereby restoring danger to a writing which was now guaranteed the benefits of ownership. (149)

According to this view of the history of texts and discourses—a view shared by most writers on copyright—the business of authorship became considerably less risky at the moment when property rights were written into law. *The Trouble with Ownership* contests this version of the history of authorship, arguing instead that if authorship had been "dangerous" in the era before authors were endowed with rights, it only became more so once they could be encouraged to step forward and take responsibility for their writings. If "penal appropriation" preceded proprietary authorship—that is, the obligations attached to ownership ensured that authors were still open to punishment for the effects of their works after they became capable of owning them—these punishments, moreover, at least in the opinion of eighteenth-century commentators, threatened to outweigh the "benefits" (the word is Defoe's as well as Foucault's) newly available to authors willing to take advantage of the "system of property."

The more that rigidly authorial property rights became recognized and then codified in law, this book argues, the more authors were exposed to penal effects. Owning one's work makes one subject to punishment not only because it makes it easier to trace texts back to their owners but also because authors who insist on a proprietary relation to their works are punishable for every subsequent, illicit appropriation to which their printed work is exposed. This point is most succinctly and humorously made by a less frequently mentioned theorist of authorship, Jacques Derrida, in his essay

"Limited Inc a b c." In this 1977 essay, Derrida offers a response to John R. Searle's "Reiterating the Differences," which was itself a response to Derrida's earlier "Signature, Event, Context."[21] In the course of his response to a response, Derrida offers an extended meditation on the relationship between writing and responsibility and, more specifically and significantly, between copyright and liability. In addition, he offers readers an opportunity, albeit a slightly elliptical and ironic one, to consider the desirability of proprietary authorship—a desirability taken for granted by historians in the liberal tradition for whom the advent of rights in any sphere of life, literary or otherwise, can only constitute a social good.

Derrida begins "Limited Inc a b c" by recounting that late in 1976—the date is important—he received a manuscript copy of Searle's essay in the mail. Two things about the manuscript—two marginal but nonetheless essential features—immediately jumped out. First, at the top left-hand corner of the manuscript, above the title, was the phrase "*Copyright © 1977 by John R. Searle*" (30). Second, at the end of the paper, Derrida found a note of acknowledgment, a note that read, "I am indebted to H. Dreyfus and D. Searle for discussion of these matters" (31). Derrida considers each of these statements—the statement of ownership and the statement of indebtedness—at some length, but, most presciently, he discusses in some detail what relationship might be said to exist between the two. He generously passes over—though not without noting it—the fact that since he has received the manuscript "shortly before Christmas, 1976," and since Searle's copyright asserts itself for the year 1977, it is not clear exactly what the status of that copyright might be at the time of the essay's arrival. Moreover, even if the date were not belated with relation to the time of the essay's circulation, Derrida poses a series of other questions that further destabilize Searle's insistent foregrounding of his authorship through the figure of copyright: "Does he make use of his rights to reply? Of his rights as an author? But what makes him think that these rights might be questioned, that someone might try to steal them from him, or that there could be any mistake concerning the attribution of his original production? How would this be possible? Can the thing be expropriated, alienated?" (30). Putting in question at the outset not only the status of authorial property rights but also the motivation behind claiming them in the first place, Derrida playfully signals to his readers—and, presumably, to Searle himself—some of the liabilities that attend every assertion of such rights. By drawing attention to his proprietary relation to his text, by insisting on his rights as an author "to the point of provoking suspicion," Searle is practically inviting readers to question him, to steal from him, and ultimately to expropriate his precious commodity (31).

This, in a manner of speaking, is exactly what Derrida goes on to do, although in doing so he is behaving more like Robin Hood than a common burglar. If the rights of an author purport to be a pure product of property and originality, as Derrida acknowledges that we understand them to be, then what are we to make of the "debts" to H. Dreyfus and D. Searle that John Searle acknowledges—but emphatically does not repay—at the end of his paper? Or rather, at the end of *the* paper, since it is not entirely clear, at this point in the investigation, *whose* paper, exactly, this is. Searle's? Which Searle's? Searles' and Dreyfus's? Derrida continues, "the debt includes my old friend H. Dreyfus, with whom I have also worked, discussed, exchanged ideas, so that if it is indeed through him that the Searles have 'read' me, 'understood' me, and 'replied' to me, then I, too, can claim a stake in the 'action' or 'obligation,' the stocks and bonds, of this holding company, the Copyright Trust. . . . 'I' therefore feel obliged to claim my share of the copyright of the *Reply*" (31). If this essay is John Searle's, it is also, by virtue of the many debts he has accumulated over the years, D. Searle's, H. Dreyfus's, and Jacques Derrida's as well. Derrida in fact feels so strongly about the importance of being precise about authorial rights—since, after all, Searle has brought them up in the first place—that he feels compelled to replace the name of the author, the authorial signature, with a more legally and ethically accurate formulation. The author of this text, he concludes, and the entity who deserves any rights accruing from the work, is "a more or less anonymous corporation (three + n authors)" (36).

> The expression "three + n authors" seems to me to be more rigorous for the reasons I have already stated, involving the difficulty I encounter in naming the definite origin, the true person responsible for the *Reply*; not only because of the debts acknowledged by John R. Searle *before even* beginning to reply, but because of the entire, more or less anonymous tradition of a code, a heritage, a reservoir of arguments to which both he and I are indebted. How is this more or less anonymous author to be named? In order to avoid the ponderousness of the scientific expression "three + n authors," I decide here and from this moment on to give the presumed and collective author of the *Reply* the French name "Société à responsabilité limitée"—literally, "Society with Limited Responsibility" (or Limited Liability)—which is normally abbreviated to Sarl. (36)

In this passage, Derrida for the first time in the essay explicitly addresses the question of responsibilities, which he, virtually alone among theorists of authorship, considers a necessary companion to the question of rights. Just as he has difficulty identifying the "definite origin" of the essay called "Reiterating the Differences," he finds himself unable, or perhaps unwilling, in a radical ethical gesture, to locate "the true person responsible for the *Reply*" either. He solves both of these problems at once by incorporating all those who might be entitled to a share in the essay—as well as those who might be liable for it—into the "more or less anonymous" entity called Sarl. This entity has limited liability for the essay—but limited how? Does each part of the entity have liability in proportion to his or her share in the origin? Since such shares can never truly be apportioned, however—since, that is, our textual and intellectual debts can never "truly" be acknowledged, let alone tallied and paid off—the authors will have to settle for collective or corporate attribution, a share in the profits, in exchange for which they are excused total or exclusive responsibility for the *Reply*.

Derrida concludes this section of the essay with some words of consolation for those addressees who may feel that they have lost something in this exchange. "I hope that the bearers of proper names will not be wounded by this technical or scientific device [three + n authors]. For it will have the supplementary advantage of enabling me to avoid offending individuals or proper names in the course of an argument that they might now and then consider, wrongly, to be polemical. And should they, perchance, see this transformation as an injurious or ironic alteration, they can at least join me in acknowledging the importance of the desires and fantasms that are at stake in a proper name, a copyright, or a signature" (36). Once again, Derrida, ever the dealer, offers Sarl a kind of trade-off. However much they may feel that they have lost by being absorbed into a collectivity for the purposes of attribution, however much they may feel that their proprietorship has been ironized, injured, and downright misappropriated, at least they will have the opportunity to sidestep any offense produced in the course of Derrida's remarks. They need not feel responsible for those things he takes issue with in "Reiterating the Differences." Since no one any longer "owns" this text, no one will be expected to answer for it.

In dissolving authorship into a corporate entity, Derrida is pursuing a strategy not unlike that undertaken by those recent historians of the book who have reread the print trade as a collaborative, collective, decentered enterprise, with no single governing consciousness. At the same time, he is (presumably unwittingly) mimicking those early modern authors who attempted to escape liability for their works by claiming that their works had been stolen by unscrupulous members of the trade, circulated by piratical printers and mischievous booksellers. He is, to return for a moment to

Foucault, refusing the attributes—both the benefits and the liabilities—that characterize modern authorship and distinguish it from the forms of attribution of texts associated with earlier eras.

In a related gesture at the end of "What Is an Author?," Foucault returns to the question of what he calls "the 'ideological' status of the author"—that is, the function the author fulfills in the regulation of all forms of expression. The author, Foucault writes, in a reversal of traditional understandings of authorship, is "a certain functional principle by which, in our culture, one limits, excludes, and chooses; in short, by which one impedes the free circulation" of ideas and expression (159). Rather than being a fountain—as Roger L'Estrange would put it—which is to say, a generative figure who "deposits, with infinite wealth and generosity, an inexhaustible world of significations" into a text, an author is a principle of limitation, "a principle of thrift" (159). Foucault concludes, "the author is therefore the ideological figure by which one marks the manner in which we fear the proliferation of meaning" (159). By understanding the Act of Anne, which definitively linked books to their authors under the law for the first time, as a response to this fear of proliferation of meaning, as well as a response to anxieties about the chaotic effects of commercial deregulation in the print trade, it is possible to see how ownership and liability came together in 1710. Proprietary authorship, in an unfortunate turn of events, made it possible for the first time to ensure an effective means of "penal appropriation." How authors recognized and responded to this change in their legal, cultural, and ideological status constitutes the main concern of this book.

Surviving Copyright: Strategies of Disownership

Early modern readers and writers, as Adrian Johns notes in the epigraph to this introduction, were well aware of the perils associated with the trade in printed books, even if later commentators have disregarded them. Authors, in particular, encountered a variety of dangers in the early modern period and were answerable for a wide range of crimes. They faced legal charges including sedition, libel, heresy, and treason.[22] On the ethical front, they might be accused of encouraging vice or circulating lies. The perilous waters of the book trade required them to negotiate greedy publishers, outright pirates, thieving booksellers, and inaccurate printers. Authors, as Gay in particular discovered in the aftermath of his publication of *The Beggar's Opera*, might be held responsible not only for their own actions but also for the actions of any reader who chose to cite a printed work as a motive for his or her criminal activity. Given the myriad dangers attached to authorship in this period, and the severity of the punishments to which crimes of writing were subject, authors had to find strategies to ensure that the costs of authorship did not outweigh its benefits.

Catherine Gallagher's influential book, *Nobody's Story*, is a study of the way in which female writers in this period survived the trials of publication and even, from time to time, managed to "thrive" despite them.[23] Gallagher begins by noting that women writers, rather than trying to deny their femininity as a means of negotiating the difficult terrain of publicity, actually "emphasized their femininity" as a means of "gaining financial advantage" (xiii). Women authors, she writes, emphasized one characteristic of female "powerlessness," their "dispossession" (xx), more insistently than any other. The fact that women had only extremely limited access to property, literary or otherwise, allowed women writers to draw attention to their "inability to *own* the text" as a means of evading some of the most pressing obligations that followed from commodification, appropriation, and responsibility—the same obligations to which male authors in general, and proprietary male authors in particular, were subject (xx).

The strategy of "capitalizing on . . . femaleness" (xxiv) by making use of the female trait of "dispossession" was not limited to women authors in this period. Gay, for instance, persistently figured himself as a vulnerable, penniless, and literally "dispossessed" author throughout his career. His rhetoric of powerlessness became particularly acute when he set about publishing the sequel to *The Beggar's Opera, Polly,* in 1729. Thanks to the notoriety of its predecessor, *Polly* promised to be an unusually controversial work, as a result of which it was banned from presentation on the stage by the Lord Chamberlain.[24] Gay nonetheless made the potentially foolhardy decision to allow the work to appear in print. In addition to rhetorically emphasizing his vulnerability in all of the petitions, letters, and prefatory material surrounding the publication of *Polly*, Gay made use of another strategy of "capitalizing on femaleness," by engaging the duchess of Queensberry as patron of his work and protector of its author. Gay relied on the fact that, as a woman, the duchess could protect him, without herself being exposed to any overwhelming repercussions from her involvement with this scandalous publication. By asking the duchess to do the public work of selling subscriptions to *Polly*, Gay managed to avoid the most immediate danger of "penal appropriation" that he feared would ensue if he himself were to appear in public as its author. Thus, Gay used the duchess as a shield, a patron, and a protector in the publication of this particularly risky work.

When Alexander Pope published *The Dunciad* in 1728, he also made use of a female intermediary to aid in the publication of his dangerous text. The danger of *The Dunciad* lay primarily in the fact that it constituted an ad hominem attack on virtually every minor author—the titular Dunces—of the age. In the first edition, Pope tried to protect himself even minimally—and to circumvent the ever more pressing libel laws—by identifying his adversaries only by coded names or initials with dashes. In the expanded 1729 edition, the *Dunciad Variorum*, he abandoned all pretense to discretion and identified the Dunces by name. Although Pope went to elaborate lengths to maintain property in these poems, he feared the reprisals of the Dunces that might result if he put his name on the works and advertised them as his own. Instead, Pope placed a false imprint on the title page, which bore the name of a female bookseller, Anne Dodd. Pope relied on the fact that Dodd would have neither the means nor the authority to prosecute him for his appropriation of her name. Thus, like Gay, he employed a woman to serve as a shield, a barrier between himself and the Dunces. The name on the title page worked exactly as Pope intended: Dodd operated as a stand-in for the anonymous author, only barely managing to escape the blows—physical as well as legal—that were meant for Pope himself. Dodd operated in this transaction among authors and readers as what Derrida, in "Limited Inc a b c," refers to as a "front," "borrowed name," "straw man," "substitute for a clandestine subject" called the author.[26] The straw woman Anne Dodd ensured Pope's survival and his access to the prerogatives of property by reducing the chance that he would be prosecuted or punished for the contents of this particularly risky work.

Through their female intermediaries, Pope and Gay tried to retain the strategy of dispossession while reaping the benefits of their proprietary rights. They tried, that is, to lay claim to the privileges of property as well as those of dispossession, by sheltering the rights of the male author behind a bulwark of feminine mediation. Pope and Gay, in an attempt to disrupt the relation between property and punishment, placed another, intermediary body between themselves and their criminal works. They relocated responsibility for the text onto a woman, out of the conviction that a female figure was best suited to reduce the risks of publication as a result of her benighted relationship to property, literary and otherwise. This relocation was quite literal, for Pope and Gay ensured that these female bodies would stand in for them in the event of reprisals against the body of the author.

In these dramatic acts of substitution, the duchess and Anne Dodd were, no less than Gay and Pope, real embodied historical figures, and one of them, not coincidentally the poor bookseller (albeit also a well-known book pirate), did not choose her role in these events. Pope, in an act of remarkable callousness, was content to expose Dodd to the rage of the Dunces and the accusation of having pirated his book, all in the service of his profit and self-protection. One might conclude from the story of Anne Dodd that the founding gesture of proprietary male authorship is an act of reckless violence against women, a willingness to let female bodies suffer in place of male ones. It is tempting, on the basis of this evidence, to see Dodd as an unwitting victim of Pope's insatiable will to manipulate the book trade, to fold her into this story as a powerless victim through whom the finer details of masculine authorship were worked out. Anne Dodd, in this version, goes down in history as nothing but a straw woman.

But this is not the story, or the history, I want to tell. By investigating Dodd's career as a bookseller and pirate, I suggest that she, too, was exploring ways to capitalize on the changing conditions of the literary marketplace. She even stood to profit from her role as Pope's "front," not hesitating to make use of the notoriety secured her by *The Dunciad*. As a "mercury"—a pamphlet seller—and as a female pirate, Dodd demands some narrative space of her own, teaching us as much about the "legitimate" roles women played in the early eighteenth-century book trade as she does about the trade's criminal underside. Like her predecessor in literary crime, Elizabeth Cellier, one of the subjects of my third chapter, she modeled for her contemporaries, both male and female, the strategic use of disownership to advance both commercial and political aims. Her story, too, reminds us that too exclusive a focus on the author at the expense of an understanding of the workings of the trade as a whole can lead us to miss much that is distinctive and important in the literary culture of the early eighteenth century, not least the participation of women in publishing and distributing those texts—periodicals, political pamphlets, criminal and other popular literatures, novels—we consider most characteristic of the changing conditions of reading and writing in the period. Finally, exploring Dodd's career, and ultimately her role in *The Dunciad* incident, allows us to put the entire risky business of the book trade in the first era of literary property into perspective. Through Dodd and *The Dunciad*, it is possible to see at once the dangers of the trade and the remarkably creative strategies developed by authors and others to elude those dangers. Through the study of Dodd, then, this book comes full circle, acknowledging the degree to which authors, under the new conditions of proprietorship governing the literary marketplace and above all the profession of authorship, became newly reliant upon members of the book trade to save themselves from what Pope calls their "dangerous fates."[27]

The book is divided into two parts, each of which contains closely related chapters. Part I, "The Trouble with Ownership," traces the interplay of possession and liability, and the relationship of each to authorship, in the period preceding the establishment of authorial copyright. In response to those critics who have located in this period a gradual transfer of rights from publishers to authors, this section locates a more fundamental transfer of responsibilities, as the author comes increasingly to be endowed with primary—if not sole—responsibility for the effects of what Henry VIII, in a proclamation of 1538, called "naughty printed books." While authors had always been considered at least partially responsible for the content of such books, structural elements in the book trade made it difficult to locate, and hence to prosecute, the author. Much of Part I is given over to exploring why, in the words of Chief Justice Scroggs in 1680, "it is Hard to find the Author," and what strategies the authorities—including licensers such as Roger L'Estrange as well as common law judges like Scroggs—developed to make it easier to locate this elusive figure. The first part of the book further establishes that the understanding of authorship as a form of ownership is less a revolutionary invention than a timely refinement of an already prevalent understanding of the relationship between authors and their works—an understanding clearly articulated by the custodians of both the common-law and the statutory traditions, and intimately tied to attempts to regulate the press.

Part II, "The Dangerous Fate of Authors," explores what happens to the relationship between authorship, property, and liability when proprietary authorship is codified in law after 1710. Despite constant frustrations, the Crown, the Parliament, and the courts had recognized for two centuries the link between ownership and liability, along with the necessity of finding the author in order to make that link explicit. Part II argues that the so-called Copyright Act attempted to solve the problem of the disappearing author in two ways: first, by insisting that in order to reap the benefits of proprietary authorship, authors would have to submit to various forms of documentation when claiming their proprietary rights; and second, by eliminating the widespread piracy that had made prosecuting and punishing authors virtually impossible throughout the first two centuries of print. Paradoxically, the act did not explicitly address itself to matters of press regulation in any way—a fact that has led to the long critical silence on the relationship between copyright and liability. Yet however difficult it has been for modern commentators to recognize this regulatory feature of the history of copyright, early eighteenth-century authors were under no illusions about the potentially disastrous consequences of stepping forward to lay claim to the full benefits of modern authorship.

The book's first chapter, "Authorship and the Regulation of the Press," offers an overview of the place of the author in ordinances, edicts, and other writings related to press regulation, from the reign of Henry VIII to that of Charles II. The first half of the chapter looks in detail at the writings and career of Roger L'Estrange, surveyor of the imprimery under Charles II and "bloodhound" of the Restoration press. L'Estrange was the single most influential voice on matters of press control after the revolution, and he instituted practices of policing and prosecution that took the control of the press out of the hands of the stationers and put it back under the care of the Crown and the courts for the first time since 1557. In his *Considerations and Proposals in Order to the Regulation of the Press* (1663), L'Estrange codified a system of rewards and punishments predicated on the belief that the author ought, whenever possible, to be punished for the appearance of dangerous or illegal ideas in print, and that all other members of the book trade should be coerced into assisting the surveyor in his task of finding and punishing the author. Should the author remain out of reach, L'Estrange continues, making explicit the link between authorship, ownership, and liability, anyone else "in whose possession" a dangerous book was found should be "reputed, and punished as the Author." Although the authorities had, for two centuries, routinely prosecuted printers and publishers for their part in the production of naughty books, the second half of the chapter argues that the desire to "find the author" had a long history in English press regulation, a history somewhat obfuscated by the notoriously difficult task of actually locating what L'Estrange calls the "First Movers," when compared with the ease of finding printers, publishers, and even readers. From its beginnings in the Tudor period, this chapter concludes, English press regulation was marked by a powerful conviction that the author was, in L'Estrange's terms, "the Fountain of our Troubles," even though the powers charged with oversight of the press continued to struggle to find ways of accessing—and ultimately cutting off—that fountain at its source.

The second chapter of Part I, "The Trials of Ownership," moves from the statutory arena of early modern press regulation to the drama of the Restoration courtroom. After an introductory section that distinguishes the forms of press regulation enacted by proclamations and edicts from those pursued in the common-law tradition, the chapter turns to three cases that demonstrate both the perils of ownership and the unceasing struggle after the Restoration to find and punish the author for offenses in print. The first case, John Twyn's 1664 trial for printing and publishing a treasonous pamphlet, ultimately resulted in Twyn's conviction and execution. Although the case seems to argue against the primacy of authorial liability, since it was for his actions as a printer that Twyn was punished, the proceedings of the case nonetheless demonstrate that it was the author the authorities were really interested in prosecuting. L'Estrange, appearing as a witness in the trial, went so far as to promise Twyn that he would be granted mercy if he would only "discover the Author." When Twyn refused, L'Estrange recommended that Twyn be punished in the author's stead because, as L'Estrange suggestively put it, "he owned the thing"—that is, he admitted his part in the printing of the pamphlet. By "owning" the pamphlet, L'Estrange indicates, Twyn opened himself to prosecution and punishment for its treasonous contents. The same language of ownership recurs again and again in the other two cases under study here, both of which were tried in 1680: Henry Carr's trial for printing, publishing, and being the presumptive author of *The Weekly Pacquet of Advice from Rome*; and Elizabeth Cellier's seditious libel trial for writing and publishing *Malice Defeated*, an account of her earlier trial for treason. In both of these cases, the judges and prosecutors asked the defendants again and again whether they "owned" their books, and the defendants sought to evade punishment by contesting the definition of ownership put forth by the court. As Cellier cheekily argued in the course of her libel trial, "I said only it was mine; not that I was the Author." Whenever possible, Cellier, like Carr, attempted to dispossess herself of her literary property at the same time that she challenged the equation between ownership and authorship on which the common-law strategies of press regulation depended.

The first chapter of Part II, "Daniel Defoe, the Act of Anne, and the Obligations of Ownership," considers the direct role that Defoe's writings played in the elaboration of a notion of authorial copyright. Rose notes in passing, in *Authors and Owners*, that Defoe's *Essay on the Regulation of the Press* (1704), along with a set of essays in his *Review* (1709–10), "influenced the London Stationers" in their attempts to get Parliament to pass an act that would seriously limit the prevalence of piracy in the book trade (35). From Defoe's writings, Rose convincingly argues, the stationers may have begun to develop the notion of authorial property rights on which the Act of Anne and its novel antipiratical strategies depended. Lost in this history, however, is the darker side of Defoe's theory of proprietary authorship: that is, its intimate link to authorial liability. The benefits that accrue from authorial property rights, Defoe insists, constitute a kind of consolation prize awarded in exchange for accountability. In fact, Defoe makes explicit the ways in which literary property responds to—rather than produces—authorial liability: "if an Author has not the right of a Book, after he has made it, and the Benefit be not his own," he argues, "'twould be very hard the Law should pretend to punish him for it."[27] Since authors are already considered legally answerable for their works—as Defoe himself discovered when he stood in the pillory for *The Shortest Way with the Dissenters* (1702)—the law should at least protect their "right" to benefit from what they have written. Defoe here proposes a relationship between literary property and authorial liability that has since been occluded, if not forgotten. Three hundred years *avant la lettre*, he makes the link Foucault himself never fully elaborated, between proprietary authorship and penal appropriation.

The final two chapters, "Revenge of the Straw Woman" and "*Hostis Humani Generis*," explore the immediate consequences for authorial liability of the 1710 statute. A comparative analysis of the publication and piracy of Pope's *Dunciad* (1728, 1729) and Gay's *Polly* (1729) illustrates the perils authors exposed themselves to by being proprietors of their own works. Over the course of a year, Pope and Gay each published an unusually dangerous work, capable of inflaming passions and inciting retribution; each attempted to retain his copyright through manipulating recent changes in the law affecting literary property; and each made use of intermediary figures to mitigate the liabilities of owning his work. To avoid the punishments they anticipated, which ranged from prosecution for sedition to the threat of physical beatings, Pope and Gay placed shields between themselves and their audience, shields who were positioned to take responsibility for the author's transgressions. In both cases, the author's human shield was a woman. Through their female intermediaries, Pope and Gay tried to appropriate the benefits of dispossession, even as they laid claim to the property rights made available by the new law. In the end, however, neither successfully avoided running into trouble in their pursuit of ownership, trouble that only accelerated with the development of copyright.

PART I

The Trouble with Ownership

The fact is that after first publication the British author usually disappeared, and if he did reappear, it was in the pillory.

—*Augustine Birrell,* Lectures on Copyright, *1899*

Chapter 1
Authorship and the Regulation of the Press

For the Authors, *nothing can be too* Severe, *that stands with* Humanity, and Conscience. *First, 'tis the Way to cut off the* Fountain *of our Troubles. 2dly. There are not many of them in an Age, and so the* less work *to do.*

—*Roger L'Estrange,* Considerations and Proposals in Order to the Regulation of the Press, *1663*

Introduction: Naughty Printed Books

In early modern England, almost anyone could be held responsible for the perceived or merely suspected ill effects of what a proclamation of Henry VIII, in 1538, called "naughty printed books."[1] So potentially toxic, so infectious and "pestiferous" were printed works deemed that merely to "buy, receive, or have" the wrong book without even opening it was at times punishable by death.[2] If one surveys the official history of press regulation before the Restoration using royal proclamations, patents, and decrees, as well as parliamentary statutes, it quickly becomes clear that liability for printed works was intended to be distributed over the widest possible field, from producers to distributors to readers themselves. The history of legal proceedings surrounding printed materials is equally heterogeneous, with printers, booksellers, publishers (a capacious and somewhat imprecise term),[3] and even bookbinders coming before the judges considerably more often than authors themselves. To be involved in any way in the production, circulation, or reception of printed materials, it seems, was to open oneself to prosecution and punishment by a state and a legal establishment determined to minimize the ill effects of the introduction into England of the plague of printing.

Nonetheless, a survey of these materials also makes clear that despite the dispersion of legal liability for printed works—the no-nonsense conviction that anyone and everyone involved in the production and distribution of undesirable printed materials should be punishable under the law—the author held a privileged place in the calculus of responsibility. Here a distinction—slippery at best, but necessary all the same—is required in the vocabulary of this analysis. While the title of this work invokes *authorial liability* in the most general terms, I use *liability* in this chapter and throughout to mean something quite specific: answerability to law. To be liable is to be bound by law and subject to it—even, in the words of the *Oxford English Dictionary*, to be "likely to suffer from (something prejudicial)."[4] Responsibility, though it can carry legal connotations, particularly in United States law, will here be used in a broader sense, to mean morally, ethically, or even economically answerable, although not specifically to institutions of the law or the state. In this usage, responsibility means something close to accountability, a term with which it is, in many ways, interchangeable.[5] Yet to be responsible for a piece of writing means something more than mere accountability: it also carries connotations of being a work's creator. When we say that an author is responsible for a particular piece of writing, we are endowing that author with a claim to a positive form of responsibility, as well as acknowledging his or her potential to suffer from any ill effects it might generate. To return to my initial claim, then, with these nuances of vocabulary in mind, although legal liability was widespread in the domain of printed works, and although all of the figures involved in the market for printed books bore *some* accountability for their participation in illicit or dangerous aspects of the trade, the author was still considered the *most* responsible of all of the participants. He or she was, in the words of the overseer of the Restoration press, Roger L'Estrange, "the Fountain of Our Troubles."

L'Estrange's comment comes in the course of his *Considerations and Proposals in Order to the Regulation of the Press* (1663), an essay published as a response to the passage of the last of the great early modern licensing acts, the Press Act (as it is commonly called) of 2 June 1662.[6] The full title of the statute—initiated by the newly enthroned Charles II and passed by Parliament—was "An Act for Preventing the Frequent Abuses in Printing Seditious Treasonable and Unlicensed Books and Pamphlets and for Regulating Printing and Printing Presses." As its title suggests, the Press Act did not address itself directly to the question of authorship. In fact, like most of the measures that had preceded it in the century and a half since the beginning of English press regulation, the act made almost no mention of authorship at all, focusing instead on the activities of printing presses and printers, as well as other figures directly involved in the mechanics of book production. Nonetheless, by reading the Press Act—and those regulatory measures that preceded it—in company with L'Estrange's essay, it becomes possible to identify the complicated role assigned the author—in legal as well as ethical-political discourse on the press—in the years leading up to and immediately following the Restoration. Through a careful review of the changing terms and provisions of press statutes and proclamations, read through the frame of L'Estrange's retrospective gloss on them, this chapter offers a history of the place of the author in the regulation of the early modern press.

L'Estrange is notable among early modern writers on the press in England for his explicit foregrounding of the matter of authorial liability. While he himself was responsible, in his formal capacity as surveyor of the imprimery and his undying reputation as the "Bloodhound of the Press," for prosecuting all sorts of malefactors in the seventeenth-century book trade, L'Estrange never wavered from his conviction that the author was the figure most deserving of punishment, the "fountain" from whom all naughty books and thus all social unrest ultimately flowed. From the moment of Charles's return to England, the mostly loyalist and certainly opportunistic L'Estrange began producing a flood of pamphlets laying the blame for "the *Causes* of our late *Troubles*" at the door of his fellow pamphleteers and printmongers.[7] "Nothing more certain," he wrote in 1661, only months after Charles's return, "than that the Freedome of the *Presse* and *Pulpit*, is sufficient to embroyl the best ordered Government in the World."[8] L'Estrange himself calculated a year later that since the monarch's "blessed" return, "Two-Hundred-Thousand Seditious Copies" had rolled off the presses, not counting reprints of the more inflammatory materials published during the Interregnum. "What this Glut of Poysonous Libels may produce," he wrote to the peers of the House of Lords, "is submitted with Just Reverence to your Lordships Wisdom."[9]

L'Estrange's invocation of the "Poysonous" nature of the documents rolling off the presses is reminiscent of the ubiquitous Tudor trope of print culture as pestilence—an image to which commentators returned again and again in the early modern period and that may even have led to the practice of destroying illicit books and pamphlets by fire. Yet despite his frequent references to the proliferation of what he calls, in *L'Estrange His Appeal* (1681), "Swarms of Libells," it is naughty authors, rather than naughty books, that for L'Estrange constitute the true carriers of this plague.[10] Lamenting in the same pamphlet the ease with which authors, the conduits of cultural disease, could decimate the entire social order with their productions, he notes, "The *Egyptian Locusts* were nothing to This Plague of our *English Scarabs*" (21). Authors in this image are both of the nation—they are "English"—and foreign to it, "Scarabs"—that is, Egyptian beetles. They circulate, verminlike, among the population, spreading seditious, ostensibly alien ideas and encouraging others to take up their pens in the service of further disorder. In order to cut short further cultural contamination, it will be necessary, in

L'Estrange's view, to focus regulation not on books themselves but on those who make books, and above all on the authors who constitute the true source of the plague.

Yet finding authors is never as simple, in L'Estrange's estimation, as one might hope. In fact, in his recognition of the problem of locating the author, L'Estrange is forced to abandon the archaic but ultimately consoling image of a plague brought by swarming insects, substituting in its stead something closer to a germ theory of cultural disease. In a passage that brings together both the image of authors as pestilential vermin and the recognition of their ultimate invisibility, L'Estrange in *A Short Answer to a Whole Litter of Libels* (1680) writes of the "Infernall Band of Libellers" who have "pelted" him with defamatory pamphlets: "They ly lurking in the Dark, like Poysonous Serpents, stinging what falls within their Reach, and blowing about their Venom, but there is no finding of their Holes. So that where there appears no Adversary, (unlesse a man will contend with a Phantome) there is no Place for a Competent Reply."[11] The author, in this passage, begins as a visible, locatable creature, a serpent, but degenerates into a "Phantome," a mysterious figure who cheats his victims of the opportunity for a "Competent"—that is, fit, appropriate, proportioned—reply. The recipient of a libel does not know to whom or to what he or she is replying, since most pamphlets are "popp'd into the world by stealth," with no name attached, leaving their creators protected from detection by the impossibility of tracing an anonymous text back to its source (1). As a result of this authorial disappearing act, L'Estrange insists, it is impossible for him to formulate a direct and sufficient response to the outpouring of malicious materials directed at him by his contemporaries.

One might pause to wonder, though, why it is that L'Estrange needs to know the name of the author of a given pamphlet in order to be able to respond to it. He could, presumably, simply respond to the allegations, without needing to know the identity of the individual who had sent any given "Vomit of a Libell" into the world (1). For L'Estrange, however, a "Competent Reply" to a libel always entails not only generating a printed response but also bringing the perpetrator of that libel before the law. Unfortunately, moreover, it is the law, rather than the reply, that is stymied by the problem of authorial invisibility. L'Estrange concludes by confessing that while he has been able to "lay open the Libeller" to his readers in the course of his *Short Answer*, he has had to stop short of his true goal, due to the simple fact that "I cannot find the Man." In this canny formulation, L'Estrange acknowledges a split in the figuration and functioning of authorship with which all those involved in the regulation of printed works—and of all written works, for that matter—have to grapple: that is, the ability of the "Man" behind any piece of writing to simply disappear, phantomlike, once that writing has been released into the world. Not content to lay aside his prosecutorial ambitions altogether, however, L'Estrange does make a final threat before closing: "I shall, however, try a point of Law," he says, "in time Convenient, with some of the Publishers and Dispersers" of these libels (13). These figures, it seems, lack the author's knack for timely disappearance, and it is they who will feel the full force of the surveyor's vengeance, standing in for the author as the recipients of L'Estrange's retributive ire.

In this series of pamphlets on a wide variety of topics, stretching from the Restoration to the early 1680s, we see hints of L'Estrange's broader philosophy of press regulation, along with some of the limitations of that philosophy when it runs up against the more pragmatic problem of enforcement. In the 1663 essay, *Considerations and Proposals in Order to the Regulation of the Press*, L'Estrange turns his entire attention to the question, presenting a systematic, if preliminary, account of his model for the management of the press. In addition, he outlines strategies to circumvent some of the problems of enforcement he anticipated from the very beginning and witnessed among those contemporaries trying to stem the tide of pamphlets that followed Charles's accession to the throne. It is worth noting that L'Estrange's essay is one of only three such systematic interventions on the topic of press regulation to appear in England in the early modern period in the form of a general address by what L'Estrange calls "a *Private Person*" to the reading public.[12] The first, Milton's *Areopagitica* (1644), simply denied the need for a practice of regulation aimed at the press per se, arguing that existing laws of treason, sedition, and blasphemy, along with the invisible hand of the marketplace of ideas, would serve to punish or silence those who overstepped the bounds of acceptable written discourse.[13] The other example of such an essay, Daniel Defoe's *Essay on the Regulation of the Press* (1704), which constitutes the subject of my third chapter, took for granted both what Defoe calls the "licentiousness of the presse" and the need for its regulation, but focused attention instead on the need to assure those involved in the production of printed works—and authors in particular—of some reward for the risks attendant upon entering an increasingly litigious literary marketplace. It is only L'Estrange's essay, then, that actually tries to anatomize and rationalize the practices of regulation and the proportioning of punishment for all of those engaged in the production and distribution of printed materials.

L'Estrange's *Considerations*

L'Estrange's essay begins with a pair of dedicatory letters, to the king and to the members of both houses of Parliament. This divided dedication makes sense when we take into account the fact that the 1662 Press Act, to which L'Estrange's essay was, in part, a response, was a joint effort of the king and the Parliament, and the first piece of press regulation to be generated collectively by all of the branches of government.[14] L'Estrange's dedications acknowledge this new spirit of shared oversight of the press, which, he believes, holds the key to successful future governance. L'Estrange's approach here is notably different from that of Cavalier contemporaries like Richard Atkyns, whose essay on the *Original and Growth of Printing* was published a year later.[15] Atkyns called for a return to a system of press control conducted entirely under the aegis of the Crown, out of a conviction, inherited from the prewar period, that the press quite literally belonged to the reigning monarch and could thus be disposed of in any way the monarch saw fit. As Atkyns concisely put it in his own dedicatory epistle to the newly enthroned king, "That Printing belongs to Your Majesty, in Your publique and private Capacity, as Supream Magistrate, and as Proprietor, I do with all boldness affirm" (B1v).

L'Estrange, whatever his Royalist leanings, stopped considerably short of this extreme and outmoded position. In fact, his dedication to the king neatly suggests that the regulation of the press is, if anything, a matter beneath royal attention, to be handled by lesser functionaries, such as, one presumes, L'Estrange himself. His essay, he tells the king, will be divided into two parts. The first is "a *Deliberative Discourse* about the *Means* of *Regulating* the *Press*"; the second offers extracts from a range of treasonous and seditious pamphlets, included, he says, "to Evince the *Necessity* of that *Regulation*" (A1v). Although the second half of the treatise is submitted directly to "Your *Royal Consideration*," L'Estrange is not, he insists, "presuming in any Sort, to Concern *Your Majesty* in the *Former*" (A1v). The nuts and bolts of press regulation need not, he generously suggests, concern the king at all. With this one swift move, L'Estrange removes the practices of press control from the purview of the Crown not by force but by flattery. While it will certainly be necessary to convince the king—and keep him convinced—of the necessity of regulating the press, the means of doing so should remain in the hands of legislators and their appointees, better suited as they are to the raw and messy business of keeping the pens and, above all, the presses of the nation in check.

From the very beginning of his essay, including the dedications, L'Estrange is equally explicit about what he considers to be the most pressing problem facing those who would restrain the press: the fact that enforcement of press controls and disciplining of members of the trade has until now been largely left to the wardens of the Stationers' Company. In his letter to the king, he notes that hundreds of pamphlets charging the king with "an Inclination to Popery" have appeared since the Restoration (A3v). Unfortunately, however, "the *Instruments* that Menage this Part of the Plot, are *Ejected Ministers, Booksellers,* and *Printers*" (A3v). Even at this early stage, L'Estrange has made clear who the adversaries are in his battle to control the press, and those adversaries, in most cases, are the very figures who are supposed to be the allies of press regulation: the printers and booksellers who make up the membership of the Stationers' Company. Later in the same letter, he is more explicit about the problems precipitated by a strategy of internal trade policing: "Diverse of the very *Instruments*, who are *Entrusted* with the Care of the Press," he writes, "*Tacitly Consent* . . . to the *Corruptions* of it" (A4v). Printers and booksellers have lost all credibility as enforcers of press regulation, and the company can no longer be trusted to take responsibility for the behavior of its own members.

Near the end of the text of the essay, L'Estrange returns to the topic of the company, wryly passing judgment on the paradox of its multiple and competing functions: "It seems a little too much to *Reward* the *Abusers* of the Press with the *Credit* of *Superintending* it," he writes (25). Neither the printers, who exist only in a "Servile and Mercenary Dependence" on the booksellers, nor the booksellers themselves can be trusted to identify those members of the trade engaged in illicit publication practices (27). Instead, L'Estrange suggests, in addition to the licensers named in the 1662 Press Act, six new government agents should be appointed, charged with "the Care of the Press," and known by the "*Title of Surveyors of the Press*" (28). These surveyors will act as independent agents, each assigned to one of the divisions of the trade already associated with individual licensers. Theirs will be the task of rooting out the corruption endemic to the book trade, primarily through the practice of regularly searching the premises of printers and booksellers believed to be engaged in unlawful practices. Unlike those company insiders in whose interest it remained to hide and protect their fellow stationers from government interference, the surveyors of the press would undertake the task of revelation, making it possible to "find the man" or men responsible for any dangerous or undesirable publication. Faced with the mutually protective practices of the stationers and the invisibility of the author, the job of the aptly named surveyors would entail finding and making visible "Phantomes" who were always threatening to disappear from sight.

As the moniker "Bloodhound of the Press" suggests, contemporaries recognized L'Estrange's talents as a tracker and retriever of literary wrongdoers. In fact, the image of tracking, of moving along a chain of clues to reveal the origin of a misdeed, perfectly describes L'Estrange's proposed plan for the regulation of the press. He begins his description of this plan by anatomizing the activities of the book trade, splitting the trade into two groups, which he somewhat confusingly calls "printing" and "publishing." Of the first set, he writes, "The Instruments of setting the work afoot are These. The *Adviser, Author, Compiler, Writer, Correcter*, and the Persons *for* whom, and *by* whom; that is to say, the *Stationer* (commonly), and the *Printer*" (1). To this list, he adds anyone who works on presses, including even the letter-founders whose liability for the production of any given printed work seems, at best, a limited one. Nonetheless, L'Estrange is scrupulous in his inclusion of even the most seemingly marginal members of the trade. Moreover, while he is clearly preoccupied with the problems associated with *print* culture in this list, his inclusion of compilers and writers suggests that he also has in mind the possibility for regulating the market in manuscripts and other scribal publications—a point to which I will return below.[16] For now, though, it is necessary to turn to the other list, of those figures he calls the "publishers": "The usual *Agents* for Publishing, are the Printers themselves, *Stitchers, Binders, Stationers, Hawkers, Mercury-Women, Pedlers, Ballad-Singers, Posts, Carryers, Hackney-Coachmen, Boat-men*, and *Mariners*. . . . Hiding, and Concealing of unlawful Books, is but in order to Publishing, and may be brought under the same Rule" (1–2). In this second group, once again, the list of agents who may be considered to be involved with the production of a given work is long and almost comically comprehensive. Even the coachmen and sailors who unwittingly transport unlawful books will be held accountable for their role in the distribution of those materials. More telling still is the inclusion in this list of those who hide or conceal such books. L'Estrange, in what might seem like a paradox, insists upon including in the list of "publishers" not only those who vend and distribute naughty books to the public but those who knowingly keep them secret as well. In these opening paragraphs, then, L'Estrange makes absolutely clear that he will hold anyone and everyone in the book trade responsible for their role in that trade, no matter how tenuous their link to the offending material may seem.

In what follows, however, L'Estrange begins to make sense of this chaotic picture of distributed liability. He does so first by creating a chain—a hierarchy, even—of responsibility, and then by engaging the members of the trade to help move himself and his fellow literary detectives along the chain of responsibility toward the holder of the original "seditious intention" (to use Marcus Nevitt's phrase).[17] L'Estrange begins by acknowledging the extreme difficulty that faces the surveyors of the press—that is, that those most responsible for dangerous books are also the most difficult to track down. His solution to this problem involves instituting a system of rewards and punishments designed to encourage or, where necessary, to force members of the book trade to assist him in his regulatory project: "Touching the *Adviser, Author, Compiler, Writer,* and *Correcter,* their Practices are hard to be Retriev'd, unless the one Discover the Other. This Discovery may be procur'd partly by a *Penalty,* upon *refusing* to *Discover,* and partly by a *Reward,* to the *Discoverer;* but let both the *Penalty,* and the *Reward* be *Considerable,* and *Certain*: and let the *Obligation* of *Discovery* run quite Through, from the *first Mover* of the Mischief, to the *Last Disperser* of it" (2). The basic contours of L'Estrange's model appear for the first time in this paragraph. He opens with the admission that the author and all of those involved with the manuscript before it enters the print trade are "hard to be Retriev'd." Once again, the language of visibility and invisibility, of hiding and retrieving, drives L'Estrange's understanding of the root problems associated with regulation. With this acknowledgment in mind, though, he assumes that the best and perhaps the only efficient means for making these originary figures reappear—and this is, for L'Estrange, the ultimate goal of any regulatory regime—involves forcing the more visible or retrievable members of the trade to "discover" those who are more difficult to track down. In the first paragraph, it is only the writers and correctors who will be forced to take part in this project of mutual surveillance, but by the end of the second paragraph L'Estrange has corralled everyone in the trade, from the "first mover" to the "last disperser" of a given book, into the system of rewards and punishments that leads to mutual discovery.

As he proceeds, L'Estrange makes clear the fact that while the "obligation of discovery" may be equally distributed, it is also unidirectional, leading inexorably toward the "first mover." It would not, that is, be all that important for L'Estrange if the printer of a work were to reveal to him the name of the letter-founder responsible for supplying that printer's type. Should the printer be able to reveal the identity of the corrector, however, L'Estrange's system of rewards would be satisfied, leaving him one step closer to his unchanging goal—the goal of finding the work's "first mover." In L'Estrange's schema, the ultimate responsibility for every work ought to and ultimately must fall on one figure alone: the figure called the author. Anyone willing to help L'Estrange locate the author, no matter how culpable he or she is in the publication of the work, will be exonerated, and perhaps even rewarded. Failure to assist L'Estrange in his plan, however, will produce dire consequences. Not only will the recalcitrant book trade member be held responsible for his or her own participation in the production of the unlawful book; he or she will have to take on the author's sufferings as well. L'Estrange thus continues, adding a new and crucial term to his vocabulary of regulation, "*If any unlawful Book shall be found in the Possession of any of the* Agents, *or* Instruments *aforesaid, let the* Person *in whose Possession it is* found, *be Reputed, and Punish'd as the* Author *of the said Book, unless he* Produce *the Person, or Persons, from whom he Receiv'd it*" (2). Failure to identify the source of an offending book will lead one to be punished as though one were its author. To be an author, then, means in this passage to be the person held responsible for a work, regardless of one's actual role in its production. Moreover, authorship in this passage is, for the first time, and in an admittedly vague fashion, directly associated with possession. To have a book in your possession is equivalent to being the author of that book, as ownership, authorship, and liability are tentatively made to stand in for each other as the crucial components of determining responsibility for printed works. What we see in L'Estrange's essay is thus, in the end, a full-fledged attempt to elaborate and isolate a notion of authorial liability, a concept that is further associated, in some as yet undefined way, with the question of the liability attached to "possessing" a printed work.[18]

The *Considerations* addresses itself primarily to the problem of keeping watch over the market in printed works. Yet, L'Estrange elsewhere makes clear that the regulation of manuscripts poses problems virtually indistinguishable from those precipitated by the print trade. In the case of manuscripts, however, regulation is made more complicated by the fact that it is precisely those figures—authors, compilers, writers—who are most difficult to locate, who are primarily or exclusively responsible for the production and distribution of such works. Those figures whose activities are easier to "retrieve"—the printers and booksellers—are either not involved at all in the circulation of manuscripts or involved to a much lesser degree.[19] It is notable, then, that L'Estrange's plan for the regulation of the manuscript trade is remarkably similar to the one he describes with relation to printed works, and it centers, once again, on retrieving the author. In a document presented to the House of Lords in 1675, preserved under the title "Mr. L'Estraings Proposition concerning Libells" and recovered by Harold Love, L'Estrange writes:

> The Question of Libells, extends it selfe (I conceive) to manuscripts, as well as Prints; as beeing the more mischievous of the Two: for they are com[m]only so bitter, and dangerous, that not one of forty of them ever comes to ye Presse, and yet by ye helpe of Transcripts, they are well nigh as Publique. . . .
>
> And for Libells in Writing, I do humbly offer this to Consideration. That although Copyes of them may passe indifferently from one to another, by other hands, yet some certain Stationers are supposed to bee ye chiefe, and profest dealers in them, as having some affinity with their Trade.
>
> And when they come to be detected, the Com[m]on Pretence is, *They were left in my shopp*, or *sent in a Letter, I know not by whom*: which may be true in some cases, though but a shift, for ye greater Part. . . .
>
> Whoever shall receive, and Conceale any such Libell, without giving notice thereof, to some of his Matyes Justices, within a certain space of time after the receipt of it; let him suffer as an Abettour of it, & if he shall not produce ye person of whom he had it, let him suffer as ye Author of it.[20]

L'Estrange notes that libels in manuscript can circulate as widely as printed libels—indeed, that there are booksellers who specialize in this particular portion of the trade. He further warns the lords that these unprinted libels are "more mischievous" than their printed cousins, since they are not required to pass the test of a licenser before they make their way to the marketplace. In what will become a familiar topos in the annals of the book trade, stretching all the way from the Restoration to the 1730s (as the cases of John Twyn and Anne Dodd will show) and not limited to the circulation of manuscripts, booksellers could, according to L'Estrange, try to claim ignorance of the origins of dangerous materials, simply by stating that they had been dropped at the shop without the distributor's prior knowledge. L'Estrange, however, serves notice that he will be neither fooled nor foiled by this familiar ruse. Any bookseller who conceals his receipt of such a libel, and who is unwilling or unable to say how it came into his possession, will, just like his colleagues in the print trade, be forced to stand in "as the author," and even more menacingly to "suffer" in the author's place, unless he or she is willing to assist L'Estrange in his unrelenting quest to bring the authors of dangerous works before "his Matyes Justices."

In print or in manuscript, then, the author is, in L'Estrange's formula for regulation, the grandest of the "Grand Delinquents" who plague the book trade (32). While L'Estrange includes printers and booksellers among the numbers of those deserving to be punished, his ultimate goal, as the epigraph to this chapter suggests, will always be first to find the author and then to bring him or her to justice. All a printer or bookseller must do in order to be excused for participating in the trade is to reveal the identity of the author—a revelation for which the collaborator may even receive a reward. Should he or she refuse to cooperate, however, the author's suffering awaits.

The *Longue Durée* of Authorial Liability

L'Estrange, of course, was just one figure in the long history of early modern press regulation, albeit a vitally important one in the context of Restoration publishing. Nonetheless, it remains to be shown whether his unflinching, almost maniacal conviction about the place of the author in the assignation of liability for works, whether printed or unprinted, was characteristic of early English regulation in general. Perhaps L'Estrange's personal campaign against authors was just that, a private quirk, motivated by revenge (given his harsh treatment at the hands of his scribbling contemporaries) or competitiveness (given his equally zealous contribution to the ongoing litter of libels) rather than by a more balanced assessment of the legal context for determining liability and responsibility for naughty books. The remainder of this chapter will be devoted to providing a context and a history for L'Estrange's unhesitating identification of the author as the "Fountain of Our Troubles."

In order to get a more general picture of the author's place in early modern English controls on the press, it is necessary to review the motley assortment of proclamations, acts, and decrees directed at the regulation of books and pamphlets, which appeared, as Harry Ransom tersely puts it, "with monotonous regularity," beginning with the early sixteenth-century proclamations against heretical writing and preaching distributed by Henry VIII and ending with the last great centralized regulatory measure, the 1662 Press Act, with which L'Estrange himself was so intimately engaged.[21] In addition, since the Stationers' Company was charged with oversight of the press and printing throughout most of this period, it is also necessary to glance at the company's part in establishing and maintaining the practices and policies of press control. The company and the central governmental bodies (whether monarchical or parliamentary) were not, by any means, the only authorities responsible for keeping an eye on the circulation of dangerous books and manuscripts in the sixteenth and seventeenth centuries; the courts, too, were busy passing judgment on the producers and purveyors of written and printed materials—as well as speech acts—deemed treasonous, libelous, slanderous, or seditious. I defer until the next chapter a more extensive discussion of the role of the courts in early modern press control, however, in order to focus attention on the limited and discreet canon of public statutes and proclamations on the topic that emanated from centralized authorities from the reign of Henry VIII to that of Charles II. I do so, once again, in the hopes of isolating a history not of individual authors and their encounters with the authorities—a history most clearly discernible in the legal judgments of the period[22]—but rather of the discourse surrounding authorship, a discourse that was crafted and recrafted by those centralized authorities as they sought to manage the perceived threat posed by the rapid growth and spread of the press and the book trade, not only in England, but throughout Europe as a whole.

For the purposes of this analysis, the view of authorship, ownership, and liability—and the relations among them—articulated in these proclamations and edicts is more important than the question of whether or not they were actually successful in halting the flow of unauthorized or undesirable books and pamphlets. In fact, as numerous commentators have pointed out, they frequently had little or no effect whatsoever—a point made concisely by Adrian Johns, in *The Nature of the Book*: "the early modern state had neither the ideology, nor the finances, nor the mechanisms, nor the police and personnel to construct a régime of censorship recognizable as such to late twentieth-century eyes."[23] Nonetheless, these proclamations and other public pronouncements continued to pour off of governmental desks for two hundred years and, taken together, give a kind of diachronic series of snapshots, if not of the actual practices of regulation, then at least of the changing cultural fantasies of how such regulation might be achieved. Moreover, in addition to providing an overall picture of what the authorities in different eras thought they were controlling when they set about controlling the press, they offer crucial evidence of the author's place in that perennially precarious system of oversight and regulation.

The content of these statutes and proclamations has, of course, been amply mined by scholars in search of their place in the history of censorship and what Fredrick Seaton Siebert calls the "struggle for freedom of the press."[24] These documents have also, since the late nineteenth century, been an object of scrutiny for those whose particular interest is the history of copyright and intellectual property. Notwithstanding the massive outpouring of work by scholars from Augustine Birrell, Alfred Pollard, A. M. Albright, and Walter Greg, to, most recently, Joseph Loewenstein, however, the place of the *author* in these proclamations and statutes has received scant attention.[25] This paucity of attention seems quite natural once one acknowledges how little, in many ways, these documents actually have to say about authorship, and how sporadically the figure of the author appears within them. More often than not, the author is just one of a string of agents being put on notice to keep within the bounds of acceptable discourse or risk punishment. Moreover, given the ease of identifying printers and publishers, the author's liability enters regulatory discourse, if at all, as a kind of aside: if you *can* find the author, prosecute him or her, but since you almost certainly will not, other regulatory expedients have been provided. As Loewenstein additionally notes, with the development of the system of prepublication oversight known as licensing, the author threatened to disappear altogether from the terrain of regulation: "the licensing of the 1530s and after turns the focus onto the press, which becomes the central site of criminality."[26] Whereas the earliest regulatory measures had addressed themselves primarily to the specific content of dangerous ideas—heresy, blasphemy—without yet having mastered how to control the proliferation of those ideas, subsequent legislation emphasized the mechanisms of proliferation themselves, or what Loewenstein calls "the specific technological challenge of the press" (55). The author, he concludes, was "much too slippery" to be a target of Tudor press regulations, inclined as that figure was to simply vanish from the scene of the crime the moment the work was handed over to the printer.

A passing glance through the annals of the *Tudor Royal Proclamations* bears out Loewenstein's arguments about the mechanistic nature of sixteenth-century attempts to stamp out naughty printed books. Yet these documents do not omit the author altogether; indeed, the author does appear, and appears consistently enough to make it possible to trace changing notions of what would later come to be called authorial liability, even in sixteenth-century regulatory measures. For alongside the abiding early modern conviction about the author's evanescence—the universal, pragmatic acknowledgment of his or her capacity to disappear—there is another conviction, already familiar to us from reading L'Estrange, that pervades documents related to the early history of the press. This second conviction holds that notwithstanding the author's disappearing acts, he or she is ultimately the one responsible for the content and the effects of naughty books. Others may share the liability, and others may be subject to punishment, but the author is the root—the fountain, in L'Estrange's formulation—of all textual troubles. In the proclamations and statutes enacted before the Restoration, it is fully possible to find this conviction about the fundamental character of authorial liability elaborated, repeated, and strengthened, alongside that other, accompanying conviction about the author's elusive nature. What these twin convictions ultimately produce, these documents show, is an increasingly urgent need to find a way to track authors down, to bring them to account for their textual indiscretions. When L'Estrange set out to discover the author, they make clear, he was following in a long line of less well-known figures, who were no less passionately dedicated to retrieving and punishing the author, notwithstanding centuries of failure to achieve that goal.

Tudor Royal Proclamations and the (Dis)Appearance of Authorial Liability

The first major Henrician entanglement with the problem of the pestilent press occurred in a proclamation of 1529, in the twentieth year of Henry VIII's reign.[27] As its title—"Enforcing Statutes against Heresy: Prohibiting Unlicensed Preaching, Heretical Books"—suggests, the proclamation failed to distinguish among various material forms in which illicit language or ideas might appear, and in this it is characteristic of early regulatory measures.[28] Books, manuscripts, and even speech acts are covered by its expansive prohibitions, because for Henry and his ministers, unlicensed preaching of heresy is indistinguishable from the distribution of heretical books. "No man," according to the proclamation, should "hereafter presume to preach, teach, or inform anything openly or privily, or compile and write any book" or even engage in public "assemblies," any of which spreads doctrine that challenges the tenets of the currently sanctioned faith (1:183). From the point of view of the production and distribution of heretical language, the proclamation makes no attempt to identify or single out particular agents responsible for that language, especially authors, about whom it is notably silent. The only indication of the particular combination of elements—authorship, liability, and possession—whose history this chapter traces comes in the mention of an additional category of persons whose behavior falls under the purview of the new restrictions: those who do not write or sell but simply *possess* the sorts of documents it proscribes: "Moreover that all and every person and persons having any books or writings of any such erroneous doctrine and opinion do deliver or cause to be delivered effectually and actually all and every such book and writing to the bishop of the diocese or to the ordinary of the place within 15 days after this proclamation [be] announced" (1:183). Later on, in a specific ban on imported heretical books, the proscription against "the having of them" is once again repeated (1:185). In this seemingly innocuous equation of the possession of banned books with liability for them, even without any mention of authorship, the history this book tells finds a kind of prologue. In what follows, it will be necessary to keep watch for all references to the consequences of "having" books—and, especially, of "owning" them—in the documents of early modern press control.

Just a year after this first foray into the terrain of legislation, Henry had occasion to speak out again on the topic of heretical language.[29] This time, however, he addressed himself directly to the prohibition of "Erroneous Books" and specifically to English books printed abroad and imported into England. The agents responsible for this black market in heresy are here termed, in an anticipation of L'Estrange, "our ghostly enemy" (1:194). Since evanescent aliens have control of the production and distribution of these "blasphemous and pestiferous" works, the proclamation instead takes aim at those who "buy, receive, or have" them (1:194). The local bishop is once again the immediate destination for "all and every person or persons which hath or hereafter shall have any book or books in the English tongue printed beyond the sea" (1:195). Unable yet again to stop these books at the ghostly source, Henry settles for policing the other end of the chain, those who merely possess prohibited books. The proclamation does, however, almost as an aside, make one provision for the regulation of production, in its insistence that anyone contemplating printing any new work on a religious theme must first offer it for examination to the ordinary of the diocese where the book is to be printed. In this very early attempt at licensing the Tudor press, the proclamation also insists that the printer place his own name along with the examiner's on the book, "as [the printer] will answer to the King's highness at his utmost peril" (1:195). The recorded name, then, is early on equated with the threat of punishment and "peril," in a pattern that will repeat itself throughout the long era of English licensing. Despite this half-hearted gesture at the regulation of production, however, the proclamation soon returns to its prior preoccupation with those who "buy, receive, keep, or have" potentially inflammatory works (1:196). The Tudor authorities here seem to acknowledge that, at least for the time being, given the "ghostly" nature of their adversaries in the print trade, the most effective way to regulate the press is to make possession, rather than dissemination more generally, synonymous with "utmost peril."[30]

The history of licensing in England is conventionally traced to the 1538 proclamation with which this chapter began, yet that proclamation is, in fact, little more than a refinement and secular expansion of the experimental system put into place in 1530 for religious books.[31] As of 1538, however, printing "any book in the English tongue," regardless of religious content, will require that it first be submitted for examination (1:271). In a further bid to make licensing capable of addressing profane books, as well as religious ones, the examiner must be either a member of the Privy Council "or other such as his highness shall appoint" (1:272). In another important innovation, the 1538 proclamation for the first time definitively connects licensing—and hence liability—with "privilege"—and hence property—in its insistence that the title page of all new printed works bear the words, "*cum privilegio regali . . . ad imprimendum solum*" (1:272). This formulation explicitly links the right to print the work, the privilege conferred by the king or his agents, with the responsibility for what is printed.[32] While the proclamation does not specify that the printer's name must be on the work, finally, as all future licensing orders would do, it does insist that at least "the effect of his license and privilege be therewith printed, and plainly declared and expressed in the English tongue" (1:272). Presumably such a license would include, if not the name of the printer, then at least that of the examiner to whom the work was shown. The effect of the 1538 proclamation, then, is first to bind privilege to license, property to liability, and then to ensure that at least some name is available to which the work can subsequently be traced, should a test of that liability prove necessary.

The 1538 proclamation, addressed as it is to rising concerns about the book trade's collusion in the production and circulation of "naughty printed books," especially those with their origins in continental heresies, makes no mention of the author in the course of its provisions for the quick suppression of such books. Nonetheless, a brief provision for the management of translations does anticipate uncannily the discourse of authorial liability that will culminate in L'Estrange's *Considerations*: "Nor shall [anyone] henceforth print any book of translations in the English tongue unless the plain name of the translator thereof be contayned in the said book; or else that the printer will answer for the same as for his own privy deed and act, and otherwise to make the translator, the printer, and the setter forth of the same, to suffer punishment, and make fine at the King's will and pleasure" (1:272). While the authorities are willing to make the translator, the printer, and the publisher or bookseller "suffer punishment," it is the translator who is singled out for particular regulatory scrutiny in these lines. Only the translator's name is required, presumably because of the greater difficulty involved in tracking down his or her role in the work's production once the work has appeared. Moreover, printers who collaborate in dangerous works with anonymous translators will be held accountable not only for their own part in the printing but for the translators' misdeeds as well. This provision suggests that the translator's is the most important "privy deed and act" of the three, the one that must be fined and punished, in order for justice to be done. In the absence of a translator, someone else may even be made to suffer in his or her place, as though what defines a translator is a function not of his or her actual role in the work's production but instead of his or her primary liability. To be a translator, in this context, is to be the person fundamentally responsible for the appearance of a dangerous work, regardless of one's actual function in the work's production. While this is the only mention of translators made in the documents of early modern press regulation under discussion here, the threat of substitution—of surrogate liability—invoked in these lines will become more and more familiar in the legislation to come.[33]

If, in 1538, the chain of liability had been traced back from possessor to examiner, to printer, to translator, only eight years later the authorities would be emboldened to complete the chain by adding the author, for the first time, to the list. A 1546 proclamation again aims at the extirpation of heretical books, first and foremost through strengthening the prohibition on "possession" of such books.[34] In an even more explicitly proprietary (and even carceral) formulation, it elaborates the consequences for anyone who has such a book "in his or their custody" (1:374). At the other end of the spectrum, however, in the realm of the production of new books, the proclamation makes its most radical innovation: "Moreover the King's majesty straightly chargeth and commandeth, upon the pain aforesaid [imprisonment, fine, et cetera] that from henceforth no printer do print any manner of English book, ballad, or play, but he put in his name to the same, with the name of the author and day of the print" (1:375). The Tudor government here expresses a new and direct interest in the identity of the author of any work to appear in print, not, in this case, to single the author out for special suffering but to put him or her on notice that the state now wishes to keep records of the "First Movers" of all new textual productions. Interestingly, there is no indication that the consent of the author is necessary, either for the use of his or her name, or for the publication of the work in the first place. This requirement, in fact, would not enter the regulatory arena at all until 1642 and would begin to play an important role only twenty years after that, in the 1662 Press Act—a matter discussed in more detail below. Without the acknowledgment of the need for such consent, the author is here, in 1546, forced to play a role in the regime of regulation, regardless of whether he or she has had any part in making public the offending words. Under such circumstances, merely to write a work for private circulation, or even for one's own edification or amusement, without any intention to publish its contents to others, becomes a distinctly risky business.

From this time forward, most proclamations concerning heretical, seditious, or blasphemous books cast the widest possible net in identifying those who may be held responsible for such works, a net that includes the author, but only in a long list of similarly prosecutable figures. As a 1555 proclamation of Philip and Mary puts it, the authorities should be on the lookout for anyone who presumes to "write, print, utter, sell, read, or keep, or cause to be written, printed, uttered, read, or kept" any manner of heretical book.[35] At the same time, however, a persistent stream of proclamations began to appear that gave special attention to the author, and to that figure's unique and privileged place in the determination of liability. Among the most interesting of such proclamations is one from 1553 that is concerned not with books at all but with speech—specifically, that most inflammatory category of speech act known as "seditious rumour."[36] Given the extreme danger to public order posed by "such lewd liberty of speaking evil doings," the text proclaims, subjects must not only "forbear to publish"—in other words, to pass on to others—any rumors to which they may be privy but must also give over to the authorities anyone known to have engaged in such unsociable speech. The penalty for failing to fulfill the latter requirement is formulated in terms reminiscent of those applied to translators in the 1538 proclamation: "If the hearers of any such light, seditious, or naughty talk, spoken in his or their presence, shall not according to this proclamation open the same to the next justice or officer (as aforesaid), that then the same person so hearing and not declaring the same, and being thereof justly convicted, shall be reputed and taken for the first author of the said rumours, and have such punishment for the same as the first author should, if he were apprehended" (2:4). Authorship is here split off from the practice of writing but retains its valence as the locus of primary liability, a primacy marked by the peculiarly redundant phrase "first author." In order for the regulatory mechanism to function, this document suggests, it is not necessary for there actually to be a first author, but it is necessary that someone be found to assume that first author's place, to function as though he or she were the prime mover. Increasingly, then, a function for the author is being defined in these proclamations, but its definition is not the one with which we are generally familiar. To be an author, these documents suggest, means nothing more nor less than being open to liability, punishment, and suffering; perhaps as important, anyone standing too close to the place of the author can and will be "reputed and taken for the first author" should that author already have disappeared.

For all members of the book trade—indeed, for anyone involved in any way with naughty books, writing, or speech—the mobility of the author function, its tendency toward slippage, must have posed a profound threat. Merely to peddle a dangerous book on a street corner or to arrange for it to be peddled, to sew it or to arrange for it to be sewn, could, according to these proclamations, open one to prosecution as if one had been its very inventor and creator. By the middle of Elizabeth's reign, the authorities had clearly taken notice of this disturbing feature of authorial mobility, as well as of its capacity to inspire alarm in members of the trade, for they began to institute a system designed to capitalize on this widespread threat, a system of rewards to go along with the punishments elaborated by their Tudor predecessors. In a proclamation of 1570 demanding the arrest of anyone caught "circulating" seditious materials, the ultimate goal, notwithstanding the practical focus on mechanisms of distribution, is explicitly and ideally to locate the authors of such pamphlets and books.[37] Any justice of the peace receiving seditious materials is commanded to apprehend "all the persons charged or suspected as authors, or anywise participants" in the dispersal of these works (2:342). To advance this lofty end, a new strategy of regulation is then introduced: anyone who can "discover who are the authors or writers, counselors, or conveyors" of these works, the proclamation promises, will be "largely rewarded" (2:342–43). Finally, in an innovation worthy of the bloodhound himself, and directly addressed to the "conveyors" and other lesser offenders in the trade, "If he have been anywise a partner in the same fault, and yet will discover the principal authors or offenders therein, he shall not only be favorably pardoned for his concealment of offense, but shall also be so well rewarded as he shall never have cause to repent of his discovery" (2:343). So important is the discovery of the author or other "principal" offender, that all other figures will be indemnified, absolved of liability and even eligible for large rewards for their part in the hunt for textuality's new prime suspect. The stakes of refusing to cooperate, however, increased as fast as the rewards. As another proclamation of 1570 put it, anyone refusing to reveal the "secret persuaders of disobedience" to the queen will be harshly dealt with: for their recalcitrance, they "shall be taken, reputed, and punished as abettors and maintainers of the principal traitors that were authors of the same."[38]

If the 1570 proclamation still wavers slightly in its willingness to settle for either the author, or some other abettor or assistant to the "principal offender," a similar measure from 1576 will stop at nothing less than locating the author him- or herself. This decree, aimed at condemning a recent rash of "infamous Libels," declares its own system of rewards and punishments designed specifically for obtaining "some certainty for the discovering of the authors thereof."[39] Those who assist in that discovery will be handsomely rewarded—one hundred pounds for a gentleman, forty pounds for those of lesser rank—while anyone caught aiding the offenders, including public officers who have been "remiss" in their duties, will be condemned to "receive such like punishment as the authors of seditious libels ought to doe" (2:401). Clearly, the hunt for the author is becoming more and more refined as time goes on, producing a need for ever more carefully crafted expedients for tracking down that elusive figure. At the same time, however, given the ability of authors to disappear altogether or at the very least leave the country before their books appear, the likelihood of actually being able to track them down seems ever more remote. A proclamation from 1583 declaring "seditious and schismatic" a collection of writings by Robert Browne and Robert Harrison gives some suggestion as to the means authors used to escape punishment for their works.[40] Given that the two authors have "fled out of the realm as seditious persons fearing due punishment for their sundry offenses, and remaining presently in Zeeland," the authorities will have to be content with burning their books and prosecuting those who in any way have helped to hide or distribute them (2:502). The authorities, that is, will have to settle for punishing the printer and bookseller, having failed to invent an effective means of catching up with the real culprit, a figure whose greatest asset is and will remain for at least a century the ability to disappear—the paradigmatic "ghostly enemy."[41]

Licensing: Printers, Authors, Owners

According to David Loades, what distinguishes Tudor regulation of the press, especially prior to 1550, from later measures is the government's comparative leniency with relation to printers and others in the book trade.[42] Attention in this period was, he relates, focused on the finished product, the book itself, which the authorities believed existed in such finite numbers that these naughty objects could be extirpated after the fact. Loades's research on clandestine printers suggests that in those cases when the government did decide to prosecute the human agents behind offending books, they saw printers and bookbinders "simply as craftsmen, who were not responsible for the contents of works which they processed."[43] As the last section made clear, no matter what threats were leveled against these secondary agents of the trade in proclamations and decrees, the author was the agent deemed primarily responsible for printed books, and it was to the apprehension of the author that these early measures most often addressed themselves. In most cases, Loades concludes, these printers were–unsurprisingly–content to take advantage of the Tudor assessment of authorial liability and "let the authors shoulder the main burden of risk" (15).

If one thing can be said to characterize the regulation of the press between 1550 and the end of a full-scale system of licensing in 1695, it is, as Loades also notes, a shift in focus onto those figures who occupied positions on the chain of liability between the originating author and the final product held in the reader's hand. Printers, correctors, binders, booksellers, hawkers: these are the agents against whom press regulation would primarily battle, from the incorporation of the Stationers' Company in 1557 until the ultimate failure of prepublication press control at the close of the seventeenth century. Scholars of licensing have pointed out repeatedly that a major innovation accompanied this transformation in the methodology of press regulation, an innovation that consisted of the introduction of a trade-off of rights for responsibilities among those now charged with oversight of the press. In exchange for a virtual monopoly over the printing of books both new and old, the company undertook to play a vital role in the maintenance of licensing. Even when, as in the 1586 and 1637 Star Chamber decrees concerning printing, authorities outside the company were given the task of examining and authorizing books prior to publication, in practice licensing responsibilities most if not all of the time fell to the members of the company. In the words of Harold Weber, the 1557 charter of the Stationers' Company represented a decision "to assign the chief responsibility for enforcing the labyrinthine complex of regulations created by the state to the individuals responsible for the production and marketing of books."[44] In the more polemical version of the same point made by Donald Thomas, "it was decided to make the book trade its own censor."[45]

The terrain of press licensing has been extremely well traveled, especially of late, often as a means of discovering what role the system of licensing played in the elaboration of a notion of stationer's copyright, that larval form of intellectual property that would, as these histories tell it, one day metamorphose into the authorial version. Siebert, for instance, notes, "it is almost impossible to disentangle the efforts of the printers to maintain their 'copy-rights' from their complacent cooperation in suppressing 'unlawful' printing."[46] Siebert's deliberate use of the term "copy-rights," undermined as it is by the double hesitation of scare quotes and the antiquated, halting hyphen, still foregrounds his investment in linking the history of trade protectionism *and* the practices of press regulation that go under the heading of licensing to the genesis of copyright. The transformation from licensing to the ostensible "freedom of the press" to which Siebert's title triumphantly alludes will coincide neatly with the development of monopoly privileges into authorial rights—a coincidence remarked again, and in even more detail, by Loewenstein. For the author of *The Author's Due*, assessing the relationship between "the ideological control of books" and the control of "competition within the nascent book trade" provokes the question, "what place do proprietary rights have in the negotiation of these two forms of press control?" (9). Proprietary rights emerge for Loewenstein, as for Siebert, as a solution both to the difficulty of successful press control and to the stifling of the free trade in ideas by monopoly capitalism.

Despite the strong focus on the genesis of intellectual property, and hence of modern, proprietary authorship, historians of licensing are most frequently content to leave the author out of the account. This is not, such histories seem to say, the author's story *yet.* However "slippery" (to use Loewenstein's term) the author's presence in regulatory materials from the mid-sixteenth to the late seventeenth century, however, licensing did have consequence for authorship, and licensing statutes did, albeit in a somewhat muted fashion, persist in the attempt to "find the author" even as they addressed themselves to the printer and publisher. Most important, they set the precedent for later regulatory systems—including those proposed by L'Estrange, Defoe, and the drafters of the 1710 Copyright Act—by establishing a deliberate and detailed system for documenting responsibility for printed works, a system that increasingly came to include identifying the author of any work one intended to bring out in print. Licensing decrees and statutes tackle the problem of liability for printed materials through the establishment of ever more elaborate paper trails. The name, the imprint, the entrance in the register of the Stationers' Company: these are the tools of press regulation increasingly sharpened in the progression of licensing mandates.

It is instructive in this regard to compare the two major Star Chamber decrees of 1586 and 1637, neither of which is particularly fulsome on the topic of authorship.[47] In the later decree, however, the cursory documentary system established in the 1586 version is expanded considerably as though the only way to address the persistent and "divers abuses" of the licensing system lamented by Star Chamber in 1637 is to keep better records (Arber, *Transcript*, 4:529). The documentation required by the 1586 decree is, after all, quite restrained: all printers will be required to "bring a true note or certificate" for each press currently in operation to the wardens of the company (Elton, 183). Provisions for the proper documentation of licensing itself are not made, however. Printers are simply ordered to refrain from printing any new book until it has been "seen and perused by the archbishop of Canterbury and bishop of London" (Elton, 185). The method for recording that the work has been so perused and authorized is not described, although the company in this period certainly had its own principles and practices of documentation, described in detail by Greg and others, in the form of the register of the company, in which all works were, at least in theory, to be entered. Most significant for the immediate analysis, however, is not the specific history of registration but rather the extent to which the general terrain of documentation was simply entrusted by Star Chamber to members of the trade.[48]

By 1637, the authorities of Star Chamber had clearly concluded that such laissez-faire reporting practices and unspecified requirements were leading to the widespread disorders associated with the trade. It is tempting, in fact, to read the 1637 decree as a triumph of Stuart bureaucracy, quietly instituting an entire system of record keeping to support the more obviously revolutionary changes it introduced—most notably, the restriction to twenty of the number of master printers and the establishment of a range of named licensers, both ecclesiastical and political, to oversee the printing of different categories of books. Yet beyond these more dramatic regulatory measures lay an important new attention to documentation, a feature of the decree that went hand in hand with a new thoroughness in specifying the exact nature of the textual objects subject to perusal by the recently appointed team of licensers. The specificity of these provisions would play an important role both in the many court cases related to printed books after the Restoration and, into the next century, in debates about the proper object of intellectual property law. The provisions of the 1637 Star Chamber decree, in other words, paved the way for the better management both of textual regulation and of copyright.

The relevant provisions of the act—no less than six of them—are most easily summarized in the form of a list:

1. Whereas previous orders had left relatively vague the exact form of the books and pamphlets to be submitted to the licenser, the 1637 decree requires the inclusion of all "Titles, Epistles, Prefaces, Proems, Preambles, Introductions, Tables, Dedications" (Arber, 4:529). This insistence on the presence of the entire paratextual apparatus of a work suggests a newfound

vigilance and critical sophistication on the part of Star Chamber. While the core of a work alone might pass regulatory muster, this provision seems to say, an introduction, a dedication, or even a mere title might have the capacity to shape the reading of a text in such a way as to make it suddenly dangerous or even downright seditious. A later provision requiring that all previously published works be presented to be relicensed seems similarly cautious, or even paranoid, about the nature of the textual object. New editions must henceforth be submitted "with all such additions as the Author hath made" (Arber, 4:533). From now on, these two clauses suggest, the authorities will leave nothing to the printer's or publisher's discretion when it comes to determining what, exactly, should be presented to the licenser's greedy eye.

2. While previous ordinances had tacitly presumed that the stationers themselves would maintain the practice of entrance in the register book of the company, the 1637 decree specifies that such entrance is mandatory. Prior to publication, all works "shall be first lawfully licensed and authorized . . . and shall be also first entred into the Registers Booke of the Company of Stationers" (Arber, 4:530). Failure to fulfill either of these requirements—licensing and entrance—will result in a perpetual ban on printing for the individuals concerned, along with "such further punishment" as the courts deem appropriate in the present case (Arber, 4:530). The mention of further punishment acknowledges that only those with something to hide—whether an infringement of others' rights to copy or an ideological infraction—would fail to openly avow their work in the form of a company-sanctioned registration. The requirement of entrance, then, takes aim at precisely those works attempting to drop below the bureaucratic radar. In addition, it puts the members of the company on notice that what had previously seemed like a tool of the company for the protection of its members' interests—the register itself—is now a tool of the state, as it would continue to be into the first era of copyright.

3. Elaborate and highly precise practices are here established for both the method of licensing and for its documentation. Item 4 specifies that two "written Copies of the same Booke" with all paratextual materials intact must be submitted to the appropriate licenser by the aspiring printer or other agent (Arber, 4:530). One of these written copies will be kept "in the publike Registries" of the designated licenser, in order to check against any later printed versions, "that he or they may be secure, that the Copy so licenced by him or them shall not bee altered" (Arber, 4:530). In both of these copies, the second of which will be returned to the applicant along with

the license, the licenser must "testifie under his or their hand or hands" that the book contains nothing objectionable (Arber, 4:530). Finally, that testimony must be "imprinted" in the version that comes from the press, along with the name of the licenser or licensers. Clearly, Star Chamber intended to be as strict with those charged with the practice of "authorizing" books as it was with those who undertook to write and print them, demanding of them that they personally vouch for the contents of any works they perpetrated upon the reading public. Although this is not the first order to specify the need to name the licenser on a printed work—indeed, the requirement dates back at least to Henry VIII's 1538 proclamation—the 1637 decree is by far the most precise attempt to articulate the exact responsibilities of the licenser, the nature of the object to be licensed, and the means for documenting that the licenser has fulfilled all of his assigned duties—all forms of documentation that could later be used to build a case against the licenser of any book that proved more inflammatory than the designated official had predicted on a first viewing.

4. The problem of regulating books imported from abroad had been a constant preoccupation for those attempting to control the spread of naughty printed books since the very dawn of printing in England. The 1637 decree for the first time attempts to solve this problem not through banning imported books, as Henry had done, but through documenting them. Item 5 specifies that anyone bringing books from abroad with the intent to give or sell them to others must "present a true Catalogue in writing of all and every such booke and bookes" to the archbishop of Canterbury or the bishop of London (Arber, 4:530). While this provision was almost certainly not enforced, and may even have been unenforceable, it represents yet another attempt to tie a human agent, through the medium of a written record, to a book that might later prove offensive to those in power.

5. Most significantly for my purposes, the 1637 decree resurrects a requirement specified only once before, in 1546, that the name of the author be placed on any new printed work—in the words of item 8, that is, of any "Bookes, Ballads, Charts, Portraiture, or any other thing or things whatsoever" (Arber, 4:531).[49] Along with the name of the "Author or Authors, Maker or Makers" must be recorded the name of the printer and of the person "by, or for whom" the work is printed, a clear attempt to force those fiscally responsible for a work to be legally responsible for it as well (Arber, 4:531). The penalty for failing to record these names is stiffer than all other penalties threatened in the decree: forfeiture of the books, destruction of the press or presses on which the books were printed, and, uniquely, "such other

corporall punishment" as the Star Chamber or High Commission "deems fit" (Arber, 4:531). The added threat of corporal punishment here is deeply resonant, reminding those reading the decree and subject to its provisions that it is their bodies, and not only their textual properties, that are destined to suffer for infractions either of the Stuart ideological code or simply of the bureaucratic mechanisms put into place to sustain that code.

6. As if in recognition of the very fragility of its own newfound faith in the word—at least in the printed word—as a guarantor of good behavior, item 9 forbids the use of false imprints on any printed work. Any attempt to "forge, put or counterfeit" the mark of a stationer not involved in the book's publication is forbidden, and in order for his or her name to appear, the printer's or publisher's "consent" must be secured in advance (Arber, 4:531). The decree is notably silent on the question of the author's consent—a concern that would have to wait another quarter century to be recognized. Nonetheless, there is an ironic undertone to this provision, acknowledging as it does the existence of a strategy for circumventing virtually all of the other measures the decree has so painstakingly laid out, especially those requiring that the name of the author, printer, publisher, and licenser be printed on all new works. Any paper trail, item 9 confesses, is ultimately susceptible to both "forg[ery]" and "counterfeit[ing]"—a limitation of the smooth functioning of press regulation and its accompanying bureaucracy vividly illustrated in the careers and trials (in every sense) of authors such as Francis Kirkman and Alexander Pope.

In the 1637 decree, then, it is possible to trace a multifaceted attempt to shore up a faltering licensing system through the establishment of methods for holding people accountable for the content of printed works with which they have in any way been involved.[50] Most notably, the same mechanisms in force for protecting printers' and publishers' rights—entry in the Stationers' Register and the public announcement of a proprietary interest entailed in the imprint—will henceforth explicitly be used (as they have implicitly been used for more than fifty years) as mechanisms for enforcing the licensing system. Anyone wanting to claim such rights will, in so doing, accrue to him- or herself weighty responsibilities; anyone willing to bear such responsibilities will, intentionally or not, also become the bearer of rights. Owning a book, the 1637 decree suggests, will require owning up to it. The reverse will also be true.

Lest I seem to be introducing a new vocabulary—a vocabulary of ownership—that is as yet unwarranted in this analysis, we need only look to the printing order of 1643, the first major statement on the topic produced during the Interregnum, for the introduction of a vocabulary of ownership into the lexicon of licensing itself. Before turning to this document, however, it is necessary to pause over an earlier order—an order that has played a crucial role in writing about the history of authorial property rights, despite its rather minor role in the larger history of press regulation. With the abolition of Star Chamber in 1641, the carefully crafted provisions of that body's 1637 decree were, in an instant, nullified.[51] Although the hiatus prior to the reestablishment of licensing and limitations on the number of presses, this time by Parliament, was only two years, the virtually unregulated interval from 1641 to 1643 had a profound effect on the output of English presses. According to at least one account, that output increased tenfold after 1640.[52] Both king and Commons looked with trepidation at the prospect of an ideologically unrestrained press, as did the stationers themselves, who watched their monopoly on printing evaporate in the presence of an equally unrestrained trade. In January 1642, just six months after the abolition of Star Chamber, the stationers had already begun petitioning anyone who would listen for a new arrangement regarding the rights of the company to print bibles.[53] Commons responded with a series of preliminary, provisional, "scattershot" responses—the term is Loewenstein's (*Author's Due*, 162)—beginning with an order dated 29 January 1642. The order declares "that the Masters and Wardens of the Company of Stationers shall be required to take especiall Order, that the Printers doe neither print, nor reprint any thing without the name and consent of the Author." It continues, in an already familiar fashion, "That if any Printer shall notwithstanding print or reprint any thing without the name and consent of the Author, that he shall then be proceeded against, as both Printer and Author thereof."[54] For Loewenstein, this order constitutes nothing less than "the single most powerful piece of evidence in support of Foucault's bibliographic hypothesis" regarding the relationship between authorship and punishment (*Author's Due*, 162). As Foucault would predict, in other words, the order recognizes the author as someone subject to punishment at the same moment that it recognizes him or her as someone with an interest—perhaps even a proprietary interest—in the work. The author's consent is secured not in order to ensure that his or her rights and privileges are respected but in order to ensure that he or she is available as "the human origin of discourse who is submissible to punitive objectification" (*Author's Due*, 162).

Loewenstein here distinguishes his reading of the order from those of Siebert and Francis Barker, who both see in it an anticipation of the authorial property rights that would be codified in law in 1710. Certainly, Siebert's reading is at least somewhat persuasive, given that, according to his account, the order followed a flood of complaints to Commons on the part of authors about the sudden increase in unauthorized printed works. For Siebert, coming as it does in response to these quasi-proprietary complaints, the requirement of authorial consent constitutes "one of the earliest recognitions of the rights of authors by the English Parliament" (*Freedom of the Press*, 171). For Barker, even more radically, it provides for "the protection of copyright vested, for the first time in English law, in the author."[55] Loewenstein ends by acknowledging, almost grudgingly, that "the ordinance makes a small contribution toward the eventual reification of authorial property," yet he fails to plumb the relationship between that tacit gesture toward proprietary authorship and the more prevalent sense in the order of authorship's "penal reification" (*Author's Due*, 163). What stands out about these accounts is their implicit suggestion that we should choose between reading the order either as a guarantor of rights or as a threat of liability. Given the knowledge on the part of all three critics of the ways in which, prior to this time, in Siebert's own formulation, it had been "almost impossible to disentangle" rights from responsibilities in the domain of press regulation, why should that entanglement not persist into the era of authorial property rights? What renders this short-lived order most significant for the present analysis, then, is its place in a genealogy neither of authorial property nor of authorial liability but instead, of the inextricably "tangled" relationship between them.[56]

The 1642 order was only one of a number of preliminary regulatory measures that would be folded into the licensing act of 1643.[57] The act, which opens by acknowledging the extent to which its formulation and passage have been delayed by what it delicately terms "the present distractions" of civil conflict, is notable for its brevity when compared to the Tudor and early Stuart measures that had preceded it (*A&O*, 1:184). It is also notable for the degree to which it explicitly and almost exclusively directs itself to questions of property in copies, reinstituting a system of licensing deliberately and self-consciously designed—at least in theory—to protect the rights of stationers rather than to monitor the flow of potentially dangerous ideas. While the act does mention a recent upsurge in "scandalous, seditious, libellous, and unlicensed" printed materials, it is more immediately and more consistently concerned with the "abounding Delinquents" who have failed to respect other men's copies: "Divers of the Stationers Company and others being Delinquents (contrary to former orders and the constant custome used among the said Company) have taken liberty to Print, Vend, and publish, the most profitable vendible Copies of Books belonging to the Company and other Stationers" (*A&O*, 1:184). The strategies for remedying such rampant proprietary delinquency include ensuring that all new printed works be licensed (the identities of the licensers to be worked out later by the Commons and lords), that they be entered in the Stationers' Register, and that the printers put their names to the copy (whether in the book itself or in the register is not recorded). Furthermore, the ordinance expands on its new language of "belonging" by specifying that books not be entered in the register "without license and consent of the Owner or Owners thereof" (*A&O*, 1:185). The requirement of authorial consent found in the 1642 order has been tellingly modified here, making consent of the *owner* rather than of the *author* necessary for entry and subsequent publication. Nonetheless, the appearance of an explicit vocabulary of ownership is crucial to the future elaboration of liability for printed works, including authorial liability, as the next chapter makes clear. From now on, participants in any of the many functions of the book trade are alerted that ownership will play a preeminent role not only in checking the misappropriation of rights to copy but also in recording a kind of baseline responsibility for the products of the press.

The Interregnum: The Eclipse of the Stationers and the Rise of the Author

Over the next decade, in 1647, 1649, and 1653, Parliament revised, refined, and revived the licensing strategies originally laid out in 1643. Much of the attention in these ordinances was directed at the proper licensing of news and newssheets, those printed ephemera that constituted the major new output of English presses in the Interregnum. In addition, these ordinances struggled to define the appropriate licensers for different categories of books until, finally, in 1653, all licensing was centralized in the Council of State. This body was further charged with "the Government and Regulation" of all printing, and the Stationers' Company was instructed to "follow and observe such Rules, Ordinances and Directions" as the council laid down.[58] The company's loosening grip on the practices of press regulation—the regulation both of rights and of responsibilities—is nowhere clearer than in these lines. Whatever power they had managed to accrue to themselves under the early Stuarts was ebbing away in the period of parliamentary reform.

Less remarked in these acts than the eclipse of the stationers is the quick ascent to prominence of another figure, a figure whose slippery, ghostly presence had lingered in the background of materials on licensing until this time. That figure was the author. In the 1643 ordinance, the only mention of the author comes in the requirement that the authorities apprehend "all Authors, Printers, and other persons whatsoever" involved in the production and distribution of "scandalous, unlicensed, and unwarrantable works" (*A&O*, 1:185). The author's name, let alone his or her consent, is not required for entry in the register, and authorship here appears only in the domain of infraction, not in the domain of attribution. The 1647 ordinance, by contrast, directed against "unlicensed or scandalous Pamphlets," offers the author a leading role in both domains.[59] The ordinance first specifies that all printed matter must be licensed, "with the name of the Author, Printer, and Licenser thereunto prefixed," thereby restoring the insistence on authorial naming that had lapsed in 1641 with the dissolution of Star Chamber (*A&O*, 1:1022). More important, the ordinance institutes for the first time a detailed system of preordained fines and jail terms for failing to license a book, a system that quantifies liability in a descending scale that makes it possible to reconstruct precisely, if somewhat comically, the degree of comparative liability purportedly attached to each individual agent involved with each book. This scale, the act confirms, gives the author absolute pride of place:

> The Maker, Writer or Composer of any such Unlicensed Book, Pamphlet, Treatise, Ballad, Libel, Sheet or sheets of News, shall forfeit and pay Forty shillings, or be Imprisoned in the Common Goal . . . until he shall pay the same, so that the said Imprisonment exceed not forty dayes; The Printer to forfeit and pay Twenty shillings, and suffer the like Imprisonment, until he pay the same, the said Imprisonment not exceeding Twenty dayes, and likewise to have his Press and Implements of Imprinting seized and broken in pieces; The Book-seller or Stationer to forfeit and pay ten shillings, or be Imprisoned in like manner until he pay the same, the Imprisonment not exceeding Ten days, And the Hawker, Pedler or Ballad-singer to forfeit and lose all his Books, Pamphlets and printed Papers exposed to sale, and also to be whipt as a Common Rogue. (*A&O*, 1:1022)

In this unique attempt to specify, proportionally, the relative culpability of the producers of unlicensed materials, the absolute cultural conviction about the author's preeminent liability is articulated and accorded material form. The author is twice as liable as the printer, four times as liable as the bookseller, and unquantifiably more liable than the poor commoners who take their place at the end of the chain of production and distribution. The entire property of these liminal figures, the ordinance seems to suggest, does not amount to the sum of five shillings, the amount it would take for the arithmetic of liability to work out exactly. Instead, they are simply sentenced to lose their livelihood and to be publicly punished through the most corporeal of indignities: whipping. Finally, unlike the Elizabethan and L'Estrangean systems described above, the 1647 ordinance does not outline an elaborate system of rewards to go along with these highly targeted punishments. Nonetheless, it does tacitly endorse such a system in its provision that one half of the fine assessed in any of these cases should be paid to "the person or persons who shall discover and prosecute the said Offenders" (*A&O*, 1:1023). This disbursement would presumably act as a major incentive not only to "innocent" bystanders but also to all minor participants in the trade and, above all, to those hawkers, peddlers, and ballad singers otherwise in danger of losing their entire livelihood—an incentive system operating within the trade that was made explicit in the 1649 version of the same licensing ordinance.

The final provision of the 1647 act seems, on the surface at least, redundant: in its final paragraph, the measure makes a point of noting that the system of graduated punishments delineated in the act in no way acquits those concerned in cases where the material is not only unlicensed but also "seditious, Treasonable, or Blasphemous" (*A&O*, 1:1023). These offenders will be subject to "such farther Penalties" as either the common-law courts or Parliament itself shall determine. Surely no one involved in the trade could really have imagined that a printer of unlicensed treasonable material would forfeit twenty shillings and twenty days in lieu of his or her head for the production of this particular naughty book. The very redundancy of the statement suggests that the drafters must have had some other motive in mind when reminding readers that an entire regime of postpublication limitations on expression existed to back up the prepublication system of licensing. Over the next half century, and especially in those periods when licensing provisions were allowed to lapse, the courts would come increasingly to supervise the output of the press. For now, however, they would remain in the background, a second line of defense designed to supplement what contemporaries still apparently believed could be an effective system of prepublication licensing.

How precarious and incomplete this system in fact was is suggested by the fact that just two years later, in September 1649, Parliament passed a renewed but much-expanded measure, with increased penalties for all members of the trade in unlicensed books and pamphlets.[60] If Parliament was to get serious about licensing, it seems, they would have to be far more strict and more deliberate in the formulation of a revised system of press oversight. In this case, interestingly, the provision calling for licensing is actually subordinated to a much more extensive description of new regulations for policing what the act calls "Scandalous or Libellous Books, Pamphlets,

Papers or Pictures" (*A&O*, 2:246). Clearly, Parliament felt the need for a category of offensive and troublesome materials falling between the allowable and the treasonable or seditious, the latter requiring a relatively high standard of proof and the imposition of potentially inflammatory punishments such as mutilation and death. Perhaps the key to controlling the press lay in the strict surveillance of such materials, which menaced the government enough—and were easy enough to produce—to require powerful, if not fatal, disincentives.

In the 1649 act, the same penalties that apply to the producers of such scandalous works will, as if as an afterthought, be applied to the producers of unlicensed printed materials, supplanting the penalties introduced in 1647. Here, too, a system of subtle but crucial changes is introduced into a scale of graduated punishments that otherwise closely resembles its counterpart of two years earlier. First, the term "Author" replaces the unwieldy formulation, "Maker, Writer or Composer" found in the previous act. Earning the more exalted title of author turns out to be costly, however, since the fine for authorship of scandalous or unlicensed materials is now increased to ten pounds, although the jail term remains the same: forty days. Printers will be charged five pounds and twenty days, and the bookseller or stationer forty shillings and ten days for their respective infractions. Hawkers, peddlers, and ballad singers are here excused from the lineup, not because they have been granted immunity but because "no such Hawkers shall be any more permitted" (*A&O*, 2:252). In their place, however, a new though no less familiar figure has entered the scene of regulation: "If any person happen to buy any such seditious, scandalous, or libelous Pamphlets or Papers, and shall not within Four and Twenty hours after knowledge thereof, bring them to the Lord Mayor of London (if the buyers resiance [*sic*] be there) or some other Justice of the Peace . . . [he or they] shall forfeit for every such omission, the sum of Twenty shillings for every such concealed Paper, Pamphlet or Book" (*A&O*, 2:246). In this partial return to the strictures of Tudor regulation, merely to buy a book or to have one in your possession is to be liable to punishment. In this instance, however, the ultimate purchaser or possessor of the book is deemed the least culpable of all these several agents, with the author occupying the privileged position—if we can call it that—in the scheme of regulation.

The author shows up elsewhere in the 1649 ordinance, in the new direction to the printer to include on the title page "the Author's name, with his quality and place of Residence, or at least the Licensers names where Licenses are required, and his own Name and place of residence" (*A&O*,

2:249). A series of graduated penalties is then introduced for those printers who fail to include these precise locating devices. The will to find the author, through recording his or her place of residence, is here already in evidence, as is the will to hold the printer responsible should the author, in L'Estrange's apt formulation, fail to be "Retriev'd," either through the choice to omit the author's name or because the author's name or place of residence turns out to be counterfeit. What this and the other Interregnum licensing acts demonstrate, then, is the double bind that has haunted press regulation and the regulation of ideas more generally at least from the time of Henry VIII: on the one hand, a deep cultural conviction that no matter who else is partially responsible for the production and distribution of naughty books, the author, as the acts of 1647 and 1649 so clearly show, is the most responsible of all; on the other, that prosecuting authors, or keeping them from disappearing altogether, is a task that remains somehow out of reach of the agents of press control.

Conclusion: New Dogs, Old Tricks, or L'Estrange and Restoration Press Control

It was into this double bind, as we already know, that Roger L'Estrange sought to insert himself with his *Considerations and Proposals* of 1663. Understanding, as no predecessor had done, both the absolute necessity of cutting off the fountain at its source and the equally absolute necessity of offering the members of the trade some tangible reward for leading him to that source, he articulated a system for policing the press that had been present but only intermittently articulated for a century and a half. Wherever possible, by any means necessary, the system declared, lay hands on the author. In order to make that slippery task more manageable, use threats and promises to coerce and cajole those who might be able to point a finger at the ultimate culprit. Finally, make clear to those implicated that, should they fail to offer the proper assistance, they will be forced to pay not only for their own crimes but for those of the author as well. L'Estrange did not invent these tenets of press regulation, but he may have been the first to bring them together in a unified scheme designed to sever the supply of naughty books once and for all.

L'Estrange was responding most immediately not to the regulatory measures of the Interregnum but to the 1662 Press Act. This act, however, is primarily notable for its total absence of innovations or new ideas for managing the press, drawing as it does almost word for word on the Star

Chamber decrees of 1586 and 1637. As Siebert notes, although for the first time, "the regulations of Charles II were issued from Parliament instead of from Star Chamber, they followed the general lines of control as devised by Archbishop Whitgift under Elizabeth."[61] One might be tempted to see this as a sign of continuing faith in the licensing methods devised by Star Chamber if only the pathetic record of success in enforcing those statutes and proclamations were not so abundantly clear. The 1662 act, like its late Tudor and early Stuart counterparts, tried to control the trade primarily by intervening in the trade's intermediary functions, slashing the number of presses from fifty-nine to twenty, carefully controlling the number of apprentices and journeymen attached to each press, and restricting the selling of books and pamphlets only to members of the Stationers' Company. Rather than controlling the fountain at its source, in other words, the Press Act sought to replace the outflow pipes draining the fountain with conduits of a smaller gauge—a strategy bound, as L'Estrange was quick to point out, to produce considerable leakage and overflow at the source, given that the supply of material proceeded unchecked. The 1662 act, in fact, did not even absolutely require that the name of the author appear on works brought to be licensed, insisting that the printer provide the author's name only if required to do so by the licenser. Given the almost complete absence of any mention of the author in the 1662 act, in fact, we might see L'Estrange's *Considerations* not as an elaboration upon the Press Act but as a corrective to it and at the same time as a remarkably canny reading of the shortcomings of most press regulation to date. His "Deliberative Discourse" is at its most deliberate in pushing into the foreground the very figure whose ghostly presence has haunted the regime of licensing to date without ever stepping forward to claim his or her deserved place in the overall scheme of regulation.

L'Estrange might have done better in the *Consideration* to turn his attention directly to the legal remedies available for the control of printed works, including blasphemy, libel, treason, and the increasingly popular accusation of "seditious libel" treated at length in the next chapter. For, while licensing measures were renewed, lapsed, and were revived continuously over the next thirty years, until the final termination of the licensing provisions of 1662 in 1695, a quiet revolution was taking place in the regulation of the press, a revolution centered in the courts. Although the shift was neither sudden nor final, its consequences could be felt throughout the 1660s and 1670s, and especially in the period from 1679 to 1685 when no licensing laws were in effect and the country was deranged by a series of purported "Popish" and Presbyterian plots.

Before turning to these courtroom dramas, however, it is perhaps fitting to close this chapter with one more royal proclamation, this one from 1679, almost at the end of Charles II's reign. This proclamation might be said to span the divide between an older era of licensing, primarily as a royal prerogative, and a new era of press control given over to the judges and the courts. In the proclamation, it is possible to hear echoes not only of ancient Tudor experiments at press regulation but also of L'Estrange's undeniable role in attempting to bring the author to the center of press regulation once and for all. That the courts would have just as much trouble getting the author to appear—let alone to suffer—as their counterparts in the regime of licensing, neither L'Estrange nor Charles could possibly have predicted. That it would take work—more work, perhaps, than they were willing to expend—to bring the author forward to take responsibility for his or her crimes, however, the 1679 proclamation already makes entirely clear.

In its stated goal of "Suppressing . . . Seditious and Treasonable Books and Pamphlets," the proclamation orders "Judges, Justices of the Peace, Mayors, and other Magistrates, to cause all Seditious and Scandalous Books and Pamphlets whatsoever, being Libels against the Government, or against any Publick or Private Person whatsoever, to be seized on, and the Makers, Printers, Sellers, or Publishers of the same, to be Apprehended and Committed to Prison, to the end they may be Proceeded against, and Punished according to Law."[62] So far, then, the proclamation is new not only in its careful attention to postpublication offenses prosecutable in the courtroom—libel, sedition, the antiquated *Scandalum Magnatum*, or libel of public magistrates—but also in its expectation that the officers of the law, rather than those of church or government, are the persons responsible for prosecuting and punishing such crimes. In its further provisions for the most effective means of achieving such prosecutions, however, the proclamation is not new at all—it is, in fact, engaged in a familiar struggle:

> And to promote the Discovery of such Wicked Offenders, his Majesty doth further by this his Royal Proclamation Publish and Declare, That if any Persons shall within the space of One year next ensuing, Discover or make known to his Majesties Privy Council, or either of his Majesties Principal Secretaries of State, or to the Lord Chief Justice, or any other Judges of his Majesties Court of Kings-Bench, the Authour or Printer of any Seditious and Treasonable Book or Pamphlet, every such Discoverer shall immediately after the Conviction of the Offender, have and receive from his Majesty the Reward of fourty pounds. . . . And his Majesty is further pleased to Declare and Assure, That his Gracious Pardon shall be granted to any Hawker, or Disposer of any such Books or Pamphlets, who shall make Discovery or Printer

from whom he or they received the same; and likewise to any Bookseller or Printer of any such Books or Pamphlets, who shall Discover and make known the Authours thereof. (1–2)

L'Estrange's strategy of rewards and punishments, and his chain of liability are all alive and well in this proclamation. Hawkers and booksellers are engaged to find printers, and printers to find authors, in what now seems a thoroughly predictable regulatory concept. Once again, the author is the figure charged with preeminent liability in these lines, and all prosecutorial energies will be directed toward "discovering" that mobile, slippery, disappearing figure.

For at least two influential recent historians of the book trade, the proclamation of 1679 and the entire atmosphere surrounding the temporary lapse of licensing in 1679 brought new attention to the author as a central figure in the regime of regulation. For Harold Weber, in *Paper Bullets*, the 1679 proclamation inaugurated an era in which "courts and judges increasingly stressed the author's preeminence in the legal economy of censorship" (175). In contrast to earlier eras, he relates, the author was increasingly singled out in this era as "the primary agent of public discourse, the unitary source from which the power of the press ultimately flowed, and the cynosure of judicial discipline" (174). Prior to this time, according to Weber, only L'Estrange had sought as deliberately as Charles and his judges to place the author at the center of the scheme of regulation. In a related vein, Adrian Johns, in *The Nature of the Book*, notes the degree to which, in the period from the Restoration to 1680, a rhetoric of authorial culpability went hand in hand with the expansion of the category of the author to cover all those involved in the book trade. "Proposals were made that not only printers but 'Binders, Stitchers, Concealers, Sellers, Publishers, & Dispersers' be legally considered authors, too" (159). Above all, in Johns's account, stationers in the mid-seventeenth century became particularly susceptible to attributions of quasi-authorial liability: "deeming the Stationer to be culpable served to crystallize attention on the concept of authorship," Johns concludes, in a move designed "to give the state someone to prosecute" (159). Both Weber and Johns, then, find the figure of the author cropping up increasingly in the documents associated with press regulation after the Restoration, especially in court documents recording trials for unlicensed printing, treason, seditious libel, and other press-related crimes. Johns, for his part, notices in these same documents a simultaneous slippage in the definition of authorship—or, to use the Foucaultian terminology, of the author function—as virtually anyone in the print trade came to stand in for the elusive figure, the source, perennially absent from that trade's center.

The coming chapter confirms these accounts of the frequency of references to the author in such court cases and finds, with Johns, a willingness to make almost anyone in the trade stand in for the author if the author cannot be found. What this chapter has shown, however, is that this rhetoric of authorial responsibility has a long history, a history stretching back through L'Estrange's *Considerations* to the beginnings of English press regulation itself. What these otherwise compelling analyses miss, moreover, is not only the long history of authorial liability but also the role a rhetoric of ownership plays in the courtroom dramas of press regulation after the Restoration. The coming chapter not only carries forward the history of the place of the author in early modern press regulation but also begins to connect that history to notions of textual ownership becoming ever more prevalent in late seventeenth-century discussions of authorship. If what distinguishes modern authorship is its proprietary nature, as eminent historians such as Michel Foucault, Mark Rose, and Martha Woodmansee, among many others, have argued, then we would do well to ask what it means to "own" a work in the period leading up to the first era of authorial copyright. The somewhat surprising answer to that question is eloquently answered in the prosecutions of John Twyn, Henry Carr, and Elizabeth Cellier, which make up the topic of the next chapter.

Chapter 2
The Trials of Ownership: Finding the Author in Court

It is Hard to find the Author.
—Lord Chief Justice Scroggs

Prynne's Ears, Again

Any attempt to trace the trials of authorship in the seventeenth century ought, by rights, to begin with William Prynne, benighted author of *Histriomastix* and hundreds of other tracts denouncing playwriting, drinking, long hair, and all things sympathetic to Catholicism, including, in his estimation, William Laud, archbishop of Canterbury, and the family of his employer, Charles I.[1] Prynne, a lawyer, managed to lose his ears not once but twice, in 1634 and in 1637, as a result of his ceaseless advocacy on behalf of Puritan causes. In addition to this, his most spectacular punishment, Star Chamber sentenced Prynne to be imprisoned, fined, branded on the face, pilloried, and exiled to the Channel Islands. As Annabel Patterson persuasively argued two decades ago in *Censorship and Interpretation*, Prynne is the very emblem of the suffering author in the early modern period, a casualty of a censorship system entirely unable to control the increasing power of the press.[2] Most significantly for Patterson, Prynne was forced by the officials of Star Chamber to bear responsibility not only for what he had written but also for subsequent interpretations of his writings. As Lord Cottington put it, during the 1634 *Histriomastix* trial, "It is said, hee had noe ill intencion, noe ill harte, but hee maye bee ill interpreted. That must not be allowed him in excuse, for he should not have written any thinge that would beare construccion, for hee doth not accompanye his booke, to make his intencion knowne to all that reades it."[3] In this remarkably broad summary of the limits—or limitlessness—of authorial liability, Prynne's "intencions" are simply beside the point. He will be forced to bear responsibility for any number of meanings attributed to him or his work by others, including those least disposed to read him generously. His words are deemed to be the origin and basis of subsequent "construccions" and misconstructions, even though those words go forth into the world unaccompanied, incapable of attesting to their author's good or ill "harte." If, for Michel Foucault, modern authorship is an insidious solution to the problem of the "proliferation of discourse," Prynne has a good case for being called the first modern author: persecuted, locked up, and mutilated for any and all interpretations visited upon his work, Prynne is a kind of poster child for authorship as "penal appropriation."[4]

Yet, Prynne's case is virtually anomalous in the annals of seventeenth-century authorship trials, precisely because of the ease with which the author was "appropriated." Prynne nowhere denied having written the book, which appeared under his own name.[5] He even seems to have adamantly insisted, against the suspicions of his contemporaries, that this enormous tome was written alone, without the help of any collaborator. The trial report notes early on, "All he confesseth to be written by himself without the helpe of any other." The next page repeats, "he confesseth hee made the booke all himselfe."[6] Prynne could hardly have denied his authorship, given that he had personally secured a license for the work, thereby exposing himself publicly as the person responsible for his long-awaited production. The book was licensed on 31 May 1630 and entered in the Stationers' Register on 16 October of that year, again with Prynne's name prominently displayed. The register entry reads, "Master Sparkes, Entred for his Copie under the handes of master Buckner and master Harison warden. A Booke called *Histriomastix* by Master William Prinn."[7] When the book finally appeared in 1633, Prynne's name was printed prominently on the title page. With his name so painstakingly associated at every stage with the work, Prynne could hardly disown it once its considerable indiscretions had come to light. This, then, would be one of those extremely rare cases in which finding the author would turn out to be no challenge at all.

For the majority of seventeenth-century cases, especially those occurring after the Restoration, however, things would not prove to be so simple. To return for a moment to Roger L'Estrange's *Considerations and Proposals in Order to the Regulation of the Press*, published on 3 June 1663, we remember the bloodhound's lament that, "Touching the *Adviser, Author, Compiler, Writer, and Correcter*, their Practices are hard to be Retriev'd."[8] In the atmosphere of fear, suspicion, and mistrust of the opposition press and its agents that accompanied the return of Charles II to the throne, it is not difficult to imagine that authors would take advantage wherever possible, and as never before, of their inherent capacity for disappearing.[9] L'Estrange must have been encouraged, if not fully satisfied, by the provision in the 1662 Press Act that required the printer of any new work to "declare the Name of the Author thereof if he be thereunto required by the Licenser."[10] Yet, L'Estrange is only secondarily concerned in the *Considerations* with the regulation of *licensed* books. Far more serious was the flood of materials printed, as L'Estrange pointed out in the epistle dedicatory, "in Defiance of the Law" (A3v). It was these unlicensed books and pamphlets that threatened to return the nation to the state of upheaval and self-destruction from which it had only recently emerged, and it was thus to their eradication that the essay addressed itself. L'Estrange's strenuous efforts at finding out and cutting off the "Fountain of our Troubles"—both in the *Considerations* and in his capacity as surveyor of the imprimery beginning in August of 1663—were overwhelmingly directed toward this single-minded end (32).

As the discussion of the *Considerations* in the previous chapter detailed, L'Estrange's strategy for finding the author consisted of a system of rewards and punishments designed to induce others in the trade to turn over the offending "fountains" to the authorities. The main penalty L'Estrange recommended for those printers, publishers, and others who refused to cooperate was that they should be "*Reputed and Punish'd as the Author*" (2). This strategy of bribery, threat, and substitution did not originate with L'Estrange but had antecedents in royal proclamations from 1642, 1553, and even 1538, as the previous chapter makes clear. Nonetheless, as the seventeenth century wore on, both the hunt for the authors of unlicensed books and the willingness to let others suffer in their place seem to have accelerated. Paradoxically, in fact, the very expansiveness of the definition of the author used by the law and the courts—its ability to cover the activities of other members of the trade—resulted in an ever more developed rhetoric of authorship as the site of primary responsibility for printed works. As Joseph Loewenstein puts it, in an article about the printer John Twyn that anticipates many of the concerns of this chapter, "the seventeenth-century press was becoming authorial: the constitution of authorial property as we know it, the legal constitution of authorship as such, is in some measure a reaction to the proliferation and dispersal of authorial functions across the field of dissemination."[11] The more printers were "Reputed and punish'd" as authors in the Restoration courtroom, Loewenstein suggests, the more the author was ensconced at the heart of the drama of attribution and liability on which press regulation depended. While it still seems early to identify "the constitution of authorial property as we know it," moreover, Loewenstein is certainly correct to find in the seventeenth century, especially in the courts, an increasingly proprietary understanding of both authorship and liability, an understanding encapsulated most economically in the repeated references to whether or not a given defendant has "owned" his or her book. It is to this new and increasingly prevalent rhetoric of ownership—and the troubles and confusions that followed from it—that the present chapter turns.

Through looking in detail at the testimony in three trials related to the press that took place between 1660 and 1680, it is possible to reconstruct one episode in the emergence of a discourse of proprietary authorship, an episode that testifies eloquently to the inseparability of possession and liability in the ongoing juridical definition of what it meant to be an author. When judges and prosecutors asked authors—and others—whether they "owned" their books, they asked the question in the hopes of establishing responsibility for an offending book. To own a book was thus to own up to it and to do so in a primary or exclusive fashion. Owning a book, that is, meant, in L'Estrange's formulation, confessing to being its "first Mover," the person whose initiative brought it into the world.[12] This was the meaning attached to the phrase in the treason trial of the printer John Twyn in October of 1664. Yet owning a book was also almost always synonymous with being its author, as was the case in the trials of Henry Carr and Elizabeth Cellier in 1680. Notwithstanding the strenuous efforts on the part of both of these defendants to disown their books, each had left indelible traces of his or her authorship on the work and elsewhere, making it difficult—though not impossible—to evade responsibility for having written them. Finally, owning a book might carry a strict proprietary meaning, denoting the person in whose name the work was entered in the Stationers' Register or, barring that, the person for whom the work was printed and published. When these three meanings of ownership—liability, authorship, and possession—came together, as they did in the trials of Carr and Cellier, it became increasingly difficult for the defendant to escape. In these three Restoration court cases, then, it is possible to see some of the perils of proprietary authorship sketched out, along with the strategies undertaken by individual authors to try to disown their books and renounce the risky business of textual ownership on which authorship was beginning to depend.

Twyn's Hand

> *I must find the Author, or be deemed Author my self.*
>
> —*Francis Smith, printer*[13]

It might at first glance seem perverse to begin an account of authors on trial after the Restoration with the case of a printer, John Twyn, convicted of treason at the Old Bailey in October 1664 and sentenced to be hanged, drawn, and quartered. Yet, Twyn's case illustrates more sharply than any other in the period both the urgency attached to retrieving the author and the dire consequences that followed for those who refused to cooperate in doing so. Precisely because the author never appeared in the Twyn case, it is possible to trace the machinations and manipulations undertaken by the authorities in an ultimately fruitless effort to make the author reveal himself. More interestingly, however, not content to make Twyn simply suffer in the missing author's place, the officers of the court went through an elaborate process of producing an author where there was none before, and that author, bizarrely, turned out to be Twyn. The court achieved this miraculous act of transubstantiation by rescripting some of Twyn's own practices as a printer—in particular, his correcting of proofs—as a form of authorship. If Twyn could be found to have had a hand in correcting the sheets that came from his press, the court argued, then he had, in the court's estimation, made himself part of the authorship of the work in question. How exactly the court went about making this argument, and what role Twyn's hand played in their strategy, will become clear in what follows.[14]

That Twyn should have been tried for treason was highly unusual, a direct effect of the extraordinarily inflammatory nature of the work he was caught printing. On 7 October 1663, on the advice of an informant, L'Estrange and a number of his assistants broke into Twyn's shop in the middle of the night. Twyn and his apprentices were caught red-handed printing off sheets of an anonymous pamphlet titled *A Treatise of the Execution of Justice; or, Mene Tekel.* This work defended the regicide of Charles I and gestured at the idea that, with the return of his son to the throne, it might be time for a repeat performance. The full title of the work, at least according to the indictment, read, "A Treatise of the Execution of Justice; Wherein Is Clearly Proved, That the Execution of Judgment and Justice, Is As Well the Peoples as the Magistrates Duty, and If the Magistrates Pervert Judgment, the People Are Bound by the Law of God to Execute Judgment without Them and upon Them."[15] As if this were not damning enough, the prosecution speculated that the work's appearance had been timed to coincide with an uprising in the north that was due to take place in early October 1663. One prosecutor, Sergeant Morton, testified that the rebels "could not be ready till that 12th of *Octob.* for *the Seditious Books that were to lead on that Design, and the Libels and Declarations could not be Printed before that day*" (12). *A Treatise of the Execution of Justice* was, according to Morton, a prime example of one of these seditious books designed to "lead on" the rebellion. The court's job, however, was to prove not only that the work constituted sedition but also that it met the considerably higher standard of treason, a capital offense of which only one other printer had ever been convicted.[16]

In 1352, a statute of Edward III defined treason as "compassing or imagining" the death of the king, waging war on the king, or assisting the king's enemies.[17] For the following two hundred years, evidence of an "overt act" against the king was necessary in order for treason to be proved. However, in the religious upheavals of Henry VIII's reign, the Parliament of 1534 extended the law to include treason "by words or writing."[18] In 1649, Parliament further extended the statute to include those who "publish, by Writing, Printing, or openly Declaring" words designed to overthrow the government, and in 1661, yet another modification to the statute was passed combining the earlier ones, which now added imagining the death of the king by "Printing, Writing, Preaching, or Malicious . . . Speaking" to the list of treasonable offenses.[19] The indictment in Twyn's case reflects this long history. It first notes, according to the old law, that Twyn "traitorously didst compose, imagine, and intend the death and final destruction" of Charles II. It goes on to specify that "these thy most wicked Treasons, and Traiterous imaginations to fulfill, thou . . . didst declare, by Imprinting, a certain Seditious, Poysonous, and Scandalous Book" (3). Lord Chief Justice Robert Hyde's summary of the case to the jury backtracks slightly by leaving printing out of the equation, simply stating, "there is no doubt in the World by the Law of the Land, the Publishing such a Book as this, is as High a Treason as can be Committed" (31). By participating in making this work available to the public in any way, Hyde concludes, Twyn has opened himself to the charge of treason.

The court, then, had a sound statutory basis for prosecuting Twyn as either the printer or the publisher of this manifestly treasonable book.[20] In addition, since defendants in treason trials were not allowed counsel, and since Twyn had actually been caught in the act of printing the *Treatise*, the case was virtually airtight. Indeed, Hyde stated at the start of the trial that "the very *Title* of the *Book* (if there were no more) is as *Perfectly* Treason as possibly can be" (5). One has to wonder, in fact, why the court went to such elaborate measures to prove anything beyond the mere printing and intention to publish the work, or its title page—why, that is, they flirted with the domain of authorship at all. Yet they did so throughout the case, repeatedly attempting to establish not only that Twyn had set the type for individual pages of the work but also that he had both known what he was printing and sympathized with its content, that he had actively participated with his whole "harte" in the work's "ill intencion," as the judges of Star Chamber would have put it. More radically still, in the face of Twyn's repeated refusal to give up the name of the author, the court retaliated by trying to make him the author himself.

In L'Estrange's testimony in the case, the surveyor recounted that on the night of 7 October, just hours after the raid, he gave the printer an opportunity to provide the name of the author and thereby save himself. Having seized the sheets still wet from the press but lacking the manuscript copy from which the sheets had been printed, L'Estrange testified, "(Mr. *Twyn* said I) it may possibly do you some good yet to bring forth this Copy, if you will be so ingenious to produce the Copy, and discover the Author you may find mercy for your self" (20). In response to L'Estrange's request, Twyn provided the copy but refused to comply with the surveyor's other request, that he "discover the Author." He had already denied any knowledge of the origins of the work, telling L'Estrange that the copy "*was brought to him by an unknown hand*" (19). He was thus, he claimed, unable to identify either the author of the work or the person who wanted it printed, although he later revealed that the hand in question, the one that had actually delivered the manuscript to him, belonged to the maid of radical printer Elizabeth Calvert. This maid, he admitted, had given him the work to be printed, but beyond that basic information, he disclaimed all knowledge of the movers behind the *Treatise*, those unknown hands "for whom" it had been brought to the press (1).

At the conclusion of the trial, moments before sentencing, Twyn was again offered the bargain L'Estrange had originally made available, this time by Hyde himself. "The best you can do now toward amends for the wickednesse you have done," Hyde cajoled, "is by discovering the Authour of this Villainous Book" (30). This time, Twyn responded by explicitly denying that he knew the identity of the author, to which Hyde, the judged-turned-detective, responded, "Did you never see the hand before, with which this Copy was written?" (30). Twyn's negative response prompted incredulity on the part of the chief justice, who suggested that only a "mad" printer would accept an inflammatory pamphlet that arrived with no identifying marks, with neither the author's name nor a recognizable sample of his or her handwriting (30). Through withholding names and deliberately proliferating claims about unknown hands, Twyn attempted to short-circuit the mechanisms used to trace works back to those individuals responsible for them.

Unfortunately for Twyn, the officers of the court had already begun to make the case that, in the absence of other culprits, Twyn himself was the person responsible for the work—that he was, in fact, in possession of the offending hand.

The first witness interviewed by Hyde was Joseph Walker, Twyn's apprentice, who had been hard at work assisting his master on the night of the print shop raid. Walker immediately confessed that he himself was responsible for "composing" a number of the offending sheets, an admission that seemingly alarmed Hyde, who asked, "What doe you mean by Composing?" (13). To Hyde's probable disappointment, the apprentice replied, "Setting the Letters," thereby clearing up any possible misapprehensions about the apprentice's unlikely authorship of the work. Hyde went on to pursue an extensive line of questioning about the correction of the proofs, questions clearly designed to ascertain the exact nature of Twyn's part in this technical process. If he was not the work's author, these questions sought to determine, how involved was Twyn in the minutia of proof correction? Yet again, moreover, in this lengthy discourse between the relentless chief justice and the surprisingly agile apprentice, an unidentified hand seemingly holds the key to the case:

L. Hide. When you had printed one sheet, were there not some mistakes of the Letters to be mended?

Walker. Yes, there were *Literals.*

L. Hide. Who made the Amendment?

Walker. Upon my Oath I cannot tell.

L. Hide. Do you believe it to be your Masters?

Walker. I cannot tell that.

L. Hide. Have you seen your Master write heretofore?

Walker. I have seen him write, but because I have heard of them that could counterfeit mens hands, I dare not swear it was his Writing.

L. Hide. Were the amendments that were brought back, like his hand?

Walker. The Letters were something like them, but I cannot swear positively, that they were his.

L. Hide. No, that you cannot, unless you saw him write them; but was it like his hand?

Walker. It was not much unlike his hand. (15–16)

Hyde never succeeds in this exchange in getting the apprentice to confirm that the sheets have been amended, or corrected, by Twyn himself. Hands, as

Walker notes, can be counterfeit, and since he has not seen his master in the act of writing, he will only go so far as to say that the writing in question is "not much unlike his hand."

Only later in the narrative, however, does it begin to be clear why it is so important for the justices to pin down exactly whose hand was involved in the seemingly mundane, admittedly "literal" task of correcting the proofs. As the prosecution made its case, proof correction came increasingly to look like a form of authorship, making the question of whose hand was involved in this quotidian task a matter of the highest importance. In an exchange that also represents the first appearance of a vocabulary of ownership in this case, L'Estrange rehearsed once again the events of 7 October for one of the other judges, Justice Keeling.

> *J. Keeling. Twyn* owned to you that he had corrected some of the Sheets, that he had read them, and said it was *mettlesome stuff.*[21]
>
> *Mr. L'Estrange.* I did ask him in the house of the Constable: Who corrected this? the Corrector must certainly know what it was. Said he, *I have no skill in correcting.* But when I speak of *correcting,* I mean who *revised* it, *overlooked* it for the Press. *I read it over,* sayes he.
>
> *Twyn.* I never said such a word. . . .
>
> *Serj. Morton.* (to L'Estrange) What did you hear him confess before Sir *Henry Bennett*?
>
> *Mr. L'Estrange.* He owned the thing, that is, he acknowledged he had printed the sheet. (21)

Twyn was willing to "own" that he had printed parts of the work, but he resisted at all costs owning his hand in correcting them. L'Estrange's comment that "the Corrector must certainly know what it was" suggests why Twyn was so reluctant to confess his part in the practice of amendment, or "revision," as it was now suggestively called. Revision suggests something more agential, more original and intentional, than mere correcting; it suggests the possibility of actual changes or improvements visited upon the text. As Mr. Dickinson, one of those who assisted L'Estrange in the raid, put it just moments later, "When you revised it, you must needs know the sence of it" (22). Correcting proofs is becoming less literal by the moment, transforming from a mechanical process of checking a manuscript page against its printed counterpart to a quasi-critical, quasi-creative act of sense making and revision. As Loewenstein aptly puts it, "According to Justice Hyde and

Surveyor L'Estrange—and they should know—to read proof is to write, or at least to share in the work of writing."[22] In a postscript to the case, in fact, correction is even more deliberately tied to authorship than it is to mere writing. The editor of the *Narrative* bemoans the fact that Twyn, who "formerly owned" having corrected the proofs, later denied it. "The next question," the editor notes, should "*Infallibly have been,* To whom was it carried? *Or,* who Corrected it? as the *Readiest way to the Discovery of the* Author" (78). Unlike the editor, however, in response to Twyn's refusal to identify any of the actual originating agents behind *A Treatise of the Execution of Justice,* the mysterious hands who brought the work into being, the chief justice and his associates were content to identify Twyn's hand as the one responsible for correcting, and thus authoring, this dangerous work.

Given that under the 1661 treason statute, the court could have convicted Twyn for his part in the printing of the *Treatise,* which he freely confessed, it remains to be explained why the prosecution was so intent on attributing to Twyn a more extensive role in the production of the work, including an authorial role. The first answer to this puzzle lies in the fact that Twyn attempted to argue throughout the trial that he was merely making a living in printing the work—that he had, as he protested at his sentencing, "never read a word of it" (33). As he repeated at the execution itself, he had printed it "barely for getting a little mony for my Family" (74). Clearly, the court was worried that the jury, at least half of whom were stationers, would be persuaded by this defense.[23] In the "Letter to the Reader" that precedes the published account of the trial, possibly written by L'Estrange himself, one of the justifications for bringing the trial account to press at all is to warn other stationers not to attempt a similar defense and to emphasize the "Hazzard of Dispersing of Books as well as Printing of them" (A4v).[24] The case is meant to serve as an example to aspiring print rebels that "*none presume to flatter themselves with an Expectation of coming off, in Cases of* Treason *and* Sedition, *upon the Plea of* Trade" (A4v). Clearly, those in charge of managing the press were worried enough about this "plea of trade" to want to publicly eliminate any expectation that such a strategy might work. If there was indeed some anxiety on the part of the court that the stationers present would sympathize with this sort of professional defense, then, this helps to explain the urgency with which the justices sought to paint Twyn as a full and knowing collaborator in the publication of his own hazardous work.[25]

A more fundamental explanation for the court's behavior can be found, however, in the strategies for press regulation laid out by L'Estrange in the *Considerations* and deliberately followed throughout the trial. Over and over, Twyn and his apprentices were asked to identify the author of the *Treatise*, and over and over, they refused to do so. As much as the prosecution knew that it *could* make its case against Twyn as a printer, there is a palpable sense in the trial proceedings of dissatisfaction with this outcome. Not to find the author means failure, or, at the very least, it means that justice has only partially been done. Twyn has, in some profound sense, cheated the court of its own "execution of justice" by refusing to provide information leading to the fountain of all textual troubles.

Just how important it was to the justices to find the author is borne out yet again in the conclusion to the trial and the rather gruesome description of the days leading up to Twyn's execution. As though temporal justice might be satisfied with an outcome that convicted the printer of a treasonous work, but divine justice would not, Hyde in sentencing the prisoner adjured Twyn to "make your peace with God, which must be done by confession, and by the discovery of those that are guilty of the same crime with you" (34). Harassed to his very grave by the court's need to satisfy its lust for authorial blood (in the name of justice and in the name of God), Twyn was pressured constantly in Newgate as he awaited execution to comply with the chief justice's last request: "*Mr. Weldon*, the *Ordinary of Newgate*, spent much time and pains upon him, to convince him of that horrid Crime, for which he was to Suffer; Particularly pressing him to a *Confession* both of his *Offence*, and of the *Author* of that Treasonable Piece, for which he was to Die. His Answer was, That *it was not his Principle to betray the Authour*; but it belong'd to others" (73). By this time, Twyn had given up all pretense that he did not know the author, or at least the way to find the author. On principle, he was keeping the information to himself, refusing to betray a figure whose punishment he knew would be as "severe" as, or perhaps more severe than, his own.[26] The last, taunting line of the passage seems to suggest that Twyn knew of others who had the information the court wanted, but that discovery of the author was, in his estimation, their responsibility—indeed, that responsibility "belong'd" to them.

Yet the line in question, "that *it was not his Principle to betray the Author, but it belong'd to others*," is open to an alternative reading. Twyn might also have been saying that the *principle* of giving up the author was not his but was a principle that belonged to others—others named, for instance, Chief Justice Hyde and Roger L'Estrange. If this reading is correct, Twyn's refusal to provide the name of the author then becomes a refusal to participate in the entire treacherous system of press regulation that encouraged members of the trade to betray each other in order to ensure their own safety. This "construccion" of the line is borne out in the court's final, eleventh-hour effort to induce Twyn, in the waning moments before his execution, to comply with their requests. Once again, they offered him his freedom in exchange for the name of the author. This bargain Twyn refused for the final time, and he did so, once again, according to a formal principle: "Mr *Ordinary* did likewise further urge him to a Confession of the *Author*, upon a Confidence, that such a Discovery might save his Life. To which he Replyed, that he neither could do it, nor did believe himself obliged to if he could; for better (sayes he) *one* suffer, then *many*" (73–74). Twyn here suggested that, even were he to expose the author, he too would probably still be one of the many to suffer for their parts in the publication of the *Treatise*. Yet his refusal to comply with the ordinary's request comes not from self-interest but from his own, alternative principle of press regulation, a principle he opposed to that of L'Estrange and others: "better one suffer, than many."

As it turns out, however, Twyn's principle is in fact very close to that articulated by L'Estrange throughout his career and passed on to those charged with oversight of the Restoration press. One need only remember L'Estrange's calculation in the *Considerations* that prosecuting the author is the most economical way to go about the business of press regulation: "There are not many of them in an Age, and so the *less work* to do" (32). Almost two decades later, in the trial of Henry Carr, Lord Chief Justice Scroggs demonstrated the persistence of this L'Estrangean doctrine when he memorably stated, "it is Hard to find the Author, it is not hard to find the Printer: but *one Author* found is better than *twenty Printers* found."[27] Twyn, then, propounded a principle that shared the calculation of L'Estrange and Scroggs—better to punish one than many—but that somehow missed the key element of their technique, that it is the *author* who must be punished in order for the regulatory arithmetic to work out in a satisfactory fashion. Twyn's own trial, in fact, offered eloquent proof of the persuasiveness of the official doctrine, for in the end, even despite its gruesome conclusion, the Twyn trial satisfied no one. Twyn went to his grave carrying the only piece of information that really mattered—the identity of the unknown hand behind *A Treatise of the Execution of Justice*. It would take more than rewards and punishments, more even than death threats aimed at collaborators, to make the author appear. Somehow, the courts would have to find a way to force authors to own their books.

Interlude: Libel, License, and the Resurgence of Royal Prerogative

> *For those hireling Scriblers . . . who write to Eat, and lye for Bread, I intend to meet with them another way, for they are onely safe whilst they can be secret; but so are Vermine, so long onely as they hide themselves.*
>
> —*Lord Chief Justice Scroggs,* The Lord Chief Justice Scroggs his Speech in the Kings-Bench

The case of John Twyn constitutes an exception to the norms of Restoration press regulation not only because Twyn was a printer but also because treason, the crime for which he was tried, was an extreme infraction requiring extreme punishments. The vast majority of press regulation from 1662 to 1679 was carried on under the aegis of the Press Act, with punishments ranging from fines and imprisonment to confiscation of presses and occasional corporal measures, including the pillory and whipping. Once licensing regulations expired in 1679, however, the government found itself without the capacity for prepublication oversight of the press and with a chaotic common-law tradition for handling prosecutions once offensive materials had actually been issued. A kind of regulatory vacuum thus emerged after 1679, a vacuum filled only after 1685 by the reemergence of statutory measures for prepublication licensing. In order to understand the trials of 1679–81 that make up the remainder of this chapter, then, it is essential to review the events immediately surrounding the expiration of licensing laws in 1679 and to detail the improvised system of oversight worked out in the wake of this transformation in regulatory regimes.[28]

The lapse of the Press Act on 26 May 1679 could not have come at a worse time for the king and his allies. The statute expired when Parliament was dissolved, only eleven days after the first bill had been introduced to prevent James, the king's brother, from succeeding to the throne upon Charles's death. The lapse thus offered "hireling Scriblers" of the Whig variety an opportunity to galvanize public opinion in the cause of exclusion. In addition, the country was reeling from the dramatic aftermath of the so-called Popish Plot, the ostensible—and almost certainly fabricated—Catholic plan to bring down the government brought to the attention of Parliament by the infamous Titus Oates and his associates in August of 1678. The end of prepublication licensing nine months later threatened to let loose a torrent of pamphlets and other printed materials stirring up the various factions concerned in and affected by all of the many purported plots and counterplots.

Recalling Parliament to reintroduce a new licensing bill was no solution, however, since with that legislation was sure to come further attempts at undermining the succession. For the time being, at least, control of the press had to be returned to the hands of those who had relinquished it a half-century before: the king, the Privy Council, and the prerogative courts, especially the Court of King's Bench, presided over by Lord Chief Justice William Scroggs.[29]

The king and his associates responded quickly to the crisis, although not quickly enough to stop what Harold Weber, in *Paper Bullets*, calls "a sudden proliferation of printed news" (162). Weber notes, "the alacrity with which the opposition took advantage of the lapsing of the Licensing Act of 1679 suggests that both an audience for political literature and the structures for producing and distributing such material had survived and even prospered during the first two decades of Charles's reign" (158). The Privy Council must have been aware of this surviving underground of opposition publishing, for on 27 May, just a day after Parliament was dissolved, the council called on that intermittently steadfast friend to royal prerogative in matters of the press, Roger L'Estrange. It had come to the council's attention that "several Seditious Pamphlets are now in the Press, and are likely to increase" as a result of the expiration of the system of licensing.[30] L'Estrange was again summoned in September 1679 and directed to begin searching immediately for such pamphlets and to seize any that might be "brought in Evidence against the offender."[31] It remained, however, for the Privy Council to determine what crime, exactly, these offensive pamphleteers were to be charged with and which participants in the trade were open to prosecution for the liberties they had taken with the press.

In order to obtain an answer to these pressing questions, the king and council decided to ask the judges of the realm what expedients might be available to them for controlling the press. The first such request came on 17 October 1679. Even before the judges as a body had had a chance to respond, though, Scroggs, apparently on his own initiative, lent his voice to the rising outcry concerning an unregulated press in a speech given before the other justices at the Court of King's Bench on 23 October 1679. On the title page of the published version, the speech is said to have been "Occasioned by the many Libellous Pamphlets which are publisht against the Law, to the Scandal of the Government, and Publick Justice."[32] Yet, Scroggs's speech, here put forth as a contribution to the public debate over press regulation, was also a transparently self-interested production. In the wake of a series of controversial trials, including Scroggs's acquittal of Sir George

Wakeman, the queen's Catholic physician, on treason charges, the chief justice had himself become the target of a veritable flood of defamatory broadsides and pamphlets.[33] The personal nature of the occasion may explain the particularly rancorous nature of Scroggs's indictment of "hireling Scriblers," quoted in the epigraph to this section. Yet, Scroggs's speech is directed not only at the cowardly, secretive, verminlike authors but at the rest of their associates in the trade as well: "Let their Brokers, those Printers and Booksellers by whom they vend their false and braded Ware, look to it; some will be found, and they shall know, that the Law wants not power to punish a Libellous and Licentious Press, nor I resolution to execute it" (4). Scroggs's outrage may be focused on the hidden authors of these libelous tracts, but his regulatory energies take aim at the publishers and booksellers, at least some of whom, he confidently states, "will be found." Scroggs here resoundingly trumpets the law's power to restrain the press and to punish whatever offenders it can lay hands on.

At the very end of the speech, Scroggs returned again to the question of the scope of judicial power, addressing himself directly to the question of the extent of the court's jurisdiction in handling matters of the press: "In short, it is the proper business of this Court, and our Duties that sit Judges here, to take care to prevent and punish the Mischiefs of the Press" (7). At this point, listeners would have been forgiven for wondering if Scroggs were not protesting a bit too much on the question of the courts' duties—and rights—with respect to the press. As it turned out, in fact, many of Scroggs's contemporaries, including some of those with whom he shared the bench, were less sure than the chief justice about the precise extent of the courts' power to punish libelers as well as the more general responsibilities of the Crown and its agents with relation to the press. These fractures emerged over the course of the decisions—three in all—handed down by the judges in response to Charles's repeated requests that they declare "what expedients may by Law be made use of to remedy the Great Mischiefs that dayly arise from ye Licenciousness of the Presse."[34] These requests were clearly designed to ascertain whether or not the Crown, acting alone, had the right to reinstate a system of prepublication licensing to curb the ongoing licentiousness. In the course of the three decisions, it is possible to trace divergent, even contradictory, opinions about the Crown's rights and responsibilities with relation to the press. Out of these contradictory opinions emerged the strange and tangled cases of Henry Carr and Elizabeth Cellier, to which this analysis will turn next.

The first time the Crown applied to the judges, on 17 October, the judges as a whole took ten days to respond, although Scroggs clearly hoped to jump the gun by making his opinions public on the twenty-third. On 27 October came back the collective reply, which, notwithstanding its strident tone, told the king nothing he did not already know: "all Seditious & Scandalous Books or Pamphlets being Libells ag[ainst] the Government or against any Publique or Private Person" could be seized by agents of the Crown. The offending "Makers, Printers, Sellers, or Publishers" could then be "proceeded against and punished according to Law."[35] The judges were clearly here recommending that the Crown use existing common and statutory law, including treason, libel, *Scandalum Magnatum*, and seditious libel, to prosecute the purveyors of offensive materials. In a blow to Charles's ambitions, however, no mention whatsoever was made of the power to reinstate licensing. On 31 October, the king issued a royal proclamation—discussed in detail at the conclusion of the previous chapter—reiterating the terms of the judges' decision and instituting a system of rewards designed to make easier the discovery and prosecution of authors and others responsible for "Seditious and Treasonable Books and Pamphlets."[36] That Charles knew how unlikely it was that this proclamation would be sufficient to curtail the recalcitrant abusers of the press is attested by the fact that he appealed to the judges a second time, only two months later, in January of 1680, only to receive the same answer. In the words of Philip Hamburger, the judges, in an even more tentative ruling, "suggested that the king use the statutes of *Scandalum Magnatum* against the Press."[37] Lois Schwoerer reports that the Crown "was so disappointed in the ruling that [the king] forbade the Clerk of the Privy Council to enter it in the council's official register."[38] The search for a renewed system of prepublication licensing was proving to be more complicated than Charles had, perhaps, anticipated.

In order to achieve a more favorable outcome on the third and final attempt, Charles actually dismissed two of the dissenting judges from the bench before his third appeal, which came on 14 April 1680. In addition, perhaps as a way of making this heavy-handed use of royal prerogative palatable to the more cautious judges, he restricted his ambitions this time to the regulation of "pamphlets and newes Bookes," asking only how this more limited category of printed material might be controlled. Finally, on 4 May 1680, he got the answer he had sought all along, in the form of a far more sympathetic ruling from the newly constituted bench: "As to your Ma[jesty's] Royall & Legall Power in Regulating the abuses of the Press by Pamphletts

& news Bookes which wee have considered according to your Ma[jesty's] Commands in Councill the 14th day of Aprill last past: Wee doe most humbly & unanimously certifye that your Ma[jesty] may by Law prohibit the printing and publishing all newes Bookes and Pamphletts of Newes whatever not Licenced by your Authority as Manifestly tending to the Breach of the Peace of the Kingdome. 4th May 1680."[39] For the time being, and without the intercession of an uncooperative and unruly Parliament, Charles had found a way to restore licensing, at least of the inflammatory, inexpensive, and popular materials that came under the heading of "newes." As Schwoerer notes, however, the decision, precisely because it circumvented Parliament, was highly controversial, provoking anxieties about "policies and practices that smacked of absolutism" at just the moment the king might have sought to conciliate an angry Parliament and a wary populace (16). In the unholy alliance between the Stuart court and the judiciary, which, for some, brought back memories of Star Chamber, onlookers saw evidence that "the judges were usurping the authority of Parliament in the lawmaking process" (90). In order to avert what was fast becoming a crisis of authority centered most immediately around the regulation of the press, the justices would have to proceed with some caution as they set about enforcing these new, somewhat shaky regulatory measures.

More important for this analysis, moreover, in reinstituting a licensing system, even if only for news, the judges left wide open the identity of the offenders to be prosecuted under the new judicial prerogative. All members of the trade—all of those involved in the production, distribution, and circulation of unlicensed materials—could and would still be open to prosecution as they had been all along. This outcome allowed the courts to continue casting as wide a net as possible in their attempts to maintain some control over the proliferation of unwanted news—a category so broad and ill defined that it could refer to virtually any new production that came off the press. Notwithstanding this comfortably expansive regulatory policy, however, the figure of the author continued to trouble this otherwise functional system. The ancient conviction, so eloquently borne out in Twyn's trial, that justice would not properly be done until the author was discovered and punished, seemed, if anything, to be gaining in power as time went on. In the trials of Henry Carr and Elizabeth Cellier, it is possible to trace not only the continuing urgency attached to finding the author in court but also the continuing ability of authors to disown their books and slip away, immediately before justice could be done.

Carr's Pacquet

> *How did you come to take it for granted that he was the Author, when he did once deny, but never owned it? Answer me that Question,* and thou shalt be a brave Man.
>
> —*Lord Chief Justice Scroggs,* Trial of Henry Carr

Just how tentative the justices—including Scroggs—were in the aftermath of the series of uncomfortable negotiations between the Crown and the courts in 1679–80 can be seen in the trial of Henry Carr for printing and publishing a periodical titled *The Weekly Pacquet of Advice from Rome.* The periodical was first brought out by Carr (or Care, or Car, as his name was sometimes spelled) and the publisher Langley Curtis on 3 December 1678, at the height of the furor surrounding the Popish Plot. The first issue was timed to coincide with the first execution of a supposed Catholic plotter, and the *Pacquet* was, at least initially, seen to be favorable to the government's cause of suppressing Catholic plots and factions.[40] Indeed, L'Estrange himself licensed the *Weekly Pacquet,* from the time of the first issue to the lapse of the Licensing Act in May of the next year. The periodical, which, as its name suggests, appeared weekly, had a format designed (as Sir Philip Sidney might have put it) both to teach and to delight. Split into two parts, the anonymous publication included the *Weekly Pacquet,* a rambling serialized history of the Roman Catholic Church and its "Treasons and Seditious Principles," along with the *Popish Courant,* a single sheet including "joco-serious Reflections of Romish Fopperies."[41] This tragicomic pair from the outset found favor not only with Parliament but also with the Stuart court itself. As Schwoerer puts it, "in the early winter of 1678, who could object to such a project as this? No one!" (50).

Less than a year later, the answer was rather different, and at the head of the list of those objecting to the paper could be found Roger L'Estrange and Chief Justice Scroggs. By the autumn of 1679, especially in the aftermath of the Wakeman trial, deep fissures had appeared in what had previously appeared to be the government's united anti-Catholic front. Now, anti-Catholic propaganda could just as easily appear to be directed against the Crown and its agents as in its defense. Scroggs, in particular, was subjected to vicious abuse in a series of anti-Catholic pamphlets, abuse carried on, in August 1679, in the pages of the *Weekly Pacquet* and especially the comical *Popish Courant* itself.[42] On the very day of Scroggs's speech against the "hireling Scriblers," 23 October 1679, he summoned Carr to appear before him for an interrogation about one such "joco-serious" portrayal of the judge, as a result of which Carr actually confessed to being the author of the *Weekly Pacquet.* Carr was imprisoned at King's Bench but released shortly afterward, in large part because of the ongoing confusion surrounding jurisdiction in matters of press regulation as well as the passage of the recent Habeas Corpus Act. Scroggs simply could not hold Carr without charging him with a crime, and he did not, as yet, have a crime with which to charge him. He did order him to appear daily at King's Bench, just in case suitable charges could be found. Finally, in February, in the wake of a series of successful prosecutions of printers and publishers for the common-law crime of seditious libel—prosecutions that nonetheless relied upon the first and second decisions of the judges—Scroggs felt confident enough to initiate proceedings against Carr once again.[43] On 11 February 1680, an information was brought against Carr in King's Bench on charges of having published a "scandalous and malitious Book."[44] Almost five months elapsed before Carr was actually tried, however, on 2 July 1680. By that time, the judges had had an opportunity to produce their third decision in response to Charles's persistent demands that they comment on press regulation, the decision regarding licensing of news. Much of the incoherence and confusion surrounding Carr's case can be directly linked to this accident of timing.

Carr's case stands out from others in the same period, according to Schwoerer, for the simple reason that Carr "was the only author the government had in its snare" (110–11). Having had success with the "brokers" of the trade, Scroggs seized this opportunity to flush scribbling vermin out of their secret hiding places as well. His job should have been rendered remarkably simple by the fact that Carr had already confessed, in October 1679, to being the author of the *Weekly Pacquet.* He had, that is, already admitted responsibility for his book and had done so in front of some of the nation's highest judicial officials. Surely this time the court would not—could not—fail to find the author. Unfortunately for Scroggs, as he himself put it in Carr's trial, in what would turn out to be a colossal understatement (and one of the only understatements of which the thundering Scroggs would ever be accused), "it is Hard to find the Author" (7). The trial's deceptively simple first question, "Did Mr. *Car* own he writ this Pacquet?" should have been answered without difficulty, since everyone in the courtroom knew that Carr had admitted to being the periodical's author and therefore, at least according to one definition of the term, that he had "owned" the *Pacquet* as well (3). As it turned out, however, getting Carr—or anyone else—to own the specific passages named in the indictment proved virtually impossible.

Stranger still is the fact that, according to the two judicial decisions used by the prosecution in making its case—the first and third decisions of October 1679 and May 1680, respectively, find that the author was not even necessary to prove the defendant's guilt. The prosecution needed only to prove that Carr had published the work—or that he had had a "hand" in its publication—in order to meet the terms of the original indictment, which did not mention authorship at all. According to the information of 11 February, repeated in the course of the trial proceedings, one Henry Carr, "the 1st day of *August*, in the 31st Year of our now Lord the King, at the Parish of St. *Pulchres, London*, a certain false, scandalous and malitious Book, Intituled, *The Weekly Pacquet of Advice from Rome*, or *The History of Popery*; malitiously and unlawfully hath Printed, and caused to be Published" (A1v). The information goes on to reprint a passage that, "among other things," is taken to exemplify the malicious and seditious content of the *Weekly Pacquet* (A1v). The passage in question describes a medicine, "truly *Catholick in Operation*," lately available in England, that "will make Justice Deaf as well as Blind" (A1v). This clear jab at the purported partiality to Catholic defendants of the judicial system was recognized by all as a slur against a public official, Scroggs himself, a slur designed to "scandalize . . . the Administration of Justice" and the workings of government more generally (A1v). Whoever had printed or published this scandalous passage was clearly subject to being proceeded against "by law," according to the terms of the first judicial decision and the accompanying royal proclamation of 31 October 1679.

By the time the case came to trial, however, the third decision concerning the licensing of news books had come down—a fact noted in his opening remarks at the trial by the recorder, or public prosecutor, named Sir George Jefferies. His introductory statement was patently contradictory in its estimation of what, exactly, Carr was on trial for. He first stated that Carr, "intending to scandalize the Government, hath caused a Book to be published"—the *Weekly Pacquet* named in the information (1). Only moments later, however, Jefferies went off on what must have seemed like an unnecessary tangent, reminding those in attendance that the judges had recently met and handed down their decision that "no Person whatsoever could expose to the publick Knowledge any thing that concerned the Affairs of the Publick without Licence from the King" (1). Further confusing his audience, Jefferies then returned to his original line of reasoning, complaining that "The Author of this Pacquet of *Advice from Rome*, or the Publisher of it, Mr. *Carr*, that is now the Defendant, he thinks he can scratch the Itch of the *Age*, and that he may Libel any man concerned in the government, if he can but call him a *Papist*, or *popishly* affected" (2). Although Jefferies stumbled over the question of whether Carr was to be tried as an author or as a publisher, in this passage he at least seemed to have returned to the original charges outlined in the indictment. Yet again, however, in concluding his introductory remarks, he muddied the case, repeating the judges' third decision, and stating, "now we are to try whether this Person exposed this thing to publick Knowledge, and that is the matter, Gentlemen, that you are to trie. The other is the Business of the Court" (2). Jefferies seems to be saying, in a moment of seriously arbitrary procedural improvisation, that the jury should decide Carr's case according to the third decision of the judges, while the judges would take up the "Business" of Carr's authorship (or publication) of a scandalous libel, according to the first decision. The unfortunate confusion surrounding what, exactly, Carr was being tried for (unlicensed publishing? seditious libel?) and in what capacity he was being tried (as an author? as a publisher?) would persist throughout the trial. In neither case, it needs to be remembered, would it have been necessary to prove that Carr was the author, although making that case ultimately took up the majority of the prosecution's time and energy. In a remarkable replay of the Twyn trial, in fact, proving that the defendant had caused an offensive work to be published might have satisfied the jury, but it would not satisfy the judge.

When the first witness—the printer, Stevens[45]—was called, the uncertainty surrounding the nature of the charges immediately became clear in two simultaneous but distinct lines of questioning. Scroggs asked, opening the evidentiary portion of the proceedings, "Did Mr. *Car* own he writ this Pacquet, had you any from him [?]" (3). With this concise formulation, Scroggs attempted to prove both Carr's authorship and his responsibility for the work's publication. Stevens admitted to having received samples of the *Weekly Pacquet* from Carr but would not swear that the particular issue named in the information was one of those he had received. More important, upon being asked whether he had received the papers in question "from *Car's* hand," he seemed to backpedal, stating that he could not be sure that they had actually come from Carr's hand, rather than from that of the publisher, Langley Curtis (5). He thought the papers in question had come to him from Carr, "this is, by him or his Order," but he could not be sure that others had not been involved (5). Once again, unknown hands were at work, confusing the orderly functioning of the book trade's paper trail.

If Scroggs found it difficult to discover whether Carr was the publisher of the *Weekly Pacquet*, he was to be even more frustrated in his attempt to discover whether he was the author. A lengthy exchange between Scroggs and the printer Stevens on the subject of the authorship and ownership of the *Weekly Pacquet* sums up perfectly the impediments that existed for all those wedded to regulatory schemes centered in the notion of authorial liability:

LCJ. [Scroggs.] Did *Carr* ever own himself to you to be the Author of this Book, or any of these Papers?

P[rinter]. My Lord, as I said in the other Case, so I say in this, I had no Occasion to dispute it, I took it for granted.

LCJ. Have you ever heard him own it?

P. I have heard him deny it.

LCJ. How did you come to take it for granted that he was the Author, when he did once deny, but never owned it? Answer me that Question, *and thou shalt be a brave Man.*

P. My Lord, there was never Occasion for that Discourse.

LCJ. Look you Sir, you must answer me in a Way agreeable to common Reason and Understanding. Why did you say just now you took it for granted that he was the Author, and yet you say he hath denyed it, and never owned it? Why should you then Believe he was the Author.

P. I don't say, my Lord, he never owned it.

LCJ. What Tricks we have in this World. (6)

What tricks indeed. Carr, universally believed to be the author, had nonetheless never "owned" himself to be such, at least, as the printer later put it, "in so many words" (6). As long as the author did not stand up and say, *verbatim,* "I own this book," he or she would remain safe from the reach of the law. Proving authorship was virtually impossible absent this sort of confession, for a whole litany of reasons: because writing takes place in private, because writing can be counterfeit, because seeing an author write one page does not mean he or she wrote another, because a page in the author's hand may simply be his or her copy of another author's work. No amount of prodding, pleading, or pressuring on the part of the court was able to amend this situation, even when Scroggs thundered at the printer, "That is the same Question asked before. Did Mr. *Car* ever own it as his or no? Upon your Oath, did *Carr* own this Pacquet to be his when you discourst with him about it?" (9) With no one to prove him a liar, Stevens simply maintained that Carr did not own his book in so many words—did not, that is, speak the discourse of proprietary authorship—as a result of which, his authorship remained stubbornly immune to legal proof.

Scroggs never succeeded in getting the requisite evidence of Carr's authorship from Stevens, and the defense continued to cast doubt on this fundamental aspect of the Crown's case. They were apparently unabashed by Scroggs's menacing comment to William Williams, Carr's counsel, "If you could, Mr. *Williams*, shew me any Author besides Mr. *Carr*, I would say something" (10). Perhaps sensing the weakness of the prosecution's case against Carr, Sir Francis Winnington, another of Carr's lawyers, began his own line of reasoning by insisting that the court return to the charges given in the original indictment against Carr—that is, "Whether or no this *Defendant*, that is *Carr*, did *falsely and malitiously* and with *design to scandalize the Government*, cause to be printed and published this false Libel, that is in the Information. Now truely, my Lord, We that are for the *Defendent*, say we are not guilty. My Lord, we very well know how penal a thing it is, for a Man to be the Author of a Libel, that relates to the Scandal of the Government" (12). If the defendant were such an author, Winnington repeated, that would be "a very penal Matter" (13). However, Carr's authorship of the particular passage in the information remained steadfastly in doubt. Perhaps the paper in question was not among those written by Carr. Perhaps, more interesting, the offending passages had been inserted by Carr's enemies; perhaps they had been put there by the Catholics themselves: "Who knows but that the *Papists*, that might have an ill will to this Mr. *Carr*, that hath been no friend to them, might shuffle in this Paragraph by that means to have Justice come upon him" (13). Even if Carr did write the passage, Winnington continued, the court had no way of proving that he intended it maliciously or scandalously. His original intention is, in fact, impossible to retrieve. "He might have some little Extravagancies in his Head in writing," Winnington admitted, but that does not mean that he acted with malice (14). The evidence that he did so, like the evidence for his authorship generally, is merely "remote and conjectural" (14).

For all his blustering in the early part of the case, Scroggs was clearly unnerved by the combination of the prosecution's unreliable witnesses and the defense's argumentation. The shift in tone is suggested by Scroggs's newly formulated question to the first defense witness, "has he disown'd he was the Author?" (15) It is as though Scroggs now believes he will have to prove Carr owned the work by default: if he did not disown the *Weekly Pacquet*, he must have been its author. The precarious state of the prosecution's case is suggested by a long and frustrated intervention made by Jefferies, in which the recorder tried to appeal to the "common sense" of the jury (18). The defendant's malicious intentions were indicated "in plain English" in the information: "It is as plain as can be in the World" (18). The proof of Carr's authorship is equally available to common sense, according to Jefferies: "The Printer himself, he comes here and saies, that *Carr* did acknowledge himself the Author" (18). No amount of "*snuffling* and canting" on the part of the witnesses can or ought to make any difference to the outcome of the case (19). In an echo of Twyn's trial, Jefferies concluded by averring, "every man that knows any thing of Printing, knows this, that after it hath first been taken to the Press, it is *always carried back again to the Author*, to see whether it be done according to his mind" (19). Since the pages were carried back to Carr, the authorship of the work must be his. Yet again, then, proofs are here offered as proof of authorship, undeniable evidence of the link between the printed sheet, the writer's hand, and the author's mind.

Scroggs, however, was not convinced. Although, he insisted, all the evidence pointed to the fact that Carr was indeed responsible for the *Weekly Pacquet*—that he was "thought the Author" and "lookt . . . upon as the Author" (22)—still, he could not be proven beyond all doubt to be the author of the scandalous and malicious passages named in the indictment. In a most improbable aside, Scroggs proclaimed, "I had rather, Mr. *Carr*, with all his Faults about him, and his Hummers, should go away with applause, and have him found not guilty, than do him wrong in one Circumstance" (22). Before releasing the defendant from his bonds, however, Scroggs had one more trick up his sleeve—a trick that put Carr and his authorship of the *Weekly Pacquet* right back at the center of the trial, although not without a little sleight of hand. Shifting attention away from the first judicial ruling, on the basis of which Carr was originally indicted, and with it the question of malicious intent, Scroggs argued that Carr should instead be tried according to the *third* decision, the decision regarding prepublication licensing of news. Remembering the decision recorded on 4 May, he noted, "we did all subscribe, that to Print, or Publish any *News-Books* or *Pamphlets of News* whatsoever, is illegal" (23). Rather than leaving it at this, however, having described an offense for which Carr, as one of the publishers of the work, could surely not have been acquitted, Scroggs could not resist putting the author back into the picture. Although no mention of authors had been made anywhere in the third decision, Scroggs paraphrased the judges' ruling, misremembering it in a manner uncannily reminiscent of his own speech in King's Bench on the subject of "hireling Scriblers." Directing his attention to the *Weekly Pacquet* once again, he argued, "Suppose, now, that this thing is not scandalous, what then [?] If there had been no reflection in this Book at all, yet, it is *illicite*, and the Author ought to be convicted for it. And that is for a publick notice to all People, and especially *Printers*, and *Booksellers*, that they ought to Print no Book, or Pamphlet of News whatsoever, with *Authority*" (23). Carr, Scroggs now stated, ought to be tried on the basis of his involvement with an unlicensed pamphlet of news and convicted (or so it seems) on the basis of his authorship of that pamphlet. No matter that the *Weekly Pacquet* was not really news, nor that it had had a license as long as licensing was in effect: what mattered now was the fact that the *Weekly Pacquets* since 28 May 1679, including the one named in the indictment, were published without license. As Scroggs told the jury in the closing moments of the trial, changing his tactics once again, "If you believe he was not the Publisher of this Pamphlet . . . you must find him not guilty" (26). The jury, clearly keen to show that they were not only honest men but also men of "common sense," found him guilty.

Scroggs, however, could never quite bring himself to settle for convicting Carr as a publisher; he wanted to find, convict, and punish him as an author instead. As he said in his direction to the jury, as if stating his own regulatory principle, "the Author ought to be convicted for it," even if he is convicted not as the author, but as the publisher. As Scroggs oddly claimed, reversing, in some sense, L'Estrange's model, "if he were the Author, no doubt, but he is the Publisher" (25). In the end, where Hyde managed to punish a printer as an author, Scroggs had to settle for convicting an author as a publisher. Moreover, in a strange twist to the conclusion of this case, Carr was never punished at all, either as the author or as the publisher. When he arrived for sentencing on 22 October 1680, not only was he not punished, but apparently his case was entirely dismissed.[46] The reasons behind this dismissal are complex, related to the larger concerns over royal prerogative, the Exclusion crisis, and Scroggs's own abuses of judicial power, which brought about attempts to impeach the chief justice in late 1680 and early 1681, beginning just as Carr's sentencing hearing was occurring.[47] More locally, though, as Schwoerer concludes, the Crown was unwilling to provoke an outcry on Carr's behalf, given that "the evidence of fact and the law were too problematic in Care's case" to allow them to be revisited (*Henry Care*, 125). Perhaps, too, the courts did not want to draw any more attention than had already been drawn to their difficulty in making their case against Carr, and against authors more generally. With no licensing statute on the books and none on the horizon for any materials not deemed to be news, the government surely did not want to advertise, yet again, their repeated discovery that "it is Hard to find the Author." What they needed, in fact, was to find an author, preferably an author who could be made without equivocation to own his—or her—book. This they believed they had finally done, in the case of Elizabeth Cellier.

Cellier's Fan

I said only it was mine, not that I was the Author.
—*Elizabeth Cellier,* The Trial and Sentence of Elizabeth Cellier

When the published version of Henry Carr's trial appeared in print in 1681, it promised purchasers two cases for the price of one. Along with the proceedings against Carr, readers could enjoy *The Tryal of Elizabeth Cellier, at the Kings-Bench Bar, July the 11th, 1680,* one of the most notorious treason trials of the era.[48] That date, it turns out, is incorrect, Cellier's case having been tried in actuality on 11 June.[49] Nonetheless, the juxtaposition of the two cases would prove to be undeniably apt. Although her first trial—the one printed with that of Carr—was unrelated to matters of the press, Cellier's later legal troubles mirrored Carr's almost exactly. In September of 1680, she was imprisoned and ultimately convicted for writing, printing, and publishing a work titled *Malice Defeated,* a scathing and inflammatory account of the treason proceedings in which she had, in a most unlikely fashion, been found not guilty earlier that same summer. When Cellier came in front of the judges for the second time, she would not escape so easily.[50]

In the fervent atmosphere of plot and counterplot that prevailed from 1678 to 1681, Cellier is one of the most colorful figures.[51] In June 1680, this midwife and Catholic convert was imprisoned and tried for treason for her part in the so-called Meal Tub Plot of 1679–80, a string of events so convoluted that it is almost impossible to reconstruct.[52] While ministering to Catholic prisoners still jailed in the aftermath of 1678 and the Oates affair, Cellier met Thomas Dangerfield, then going by the name of Captain Willoughby, a seeming Catholic sympathizer who became Cellier's ally, employee, and possibly lover. When Dangerfield, with Cellier's help, was released from prison, he became embroiled—apparently at Cellier's urging—in the Meal Tub Plot, a scheme to plant papers incriminating the Whigs in a plot to kill the king in the house of a prominent Whig politician, Roger Mansell (figs. 1–2).[53] When questioned by the Privy Council about his part in the affair, Dangerfield turned the tables on Cellier and her aristocratic Catholic associates, accusing them not only of concocting this sham Presbyterian plot but also of initiating their own plan to kill the king and overthrow the government.[54]

Figure 1. Elizabeth Cellier and Thomas Dangerfield, from *The Popish Damnable Plot against Our Religion and Liberties, Lively Delineated in Several of Its Branches* (London: printed for Richard Baldwin, 1681). Beinecke Rare Book and Manuscript Library, Yale University.

On 29 October 1679, Cellier was arrested and made her own appearance before the Privy Council. As Frances Dolan sums up the subsequent game of "He said, she said": "Cellier claimed that she had hired Dangerfield to provide information on how Catholic prisoners were being treated in Newgate and to work as a servant, courier, and informant; he claimed that she had hired him to fabricate evidence of a Presbyterian plot to replace Charles II with his illegitimate son, Monmouth, and to plant material incriminating the Earl of Shaftesbury in a plot against the King."[55] Ultimately, after lengthy investigations, the Privy Council accepted Dangerfield's tale, although not without some misgivings. On 11 June 1680, Cellier appeared before Lord Chief Justice Scroggs at the Court of King's Bench, indicted, according to the ancient statute, on the grounds that she and her associates "trayterously did compass, imagine, and intend the killing, death and final destruction of our said Lord the King."[56]

Figure 2. The Meal Tub Plot discovered, from *The Popish Damnable Plot against Our Religion and Liberties, Lively Delineated in Several of Its Branches* (London: printed for Richard Baldwin, 1681). Beinecke Rare Book and Manuscript Library, Yale University.

Cellier, like Twyn and all others accused of treason in this period, was required to defend herself at the trial without assistance of counsel. That she did so successfully is a testament not only to the chaotic origins of the charges against her but also to her quite remarkable capacities at oratory, fact finding, and legal argumentation. Most pertinent to the successful outcome of her trial was her contention that Dangerfield could not act as a witness against her (two witnesses being required to ground any accusation of treason)[57] because he had committed a number of felonies in the past, including burglary, perjury, and "uttering counterfeit Guines."[58] Scroggs replied that the court had evidence that Dangerfield had been pardoned for his crime—turning state's witness had advantages then as now—whereupon Cellier demonstrated in no uncertain terms that the court should not underestimate the "hair-brain'd *Amazon*" they thought they saw before them.[59] Cellier contended that although Dangerfield had indeed received such a pardon, "she had a copy of the said Pardon in Court, but it did not extend to some of the Crimes for which he was convicted, and then produced a Record, wherein it did appear, he was outlawed upon a Fellony."[60] Dangerfield was required to produce a copy of his pardon, and when he did so, Cellier's case was made: the pardon omitted the Latin phrase, *pro Felloniis*, for felonies, "which Omission had made the Pardon Defective."[61] Cellier was released, and, in a satisfying turn, Dangerfield was committed to Newgate in her place, protesting his innocence and honesty all the way to prison. In dismissing the witness-turned-defendant, Scroggs railed at the hapless and discredited Dangerfield, "I wonder at your Impudence."[62]

An otherwise derisory broadside verse published later in the year, primarily taken up with Cellier's later legal difficulties, nonetheless took time to praise the midwife's performance in her treason trial in unequivocal terms:

You taught the *Judges* to interpret Laws
Shewd Sergeant *Maynard* [a government prosecutor] how to plead a Cause,
You turn'd, and wound, and Rogu'd 'em at your will,
'Twas Trial not of Life and Death, but Skill.[63]

Had Cellier been content to quietly cherish her procedural triumph, these lines suggest, she might have had some chance of being received as a popular heroine, safeguarding the rights of commoners in an era of remarkably arbitrary judicial proceedings. This, however, was not Cellier's way. Tried and acquitted on 11 June, she spent the next three weeks composing a pamphlet the full title of which was *Malice Defeated; or, a Brief Relation of the Accusation and Deliverance of Elizabeth Cellier, Wherein Her Proceedings Both before, and during Her Confinement, Are Particularly Related, and the* Meal-Tub *Fully Discovered. Together with an Abstract of Her Arraignment and Tryal, Written by Her Self.*[64] The work contained, in addition to the account of her treason trial, a sketchy personal history, including the reasons behind her conversion to Catholicism; her decision to aid distressed Catholics in Newgate; her allegations concerning the practice of torture—here called "Tyrannical Barbarisme" (5)—at Newgate; her own version of the events of the Meal Tub Plot; and a blow-by-blow account of her multiple appearances before the king, the Privy Council, and various committees of lords in the seven months preceding her trial. Whatever truth-value might be contained in the pages of *Malice Defeated*—and Cellier continued to "justifie the truth thereof" both in the work and in all her writings after it[65]—the work was without question an irreverent, possibly foolhardy, production, replete with aspersions on the judicial system, accusations of extralegal punishment and witness tampering, and questionable reflections on a range of important figures in government and the legal profession. It hardly seems surprising that the book caught the attention of the guardians of public morality and security, even before it reached its intended audience.

Whether those charged with keeping an eye on the press happened upon Cellier's book by accident in the course of a random raid or, as seems more likely, they were tipped off to its imminent appearance, remains unclear. What is known is that in late August, one of the messengers of the press, Robert Stevens, burst into the shop of Cellier's first printer, William Downing, and seized sheets of the book as they were being printed off. Cellier and Downing—who had printed only half the book—were forced to appear before Secretary of State Leoline Jenkins, who instructed them to come before the Privy Council, "and in the meantime not to print any further."[66] Undaunted, Cellier immediately found another printer willing to finish the book, which was for sale by the beginning of September.[67] The title page of the work audaciously identified it as "Printed for Elizabeth Cellier, and are to be sold at her House in *Arundel-Street* near *St. Clements* Church." The work thus not only admitted her continuing participation in its production but kindly gave directions on how to locate both the book and the woman responsible for it. In due course, on 10 September, Cellier was arrested and sent to Newgate. The very next day, she was brought to trial at the Old Bailey, before a new judge, Richard Weston.

As in Carr's case, considerable confusion persists surrounding the precise nature of the charges brought against Cellier. This confusion is present not only in the proceedings themselves but also in modern accounts of the trial. All four recent accounts of the *Malice Defeated* proceedings, for instance, confidently aver that Cellier was tried and convicted on charges of libel. One particularly symptomatic, if muddled, version states, "she was guilty of libel, even if every word in her book was true, for she had ignored the Licensing Act, which curtailed the freedom of the press."[68] The Licensing Act had, as we know, lapsed in 1679, so Cellier can hardly be accused of having ignored it. Moreover, if Cellier had been tried for libel, she would have been tried regardless of existing licensing provisions, according not to statutory but to common law—specifically, the body of law that would come to be known as seditious libel. Philip Hamburger, the leading historian of that body of law, notes that Cellier's trial actually appears, like Carr's, to be one of the "so-called seditious libel trials for unlicensed publishing of news" that took place between 1679 and 1685.[69] In such cases, the charges seemed to be based on the law of seditious libel but actually turned out to refer back to the third decision of the judges concerning licensing of news. Hamburger notes how slippery and easily misunderstood are the proceedings in this group of cases: "in one trial—Cellier's in 1680—the third opinion of the judges was mentioned, almost casually, as the basis of the charges" (689).

Just how casually, the official account of Cellier's trial demonstrates.[70] It was not until the very end of the proceedings, after all the witnesses had been heard from and immediately before Weston summarized the prosecution's findings, that the judge mentioned, almost as an aside, and with what can only be described as intentional imprecision, "you are to take notice, that the King hath set out a Proclamation, that no books shall be Printed without a License" (29). Licensing had never been mentioned in the original indictment, and it was not mentioned again, including in the prosecution's summary of the fact of the case to the jury. Even when the jury returned, the clerk asked them only whether they had found Cellier "guilty of the Writing, Printing, and Publishing of the *Libel* for which she stands Indicted" (34), without ever alluding to the question of the work's license. In finding against the defendant, the jury did not have to specify the grounds for their verdict, a fact that left open far more questions than it answered—questions that fall roughly into two groups. First, there is no way to be sure, as Hamburger seems to be, that the jury had the licensing proclamation in mind when they found against Cellier; nor can we state with any more assurance, as recent commentators have done, that the jury was basing their conclusions on the common-law crime of seditious libel. Was Cellier guilty of producing a book that scandalized the government and defamed prominent individuals, as the original indictment charged, or was she simply guilty of bringing out a book that, regardless of content, contained "newes" and bore no license?[71]

The other set of questions left open at the end of Cellier's trial—questions already familiar from the proceedings against Twyn and Carr—concern the problem of Cellier's authorship of *Malice Defeated.* While much of Cellier's trial—an inordinate proportion, in fact—was devoted to establishing definitively her authorship of the work, the jury's verdict was naggingly silent on this crucial issue. In order to find Cellier guilty of "Writing, Printing, and Publishing" *Malice Defeated*, the jury actually, as the judge and the attorney general repeatedly reminded them, only had to find her guilty of one of these. Since her responsibility for publishing the work was definitively established by the first witness, John Penny, who testified that he had purchased copies of the book from her at her house—an event Cellier acknowledged—the trial could, in theory, have been over in moments. Indeed, the very title page of *Malice Defeated* advertised the work as *printed for* Elizabeth Cellier, an admission of liability for publishing that Cellier nowhere attempted to deny.

Notwithstanding this flood of evidence confirming her activities as a publisher, and thus as the person "for whom" the work was printed, it was yet again *as an author* that the court clearly hoped to convict the Popish midwife. From the very outset of the trial, in fact, the prosecution's case revolved around the fact of Cellier's authorship of the work, a fact the prosecution should also not have found difficult to prove, given that, as Weston reminded Cellier, "you said you writ it every word of it your self, and so owned the issue" (16). Much of the outrage leveled at Cellier in the course of the trial apparently came from the openness and publicity with which she had proclaimed her authorship of the work—"owned" it, in Weston's crucial phrase—including on the title page, which advertised at least the "Abstract of Her Arraignment and Tryal," and possibly the entire book, as "Written by Her Self." The prosecutor, Robert Dormer, opened his case by sarcastically drawing the jury's attention to this aggressive owning of the work, a practice he found particularly shocking, given the work's content: "She will appear to you to be so Criminal, that nothing can aggravate her Offences, unless the Impudence of the Delinquent, who hath set her Name to almost every Page of this Scandalous Libel; and since the Indictment hath been depending, Owned, Published, and put a value on her self, for being the Author of so Excellent a Book" (14). Cellier's impudence—a trait of which she was repeatedly accused in the pamphlet literature surrounding her case[72]—can be usefully compared to the impudence of which Dangerfield was accused by Scroggs at the conclusion of Cellier's treason trial. Dangerfield erred by attempting to insert his roguish self into public discourse, when in fact he had been barred from participation in such discourse by his lying ways and his felonious misdeeds. Had Dangerfield not lied, however, and had he not committed such deeds (or had he truly been pardoned for them), the charge of impudence would never have come up. Cellier, by contrast, is impudent precisely because she has so successfully made a place for herself in the public debate. She has "set her Name" to her book and, most damningly, "put a value on her self" for being an author—an author, in this case, of a transparently "Criminal" book. Put another way, Dangerfield is impudent because he has failed to own up to his misdeeds; Cellier is impudent because she has so outrageously and flamboyantly owned hers.

That Cellier's impudence takes a particularly gendered form is suggested by Weston's later assertion that she is an "impudent lying Woman" (24) but most clearly articulated by the charge that she has "put a value on her self" by owning her book. Even in the turbulent, arbitrary atmosphere of 1680, self-valuation was not a crime and had no proper place in a court of law, let alone in a prosecutor's opening statement. Dormer had no need to inflate or exaggerate Cellier's offences, there being so many already, and his doing so, particularly through the charge of overvaluation of the self, is a uniquely gendered attack. For anyone to own such a book would have been criminal; for a woman, however, the specific charge is aggravated by a more cultural infraction of propriety, decency, and appropriate female behavior, an infraction related to ownership more generally. By owning her book—this book or any book—Cellier was guilty of valuing herself, and of valuing herself specifically as an author. For the participants in the trial, and for many of Cellier's contemporaries, for a woman to own her book and to lay claim to value on the basis of that ownership was problematic not just when the book in question was a "delinquent" one but when the book in question was any book at all.

That gender norms profoundly influenced the court's response to Cellier—and especially to Cellier as an author—is confirmed by the fact that notwithstanding all of the evidence pointing to her responsibility for the work, questions surrounding who wrote *Malice Defeated* persisted throughout the trial. Given the circumstances of Cellier's brazen ownership, it seems incredible that the court could have been left with any lingering uncertainty about who exactly wrote *Malice Defeated*, and yet they remained obstinately unconvinced. Repeatedly, the prosecutors and witnesses expressed skepticism that Cellier could possibly have concocted such an elaborate piece of polemic, well stocked with juridico-legal musings and political reflections, without the assistance of others, by which they meant men. Surely, as one unofficial account of the trial put it, she was "by some of the Hellish Crew of *Jesuits* and *Fryars* put upon owning and publishing" the pamphlet.[73] Weston himself averred, "I do verily believe there are more Wits than yours concerned in this Book. [T]ho you bear the Name, yet the Book is not the Effect of your Wit only" (29). He went on, "I . . . have reason to suspect, that this is not acted only by you, tho you bear the name of it, but some of your wicked Priests are the Authours of it, as I am sure they are" (30). In "bearing" the text, this loaded reproductive language suggests, Cellier is only acting as a vessel for male authorship. She cannot ultimately be responsible for the work's creation, even if she is the person charged with bringing it into the world. The final product does bear her name, in a somewhat surprising twist to the old story of literary paternity; nonetheless, in the end no one can really believe that it is truly an "Effect" of Cellier's own "Wit."[74] Indeed, in what now seems an utterly predictable turn at the end of the trial, Weston made her an offer of leniency based upon this solemn conviction that the work could not, after all, really be hers: "If you will tell us who it was that set you on work, and assisted you in this wicked Business, that will be something towards the mitigation of your Fine" (30). Elsewhere in the trial, finally, the question of Cellier's sole authorship of the book was further complicated by the fact that she herself was reputed to have told the messenger Robert Stevens, on the night Stevens raided Dormer's print shop, "it was her Book, and she kept a Man to write it, and she Dictated it to another that sate by her" (19). A kind of unnatural inversion is suggested by this portrait of a female author instrumentalizing her male servants in order to produce her text. Whereas the court wanted to prove that Cellier was not the originator of the work but simply "midwife[d] it into the world," her account of using male scribes renders them midwifes to her act of creative origination.[75]

Yet it was not only these highly gendered contentions about the limits of female literary capacity that threw Cellier's authorship into question. She herself manufactured and cultivated skepticism throughout the trial about whether she had actually written *Malice Defeated.* She did so through engaging in an extended and frankly ingenious interrogation of one key concept that cropped up repeatedly in the course of the proceedings: the concept of ownership. Over and over, the court insisted that Cellier had owned her book; over and over, she contested the meaning of ownership in such a way that she could at once impudently lay claim to her book and simultaneously avoid responsibility for it. As Dormer's opening remarks in the case demonstrate, establishing that Cellier had owned her book was absolutely crucial to the prosecution's case, and cognates of the verb *to own* show up no less than a dozen times in the course of the trial proceedings. Weston, too, began with a similar announcement, stating that the evidence must prove "First, that the Book was Owned by her, and Published by her" (14). Neither of these proofs would have seemed, at the start of the trial, to offer the prosecution much of a challenge. By the end of the interrogation of the first witness, however, Cellier had changed all that.

The prosecution's first witness was John Penny, who came forward to testify that he had purchased a copy of *Malice Defeated* from Cellier at her house. "Did you ask her for the Book she published and set out?" Weston inquired, to which Penny responded, "Yes, and she did acknowledge that was her Book" (15). Anticipating the need for further clarification, Weston repeated, "What, she did own the Book she sold to you, to be hers?" (15) As Penny formulated his response, however, Cellier interrupted the proceedings with a question of her own:

Cellier. I desire to know if I said any more than you may have a Book, or there is a Book. And who asked for a Book?
Mr. *Bar. Weston.* Did she say any more than you may have a Book, or this is the Book that I have published?
Mr. *Penny.* When I got the Book and paid for it, I turned about again, and asked her if it was her own. She told me it was, and more that that, if occasion were she could have put more in it. (15)

Immediately following this apparently unequivocal testimony concerning Cellier's ownership of the book, Weston felt compelled to remind her that the issue had never in fact been in doubt: "you owned you writ it your self every word with your own hand" (16). Yet the defendant refused to be distracted from her own line of questioning, either by the judge's astonishment at her behavior or by her previous confession. Turning to Penny, she resumed her interrogation of the witness, again provoking Weston's incredulity and, increasingly, his anger, once the import of her questions became clear:

Cellier. Did I say I writ it?
Mr. *Penny.* You told me that was your Book
Cellier. I told you? Pray my Lord, put one Question to him upon the Oath he hath taken; did I say any more, than that it was mine and I sold it, not that I writ it, or was the Author of it.

Mr. *Bar. Weston.* Mrs. *Cellier,* This is a Book that is Intituled with your Name, and sold by your self. Now in any ones Judgment, this is both an owning of the Book, and publishing of the Book. When you Sold it, you gave it out as your Book, and it hath in the Title Page your Name, as the Author of it. (16)

Further quibbling about the meaning of these terms makes no sense, he suggests, when all the available evidence points against her. According to Weston, by any definition, Cellier owns this book: she is its author; she is its publisher; she has claimed responsibility for it. The title page itself bears witness to all of these forms of ownership and remains the prosecution's most damning piece of evidence against her.

Cellier was undeterred. Without answering these paper charges, she once again insisted that Weston return to the witness's testimony: "I hope you will please to remember," she instructed the judge, "I said only it was mine, not that I was the Author" (16). Here, attempting to finesse further the meanings of ownership, in an act of radical disidentification with her book, Cellier split off possession from authorship. In case the judge failed to follow her reasoning, she then provided him with an example: "I said it was my Book, and so it was because it was in my possession, but not that I writ it. This is my Fan, but it does not follow that I made it" (17). By this indisputable explication of the distinction between possession and creative origination, Weston was clearly dumbfounded. "But the Question was concerning the Author of the Book," he responded, palpably trying to see his way through this vertiginous exchange (17). In what may have been her ultimate coup, Cellier returned, "He did ask me no such Question":

Cellier. Did you ask me if I was the Author?
Mr. *Penny.* No, I did not.
Mr. *Bar. Weston.* But what did you ask her?
Mr. *Penny.* I did ask her whether it were her Book.
Mr. *Bar. Weston.* And did she own it?
Mr. *Penny.* Yes, she did.
Cellier. So it was mine, in possession.
Mr. *Bar. Weston.* Did you mean by your Question whether that Book was hers in property, or were she the Author and Publisher of it?
Mr. *Penny.* I would know whether it was hers or no.
Mr. *Bar. Weston.* But what was your intention in asking, was it whether She or any other Person made it?

Mr. *Penny*. I don't know who made it, she told me it was hers.
Mr. *Bar. Weston*. But what was your meaning in it?
Mr. *Penny*. My intentions was for fear she should have given me some other Book, to know whether it was Writ by her or no.
Cellier. My Lord, I am not to be judged by his meaning, but by his Question and my Answer. (17)

Penny, Weston, and the judicial system as a whole no longer know which question to ask in order to establish proof of authorship. Whereas in Carr's case the prosecutors could not establish ownership definitively, here they establish ownership but then falter over the question of what exactly it means to own one's book. When Robert Stevens later testified that Cellier "often owned it was her Book, and she the Author of it," she was able to respond, "I never said so in my life" (19).

By the end of the case, Weston was apparently convinced, if not that someone else had written the book, at least that it could not be proved that Cellier had. "The Question is but *Guilty or not Guilty*," he told the defendant, "whether you published this Libel or not" (29). Authorship was not, in his estimation, in question. In summarizing the case to the jury, he expressly alluded to the fact that this part of the government's case had, in legal terms, fallen apart: "Now whether or no you can doubt she was the Author of the Book, when in a manner she did own it at the Publication, by selling it as hers, I leave to you, though I must tell you plainly, I leave it as that which is to me under the Notion of Express Evidence; but I must leave it to you as Judges of the Fact, and expect your Verdict in the Case" (33). The jury, as we know, responded with a verdict of guilty, but they did so without ever stating the grounds for their judgment, including the question of whether or not Cellier had been the work's author. As the attorney general reminded them just before they withdrew, "if [they were] not satisfied that she was the Author," they were free to convict her as the publisher instead (34).

While the proceedings and verdict in Cellier's case thus possess a striking resemblance to those in the Carr trial, the Popish midwife would not come off so easily as her anti-Romish counterpart. She was sentenced just two days after her trial, on 13 September, and her punishment was both harsh and clearly designed to expose her to the maximum public humiliation for her "impudence." She was fined a thousand pounds and sentenced to be imprisoned until she could pay that enormous sum. In addition, she was condemned to stand in the pillory three times, "in three several publick Places" (35). Publicity was clearly deemed to be an integral and fitting part of her punishment, for the places and times were chosen carefully: the first time, "at the *May-Pole* in the *Strand*, on the most Notorious day"; the second, "in *Covent-Garden* on a Publick day"; and the third, "at *Charing-Cross*, on the most Publick day" (35–36). Each time, copies of *Malice Defeated* were to be burnt in front of the pillory on which Cellier stood. Later pamphlet accounts and woodcuts suggest that Cellier was harshly dealt with on these occasions by the assembled crowd.[76] So many people turned out to throw rocks and other missiles at the exposed prisoner on the first occasion, in fact, that on the two subsequent days of her punishment, she was allowed to keep her head and hands free from the stocks and to carry in front of her a kind of wooden shield. Given the ferocity with which she defended herself on both occasions in court, parrying accusations hurled at her, dodging evidence, redirecting prosecutorial assaults, fan in hand, the image of Cellier seated on the pillory with her gigantic shield seems remarkably apt (fig. 3).

In looking back over the events of the *Malice Defeated* trial, Frances Dolan sums up the double, triple, or even quadruple bind that Cellier faced as a woman author in the seventeenth-century courtroom: "Cellier is held accountable for the book (and held in contempt for trying to avoid that accountability), while she is yet dismissed as an author (and held in contempt for claiming to be one)" (228). In other words, Cellier is freighted with all of the responsibilities of authorship without being afforded any of its privileges, or, loosely put, its rights. She discovers "how penal a thing it is to be an author" without having an opportunity to participate in or profit from authorship's considerable benefits, not least the ability to "put a value on her self" that the position of the author enables.

Yet this description of the events of the trial, though compelling, glosses over entirely the degree to which Cellier took advantage of the very cultural and legal preconceptions and assumptions visited upon her as a woman author during the trial. At least as far as authorship was concerned, she not only resisted but also encouraged and profited from the court's ambivalent tendency to "dismiss her as an author." When it suited her, in fact, Cellier *dismissed herself* as an author, in a blatant attempt to disburden herself of the responsibilities that went along with authorship's more positive attributes. Indeed, throughout the trial and especially at the end, she abruptly shifted from her usual posture of bold impudence to a kind of studied impotence, in a manner that capitalized on the very attitudes about female powerlessness she elsewhere seemed to scorn. Near the beginning of the trial, for instance, upon being confronted by Weston with the fact that she had already confessed to writing the book, Cellier responded, "My Lord, If

I was a foolish vain Woman, and did seem to speak some vain words about my self, which I did not understand the Consequence of, I hope a word vainly spoke by me, shall not be brought against me to convict me of a Crime" (16). Emphasizing archetypal feminine traits such as vanity and foolishness, Cellier here tried to encourage the court's tendency to dismiss her as an author and a woman, and above all as a woman author, rather than resisting that tendency.[77]

Figure 3. Elizabeth Cellier seated in the pillory, from *The Popish Damnable Plot against Our Religion and Liberties, Lively Delineated in several of its Branches* (London: printed for Richard Baldwin, 1681). Beinecke Rare Book and Manuscript Library, Yale University.

After her sentencing, Cellier attempted another, similarly self-effacing ploy, but this time both her ambivalence and her highly strategic mobilization of these discourses about femininity were clear: "What I would say is only this. That I am a Woman, and wherein I offended, I offended out of Ignorance, and did not know it was an Offence, and if the Offence be mine, let not others suffer for me" (34). Here again, Cellier emphasizes her ignorance, suggesting that she should receive lenience based upon her inferior womanly capacities. Yet, like Twyn before her, she also insists on her willingness to suffer, and to suffer alone. Cellier even makes a proprietary claim in these lines—"If the Offence be mine, let not others suffer for me"—and states her willingness to be punished on the basis of that claim. Yet she embeds her claim to ownership in the middle of a statement that rehearses dominant cultural stereotypes about female dispossession, in a strategy clearly designed not only to mitigate her own punishment, but to protect others from suffering more harshly than a "foolish vain Woman" ought to do.

Cellier is thus neither a victim of cultural attitudes about female authorship nor an Amazonlike crusader against them. She is, instead, a scheming, slippery manipulator who takes control of and profits from already existing instabilities in the discourses about the relationship between authorship, ownership, and liability that combined to bring her to trial in the first place. These discourses are particularly visible—they come to the surface—in the case of a woman author, because for a woman to own anything at all, especially a book, creates a kind of cultural disruption, a disturbance in the emergent norms that link originative agency with proprietorship as essential attributes of modern authorship. As the cases of Twyn and Carr demonstrate, however, these instabilities were not peculiar to women authors, and women were neither the only ones to suffer from them nor the only ones to profit from them. Owning one's book was, for male authors as for female ones, a liability as well as a privilege, as capable of inciting suffering as it was of conferring value. Moreover, and most important, owning one's book was not a voluntary act, something one chose to do in the fullness of one's originative agency, in order to take advantage of authorship's rights and prerogatives. More often than not, owning his or her book was something an author was forced to do by a not particularly benevolent authority intent on keeping track of responsibility for naughty printed books rather than on protecting the rights of those who brought those books into the world. If, as Scroggs lamented, it was, in the end, simply too hard to find the author in the decades following the Restoration, by the turn of the century, the authorities had finally begun to elaborate a fail-safe system for finding authors, a system more firmly based in ownership than any that had preceded it. The name of that system was copyright. Whether such a system would turn out to be for the benefit of authors, who would never again be able to escape the troubles associated with owning their books, the second half of this book will inquire.

PART II

The Dangerous Fate of Authors

I believe, if anyone in his life should contemplate the dangerous fate of authors, he would scarce be of their number on any consideration. The life of a Wit is a warfare upon the earth; and the present spirit of the age is such, that to attempt to serve it (any way) one must have the constancy of a martyr, and a resolution to suffer for its sake. I confess it was want of consideration that made me an author.

—Pope, Preface to The Works, *1717*

Chapter 3
Daniel Defoe, the Act of Anne, and the Obligations of Ownership

A person writing a great deal on various Subjects, should be as cautious in owning all his Performances, as in revealing the Secrets of his most intimate Friend.

—*Defoe,* A Vindication of the Press, *1718*

Introduction

Five years before the passage of the Act of Anne, Daniel Defoe definitively sketched out the potentially hazardous consequences for an author of "owning all his Performances."[1] His study of the inextricable relationship between authorial rights and their attendant responsibilities appeared under the title *An Essay on the Regulation of the Press* (1704) and, along with a series of articles in the *Review,* contributed to debates then brewing in Parliament and the press about how best to restrain the disorderly business of the book trade. Yet, Defoe's involvement in the history of press regulation in this period was as much experiential as textual. He could claim some expertise on the topic of authorial liability, as is well known, after finding himself pilloried just months before for his satirical tract *The Shortest Way with the Dissenters* (1702). Less commonly noted is the fact that in the same brief period, stretching from December 1702, when *The Shortest Way* appeared, to January 1704, when *An Essay* was published, Defoe experienced the sting of proprietary infringement when, while the embattled author languished in prison, the minor printer John How brought out an edition of Defoe's works without his knowledge or consent.[2] As Defoe set about writing his essay, then, he had both his martyrdom at the pillory and his sufferings in the marketplace in mind. Out of the confluence of these two highly personal experiences of what Pope calls "the dangerous fate of authors," Defoe's theory of press regulation emerged.[3]

Defoe's *Essay* opens with the admission—one might even say, confession—that the spread of printing has led to "the Licentious Extravagance of Authors."[4] Although printing deserves to be hailed as "the most useful Invention ever found out," productive of immeasurable social and cultural benefits, it is nonetheless an undeniable fact that printing has caused at least as many problems as it has solved, largely as a result of misdemeanors he attributes specifically to authors: "'Twould be endless," he admits, "to examine the Liberty taken by the Men of Wit in the World, the loose they give themselves in Print, at Religion, at Government, at Scandal" (3). Defoe's essay was written in opposition to a proposal that the Licensing Act of 1662 be resurrected, a proposal that would have led to the reestablishment of prepublication oversight of printed works. Yet his strategy in the essay is in no way to deny the "Licentiousness of the Press" or the endless array of challenges to the authority of religion and government posed by the "looseness" of authors (3). He even admits that printing "well deserve[s] a Regulation" (3). Like Milton in *Areopagitica* (1644), Defoe is simply concerned that the goal of stopping the extravagance of some pens will not be achieved by subjecting all works to the inevitably partisan eye of the licenser before they appear in the world.

Defoe's objection to prepublication licensing stems in part from his sense that the legal canon surrounding authorial liability is so vague that authors simply cannot predict, on the basis of any authoritative legal text, whether or not they have written a work that deserves to be suppressed. "The Crime of an Author is not known," Defoe complains, but criminality nonetheless constitutes a kind of omnipresent potentiality endemic to the practice of authorship (15). With the help of a "cunning Lawyer," or even one "of no great Cunning," it is possible to read any text in such a way as to "make some part of it Criminal" (15). Moreover, the vagueness of the existing laws surrounding authorial liability not only makes every author subject to the accusation of criminality but actually encourages authorial license: "the uncertainty of the Crime seems to be the greatest Occasion of the Crime, for Men are apt to be bold in a thing they cannot find expressly Condemn'd by the Letter of the Law" (15). Given the inevitability that authors will be taken for criminals—indeed, that they will behave like them—Defoe suggests that legislators try to make a law that specifies both the content of authorial transgressions and their respective punishments, so that "Men might know when they Transgress, and when they do not" (14).

Defoe offers a further novel solution in *An Essay*, which, he believes, will compensate for some of the suffering caused by the inevitable criminalization of authorship, even if it cannot stop the tendency. Since authors are considered to be responsible for the effects of their works, whether or not they are really guilty of any misdemeanor, Defoe argues, their ability to profit from their works should be both protected and encouraged: "'Twould be unaccountably severe," he writes, "to make a Man answerable for the Miscarriages of a thing which he shall not reap the benefit of" (21). In a fuller elaboration of this protest, Defoe continues, "if an Author has not the right of a Book, after he has made it, and the Benefit be not his own, and the Law will not protect him in that Benefit, 'twould be very hard the Law should pretend to punish him for it" (21). The form this "Benefit" ought to take progresses in the essay from a loosely defined concept of authorial rights to a full-fledged articulation of literary property, designed to put a stop to the rampant tendency on the part of members of the trade to "print . . . Copies none of their own" (19). Defoe's innovation here is his conviction that printing an author's work without his or her consent is just as much an invasion of property as printing works that belong to other members of the trade. Printing without consent, he writes, with a nod to his own recent experiences, "robs the Reader, by printing Copies of other Men uncorrect and imperfect, making surreptitious and spurious Collections, and innumerable Errors, by which the Design of the Author is often inverted, conceal'd, or destroy'd" (19). Since an author can be held responsible—as Defoe believed he himself had been—for the unintended, "inverted," or simply misunderstood meanings attributed to him on the basis of works made public, whether consensually or not, he should at least be allowed to lay claim to whatever rights or benefits follow from those texts and should be empowered to bring actions against those whose depredations of the author's property both rob him and open him to severe and often arbitrary punishment.

In yet another anticipation of the provisions of the Act of Anne, Defoe proposes a form of universal registration as a means both of combating piracy and of documenting liability—that is, of keeping rights and responsibilities in balance. Defoe takes it for granted that the most effective means of keeping track of liability for printed works is to insist that authors put their names on those works, because, he notes, in an echo of L'Estrange, "there are many ways to commit this Crime, and lie conceal'd; The Crime may be committed, and the Malefactor hard to be found" (16). Printers and booksellers may choose to use their own names in the disappearing author's place, but, in Defoe's scheme, doing so means that they will be required to "answer for" the work as though they were its authors (16). Indeed, Defoe concludes, anyone willing to engage in the risky business of publishing anonymous works must clearly be invested in and sympathetic to the content of those works and thus "has some Title to pass for the Author," as printers and publishers had done for two hundred years (17). Now, however, authors have a real incentive for claiming responsibility for their works, because their assumption of responsibility can instantly be parlayed into the form of a benefit: "every Author being oblig'd to set his Name to the Book he writes," Defoe concludes, "has, by this law, an undoubted exclusive Right to the Property of it" (21). What Defoe calls for here is a kind of balanced trade-off between authorial property rights and authorial answerability. Since authors, who cannot help but be criminals in his estimation, live in perpetual danger of the law's severity, they should at least be able to rely on the legislative authorities to give them something in exchange for the very considerable risks they take.

Whether or not Defoe's essay directly influenced the drafters of the Act of Anne remains a question. Although some commentators, most notably Mark Rose, have seen Defoe's influence at work in the notion of literary property articulated by Parliament in 1710, the overall logic of Defoe's essay—that rights and responsibilities are and should be inseparable—is never made explicit in the act, which avoids the topic of press regulation and the determination of liability altogether. When Rose notes that "Defoe's agitation on behalf of authorial rights seems to have influenced the London Stationers," who in turn influenced the legislators in charge of drafting the act, he gives the aspiring regulator his due.[5] Yet he fails to mention what the stationers and legislators made of the rest of Defoe's *Essay*, the portion concerned not with property but with crimes and punishments. Rose's version of events concludes that the drafters of the Act of Anne read Defoe highly selectively, taking only his notions of authorial property rights and leaving aside his more nuanced theories concerning the necessity of regulation and, above all, his proposed technique for achieving that regulation through exploiting proprietary authorship. "The Statute marked the divorce of copyright from censorship," Rose definitively concludes, as though somehow these two forms of regulation, bound together through two centuries of coevolution, had spontaneously become uncoupled (48).[6]

Closer attention to the genesis of the Act of Anne—the documents and debates leading up to its passage, including those generated by Defoe—suggests otherwise. The act was, after all, a direct descendant of debates about how best to manage the press after the lapse of the Licensing Act in 1695 and the consequent loss of power of the Stationers' Company. In the ensuing fifteen years, parliamentarians, printers, publishers, and polemicists argued back and forth about the best means to manage the regulation of the press, by which they meant both ensuring economic order and settings limits to what Defoe terms the press's excessive "Licentiousness." Given that each of the repeated attempts to come up with a strategy for regulation tried to achieve both of these ends at once—indeed, imagined them as inextricable—the claim that the Act of Anne simply abandoned the pursuit of ideological oversight in favor of cementing property rights seems questionable at best. This chapter rehearses many of these debates over regulation while offering Defoe's career and writings as further evidence of the ongoing perils of ownership. It argues that Defoe's notion of the complementarity of property and ideological regulation in the *Essay*, while synthesizing contemporary beliefs in novel ways, was in fact characteristic of a large number of proposals for managing the press generated between 1695 and 1710. Like L'Estrange, when Defoe set about synthesizing his proposals for the regulation of the press, he articulated convictions that had been developing for decades, and that would, in turn, influence the legislation that followed.

With these findings in mind, the chapter turns to the Act of Anne itself, in order to test and ultimately challenge the claim that the statute exclusively privileged "copyright" over "censorship." In order to substantiate the contention that ideological oversight was not split off from proprietary authorship and was, if anything, made easier by this new innovation in the literary marketplace, it is necessary to look not at the act itself but at the decades following its passage. The last section of this chapter and the remainder of the book turn to the cases of individual authors who found their hazards increasing in proportion to their willingness to take advantage of the promises of proprietary authorship. Choosing to own their books, as Alexander Pope and John Gay—the subjects of the next two chapters—discovered, was the only way for authors to protect their "Benefits" in the face of rapacious booksellers and mercenary pirates. More often than not, however, as Defoe's case—like those of Twyn, Carr, and Cellier—amply demonstrates, owning one's book was no choice at all. All of those figures who assumed the risks of proprietary authorship, voluntarily or not, had to be "cautious in owning," as Defoe puts it in *A Vindication*, lest they find themselves held responsible for the predictable or unpredictable "Miscarriages" of their performances. In the midst of these shifting conditions, early eighteenth-century authors mapped out a series of not always successful strategies for managing their risks and maximizing their benefits. It is to these strategies that the remainder of this book turns.

"All the Adverbs": Defoe's *Shortest Way*

The furor over *The Shortest Way with the Dissenters* and its author's subsequent punishment have been treated by numerous critics over the past half-century. Indeed, Paula Backscheider begins her own contribution to the discussion by noting that "almost as many people know that Daniel Defoe stood in the pillory as know that he wrote *Robinson Crusoe*."[7] Whether or not this holds true for the general public, critics and biographers of Defoe have certainly been unanimous in their conviction that the author's stint in the pillory, which took place from 29 to 31 July 1703, was a crucial moment in the author's early life and even, in the words of J. R. Moore, "the crisis in his personal career." Moore continues, in surprisingly hyperbolic tones, "by this crisis, through [Defoe's] far-reaching influence, the whole course of modern literature has been affected."[8] This is a remarkable claim, and one to which I will return in what follows. Before assessing their true significance, however, and turning to their importance for this history of authorial liability, it is necessary to outline these much-rehearsed events yet one more time.[9]

On 1 November 1702, permission was obtained to introduce a bill in Commons against a practice called "occasional conformity." Since the passage of the Municipal Corporations Act in 1661, a measure strengthened by the Test Act of 1673, all those aspiring to public office of any kind had been required to pass a series of tests in order to be eligible for a position. In an effort to prevent the resurgence of rebellion, Dissenters were required to swear allegiance to the monarch and to testify that they took Communion regularly in an Anglican church. Some Dissenters, including high-ranking public officials, saved themselves from perjury and excessive public scrutiny by attending services with Dissenting congregations while more sporadically receiving the Eucharist at Anglican churches and showing other outward signs of calculated "conformity." In 1697, Defoe raised the eyebrows and, in some cases, the ire of his Dissenting colleagues by writing *An Enquiry into the Occasional Conformity of Dissenters, in Cases of Preferment*, a direct address to one such public officeholder.[10] The work's *Preface to the Lord Mayor*, addressed to the then lord mayor of London, Sir Humphrey Edwin, a Dissenter, took to task all those who, in Defoe's opinion, weakened the Dissenting cause by committing blatantly opportunistic acts of conformity, even as they claimed to represent Nonconformist interests in public life. In the text of *An Enquiry*, Defoe scathingly dubbed this practice "*playing Bopeep* with God Almighty" (11). Predictably, Dissenters responded that it was better to risk the minor hypocrisies or acts of strategic conformity demanded by the Test Act than it was to face a government and civil administration governed by none but Anglicans. Defoe, however, remained unmoved by such pragmatic considerations.

Thus, when the proposal for a bill banning occasional conformity was introduced in Commons in November 1702, Defoe was quick to respond. Even before the bill had made its way through the parliamentary process, he had prepared *The Shortest Way with the Dissenters.*[11] The tract is written in the voice of an Anglican High Churchman and advocates not only the end of the practice of occasional conformity but the destruction of the Dissenting population as a whole. It responds to events unfolding in the political sphere while more generally pointing out through mimicry the increasing intolerance being publicly expressed toward Dissenters under Queen Anne, who took the throne in March 1702. This intolerance was personified for Defoe by Henry Sacheverell, an Oxford preacher who spoke out publicly in the summer of 1702, in the pulpit and in print, against "these Crafty, Faithless, and Insidious Persons."[12] In *The Shortest Way*, Defoe parodied Sacheverell's style, along with his only barely masked conclusions about the best way to handle these enemies of the state. If anything, *The Shortest Way* argues that a measure against occasional conformity does not go far enough in addressing the social and political problems caused by Nonconformity. In one of its more scandalous passages, *The Shortest Way* reads,

> 'Tis vain to trifle in this Matter; the light, foolish handling of them by Mulcts, Fines, &c.; 'Tis their Glory and their Advantage, if the Gallows, instead of the Counter, and the Gallies, instead of the Fines, were the Reward of going to the Conventicle, to preach or hear, there would not be so many Sufferers, the Spirit of Martyrdom is over; they that will go to Church to be chosen Sheriffs and Mayors, would go to forty Churches rather than be hang'd.
>
> If one severe Law were made, and punctually executed, that whoever was found at a Conventicle, should be banish'd the Nation, and the Preacher be hang'd, we should soon see an End of the Tale, they would all come to Church, and one Age would make us all one again.[13]

Lest readers find this passage too oblique, the narrator of the tract elsewhere notes even more directly that "God has suffer'd us to bear them as Goads in our Sides, for not utterly extinguishing them long ago" (9). It is no surprise, given passages such as these, that virtually everyone who read the tract—from Dissenters intent on keeping their meager public liberties to High Churchmen keen not to alienate more moderate members of the Church, to all those charged with keeping the peace of the nation—condemned it.

Defoe's precise literary strategy in the pamphlet—and the options, as one critic put it, might include but not be limited to "hoax, parody, paradox, fiction, irony, and satire"[14]—has puzzled and consumed critics for decades. Perhaps the most straightforward answer to the question of the work's genre, if not to its author's intentions, is given by Ian Watt, who argued that *The Shortest Way* should be read as "a masterpiece not of irony but of impersonation."[15] James Sutherland pursues a similar line of argumentation when he writes that *The Shortest Way* offered Defoe a chance to practice and even "perfect . . . the technique of putting himself in someone else's shoes and proceeding to write consistently from that person's point of view."[16] Defoe's plan, as he later explicitly argued, would thus seem to have been to pass the work off as the genuine production of a "High Church fanatic," as Sutherland puts it, and by so doing, to make others who took it up and made it their own complicit in the work's advocacy of discrimination, banishment, and even murder (43). "The Case the Book pointed at," he wrote in 1712, "was to speak in the first person of the Party, and then, thereby, not only speak their language, but make them acknowledge it to be theirs."[17] Defoe, in an echo of *An Essay on the Regulation of the Press*, suggests that his plan was that any churchman who read, recognized, and endorsed the sentiments articulated in the work would "ha[ve] some Title to pass for the Author." He clearly believed that if he could succeed in making these clerics "acknowledge it to be theirs"—that is, if he could get them to *own the work*—no one would force him to acknowledge the work as *his*, or, if they did discover the true author, no one would make him suffer for having written it. Instead, those in power would recognize the true criminals in the High Church fanatics who were fooled into owning the book for him.

Defoe miscalculated. From the moment the pamphlet came to the attention of the authorities, the most powerful men in the nation set about suppressing it. From the beginning, moreover, they single-mindedly addressed themselves to finding the author, apparently not considering the printer or publisher worthy of mention. An undated letter from December of 1702, from the Lord Treasurer Sidney Godolphin to the secretary of state for the southern region, Daniel Finch, earl of Nottingham, relates that Godolphin had already discussed the matter with Robert Harley, who had recently assumed the post of speaker of the House of Commons. Godolphin writes, "I had last night some talk with the speaker [Harley], & he has had a mind to speak with you abt. a book lately Come out, call'd, *a short way with the Dissenters.* He seem'd to think it absolutely necessary to the Service of the Government that your Lp. Shd endeavour to discover who was the Author of it."[18] The letter's focus on the author stands out from similar documents produced in the era of licensing and discussed earlier in this book. Gone are the familiar long lists of those to be apprehended in addition to the author: the seller, publisher, printer, or those for whom the work was sold, published, or printed. Regulatory attention here seems singularly fixated on the figure Roger L'Estrange called the "Fountain of our Troubles." With the absence of a system of controlling the press, such as licensing that depended primarily upon the members of the book trade for enforcement, the authorities—most notably, the secretaries of state, under whose aegis the press now fell—were left to find the shortest way, as it were, to effective regulation.[19] The figure to whom they turned was, not surprisingly, the author.

Lest the letter seem anomalous, one need only turn to two advertisements published in the *London Gazette* on 10 and 14 January to see the figure of the author singled out once again. By this time, Nottingham had discovered the identity of the author, if not the man himself. He had had Edward Bellamy arrested on 2 January as the man responsible for delivering *The Shortest Way* to the printer, George Croome, who was himself arrested on 15 January. Under interrogation and in danger of prosecution himself, Bellamy did not hesitate to name the author. Immediately after doing so, he was released, as Croome would be, upon promising to testify against the author when he came to trial. On 9 January, Defoe wrote to Nottingham, declaring himself "Perfectly Free from any Seditious Designs" but remained in hiding, where he had been since late December (*Defoe Letters*, 2). Nottingham, unimpressed, resorted to the advertisements, which called for any information the public could offer leading to the arrest of "Daniel de Fooe," author of a "scandalous and seditious pamphlet." In exchange for information leading to the capture of Defoe, the advertisements offered a reward of fifty pounds, the standard sum for the apprehension of an author specified in royal proclamations from 1692 and 1702 on the topic of seditious books and pamphlets.[20] At least one critic has argued that the reward was exceptionally high, "a notable sum for a pamphleteer," yet, as these proclamations suggest, fifty pounds plus indemnity from prosecution was the going rate for information leading to the arrest of a seditious author in 1703.[21] The sum was a large one, but nothing, as the government saw it, compared to the costs of open warfare between the Dissenters and the High Church faction, let alone schism within the Anglican Church itself.

On 24 February, Defoe was indicted at the Old Bailey for having written, composed, and caused to be printed "a Certain criminal document, a Seditious, pernicious and Diabolical Libel." The danger posed by this "criminal document" is made explicit in the opening lines of the indictment, which condemn Defoe for "perfidiously, mischievously, and seditiously contriving, practicing, and purposing to make and Cause discord between . . . the Queen and her . . . Subjects."[22] The following day, after a complaint against the pamphlet was delivered to Parliament, copies of the work were burnt at Westminster Hall by the public hangman. As Maximillian Novak nicely puts it, Defoe's "body being absent, Nottingham decided to punish the text."[23] On 21 May, an informant finally gave Nottingham the information he was seeking, and the verminlike author was, in a manner that would have made L'Estrange proud, flushed from his hiding place, the house of a French weaver. He was released on bail and ordered to appear at the Sessions of Oyer and Terminer on 7 July. When Defoe finally came before the judges, however, he had a surprise for the court: unlike any other figures described in this book, Defoe decided to plead guilty. In the words of Moore, he was "induced to acknowledge his responsibility" for the work, leaving him open to any punishment the court deemed appropriate.[24]

Defoe described his decision, with something close to gallows humor, in a letter to William Penn written only a few days later, "I agreed to give the Court No Trouble but to plead Guilty to the Indictment, even to all the Adverbs, the Seditiously's, The Malitiously's, and a Long Rapsody of the Lawyers et Ceteras, and all this upon promises of being us'd Tenderly" (*Defoe Letters,* 8). Because Defoe made the unusual choice of pleading guilty, historians are left without the lengthy and detailed accounts of the proceedings left by other, less bold (or less honest) defendants.[25] In trying to assess what led Defoe to believe he would be treated "Tenderly," however, there is one document that can assist: Defoe's *A Brief Explanation of a Late Pamphlet, Entitul'd, The Shortest Way with the Dissenters*, published in February 1703 along with a new edition of the pamphlet itself.[26] This time, Defoe slightly altered the pamphlet's title, as if to offer his sluggish compatriots some remedial hints to prepare them for how to read the work to follow: *The Shortest Way with the Dissenters*, the title page now helpfully prodded, *[Taken from Dr. Sach—ll's Sermon, and Others]*. Even as the authorities hunted for Defoe, he was reprinting his pamphlet with clues for how to read it better and putting copies up for sale on the open market. Either he had great faith in his own *Explanation*, or he had seen an unprecedented commercial opportunity and sought to exploit that opportunity to the fullest. Already, it seems, he had begun to develop his conviction that if an author is to be held responsible for his or her work, he or she might at least be allowed to profit from that work as much as possible.

In *A Brief Explanation*, Defoe accuses both the public and the authorities of "mistaking the Author's Design" (19). Any criminality to be found in the work, he suggests, is to be attributed to its inept readers and not to the text itself or its author, both of which he declares "free from any seditious design" (17). He goes on to lament at length the irony that he is being prosecuted for words which, when spoken or written by the High Churchmen themselves, incur no punishment:

> When the Persecution and Destruction of the *Dissenters, the very Thing they drive at,* is put into Plain *English,* the whole Nation will start at the Notion, and condemn the Author to be hang'd for his Impudence.
>
> The Author humbly hopes he shall find no harder Treatment for plain *English, without Design,* than those Gentlemen for their plain Design, in duller and darker English. (18)

Defoe here suggests that whereas his pamphlet may appear to be a convoluted piece of artifice, sinisterly hiding its true "Design" behind a literary device of deliberately obfuscating ventriloquism, it is he who is the plain speaker, "*without Design.*" The clerics, by contrast, hide their dark designs in "duller and darker English" as a result of which he risks hanging while they escape punishment altogether. "For making other Peoples Thoughts speak in his Words," he continues, which is to say, for making their thoughts appear to be his own, the author (again, rather than the printer or the publisher, as might have been the case in the past) is held liable and in danger of his life (19). Since no one appears to be capable of seeing through either Defoe's plain design or "*the Honesty of his Intention,*" he will throw himself on the mercy of the court "rather than others shall be ruin'd for his Mistakes" (20). He maintains to the last, however, that the real fault associated with *The Shortest Way* is a crime not of writing but of reading, a crime for which he alone, as the one person who has rightly understood the work, should surely not be held accountable.

Defoe's logic may have been finely wrought in this passage, but the secretary of state and the judges remained unimpressed. On 7 July, Defoe was tried and sentenced at Justice Hall at the Old Bailey, and he was not, by any means, "us'd Tenderly," as he had hoped he might be. He was condemned to pay 200 marks (about 134 pounds), to stand in the pillory three times for an hour, to stay in prison until his fines were paid (for many, this would have constituted a sentence of life imprisonment), and to be of good behavior for seven years following his release. Defoe critics have been as quick to point out the severity of the penalty as they were the reward for his initial arrest: Backscheider, for instance, dubs it "unusual." Moore goes much further, writing, "as for the sentence—if we except the strikingly similar one against William Prynne seventy years before—it was the most severe of its kind in English literary history."[27] Moore's contention is, as we know from the previous chapter, factually untrue (unless, of course, we consider the punishment of Elizabeth Cellier and others like her not to have been of "literary" significance). More interesting, however, is the question of why critics have been so quick to see Defoe as unusually victimized by the authorities. The comparison with Prynne is especially striking, for surely losing one's ears (twice) is a far more severe hardship than standing in the pillory (three times) without disfigurement. Moore was not alone in confusing the Dissenter Defoe with the Puritan Prynne, however, and perhaps he was himself momentarily distracted by Pope's vision of the pamphleteer in *The Dunciad*: "Earless on high, stood unabash'd De Foe" (II.147).[28] To his contemporaries, as these lines suggest, Defoe's would have ranked as a heavy punishment, obviously designed to deter others from similar behavior. Yet it was not, in any sense, an "unusual" one for someone convicted of mocking the government in print. In "What Is an Author?," Foucault wonders "at what point we began to recount the lives of authors rather than of heroes."[29] Defoe's story suggests that we would do better to ask when the lives of authors began to be recounted in the mode of heroism. Defoe's status as a major figure in literary history may make it tempting to emphasize the epic proportions of his punishment and recovery, but that should not blind us to the fact that in his own time, Defoe was treated as any other author of a particularly inflammatory libel might have been.

Like so many defendants before him, Defoe was given the opportunity to mitigate his sentence by revealing to the authorities those with whom he was in league in the preparation of his pamphlet. Since the government had already apprehended and subsequently released both the printer and the publisher, their hunt must have been for those they believed to be Defoe's coconspirators and sympathizers rather than for anyone immediately concerned in the production of the pamphlet. Defoe's unhelpful response to the request seems, unlike those of his predecessors in the Popish plot years, to have been a genuine one. As he wrote to William Penn five days after his sentencing,

> Sir The Proposall you are pleas'd to hint By your Son from My Ld Nottingham, of Discovering Partyes is the same which his Lordship has often Put upon me before.
>
> Sir in some Letters which I have Sent his Lordship I have Answer'd him with the Same Assurance I did to the Privy Council, Vizt. That in the Manner which they Proposed it I really had No Person to Discover. (*Defoe Letters*, 8)

Even when the secretary of state reached the end of the chain of liability and finally had the author in custody, he was hesitant to believe that he had truly found the source of the trouble. Defoe's comic-pathetic-defiant answer, that there was in the end "No Person to Discover" beyond himself, suggests that L'Estrange had been correct to give the place of precedence to the author. Once the author had been induced to take responsibility for the work, Defoe's case suggests, there was really no one else to blame.

Defoe's stint in the pillory in late July 1703 offers a particularly vivid example of the dangers of using public punishment to chastise those whose crimes are primarily political.[30] Perhaps to Defoe's surprise, given his contention that his audience had universally misunderstood his book, the crowd used him more "Tenderly" than he could possibly have hoped. As a much later print perhaps fancifully remembers, Defoe was "pelted with flowers instead of stones" as he stood in the contraption (although a contemporary woodcut on a pirated edition of *Jure Divino* showed the author in the same position, flowerless, looking miserable and surrounded by officers holding pikes) (figs. 4–5).[31] More notable still is the fact that Defoe seems to have turned even this moment to his advantage, engaging associates to sell copies of his works, along with a new production, "A Hymn to the Pillory."[32] Charles Leslie, one of the particularly intolerant High Churchmen to whom Defoe was responding in *The Shortest Way*, wrote, aghast, of Defoe's gentle treatment, and of "the Party causing his Books to be Hawk'd and Publickly sold about the Pillory, while he stood upon it (in Triumph!) for writing them."[33] Although there is little doubt that Defoe encountered a mixed treatment at the hands of the assembled crowd, and that not all those present came to buy his books and strew flowers in his path, he nonetheless came away from the experience uninjured, with the added benefit that more Londoners than ever were buying and reading his works.

In attempting to sum up the lessons to be learned from the debacle surrounding *The Shortest Way with the Dissenters*, Moore concludes that Defoe was mistaken both in pleading guilty and in having confessed to be the author of the work in the first place. He writes, "Defoe might well have escaped through the inability of the prosecution to establish his responsibility for the publication. But once Defoe could be induced to acknowledge his responsibility he was at the mercy of the Court."[34] As long as Defoe refused to admit his responsibility for the work, Moore rightly concludes, which is to say both his authorship and his answerability for the work's contents, he was probably safe from prosecution. Like their counterparts since the era of Henry VIII, Defoe's adversaries might have found it difficult, even with a system of fines and rewards, to find the author, or, having found him, to make him own his book. In the end, Defoe put himself at the mercy of the judges through his own, calculated choice to acknowledge his book. Had he simply withheld such acknowledgment, he might have avoided his "dangerous fate."

Why, then, did Defoe ultimately own his book, practically assuring himself of punishment? Backscheider concludes that he would almost certainly have been discovered, and having been discovered, that he would have had, as she concisely puts it in an article of that name, "No Defense." Yet as the cases of Henry Carr and Elizabeth Cellier make clear, even authors who had accidentally or impetuously owned their books might later disown them and so, at least in the case of Carr, escape punishment. Defoe the speculator, who had never acknowledged the work publicly, might have been expected to take the risk of refusing to own his book and at the very least force

Figure 4. Defoe in the pillory being pelted with flowers, engraving by J. C. Armytage from a painting by Eyre Crow (n.d.). Guildhall Library, Corporation of London.

JURE DIVINO:
A
SATYR.

The First BOOK.

By the Author of the True-born-Englishman.

O Sanctas Gentes, quibus hæc nascuntur in hortis
Numina! ——Juv. Sat. 15. lin. 11.

London: Printed by *P. Hills* in *Black-Fryars*.

Figure 5. Defoe in the pillory, from a pirated copy of Defoe's *Jure Divino* (London: printed by P. Hills, [1706]). William Andrews Clark Memorial Library, University of California, Los Angeles.

the court to try to prove that it was, indeed, his. Of all of his performances to date, in fact, this should have been the one to prompt him to be most "cautious in owning."

Instead, embracing "all the Adverbs," he owned his book. That he did so, however, was less the efiect of a gross miscalculation concerning Nottingham's tenderness than it was a desperate response to a greater risk even than "penal appropriation": the risk that his works would be appropriated by unauthorized members of the book trade and that he would, as a result, lose any "Benefit" ever to accrue from them. On 17 April, while Defoe was still in hiding and thus before he had made the radical decision to take responsibility for *The Shortest Way*, he watched in exasperation as a pirated collection of his works appeared under the title *A Collection of the Writings of the Author of the True-Born English-Man.* The work, which contained thirteen pieces either by Defoe or attributed to him, sold for 2s. 6d.[35] Among those works the publisher, John How, chose to include in the volume was *The Shortest Way with the Dissenters.* On 22 July, just two weeks after he pled guilty and before he had even undergone his punishment, Defoe responded at last to this abuse of what he clearly saw as his exclusive right to control the printing and publishing of his works. He produced his own volume, cannily titled *A True Collection of the Writings of the Author of the True Born English-Man.*[36] His version, which contained 22 titles, sold for 6*s.*, more than twice the price of his competitor's. It also contained *The Shortest Way*, as well as *A Brief Explanation.* Yet its most important contribution to the Defoe archive is elsewhere, in a lengthy preface in which he excoriates his competitor for stealing his property and endangering his life. In this preface, which, though it has received very little critical attention, nonetheless stands as his first major statement on the subject of authorial property rights, Defoe anticipates many of the arguments he would make in the 1704 *Essay*, including sketching out his theory of the complementary relationship between property and liability. Here, too, he offers an answer to Moore's baffled question about why an author in danger of severe punishment would step forward to voluntarily take responsibility for the very work for which he was indicted. If there is any truth to Moore's claim that "the whole course of modern literature has been affected" by the prosecution of *The Shortest Way*, it lies in the accident of history that led Defoe to face penal appropriation and proprietary depredation simultaneously, and from that miserable experience, to propose what he saw as a more efficient and more just means to regulate the press.

Defoe's Suffering and the Argument for Ownership

Defoe opens his *True Collection* with a note to his readers: "N.B. There being a pretended Collection, of some of these tracts, published under the same Name, 'tis thought fit to give notice, that there are several things inserted in the said Book, which were not his, and those that are, being full of Errors, Omissions, and Mistakes, which in many Places invert the Sense and Design of the Author; This Collection has been corrected, and contains above double the number of Tracts that were printed in the said sham Collection, as more at large expressed in the Preface" (A2v). While Defoe had barely corrected most of the tracts reprinted in the *True Collection*, and while it did not, after all, contain quite "double the number of Tracts" in How's volume, the intention of the advertisement is clear: to discredit the competing anthology and bolster the authoritative status of his own. The advertisement, however, operates as a statement of disownership rather than of ownership. The problem with the prior volume, according to Defoe, is not that someone has stolen his property but that someone has tried to force him to own that for which he is not responsible. How's *Collection* contains "several things . . . that were not his" while so butchering the tracts that are Defoe's as to "invert the Sense and Design of the Author." Given what Defoe has already said in *A Brief Explanation* of the dire consequences of having your "design" misunderstood, the advertisement only confirms that the problem of piracy is twofold: at least as threatening as the loss of property is the attempt to make the author responsible for that which he or she is unwilling to own.

In the preface itself, Defoe turns more extensively to the question of the relationship between his property and his present and future "suffering," a word repeated three times in the first two pages. He complains at the outset that he has no "Fondness of appearing in Print having so lately suffered for it" (A3r)—a claim one might be tempted to dismiss as typically calculated authorial self-deprecation if it were not for the fact that Defoe was in the middle of such extended, unpleasant, and potentially disastrous legal proceedings. He is publishing, he says, solely "in order to do my self Justice to the World," by which he seems to mean: in order not to have further unpleasant encounters with the law based on someone else's "dismembere[d] and mangle[d]" version of his productions (A3r–v). He dismisses How's work, in language replete with proprietary terms, as "a spurious Collection of what I have no Legitimate Claim to, and an erroneous Copy of what I have" (A3v). He is forced to offer a competing volume, he continues, not simply to protect his property but to save his skin: "Nor is this all the Injury done me, by the piratical Printer, as such are very rightly called, who unjustly print other Mens Copies; but I think 'tis a most unaccountable piece of Boldness in him, to print that particular Book call'd, *The shortest Way with the Dissenters*, while I lay under the publick Resentment for the same Fact. And though the Government, indeed, may punish one Criminal and let another go free; yet, it seems a little hard, That I should suffer for printing a Book, and another Print it in the Face of the Government to get Money by it" (A3v). A year later, Defoe would claim, with no explicit reference to his own experience but in almost identical terms, "if an Author has not the right of a Book . . . 'twould be very hard the Law should pretend to punish him for it" (*Essay*, 21). In the preface to *A True Collection*, then, and hence in Defoe's immediate experience, it is possible to trace the origins of his *Essay on the Regulation of the Press.*

Defoe goes on to impress upon his audience yet again that "I am a large Sufferer for writing that Book" called *The Shortest Way with the Dissenters*, making How's decision to print it in his volume not just bold but, by all accounts, criminal (A3v). Why should How—like the High Church polemicists attacked in *A Brief Explanation*—be excused for printing the same words for which Defoe is prosecuted and punished? And how can this pirate be allowed not merely to escape but to profit from his exposure of the author? The latter question helps to explain one of the more curious features of *A True Collection*, which is that notwithstanding Defoe's endless complaints about his current vulnerability to legal action in the preface, *A True Collection*, like *A Collection* before it, reprints a copy of *The Shortest Way*. This was, then, along with the first edition of December 1702, and the revised, user-friendly version of February 1703, at least the third occasion on which Defoe had published the inflammatory pamphlet in half a year and certainly, given that he was in prison at the time awaiting his punishment, the boldest of the three. Clearly, Defoe could not stand the thought that a rival would profit from his works but be excused for publishing them, even as he lay in prison for the identical act of publication. He could not tolerate, that is, the splitting off of authorship's liabilities and benefits, such that he exclusively suffered, while another man exclusively took the profits. At the very least, if he was going to suffer largely for *The Shortest Way*, any money to be made from the book ought to be his. The mystery of why Defoe acknowledged his book, then, is apparently solved in the preface to *A True Collection.* Defoe was taking an admittedly perverse stance on the issue of the rights of the author, making what he saw as a "Legitimate Claim" to his work, even as he recognized the high toll that claiming his book in this way was bound to exact.

Two years after these events, in the summer of 1705, Defoe reflected in the *Little Review* on the miseries of 1703. He gives notice to his readers not to pay any attention when they hear "Mob Printers, Pirates, and Hawkers, crying his Name about [the Street]," claiming to have one of "D.D.F.'s" pamphlets or broadsheets for sale.[37] He assures his readers, albeit somewhat disingenuously, that they can depend upon the fact that these works are unauthorized and thus save their money, for "he writes nothing but what he publickly owns, shows his Face to, and professes to be his" (18). Just at the moment when Defoe realized fully the high costs of owning his works, this passage suggests, he also learned the costs of not owning them and resolved to take his risks openly rather than lose his livelihood through acts of proprietary infringement committed by unscrupulous stationers. Whether or not he actually lived up to this lofty aim of full disclosure—and subsequent publications as well as the argument for disownership offered by the *Vindication* in 1718, suggest he did not—matters little. Whatever his actual practices, he was at this time using the *Little Review*, as he used the *Essay* and the *Review* itself, to propound a theory of textual ownership for authors that recognized the costs of that ownership and tried to bargain for compensatory benefits—benefits that took the form of proprietary rights. It was this proposed exchange of rights and responsibilities that constituted Defoe's contribution to the discussion about the best means to regulate the press that had been brewing since 1695 and that would ultimately find a tentative resolution in the Act of Anne. Defoe's innovation was to take an already antiquated system of rewards and punishments—the very same trade-off of rights and responsibilities with which the stationers had been operating since the Star Chamber decrees of 1586 and 1637—and to put the author at the center of that regulatory scheme. As John Feather suggests, in assessing Defoe's contribution to the debates in this period,

> [Defoe] was suggesting a different approach to the whole problem of copy protection. He saw it as being a matter for the author. This was an unusual perception at a time when the whole public debate had revolved around censorship on the one hand, and the property rights of publishers on the other. . . . In a sense, Defoe's arguments opened the way for a reconsideration of the whole issue of copy protection, by suggesting a slightly different case which might be made for it. Despite Defoe's emphasis on the need for some control of the press, he had also added a further argument in favour of the protection of property. It was, of course, precisely this with which the booksellers had been concerned, and it was central to their various

petitions on the Bills which had been discussed since 1695. Defoe, however, added a new element: the idea that protection was beneficial to authors as well as to the trade.[38]

Defoe, Feather rightly notes, made the case for authorial property rights as a solution to both of the problems posed by the unregulated press: proprietary infringement and ideological license. Those rights, in his novel proposal, would be offered to authors as a kind of consolation prize in exchange for accountability. Giving up the publication practices that had made it so "Hard to find the Author," in the words of Chief Justice Scroggs, would necessitate other forms of protection, including what Feather calls "the protection of property." Newly exposed by their ability to claim a proprietary interest in their works, authors would at least be able to rely on one form of protection—"copy protection"—to shield them from complete devastation in the market for printed books.

While Defoe's solution to the problem, as Feather suggests, was an "unusual" one, including elements that were "new" in the sense that they had not been articulated in such a straightforward manner before, he was not the only writer of his generation to argue either for the rights of authors or for their compatibility with authorial liability. As Joseph Loewenstein notes, in fact, Defoe's writings on the press in this period are most revolutionary in their synthesis, their ability to draw on other changes in the culture of authorship to provide an unprecedented solution to the problem of regulation. Loewenstein writes,

It may be worth musing on the eloquence of Defoe's protest. To write and to be published were no more dangerous at the turn of the eighteenth century than at earlier moments in the history of print. Defoe attests, nonetheless, to a powerful sense of authorial implication in the printed book, an implication variously produced—by a culture of libel, by the development of the author as a trademark, and by the proliferation of sites and occasions at which the assertion of authorial property in stationer's copy and, residually, even in printed books was made to carry significant polemical and practical weight.[39]

Given these ongoing changes in what Loewenstein eloquently calls "authorial implication in the printed book," Defoe's authorial *solution* to the problem of regulation comes to look less revolutionary and more timely. His was, if anything, Loewenstein suggests, a "late development" in a series of transformations in the relationship between books and their authors that had been occurring over a long period, transformations mapped out in Part

I of this book (215). Defoe's distinctiveness, however, lay in his ability to recognize that those changes in the culture of authorship had been driven by the author's increasing liability rather than by a more naturally evolving or spontaneously emergent notion of proprietary rights.

In order to understand how authorial property rights, in Loewenstein's formulation, could rather suddenly, at this time, "be represented as an actual *absence* in the legal system," it is necessary to look beyond the immediate context of Defoe's works, to other contemporary proposals for regulating the press (216). Above all, it is necessary to understand how, in the aftermath of the lapse of the Licensing Act, "authorial implication" for printed works came to take on such increased importance in virtually *all* writings about the press, not simply in Defoe's. These proposals, unlike Defoe's, constituted failed experiments and offered tentative solutions that were ultimately deemed either unworkable or unacceptable. They nonetheless help to demonstrate Defoe's key insight, which is that with the end of a system of prepublication oversight of the press, and thus with the end of a system of universal registration for printed works, a vacuum was left not only in the system of ownership of texts but also in what had been an elaborate bureaucracy for establishing liability. The link between copyright and censorship, that is, had been temporarily broken. Among the ultimately unsuccessful proposals for remedying this situation, it is possible to make out just how difficult it was to regulate the press without bringing these two terms back into alignment. Until the government came up with a system that reestablished the relationship between ownership and obligation, the press would remain in turmoil.

The End of Licensing and the Fate of the Author

At the end of the *Little Review* essay where he recited his pledge of allegiance to textual ownership, Defoe addressed himself directly, and ironically, to his former antagonist John How:

> However, the Author desires Mr. J[ohn] H[ow] the Printer and Publisher of the [Observat]or not to think himself concern'd in this Reflection; for that he owns he does not Pirate in this Mechanick Manner, but when he finds an Author in Trouble, and unable to help himself; then like a thorough pac'd———*Printer*, he makes a whole Prize of him at once, and Prints his Works altogether; so getting Money out of other Folks Pockets, much about as honestly as others do on the High Way, and then Justifies it by an old Statute Law, *that if he could but find it, would say*, An Author has no Right to his own Copy, because he was not Apprentice to a *Printer*. (20 June 1705, 2:18–19)

Defoe here excoriates How for taking advantage of the author's misfortunes, attempting to profit from those misfortunes not merely by stealing the author's individual works but by taking the collection as a whole. Even more offensive to Defoe, however, is the manner in which How (at least in Defoe's fantasy) justifies his actions, by inventing statutory precedents for the disenfranchisement of authors, to the benefit of printers like himself. By clinging to the historic rights of the Stationers' Company and its attendant monopoly on the copying of printed works, Defoe suggests, How, like printers and publishers for centuries, steals money from authors' pockets and cheats them of their legitimate rights while leaving them to face the consequences of their works alone.

However, notwithstanding Defoe's attempt to lump him with the monopolistic stationers, How's relationship to the matter of copy ownership is not quite as simple as Defoe's barbed attack would suggest. How was a member of the Stationers' Company but was an outspoken critic of many of the company's practices throughout his professional life. Raymond Astbury notes that in 1693, when the Licensing act was due to lapse, "John Howe [*sic*] asked to speak against" the possibility that the act might be renewed. "Like many independent Stationers," Astbury continues, "he projected that the lapse of the Act would break the Company monopoly."[40] How stood to benefit from the lapse of the 1662 Press Act because, as he rightly projected, the end of licensing would mean the end of the stranglehold on the production of printed matter held by the most powerful stationers. Renewal of the Licensing Act, he thought, would condemn him for the rest of his career to operate on the illegal or unremunerative fringes of the trade. Ultimately, however, the lapse of the act only made the situation worse, since copy ownership was now entirely unregulated and printing a free market. The richest printers were at liberty to produce competing editions and to club together to drive lesser members out of the trade. Thus, an unregulated press was as economically disastrous for minor printers such as How as it was for an author like Defoe.[41]

With the lapse of the Licensing Act, then, not only would prepublication oversight come to an end, relieving the stationers for all time of one of their main duties since 1557, but so too would the company's monopoly on the production of printed books. As Laurence Hanson writes, "the importance of the Stationers' Company in the control of the press rapidly diminished."[42] Almost everyone agreed that neither of these forms of disorder in the book trade could be allowed to persist and that some other solution would be required to bring the trade under a proper management. Here, however, the agreement stopped. Turn-of-the-century attempts to find a solution to the problem of press regulation failed again and again, but these failed solutions are not without interest for the information they offer about the difficulty—perhaps even the impossibility—of severing the two historic functions of the now virtually obsolete company: copy protection and control over the content of printed works. In order to understand how it was that the Act of Anne ultimately succeeded as a kind of compromise measure, it is necessary to review some of these failed measures, measures which are characterized by two broad trends: on the one hand, the repeated attempt to disentangle copyright from censorship, and on the other, an increasing focus on the author as the sole site of liability for the content of printed works.

The act, which had come into effect originally on 10 June 1662 and had lapsed from 1679 to 1685, came up for renewal in the spring of 1693.[43] In January of that year, as the lords began to prepare their campaign to keep the Licensing Act alive, John Locke wrote a memorandum designed to convince the Commons that the act should not, under any circumstances, be allowed to remain in effect. Locke's proposals have received attention as a kind of opening salvo in the long struggle for "freedom of the press" and, in associated fashion, for "freedom of speech." As Locke's nineteenth-century biographer Peter King stirringly put it, "if the unanswerable objections which Locke stated against every part of that act [of 1662] contributed in any degree to prevent its further reenactment, his exertions may be regarded as no small service rendered to the cause of liberty and truth."[44] Yet, Locke's recommendations, however revolutionary, nonetheless practically invited the authorities to turn their attention directly to the author and to seize him or her for any "transgress[ions]" committed in the course of the text. It is hard to know, in the end, at least from the author's perspective, what kind of "liberty" is being advocated in these lines:

> I know not why a man should not have liberty to print whatever he would speak; and to be answerable for the one, just as he is for the other, if he transgresses the law in either. . . . To prevent men being undiscovered for what they print, you may prohibit any book to be printed, published, or sold, without the printer's or bookseller's name, under great penalties, whatever be in it. And then let the printer or bookseller, whose name is to it, be answerable for whatever is against law in it, as if he were the author, unless he can produce the person he had it from, which is all the restraint ought to be put upon printing.[45]

Locke never questions that it is the author who ought to be held responsible—whose "liberty" is indistinguishable from his "answerab[ility]"—even as he acknowledges that the author, at least under current conditions, cannot always be induced to appear. It is somewhat uncanny to hear the tones of Roger L'Estrange echoing in the words of this great advocate of "the cause of liberty and truth." Compare, for instance, L'Estrange's statement in *Considerations*: "*let the* Person *in whose Possession* [an offending book] *is* found, *be Reputed, and Punish'd as the* Author *of the said Book, unless he* Produce *the Person, or Persons, from whom he receiv'd it.*"[46] In the foundations of the liberal commitment to freedom of expression, then, it is possible to trace the unlikely influence of the "Bloodhound of the Press." Here, too, is Milton, whose offer of "the fire and the executioner" for books merely deemed "mischievous and libellous" in *Areopagitica* is recalled in Locke's willingness to let authors and others suffer "great penalties" for what they write "against law."[47]

The point to be taken from Locke's *Memorandum* is not that prepublication and postpublication restraints upon the press are indistinguishable, nor that Locke's proposals should be exposed as tainted, but that one person's freedom of the press is another's censorship. For advocating virtually identical restraints to those of Locke ten years later, Defoe's *Essay* is charged with being still mired in an outdated notion of the relationship between rights and responsibilities; Rose, for instance, asserts that the proposals in *An Essay* are based on a system of "rewards and punishments," derived "from within the framework of traditional society," in contrast to the "more Lockean" notion of property articulated in the Act of Anne.[48] Once it becomes clear that Locke, too, is working from within a framework in which the rights to the fruits of one's labor simultaneously bring with them obligations with relation to the law, the proximity of Locke's proposals to Defoe's—and thus to the older system of rewards and punishments—begins to emerge. If, as so many critics have done, one is tempted to trace the genesis of authorial property rights in the 1710 act to its Lockean origins, then it is important to bear in mind Locke's somewhat sobering vision of authorial "answerab[ility]" in *Memorandum* before concluding that the first copyright statute announced the end of the state's interest in linking property with liability.

Despite Locke's intervention, the 1693 Parliament adjourned without coming to any conclusive decisions about the renewal of licensing. Instead, they simply extended the Press Act for one more year, deferring further discussion until the next session. In February 1694, after a vote to renew the act yet again failed, the house appointed a committee to look for new and better solutions to regulate printing. The bill drawn up by this committee is unique among measures since the mid-sixteenth century, in that it attempts to institute a system of regulation without any form of copy protection whatsoever. As Astbury notes, the proposed bill thus "severed the historical link between censorship and copyright," advocating ideological regulation over proprietary concerns.[49] In a move that abolished the privileges of the Stationers' Company entirely, anyone could own and operate a printing press as long as the press was registered with the appropriate authorities. Books in specified fields, including science and the arts, would be exempt from licensing, but those in "the highly sensitive areas of politics, law, and religion," as Astbury puts it, would be examined sheet by sheet once printing had begun (311). In an echo of Locke, finally, the bill provided that "anyone whose name was in the imprint of such a work would be answerable as if he were the author, and the author would also be liable to prosecution, if he could be found" (311). The bill made no provisions whatsoever for copy protection and contained no mention of the Stationers' Register or any other form of central record-keeping authority. Thus, the 1694 bill, which ultimately, predictably, failed, was the first such measure to experiment with a system of regulation based exclusively on oversight, regardless of proprietary interest. Of course, the role of the imprint as a marker of liability for the work's content still preserves a notion of the unbreakable link between ownership and responsibility; to put one's name on a work is still, even here, to be obliged to answer for its content. Nonetheless, without any proposed system for protecting the proprietary interests of members of the company and others involved in the print trade, leaving them free to invade each other's property regardless of the imprint, this measure was sure to fail, and with it, attempts to modify or renew the existing legislation. On 3 May 1695, just over thirty-three years after its original passage, the Press Act finally lapsed for good.

Numerous attempts at developing a more acceptable system of regulation followed, beginning in November 1695 and continuing almost without a break until the 1710 act was finally passed.[50] The next significant episode occurred in 1699 when the House of Lords attempted to bring in a bill that would try a new tactic: regulation of content without licensing. Rather than leave postpublication oversight to the common-law courts, the lords suggested that there should be a statutory basis for the prosecution of offenders who printed "any matter that is treasonable, seditious, atheistical, or heretical"—all the adjectives, as Defoe might have put it.[51] Their proposed system, which owed much to the 1694 bill, operated primarily through the registration of presses. Anyone wanting to print a work of any kind in or around London had first to enter his or her name, along with both the location of the printing press and his or her residential address, in registers to be kept both at the Court of Aldermen of the City of London and at Stationers' Hall. Similar provisions were made for presses in the university towns of Oxford and Cambridge, while all other presses around the country were to be registered with the mayor of the town in question (3:271–72). Interestingly, the bill makes few references to "printers," instead referring repeatedly to the "owner[s] or master[s] of such printing-presses" who will not only be responsible for registering the presses in question but will be liable if anything objectionable emerges from their shop. Ownership is, then, directly tied to liability in this bill, although the liability in question seems to attach to the printer rather than to the author.

Later in the bill, however, the author does appear, only to be made, as Loewenstein notes, "the primary subject of regulation."[52] An early version of the bill, submitted 4 January, contains a number of proposals that were later eliminated, all of them vestiges of earlier regulatory systems, including compulsory registration of all works with the aldermen and the stationers, and widespread powers of search and seizure for the secretaries of state and their assistants. This early version of the bill makes numerous references to the author, always and exclusively in terms that address both that figure's liability and his or her presumed absence from the scene of the crime: "If any person or persons whatsoever shall . . . print or publish . . . any matter that is treasonable, seditious, atheistical, or heretical, . . . then the master or owner of the said press where such book, pamphlet, paper or thing was printed, shall be subject and liable to the same punishments as by law might have been inflicted upon the author thereof" (3:273). In cases where such materials are found as the result of a search, the owners of the presses may be "prosecuted and punished as the authors thereof, in case he or they shall refuse to discover or make known the author or person that brought the same to him" (3:274). Finally, anyone importing seditious or heretical books from abroad will be "taken and deemed as the author thereof" (3:274). In all of these passages, the author has always already disappeared, and his or her sole purpose in reappearing is in order to shoulder the blame for the work. The author's function, that is, has been reduced to one of obligation without benefit; as long as he or she does not need to be punished, the author need not appear.

When the bill emerged from committee on 23 January, many of these passages and requirements had been eliminated, but two features of the earlier version remained intact: the compulsory imprint and the invocation of the author as the figure who must be prosecuted for the work, if at all possible. All works must bear on the title page "the true Christian and surname in words at length, together with the place of habitation of the publisher and owner of the press" where the work was printed. While the name of the author would not have to be present on the imprint, the printer or owner of the press would be required, upon demand, to "discover and make known the author of such book." Should the printer or owner refuse, he or she "shall be subject and liable to the same punishment as by law might have been inflicted upon the author thereof" (3:276). The imprint, then, becomes a means of announcing responsibility for the work, in the absence of a system of registration of copies. The names found on the title page belong to those who have committed resources and time to the production of the work, and who thus stand to profit from it. At the same time, however, the imprint demarcates liability, by making it possible to trace the work's owners, and ideally its author, in the event of any transgressions of which the work is accused. The purpose of the imprint, then, like that of the Stationers' Register before it, is twofold: to record the makers—if not the owners—of the work and to expose those responsible for its appearance in the world to prosecution and punishment, if necessary.

One rather obvious question that emerges from consideration of this document is why the lords did not require the author's name to be included in the imprint if they wanted to assure themselves of always being able to find the culprit when necessary. Defoe, we remember, made such a recommendation in his *Essay*, when he extolled the benefits of a more extensive system of compulsory imprints. If such a system were put into effect, he promised, "Authors would be known as soon as the Book, because this Law would oblige the Printer or Bookseller to place the Author's Name in the Title, or himself" (18). Defoe vacillates about whether the inclusion of the author's name should be mandatory or only recommended, but he is quick to point out the consequences of choosing to withhold the desired information. The law, he insists, must state that should the author's name be voluntarily omitted, the printer or bookseller assumes the author's liability, so that there will always be "some body found to answer for" the work (16). Ideally, though, authors should simply fulfill their "obligations" and put their names on their works in the first place, in order to provide the most efficient system of answerability to the law.

In late 1703, a new attempt at legislation was introduced that shared Defoe's recommendation concerning the imprint, and this one, at least, reached a second reading. The bill proposed that the names of printer, publisher, and author appear on the imprint—a suggestion that provoked an immediate response from the Whig Matthew Tindal in his *Reasons against*

Restraining the Press.[53] In the first of a long line of such appeals, Tindal concluded his lengthy call for "Liberty of the Press" with a defense of the right of authors to remain anonymous:

> As to the obliging Authors to set their Names to their Works, that can only serve to hinder the publishing of most useful Books, *viz.* those designed to rectify Abuses. Besides, this prejudices People for or against a Book, and serves as a Handle for fulsome Flatteries, or gross Abuses; and we have too frequent Instances of mens thinking to atone, for not answering the Arguments, by railing at the Authors. And therefore those Writers, such as the Author of *the Whole Duty of Man, &c* that design the utmost good, have industriously concealed their Names. (14–15)

Tindal wants to spare those who set out to "rectify Abuses" from the necessity of identifying themselves. Such critics of the status quo are virtually bound to alienate, if not offend, both the contemporaries who commit such abuses and the authorities who allow them to go unpunished. In addition, he wants books to be judged on their own merits and not on those of their authors. In the final lines, though, he returns to those social reformers whose anonymity, he believes, requires the most careful defense. Turning on its head the usual arguments about the necessity of "finding the author," Tindal argues that it is those writers who "design the utmost good" rather than those who seek to conceal their "miscarriages" (to use Defoe's term) who require the protection offered by "concealing their Names." True liberty of the press, then, resides for Tindal not in creating a climate in which authors are free to own their works with impunity but in establishing a system that allows authors to disown them, when necessary.

While the 1704 bill died in Commons, the problem of the author's name did not. The authorities had finally discovered an efficient means for finding the author, but a broad cultural consensus, exemplified here by Tindal, argued against requiring authors to set their names to their works, and the proposal would not be made again in Parliament for nearly a decade. In 1711 and 1712, when a renewal of the Licensing Act was yet again proposed in Parliament, authors and others would revisit the viability of compulsory authorial imprints in pamphlets and periodicals, and would once again argue vehemently against the requirement that the author name him- or herself. I will return to these debates below after pausing to take note of the fact that one figure did continue to argue for compulsory imprints throughout the years leading up to the Act of Anne: Daniel Defoe. Unlike his contemporaries, Defoe in his periodical writings exhibited an increasingly strong conviction that the matter of regulation would be enormously simplified if authors could be induced to step forward and own their books up front—that is, on the title page. In the years leading up to the passage of the Act of Anne, especially after the publication of his *Essay*, Defoe returned to this commonsense recommendation repeatedly, in a clear effort to convince his contemporaries, including those charged with drafting new press regulation, of the wisdom of his recommendations. At the same time, however, Defoe himself was engaged in numerous acts of anonymous and pseudonymous printing, giving the lie to the *Little Review* claim that "he writes nothing but what he publickly owns." In the years and months immediately preceding passage of the Act of Anne, Defoe was still struggling with the problem of the relationship between ownership and obligation, and the necessity of being "cautious in owning," if not in his theoretical writings, then in his daily life. He seems, that is, to have been willing to suffer the consequences of owning his productions in some cases but wanted to be allowed to disown them in others. Ultimately, the Act of Anne came up with a similar solution.

The Name of the Author and the Act of Anne

While Defoe's *Essay on the Regulation of the Press* and his periodical writings on the topic have received considerable attention in the past decade from Rose, Loewenstein, Feather, and others intrigued by the strong and systematic case he makes for author's rights and responsibilties, these are not the only works in which Defoe addressed himself to the problem of the licentiousness of the press.[54] In April 1704, just months after his release from prison, as he was attempting to obtain a complete pardon and to ingratiate himself with his new employer, Robert Harley, Defoe apparently penned a rather different production, one that he certainly never owned. On 1 April, according to J. A. Downie, who discovered the work, an anonymous informant, who was apparently unaware of the increasingly close relationship between the speaker and Defoe, wrote to Harley to tell him a tale about his protégé designed to bring about the writer's permanent downfall. The informant claimed that he had accidentally wandered into a meeting of Disenters, and, going unnoticed, had been given a copy of a broadsheet titled *To the Honourable the C—s of England Assembled in P—t. The Humble Petition and Representation of the True Loyal and Always Obedient Church of England, Relating to the Bill Restraining the Press.*[55] The members of the meeting, the informant writes, informed him that "Danl. De:Foe" was the author of the enclosed inflammatory tract (52).

The work, which purports to be a defense of the renewal of the Licensing Act, is a self-consciously satirical production. In describing the style and tone of the letter, Downie uses terms that only accentuate its uncanny resemblance to a slightly earlier Defoe production, *The Shortest Way with the Dissenters*: "Under the guise of a rabid High Churchman, the author ironically condemned himself out of his own mouth in rehearsing the dubious motives of men of his kidney for muzzling the Whig press" (52). Downie downplays the comparison with *The Shortest Way* by arguing that an "actual impersonation of a High Churchman . . . was not attempted," so that here, in contrast to the former work, the author's "true stance is never in doubt" (52–53). Nonetheless, given his recent run-in with the law, Defoe's decision to produce this work, let alone to allow it to be printed (even if he planned to circulate it privately), is extremely surprising, especially for a man who was still supposed to be "on his good behavior," which is to say, on probation. The work, like its naughty predecessor *The Shortest Way*, is peppered with references to the intolerance and cowardice of the High Church party and their blatant disregard for the most basic rights of their countrymen. In a characteristically irreverent passage, the speaker charges that licensing must be renewed, "Because at present the Whigs and Moderate Church-Men, *a worse sort of Enemies than the Fanaticks*, are continually affronting us, and Bullying the CHURCH of *England* in their Pamphlets and Writings about Law, Liberty, Property, and Conscience, things we find it absolutely necessary, our present Circumstances Considerd, not to be so much concern'd about as we use to be, and which perhaps we may be a little oblig'd to entrench upon" (56). Among those measures that must be taken under the present circumstances are "some few Incroachments . . . on those Trifles call'd Liberty of Conscience," including both religious freedom and liberty of the press (such as they were) (56). The work goes on to propose specific "Incroachments," including limiting what may be said from the pulpit and subjecting all proposed printed works to scrutiny by members of the Church, a measure which is represented as tantamount to complete censorship: "if they attempt to print, we shall take care to smother the Impression at the Printers and fright the Authors from appearing" (57). The Whig press is especially threatening, the speaker admits, in one of the pamphlet's funnier moments, because "we do find that these damn'd Whigs are a little too hard for us" (56). Renewing licensing, the letter makes clear, especially if the Church is allowed to participate in the oversight of the press, will bring about the High Church's most cherished desire by effecting a total silencing of the opposition.

As far as we know, Harley simply ignored the pamphlet, and Defoe seems to have come out of this dangerous experiment unscathed. Unlike many of his other anonymous works, however, this one was never printed in a collection, nor did he ever refer to it in his letters or periodicals. The work has no imprint and, as Downie notes, "furnishes no clues to its place of origin, its printer, or its date of publication" (54). It goes without saying that the work is also silent on the subject of its author. Clearly, Defoe intended and needed to be more cautious than ever not to be associated with this particular production. He must have been willing to forego both any profit from selling the work and any reputation from circulating it beyond his most immediate friends. The work was apparently made public only on that one occasion, perhaps because Harley himself "smothered" it with a note of rebuke. Here, anyway, is one rather flagrant example of a work even this advocate of compulsory imprints could not be induced to own.

It is somewhat ironic, then, to find Defoe a year later excoriating the High Church party for the very offense he had committed in the spoof of 1704. The *Review* of 8 November 1705 contains an extended plan to restrain what Defoe sees as the particularly flagrant abuses of the press committed by the High Anglicans. In this short diatribe, a kind of *Essay on the Regulation of the Press* in miniature, Defoe spends an extended period discussing the means of controlling the excesses of the press, only to turn in his conclusion yet again to a call for property rights as a necessary part of the remedy. The piece is distinguished from *An Essay*, however, in its particular and sustained attention to the problem of anonymous publication. Defoe writes of "how dishonourable it is in a Government, to have the Subjects permitted to print every malitious and embroiling Notion, under Allegorick Titles, and in the Dark" (2:422). Lest his readers are confused by the phrase "in the Dark," he goes on to specify that the problem lies in "concealing the Authors," which leads to the impossibility of prosecution and punishment (2:422). New solutions are necessary, he writes, "That no Authors *in nubibus* [in the clouds] may fight in the dark with the Government, Constitution, Peace, Moderation, and with every Good thing; and having perform'd the Mischief, avoid the Punishment: These, may it please the Honourable House to reflect, are Incendiaries in a Cloud" (2:423). Defoe is addressing himself in this passage directly to the members of Parliament whose task it is to come up with a new means of restraining the press, and the method he proposes depends entirely upon requiring the author to acknowledge "all his performances." When authors remain in the dark, Defoe concludes, both licentiousness and proprietary infringement inevitably occur. In a subsequent passage that brings these concerns together, and that offers a narrative in miniature not only of Defoe's literary life but also of the entire history of the book trade, Defoe writes, "Books are Printed by no body, and Wrote by every body; one Man Prints another Man's Works, and calls them his own; again, another Man Prints his own, and calls them another Man's. *A.* is Loaded with *B.*'s Crimes, and *B.* Applauded with *A.*'s Virtues—*A.* Prints a Lampoon, and lays it to *C*; *C.* prints *D*'s Works, and sets *E*'s Name to them; continual Roberies, Piracies, and Invasions of Property, range among the Occupation" (2:424). One comes away with the sense that Defoe could have kept going here until he ran out of alphabet. The only remedy for this rampant disorder, Defoe concludes, and the only hope of settling both the proprietary and the regulatory issues at hand, is a statute: "these things call for an Act of Parliament," he unhesitatingly concludes (2:424). In such an act, Defoe counsels the lawmakers, "the Property of Copies may be secur'd" and "Publick Affronts upon the Government Condemn'd and entirely Crush'd" (2:424). In Defoe's proposed statutory remedy, that is, copyright and censorship would once again be bound together and the unsuccessful attempts to sunder them put to rest for all time.

For the next five years, Defoe kept after his contacts in Parliament to follow his plan for a new kind of statute. In March 1707, as yet another bill met with failure, he wrote to Harley, "I hear the Bill for Secureing the Right of printed Coppyes is stopt. I beg of you Sir in your Respect to Encouragement of Letters and Dilligence in Learning to give it your help" (*Defoe Letters*, 212). Defoe's use of the phrase "Encouragement of Letters" indicates how close the trade and the legislators had finally come to the form the "Act for the Encouragement of Learning" would ultimately take. Indeed, in February 1707, thirteen members of the trade, perhaps with Defoe's recommendations in mind, had petitioned Commons "for the better securing the Rights of Copies of printed Books," and for the first time the petition was formulated on behalf of the rights of authors. Feather writes,

> The [petitioners] pointed out that time and money had been spent in writing books, and in printing and selling them, but that the pirates, both English and foreign, were making serious inroads in this property. They therefore asked that what they called "literary property" (another new phrase) should be secured to the writer or his assignees, or to the purchaser of the copy. The last would, of course, normally be a publisher, but the petition was worded so that the petitioners gave prominence to the protection of authors without in any way compromising their own interests.[56]

Although the bill failed, here, at last, was a formulation of the problem that seemed to follow at least some of the guidelines laid out by Defoe. "Securing" property to authors and their assignees would at least solve the problem of those continual "Roberies, Piracies, and Invasions of Property" that had plagued the trade since its inception.

Defoe must have experienced some frustration, however, at the fact that the petitioners and the drafters of new legislation had failed to include what he saw as the primary justification for recognizing authorial property rights: the ease with which they led to a restraint of the press. In late November 1709, in a last-ditch effort to get his contemporaries to understand his proposals and thus to draft a more "effectual" bill, he yet again reiterated his theory of complementarity in the *Review.* He had now managed to reduce his proposal to an extremely concise form: "I undertake to propose several steps which may be effectual," he wrote, "both to restrain the licentiousness of the Press, and to secure to the Authors of Books their Right of Property" (26 November 1709; 6:403). Ten days later, he elaborated on his plan, offering a virtual manual for drafting the proposed legislation:

> To say that we know not how to prevent [piracy], is saying what is very foolish—This, and the Printing seditious or heretical Books, is easily suppress'd by an Act of Parliament of but two clauses.
>
> 1. That no Man shall presume to print, or sell when printed, any Book that has been printed before, without the Consent or Agreement of the Author or Proprietor of the said Book. . . .
> 2. For the publick Part. That every Author, who causes any thing he writes to be printed or publish'd, shall be oblig'd to cause his Name to be printed in the Frontispiece of the Book, and to give a note under his Hand to the Printer of the said Book, sign'd by two Witnesses, acknowledging and owning himself to be the Author of the said Book, and authorizing him the said Printer to print and publish the same—Which Note and Acknowledgment shall be allow'd to discharge the said Printer in Law—and shall, on the Printer's producing it upon Oath, together with the Oaths of the Witnesses, be sufficient to convict the said Author. (4:420)

If anything, Defoe's sense of the obligations the author owes in exchange for having his or her proprietary interests recognized has increased over the five years since *An Essay.* All vacillation about the question of the author's name on the imprint is gone, and in addition to the imprint, the author now has a second requirement to fulfill, in the form of a "note" signed by witnesses. Rather than the printer being required to keep a record of the author's permission to publish, the author is here required to testify to his or her liability for the work, not once but twice, and that testimony will be, in a most menacing formulation, "sufficient to convict." In Defoe's frightening vision of the consequences of literary property, owning one's work mandates signing what amounts to a confession of exclusive responsibility for the work's contents.

A month after Defoe's bleak vision of proprietary authorship was published, the Commons offered their own version of a statute to regulate the press—the bill that would come to be known as the Copyright Act. In comparison to Defoe's proposed version, the parliamentary "Bill for the Encouragement of Learning, and for Securing the Property of Copies of Books to the Rightful Owners thereof" seems downright benign.[57] There is no mention anywhere of conviction, punishment, suffering, or any other consequence of owning one's book, and the entire focus of the bill is on "security" of property rather than on liability. The same is true for the version that was ultimately written into law, titled "An Act for the Encouragement of Learning, by Vesting the Copies of Printed Books in the Authors and Purchasers of the Copies during the Times therein Mentioned."[58] This final version eliminated the language about security, offering instead the promise of "Vesting" copies in their authors, suggesting that the act conferred a right rather than recognizing a preexisting one—a feature that would take on increasing importance in subsequent debates over the nature of copyright that persist into the present.[59] Copyright remained with the proprietor for a limited term—twenty-one years in the case of works already in print, fourteen years for new works, with the copyright reverting to the author for another fourteen years if the author was still alive at the expiration of the first period. However hesitant the act was about specifying the precise nature of the proprietary interest authors held in their works—"natural" or statutory—it still required that printers and publishers obtain "the Consent of the Authors or Proprietors" of books and writings before printing them, the first time such a measure had been in effect since 1642 (9:256).

It is easy to review the text of the act and conclude, as most commentators have done, that it marks the end of the relationship between property rights and press control. Rose and Fredrick Seaton Siebert both refer to the act as a "divorce" of these two regulatory systems, and Lyman Ray Patterson describes this as the period in which censorship became "irrelevant" to copyright.[60] Reading the act, in fact, it is possible to conclude that Defoe had simply wasted his time in berating his contemporaries about the benefits of liability and the obligations of ownership. The drafters of the act, it seems, were willing to recognize an author's proprietary interest in his or her work without exacting the high costs Defoe was prepared to demand of his fellow authors.

As appealing and persuasive as this reading of the act remains to virtually all commentators, however, it misses one crucial feature of the statute: the role played by the Stationers' Register in ensuring copy protection. The provision concerning the register is, admittedly, a confusing one, for it seems to require entrance in the register as a condition of *publication*, when in fact it requires only such entrance as a condition of *protection*. Entry, that is, was voluntary, but anyone who failed to enter a work was, in effect, giving up the rights promised by the statute. The second provision of the act, which addresses the question of registration, actually operates through a kind of negative logic, specifying the consequences for those who do not enter their works rather than spelling out the benefits for those who do: "Nothing in this Act contained shall be construed to extend to subject any Bookseller Printer or other Person whatsoever to the Forfeitures or Penalties therein mentioned for or by reason of the printing or reprinting of any Book or Books without such Consent as aforesaid *unless the Title to the Copy* of such Book or Books hereafter published *shall before Publication be entred in the Register Book* of the Company of Stationers in such Manner as hath been usual" (9:256; emphasis added). Rather than mandating entrance in the register as a precondition of publication, then, this provision merely recommends entry, in the words of Feather, as a "precondition of claiming and defending rights."[61] So important is it that authors and other owners should be given an opportunity to complete this entry, however, that the statute is careful to make provision for entering books in cases where the register is for some reason unavailable, or the clerk of the register uncooperative. In such cases, which require two witnesses to testify to the unavailability of the register, the "author or proprietor" may take out an advertisement in the *Gazette* announcing his or her title to the work instead. This advertisement, like the entry in the register, can then be used at a later date as evidence of copyright. Thus the act ends up sending a slightly mixed message: formal registration of copyright is not mandated, but for those who do choose to fulfill those provisions of the act, the requirements for doing so are highly specific and carefully legislated.

Patterson has rightly argued, on the basis of his reading of the Act of Anne, that "the radical change in the Statute . . . was not that it gave authors the right to acquire a copyright—a prerogative until then limited to members of the Stationers' Company—but that it gave that right to all persons."[62] More radical still, however, is the fact that the act gave authors and other prospective proprietors a *choice* in addition to their *right*: they could record their proprietary interest in a work in the register or *Gazette*, in which case their rights would be protected, or they could forego that act of record keeping and have no recourse to legal remedy in the event of subsequent depredation. It is only through reading Defoe—and through studying the aftermath of the passage of the Act of Anne—that it becomes clear why authors and others might have foregone this process of registration, and hence of protection against piracy, as so many of them did.[63] Anyone who had reason to be "cautious in owning" a particular work would have been loath to make a public record of such ownership, a record to which the authorities could later refer for evidence of liability. Authors could, if they were so willing, go some way toward protecting themselves from their "dangerous fates" through refusing to own their books, or they could, if they were willing to take the risk, own their productions and submit to the potentially hazardous consequences that might ensue.

Of course, as Defoe well knew, and as the cases of Cellier, Twyn, and others amply demonstrate, refusing to own one's book was not necessarily proof against prosecution. Authors who chose not to protect their proprietary interest in their books might still find themselves pursued by the law. The important lesson to be drawn from the Act of Anne, however, is that those authors and others who *did* choose to own their works were *required* to expose themselves to the authorities by providing documentation of their ownership in the form of an entry in the register or an advertisement in the *Gazette.* Some public record of the name of the author or proprietor was thus required as a condition of copy protection. The new benefit of proprietorship was thus offered to authors at a price: by stepping forward to own their works, they also put themselves into a vulnerable relationship to the law. Put otherwise, under the provisions of the Act of Anne, as the cases of *The Dunciad* and *Polly* will also demonstrate, there was simply no way to be "cautious in owning." To own one's work was synonymous with a willingness to suffer.

The Perils of Ownership: Two Case Studies

Before turning to the events of 1728 and 1729, when *The Dunciad* and *Polly* were published—events in which the consequences of the Act of Anne for authors are most fully elaborated—it is instructive to look very briefly at two moments that occurred closer to the passage of the act, which also shed light on the troubles that followed from the new system of ownership. These events are, first, in 1711 and 1712, a renewed debate about making the name of the author compulsory on all imprints, and second, in 1720, the first case in which an author's rights were defended in court under the provisions of the new statute. Both of these moments, albeit in rather different ways, serve to substantiate the proposition that ownership of printed works put authors in a perilous relationship to the law by requiring them, for the first time, to dispense with their capacity to disappear. As long as authors could be induced to claim the new benefits of proprietary authorship, these case studies suggest, it would never again be difficult to find the author and, if necessary, to convict and punish that newly exposed figure.

In 1711, both the queen and Parliament applied themselves yet again to the question of the best means of restraining the press. The Act for the Encouragement of Learning had restored at least some order to the commercial trade in printed matter, but the problem of seditious and scandalous publications—especially periodicals—continued unabated. In 1710 or 1711, according to Siebert, Henry St. John—Viscount Bolingbroke, one of the two secretaries of state—devised a scheme to raise revenue and control the press simultaneously by taxing newspapers and pamphlets. This proposal would ultimately result, in April 1712, in passage of the first Stamp Tax.[64] In January 1711, the queen encouraged the new movement for regulation when she complained to Parliament of the "great License . . . taken in publishing false and scandalous Libels" and called for some "Remedy equal to the Mischief."[65] Immediate responses from members of the trade poured off the presses, arguing against any attempt to tax printed matter and proposing other, more effective and less costly measures for controlling the content of printed works. To the dismay of Whig onlookers, proposals were even made to reintroduce licensing as the only effective means to regulate the press without the introduction of a potentially ruinous financial solution.

One of those who spoke out during this new flurry of publications concerning regulation was, predictably, Defoe, who railed against the Stamp Act in the *Review* and proposed alternative methods of regulation. His main argument against the Stamp Act was that it would leave handwritten newssheets untouched while encouraging those who had formerly printed their periodicals either to continue to print them surreptitiously or to move to a manuscript format. Printed newspapers, he argued, as L'Estrange had done fifty years earlier, were far easier to track than their counterparts in manuscript, because their "Authors are known, and . . . are answerable for what they write, and may by a few Clauses, be made more liable" (29 March 1711; 8:7). Defoe is here characteristically willing to offer up the author of any printed work to the authorities and even to make him or her more liable, if necessary, than is already the case. In addition, Defoe suggests, the government should become even more stringent about the matter of the author's name, at last putting into effect the one recommendation he had been making continuously since the publication of *An Essay* in 1704. "Some Restraint should be put to Scandal, Ribaldry and Reproach, villifying Ministers of State, Invading Men's Reputations, and the like," he insists, "by obliging every Man to *set his Name* to what he writes" (8:7–8). In addition, in a recommendation that, had it been accepted, would have had profound effects on Pope's *Dunciad* in 1728, Defoe counseled prohibiting "Printing Initial Letters of Names, and oblique pointing at Persons in Matters Scandalous" (8:8). With the author's name on the title page, anyone named in the work would know whom to prosecute, and "Amends to the Injur'd" would be easier both to adjudicate and to reward (8:8). If the government wanted to introduce other specific prohibitions, including disallowing the printing of matters related to politics, Defoe would be "the first to lay down" his pen (7). Rather than a "Prohibition in general" (should licensing be reintroduced), or a tax on particular printed matter, these specific recommendations—especially the one concerning the compulsory use of the author's name in the imprint—would answer the government's ends with regard to liability without muzzling the press as a whole.

Defoe was not alone this time in his recommendation concerning the author's name. John Asgill, in a short *Essay for the Press* written in 1712, argued that a tax was impractical and licensing ineffective, since works could always be "clandestinely printed and dispers'd."[66] Instead, Asgill suggests, just one solution is necessary to solve the problem posed by the press: "The present Licentiousness being chiefly occasion'd by concealing the Names of the Authors," he writes, "the most just and natural Remedy, seems by prohibiting the Prints without the Names of the Authors to them" (7). Even those who advocated a return to licensing identified the anonymity of authors as the primary problem afflicting the press. Thus, the (*anonymous*) author of *Arguments Relating to a Restraint upon the Press*, also from 1712, complains that "the libelers never appear, whether they shoot at Random or at a Mark, their Mein or Style are as incogniscible as their Faces."[67] These authors, he or she laments, are worse than "Highway-men in Masks" (26). In addition to renewing the system of licensing, he or she concludes, some means should be found for detecting the identity of all "libelers" before allowing their works to go forth "incogniscible" into the world.

Given the widespread consensus across deep political divisions about the primary reason for the difficulty of prosecuting offensive printed works, it is instructive to discover, nevertheless, even more widespread agreement that making the author's name a compulsory part of the imprint is absolutely unacceptable. Like Tindal, the anonymous author of *The Thoughts of a Tory Author, Concerning the Press*—possibly Joseph Addison—took it for granted that authors would want to conceal their names and that they should be given the opportunity to do so.[68] The tract returns again and again, and with some urgency to the matter, insisting repeatedly that authors should continue to be allowed to remain anonymous—that is, to disown their productions—should they choose to do so. "There can be a convenient Restraint put upon the Press," the author counsels, "without obliging Authors to own themselves" (5). The terms *obligation* and *ownership* occur together throughout the tract: "what need there is of the Author's being oblig'd to put his Name, when you have a good Printer's and Bookseller's," the author complains, "I do not see"; "there may be a Thousand Things both Lawful, and indeed Useful to be Printed," he continues, "which the Writer may not be willing to own" (2). Authors do not need to put their names on their works in order to fulfill regulatory goals, the author suggests, as long as printers and publishers are required to do so in their place. Should they simply be "oblig'd to answer for whatever Faults their Authors commit," these members of the trade would be more careful about what they allowed to come out in print (3).

The pamphleteer defends his willingness to make printers and booksellers liable in the author's place by asserting that most authors would rather not publish at all than set their names to their works: "If we shou'd ever be debarr'd from Publishing our Fictions and Invectives, which will be the sure Consequence of compelling Authors to own what they do, we shall be routed for ever" (22). Silence is here posited as preferable to owning one's work, although the reasons for authorial reticence about the use of their names are never fully explained. Invoking a kind of mystification of the authorial arts, the Tory author simply avers that there are "a Thousand Reasons which none but Authors can so well account for, why all Men should not at all time own what they write" (28–29). In place of an actual explanation of the preference for anonymity, the author simply offers statistics: since only "One Part in Ten" of books currently published bear the author's name, "a force upon Authors to own Themselves" will result in the destruction of the trade—and thus of all literate culture—in one statutory blow (28).

Despite the fact that they were left, according to this logic, to suffer in the author's place, printers seem to have agreed with the conclusions of the Tory author and others like him about the ultimate outcome of requiring authors' names on their works.[69] In *The Printer's Case Humbly Submitted to the Consideration of the Honourable House of Commons* (1711?), which contained a series of proposals for the better management of the press, a group of printers spoke out against being required to name the author, offering themselves as substitutes to be named in the author's place.[70] The correct solution to the management of the press, the printers suggest, is to be found in "obliging the *Bookseller* and *Printer* of every Paper, to set their *Names* and *Places of Abode* to the said Papers" ([1]). The authorial solution, they continue, is a deeply unsatisfactory one, bad for both the trade and the production of knowledge more generally. Printers should thus be allowed to continue their profession as they have always done, "Without being oblig'd to Print the Name of the AUTHOR in the Title Page of every Book, which will very much discourage the Publication of many excellent Treatises, through the Excess of Modesty in some, who will rather stifle their Performances, than suffer their Names to appear in Print" ([2]). The "stigma of print" is invoked here as an ongoing condition of authorship, although it remains a question just how seriously we are to take the assumption of authorial "modesty" propounded in these lines.[71] It does seem clear, however, that regardless of their humility, authors and others in this period recognized the exposure, the heightened vulnerability, and the easily traceable liability that followed from printing one's name on a work. In other words, authors knew quite well the obligations that follow from ownership.

Understanding how hesitant particular authors were to reveal their names in 1711–12—and how hesitant printers assumed authors in general would be to do so—offers compelling evidence for the theory that the Act of Anne put authors in a perilous position by requiring them to enter their claim to their works in the Stationers' Register in order to have their rights protected. That the act might have hazardous consequences for those who attempted to benefit from it is suggested as well, by the first case ever brought in defense of the rights conferred in the act, the case known as *Burnet v. Chetwood*, which was tried in 1720.[72] Rose begins his discussion of the case by noting its significance both for the history of the Copyright Act and for the history of proprietary authorship: "What was novel about the Statute was that it constituted the author as well as the bookseller as a person with legal standing. After 1710 an author could, in his own capacity as author, go to court in pursuit of his rights as the proprietor of his works; and, indeed, the first case to arise under the Statute, *Burnet v. Chetwood*, was an author's case" (49). There is no question that Rose is correct about the novelty of an author's proprietary rights constituting the grounds for legal proceedings. Just what might happen to an author who went to court "in pursuit of his rights," however, becomes clear in the course of the trial proceedings, which deserve to be remembered not solely for their endorsement of authorial property rights but also for their illustration of the hidden dangers posed by claiming such rights in court.

The plaintiff in the case was not the author himself, Dr. Thomas Burnet, but his son and the executor of his estate, George Burnet. Thomas Burnet was the author of a work titled *Archaeologiae Philosophicae*, which brought together the fields of natural history and theology. The work was written in Latin and published in 1692 in the Netherlands. As Rose notes, the purpose of the work was, at least in part, to try to reconcile Burnet's "proto-geological" notion that the earth went through various transformations at the time of Noah's flood with the contents of the Book of Genesis. Among the work's more bizarre contents, Rose recounts, was "a facetious conversation between Eve and the serpent, which became widely known and caused Burnet considerable embarrassment when excerpts were published in English without his permission" (49). Despite the somewhat scandalous reception of the original work—or perhaps because of it—a group of English booksellers led by William Chetwood decided, in 1715, to make an English version of the book. George Burnet countered, as the trial account relates, by seeking "an Injunction to stay the printing and publishing a translation of the said book, suggesting it to be an injury to the executor, in whom the property of the book was vested by 8 An. c. 19."—that is, by the Act of Anne (1008). The first case brought on behalf of an author under the Copyright Act thus involved the difficult question of whether a translation constitutes a new work or simply a version of an existing one.

The booksellers argued in court that a translation "may be called a different book, and the translator may be said to be the author" (1009). On this textual argument, they grounded their case that the injunction against them should not be granted. The presiding judge, the Lord Chancellor, Lord Macclesfield, concurred with them, arguing that "a translation might not be the same with the reprinting the original, on account that the translator has bestowed his care and pains upon it" (1009). Macclesfield thus made the Lockean argument that the translators had mixed their labor with the text in question and thus could be said at least in some degree to be the new work's proprietors. However, notwithstanding this argument for the distinctiveness of translations, Macclesfield found against the defendants and granted George Burnet his injunction. He did so, moreover, on grounds that seemingly had very little to do with the original elements of the case: "Yet this being a book which to his knowledge (having read it in his study) contained strange notions, intended by the author to be concealed from the vulgar in the Latin language, in which language it could not do much hurt, the learned being better able to judge of it, he thought proper to grant an injunction to the printing and publishing it in English; that he lookt upon it that this Court had a superintendency over all books, and might in a summary way restrain the printing and publishing any that contained reflections on religion or morality" (1009). Despite the fact that the defendants had successfully made their case concerning the nature of translation and the rights of the author, Macclesfield found against them and against his own inclination. What changed his mind, moreover, was reading the book, an activity that took place, suggestively, "in his study," as though the material were clandestine. In his own reading practice, Macclesfield exemplifies his ultimate, Miltonic judgment that the work, while not worthy of an all-out prohibition, "contain[s] strange notions" and is appropriate only for a limited and highly selective reading population rather than for public consumption. Most significant here, however, is Macclesfield's concluding remark about the moral and social obligation of the courts—even in cases concerned not with morals but with property rights—to "superintend" and "restrain" printing and publishing. Authors and others are put on notice in Macclesfield's conclusion that should they come to the courts seeking redress for proprietary infractions, they must be prepared to have the content of their works scrutinized and, if necessary, restrained. "Copyright" and "Censorship," it seems, have here effected a court-ordered rapprochement, if not a complete reconciliation.

In reflecting on the events of *Burnet v. Chetwood*, Benjamin Kaplan, a historian of copyright, argues that this first defense of the rights of the author was a "strange" one, residing "on the periphery of enactment," because it concerned a translation. More important, he insists, the case "went off on an erratic ground" when the judge engaged in an ideological assessment of the work rather than arguing the case on its proprietary merits.[73] Rose more concisely and forcefully concludes, "of course . . . the lord chancellor's assertion of the court's moral superintendency over books is beside the point" (50). The evidence of this chapter, however, suggests that Macclesfield's pronouncement in the trial was not beside the point at all—was, if anything, quite to the point. Only if one has already decided that the Act of Anne sunders commercial regulation from its ideological or moral counterpart does the conclusion to *Burnet v. Chetwood* come as a surprise. Surely no eighteenth-century author—least of all, Daniel Defoe—would have found the judge's insistence on his responsibility for overseeing the content of printed works the least bit unusual or unwarranted. From Defoe's standpoint, in fact, the judge's approach to the ruling was only fair and possibly quite generous. If Burnet (or his heirs and assigns) wanted to reap the full benefits of ownership of *Archaeologiae Philosophicae*, he or they had to be willing to "answer for" the work's contents. Such answerability constituted the prime obligation of proprietary authorship and, at least in Defoe's conception of the matter, a necessary price to pay for the benefits that followed.

The plaintiff in *Burnet v. Chetwood* escaped without punishment while also retaining his proprietary interest in the work—an excellent outcome, to be sure, given the judge's negative assessment of the merits both of Burnet's case and of his father's work. Yet the case should have put contemporaries on notice that the costs of going to law in defense of one's rights as an author might be more than monetary, if the courts decided to exercise their regulatory obligations with regard to printing and publishing. The next two chapters demonstrate that Burnet's case was not anomalous in the annals of early eighteenth-century law and that others who came forward to defend their proprietary interest in their works also risked scrutiny from the government and the courts. That they did so knowingly only goes to show that those who lived in the immediate aftermath of the elaboration of proprietary authorship in law understood it better than those of us who have come after. Two decades after the passage of the Act of Anne, authors like Alexander Pope and John Gay not only recognized the risks of proprietary authorship but embraced them, even as they began to develop strategies to minimize—if not to eliminate—those risks. They tried, that is, in the face of the many obligations laid down for them by the version of authorship made available in the Act of Anne, to own their works but to be scrupulously cautious in that owning.

Chapter 4
Revenge of the Straw Woman: Disowning The Dunciad

Mr Pope is well. he had gott an injunction in chancery against the printers who had pyrated his Dunciad; it was dissolv'd again because the printer could not prove any property, nor did the Author appear, that is not Mr Gays case for he has own'd his book.

—John Arbuthnot to Swift, 9 June 1729

Introduction

The next two chapters tell a story about doubles: two authors, two piracies, two suits in Chancery,. and two injunctions. Arbuthnot's letter concisely captures the main events, which stretched for just over a year, from May of 1728 to June of 1729, of the publication and piracy of Pope's *Dunciad* and *Dunciad Variorum*, and Gay's *Polly*.[1] This story's most striking feature is its doubleness: Pope and Gay each published a dangerous work; each attempted to retain his "copyright" through manipulating recent changes in the law affecting literary property and authors' rights; each broke with tradition and paid his own printing costs; each prepared elaborately for the reception of his work through the use of advertising, well-placed gifts, and subscriptions; each found his work pirated not once but a number of times; and each made recourse to the law to try to stop the piracies.

This is the story of why Gay won his case in Chancery while Pope lost his and of the part played in Gay's victory by "own[ing] his book." It is also the story of why two financially "independent" authors—this independence will receive some scrutiny in what follows—made recourse to patrons to get their works published and to female patrons in particular. It occurs at a turning point in literary history and brings together, in a remarkably concise fashion, the factors most central to the elaboration of the professional author: the end of prepublication censorship, the development of authorial property rights, the transformation of literary patronage, the growth of a market for printed materials capable of supporting authors, and the gradual disappearance of the stigma attached to both printing and profiting from one's literary labors. As such, it dramatizes a full range of legal, economic, and ethical questions confronting the early eighteenth-century author. Yet the publication history of *The Dunciad* and *Polly* subverts the linear narrative evoked by a phrase like "the rise of the author" or "the development of literary property." This is a chaotic story, a story of authors truly caught between two worlds: one finds his work "supprest" despite every attempt to remain within the realm of the law; the other finds himself exposed to an onslaught of personalized attacks by his readers despite publishing his book anonymously. Both discover that retaining literary property can prove more costly than selling the copy outright, and both resort to the use of patrons despite their avowed "independence."

If the publication histories of *Polly* and *The Dunciad* illustrate the unruly beginnings of professional authorship in the early eighteenth century, they also provide proof of the innovative strategies authors used to deal with the economic and legal conditions confronting them. These chapters, with their emphasis on what may initially seem like the minutiae of literary production and the relations of the literary marketplace, provide the opportunity to observe in detail how practices of authorship and publication were transformed when authors gained even minimal proprietary rights to their works and when the literary marketplace began to be organized in such a way that authors could achieve financial independence through the sale of these works. These transformations had consequences for the status as well as the practices of authorship, and it is these consequences that I explore below.

Catherine Gallagher argues in her influential study of female authorship, *Nobody's Story*, that a writer's "inability to *own* the text" ensures the authorial subject a kind of innocence.[2] Female authors—and male authors, too, before the advent of a notion of literary property—were able to capitalize on the traditional association between innocence and dispossession to evade responsibility for their works. Now that authors had secured the possibility of "*own*[ing] the text," they could no longer simply claim dispossession as an alibi when accused of circulating dangerous works. As the preceding chapters have argued, during the period of press licensing and into the first decade of the eighteenth century, authors had been cushioned from the full effects of what Michel Foucault calls "penal appropriation" by the fact that they did not own their works.[3] In order to take advantage of their newly acquired access to property, authors would seemingly have to forgo the privilege of dispossession, receiving the prerogatives of property in its stead.

The Faustian bargain by which authors gained the rights of property through relinquishing freedom from responsibility for their works is anything but theoretical in the case of *The Dunciad* and *Polly*. These are more than usually dangerous works, works whose publication threatened to inflame passions and incite retribution. In the case of *Polly*, the play had already been banned from the stage, on Walpole's orders, by the Lord Chamberlain. By publishing it, Gay must have seemed to his contemporaries to be displaying a foolhardy defiance in the face of the most powerful minister in the land. In a letter to Swift written between the date of *Polly*'s banishment from the stage and its publication, Gay writes of his play, "what will become of it I know not, but I am sure I have written nothing that can be legally supprest."[4] Gay's phrasing reflects the contemporary uncertainties surrounding authorial liability: even though he feels relatively certain that he has remained within the bounds of legally publishable expression, he cannot be sure "what will become of" his play or, we might add, of Gay himself, whose name appeared on the title page as both author and publisher.[5] Pope, as Arbuthnot mentions, did not "own" his book openly—his name did not appear on the title page at all—yet he, too, tried to manipulate the terms of publication in such a way that he retained control over his property without exposing himself to the angry mob. Though his *Dunciad* was not in any immediate danger of political suppression, the poem, as Pope himself recognized, was likely to make violent the scores of Dunces ridiculed in its pages. In the second edition, published in 1729, Pope opened himself to legal prosecution for libel by identifying the Dunces formerly referred to only by their initials. However different their enemies, then, both Pope and Gay had written works that threatened to end not only their careers as authors but their very lives as well.

In addition to the threat of violence or legal action leveled against their authors, both *Polly* and *The Dunciad* fell prey to a range of potentially dangerous appropriations.[6] These works exposed their authors to risks even greater than those they could have predicted as a result of the uses to which the works were put by readers, publishers, and rival authors. The costs of such appropriation might be exclusively financial, as when unauthorized editions were introduced into the marketplace by literary pirates expert at capitalizing on the popularity of particularly scandalous works. Owning one's work, in the sense of maintaining copyright or selling the copyright for a profit to a designated publisher, might constitute a solution to this particular form of appropriation. Yet owning a work might also pose more problems than it solved, in cases where appropriation took a less material form. In the worst of such cases, unscrupulous readers and partisan critics could make authors accountable for what were in fact a diverse array of crimes of reading. In Gay's case, for instance, readers went so far as to justify their own criminal activities on the basis of the fact that they understood *The Beggar's Opera* to be a defense of criminality. Gay was also plagued by the problem of opposition journalists who used the play's comparatively subtle critique of the Walpole administration as the basis for their own flagrant antiministerial propaganda. Pope had his work turned against him when rival authors offered an array of works such as *Popiad* and *The Key to the Dunciad* which made use of Pope's own techniques of satire to render the author as ridiculous as the Dunces he mocked. In cases such as these, owning one's work might expose one to even greater punishments than those one was originally prepared to risk. Appropriation, then, made the terrain of authorship fraught with difficulty, placing authors in a double bind with respect to ownership that would require careful and novel strategies of preparation, publication, and marketing.

To avoid the punishments they feared were awaiting them and to guard against those they could not adequately predict, Pope and Gay adopted remarkably similar strategies. In their confrontation with the law and the populace, each author placed a shield between himself and his audience, a "front," or "straw man," who, voluntarily or not, was positioned to take responsibility for the author's transgressions.[7] In each case, however, the author's shield, the figure chosen to do the work of mediation, was not a straw man but a straw woman. Pope in 1728 used a false imprint when he published his anonymous *Dunciad*, an imprint bearing the name of a woman pamphlet seller: "Printed in Dublin," the octavo deceptively proclaimed, "and Re-Printed for Anne Dod" (fig. 6).[8] Anyone wanting to take revenge on the author of *The Dunciad* would be unable to locate him from the printed work alone and would have recourse only to his supposed literary assign, Anne Dodd. Dodd, we might say, was expected to act as a human shield between Pope and the Dunces. In Gay's case, the duchess of Queensberry stepped in as protector, selling subscriptions of his book and even distributing copies at court in defiance of the ministry. Should members of the government or the legal establishment choose to prosecute Gay for his inflammatory work, they would have to be willing to engage in open warfare with a woman of wealth, title, and great social prestige.

Through their female intermediaries, Pope and Gay tried to retain the privilege of dispossession while reaping the benefits of their proprietary rights. They tried, that is, to have the privileges of property as well as those of dispossession, by sheltering the rights of the male author behind a bulwark of feminine mediation. In what we might see as a reversal of the terms of eighteenth-century gender ideology, Pope and Gay adopted *female* fronts

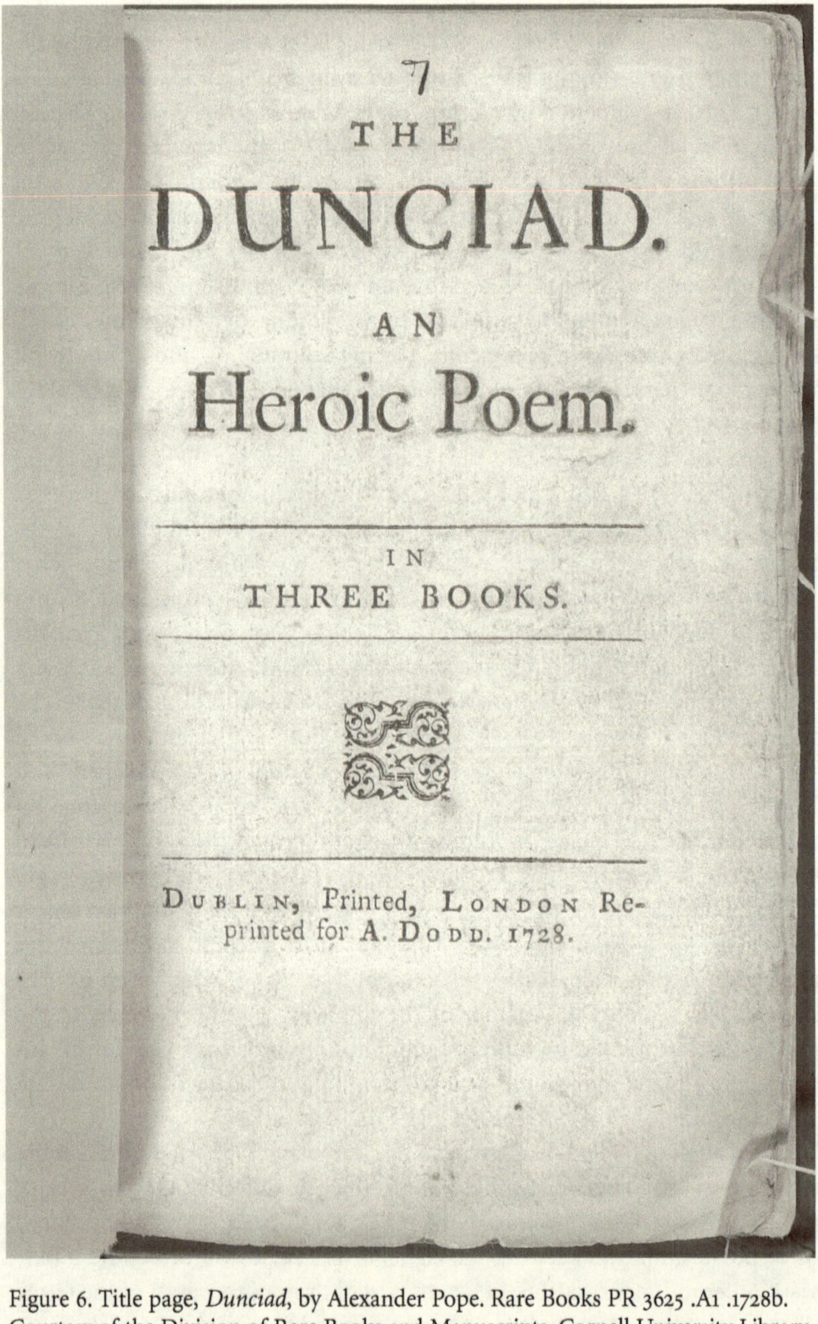
7

THE

DUNCIAD.

AN

Heroic Poem.

IN

THREE BOOKS.

DUBLIN, Printed, LONDON Re-
printed for A. DODD. 1728.

Figure 6. Title page, *Dunciad*, by Alexander Pope. Rare Books PR 3625 .A1 .1728b. Courtesy of the Division of Rare Books and Manuscripts, Cornell University Library.

to do the *public* work of authorship. Literary historians until quite recently have tended to assume that women authors are those for whom the terrain of publicity is fraught with danger, those who must, in Gallagher's terms, split off disembodied "author-selves" in order "to keep themselves alive" as embodied writing subjects (xix). The events of 1728 and 1729 suggest, first, that this necessity was not limited to women and second, that the urgency attached to staying alive as an author in the eighteenth century was more than metaphorical. The publication histories of *Polly* and *The Dunciad* further demonstrate that literary property collapses the distance between the embodied writing self and the disembodied author-self: when the author retains a proprietary right in his or her work, that author is open to appropriation because of the ease with which the work may be traced to its proprietor through documents and signatures. Pope and Gay, in an attempt to disrupt the relation between property and punishment, placed another, intermediary body between themselves and their criminal works. They relocated responsibility for the text onto a woman, out of the conviction that a female figure was best suited to reduce the risks of publication. This relocation was quite literal, for Pope and Gay ensured that these female bodies would stand in for them in the event of reprisals against the body of the author. This chapter explores why proprietary authorship relies on an act of substitution and why a female body—a straw woman—should provide the most effective front to guard against what Pope calls "the dangerous fate of authors."[9]

"A Warfare Upon the Earth": Copyright and Accountability

Given the complexity of the publication histories of *Polly* and *The Dunciad*, Arbuthnot's letter to Swift is a masterpiece of clarity and concision. Arbuthnot not only offers a summary of the main events but also unwittingly gestures at one of the incident's most significant implications for our understanding of authorship in the early eighteenth century: the relationship between literary property and authorial liability. What differs about the two cases, according to Arbuthnot, and what determines their different outcomes, revolves around a question of property or, more accurately, "own[ership]": Gay "has own'd his book"; Pope, apparently, has not. Arbuthnot's phrasing bears repeating: the author of *The Dunciad* not only has not "own'd his book" but has failed to "appear" at all. The problem of the author's nonappearance comes down to two senses of the verb *to own*: we do not know whether Pope has failed to own his book in the sense of being unable to "prove his property" or has failed to own it in the sense of stepping forward to take responsibility for it. Gay has "own'd his book" on both counts.

The Dunciad and *Polly* demonstrate with unparalleled clarity the immediate consequences for authors of the passage of the Copyright Act of 1710 and its broader implications for the development of professional authorship in Britain. These two cases are particularly useful for demonstrating the mixed blessing bestowed by authorial property rights, which opened the way both for profit and for what Pope describes as the author's "dangerous fate." Pope and Gay are especially interesting for their innovative solutions to what David Saunders and Ian Hunter call the "monstrous contingency" of authorship in the early eighteenth century.[10] Saunders and Hunter argue that copyright law has been misunderstood by historians of authorship, who have tended to ignore the degree to which it never addressed itself to authors in the first place: "copyright law," they write, "is less the pliable instrument through which 'history' writes economic interests into subjectivity than a contingent legal invention aimed at solving a specific set of gritty and intractable problems" endemic to the "unstable technical, cultural, and economic relations" structuring literary production (497). Saunders and Hunter offer a valuable caveat to those who would define copyright law in general, and the Act of Anne in particular, as nothing more than ordered steps in the gradual rationalization of the profession of authorship. My project in what follows, however, is to show how two authors made use of this "contingent legal invention" and to argue that in spite of the fact that the statute was not addressed exclusively to their "interests," and may even at times have worked against them, authors used copyright law to buttress their economic position even as they resisted the ways in which it inscribed the regulatory interests of the state onto their profession.

It is evident from Pope's elaborate attempts to evade responsibility for *The Dunciad*, and to a lesser degree from Gay's use of his patrons, that however vague the law remained on the question of liability, authors considered a claim to copyright to be a sure means of tracing responsibility for a literary work, especially one that might by its very nature invite reprisals. In the early eighteenth century, as Pope and Gay both knew, it was virtually impossible to profit financially from the publication of a literary work unless one could maintain control over the work's distribution, and yet distribution was the component of publication that opened the author most immediately to responsibility: "it was those who disseminated ideas," as Susan Stewart puts it in *Crimes of Writing*, "who reaped any rewards or punishments prompted by such ideas."[11] The only choice for the author of a risky work intent upon avoiding his own "martyrdom"—in Pope's evocative terms—was to find someone else to distribute the work, ideally someone on whom the author could depend to shield him or her from the consequences of publication while protecting the author's profits. For the early eighteenth-century author, however, whose financial independence was the distinguishing mark setting him apart from the scribblers of the past and the hacks of the present, the terrain of dependence was fraught with difficulties.

Pope, Gay, and a "Passionate Aversion" to Dependence

> *The more [the literary text] strove to be "independent," the more the author needed to deny the patron, the audience, the collaborators, and even the readers upon whom he was dependent. In fact the author remained, like the dyer's hand, subdued to the elements he worked in, but these appear as negated or denied elements, taking on a new and different form under the sign of their negation.*
>
> —*Peter Stallybrass and Allon White,* The Politics and Poetics of Transgression

"If Pope is not the greatest among English poets," wrote R. H. Griffith in 1927, "he is the greatest advertiser and publisher among them."[12] This may seem a strange and muted judgment to pass on one of the Augustan period's most cherished canonical figures, but Griffith is only one of many critics who has described Pope's legacy as a contribution more to the history of authorship than to the history of poetry. More than any other figure of the eighteenth century except perhaps Johnson, Pope is known for taking advantage of the economic, legal, and technological transformations of his age to invent the role of the professional author. Thus for Arthur Collins, in *Authorship in the Days of Johnson*, Pope was "the pioneer of literature as an honorable and remunerative profession."[13] His revolutionary achievement, the "triumph" that set him apart from his contemporaries was, for Collins, his "independence" (123). In biographies and critical studies of Pope and his work, the word "independence" recurs with uncanny frequency. To take only the work of recent scholars, Laura Brown notes that Pope "acquired a substantial financial independence early in his career"; David Foxon devotes an entire chapter of *Pope and the Early Eighteenth-Century Book Trade* to "The Problems of Independence"; and Maynard Mack, in his massive *Life* of Pope, hails his subject's "determination to preserve his poetical independence" and his "passionate aversion to dependence."[14]

Arbuthnot's letter suggests that already, at the dawn of the eighteenth century, Pope's reputation for independence had set him apart from his contemporaries, rendering him the author against whom all others would be judged. Notwithstanding the different outcomes of the two cases, Arbuthnot's letter tells only Pope's side of the story in any detail; "Mr Gays case," the reader is left to conclude, is in all its important details the same as Pope's. Arbuthnot's erasure of the specificity of Gay's story is symptomatic of the role Gay plays with relation to Pope in both biography and criticism: Gay is the lesser figure, the sidekick, the *un*professional author. Pope's reputation as "the greatest advertiser and publisher," in fact, as often as not relies upon this comparison with Gay. The myth of Pope's greatness and his status as the first professional author rise up out of the specter of Gay's mediocrity and amateurism; Pope's independence is inseparable from Gay's dependence.[15]

When critics and biographers praise Pope for his independence, they are praising what they see as an ethical stance as much as an economic one. When Pope began writing and publishing in the first decade of the eighteenth century, two options were available to support a writing career for those who, like Pope, were born without the means to finance their own literary productions. On the one hand, although the old system of court patronage had effectively become "moribund" since the Hanoverian succession, authors could still patch together a living through some combination of aristocratic and political patronage.[16] In order to do so, however, they had to be willing to write at the behest of a party or to please an individual patron. These, as Mack stirringly puts it, were "the rituals of obeisance Pope rebelled against," the concessions to which, more than any author before him, Pope had a "passionate aversion" (270). On the other hand, authors could, in the loaded words of Ian Watt, resort to "pandering to the tastes of the masses," as did the hacks ridiculed in Pope's *Dunciad*. Clearly, as Watt points out, Pope "could hardly identify himself with the emergent class of professional writers," whose dependence on the reading public was as ignoble as, and probably less lucrative than, dependence on a more traditional patron.[17]

Notwithstanding his ultimate aversion to all of these forms of dependence, Pope was actually the beneficiary of both aristocratic and political patronage, if not of popular acclaim, in the early part of his career. As Collins euphemistically puts it, prior to his "triumph" of independence, Pope had to undergo "a struggling public career of about fifteen years" (123). "Public" here means willing to write for someone other than oneself and, more particularly, willing to write for money. In Pope's case, his public career was a hybrid of new and old forms. Most significantly, he secured his fortune after 1714 by publishing his translation of the *Iliad* by subscription, a method that required Pope to solicit donations from wealthy friends, some of whom, like the traditional patron, were expected to support the enterprise solely for the sake of social cachet, regardless of the project's literary merits. Foxon notes the radical change in Pope's circumstances that took place once his "friends and patrons" supported his *Iliad*: "The contrast between the 30 guineas or so a year that Pope received in those early years and the 800 or more a year that the *Iliad* produced is indeed remarkable. It seems to me as much an example of collective patronage as a sign of the rise of the man of letters."[18] Pope's much-touted independence, then, was secured by an act of "collective patronage." Yet subscription publication was only in part a throwback to a former era, for it also took advantage of the new conditions of printing and publishing to make serial publication not only possible but also extremely lucrative. Moreover, Pope added a new and distinctively modern twist to the art of publishing by subscription by selling his copyright for an extremely high sum, 1,200 guineas, to his bookseller, Bernard Lintot. He drew up terms for the sale that encouraged further subscriptions and limited Lintot's ability to profit from copies of the *Iliad* sold on the open market. What distinguishes the publication of the *Iliad*, then, is not only its combination of new and old methods but also the fact that Pope was able and willing to sell himself simultaneously to both aristocrats and businessmen, patrons and public, and to secure whatever profits he could from each of these groups.

Pope's use of patrons did not end with the *Iliad.* When in the mid-1720s he set about publishing his *Odyssey*, Pope again turned to soliciting subscriptions—in this case, multiple subscriptions from the same individual, who then gave or sold the copies to someone else. In Foxon's estimation, "there seems no doubt that such subscriptions are a form of patronage," and a very canny form of patronage at that, given that Pope effectively instrumentalized his wealthy patrons by turning them into either booksellers or lending libraries (100). The patrons this time included both aristocratic and political figures: among those who purchased multiple copies of the *Odyssey* translation was Sir Robert Walpole himself.[19] Pope received further proof of the ministry's support of his *Odyssey* when, in April of 1725, his name appeared on the Civil List as a recipient of a government pension of two hundred pounds, "as his Ma[jes]ty's Encouragement . . . of translating the Odysses [*sic*] of Homer into English verse."[20]

Pope was careful throughout the 1720s to guard against accusations that this recourse to patrons, and particularly to governmental figures, constituted "pandering." In a letter to Lord Carteret written in February of 1723, Pope refers specifically to the threat that he might be expected to compromise himself out of gratitude for governmental support of his literary enterprise: "Give me leave my Lord to pay you my thanks for your Intentions to promote my design on Homer; but allow me to add, that if I am (however innocently) under the least displeasure of the Government: I desire not to be oblig'd by those that dislike or think me unworthy. . . . I take my self to be the only Scribler of my Time, of any degree of distinction, who never receiv'd any Places from the Establishment, any Pension from a Court, or any Presents from a Ministry. I desire to preserve this Honour untainted to my Grave" (*Pope Letters*, 2:160). However hollow Pope's claims sound, especially when we know that only two years later he would accept just such a "Pension" or "Present," via a minister, from the court, it is important to notice the very precise terms in which he delimits what he is willing to do for money. For instance, as long as he receives assurances that he is not under any governmental "displeasure," he is as willing to be "oblig'd" as any other "Scribler." Clearly, Pope wants to distinguish between the form of "public" authorship called subscription publishing and the all-out "pandering" against which he ostentatiously pronounced throughout his career. At times, though, he was led to make what his contemporaries would have called "nice" distinctions between himself and other poets. In the words of the "Epistle to Arbuthnot," published in 1735, long after critical and biographical accounts tell us he had abandoned dependence of any kind, he considered himself "Above a Patron, tho' I condescend / Sometimes to call a Minister my Friend" (ll. 261–66).[21] Whatever name is attached to Pope's relentless pursuit of financial stability—patronage, friendship, or simply the desire to secure "independence" from profit-seeking members of the book trade—one can only conclude that the pioneer of professional authorship was, even in 1735, not entirely ready to give up the benefits of dependence.

Pope's summary of his attitude to patronage in the "Epistle to Dr. Arbuthnot," with its accompanying apostrophe to independence ("Oh let me live my own! and die so too!" [l. 261]), appears immediately after another apostrophe, this one to his recently deceased friend John Gay. The invocation of Gay is in fact somewhat jarringly sandwiched between two references to patronage: the first, an indictment of "*Bufo*," the dedication-fed patron and the poet "*Bavius*" who provides him with flattering verses; the second, Pope's account of his own transcendence of the patronage form. Most interesting in these lines is the progression that lands Gay in the middle. Unlike those *Baviuses* who are taken up by great men in exchange for flattery, Pope makes Gay an example of those whom patronage has passed by: "Blest be the *Great*! for those they take away, / And those they left me,—for they left me GAY" (ll. 254–55). The tragedy of Gay's "neglected Genius" (l. 257) is mitigated only by the fact that he was able to live a "blameless Life" (l. 259). The only "Return" Gay ever received for his "Genius," according to Pope, was "My Verse, and QUEENSB'RY weeping o'er thy Urn!" (ll. 259–60). One might wonder, though, why Pope would bring up the duke and duchess of Queensberry in the midst of a paean to Gay's independence: Gay, in Aubrey Williams's fitting phrase, was "under the protection of the Duke and Duchess of Queensberry" for most of his adult life.[22] Pope cannot have been unaware that the only possible name for the relationship between the poet and the Queensberrys was the very "patronage" from which he claimed Gay was exempt, a patronage that brought Gay financial "Returns" as well as friendship and ease. Yet, Gay was no *Bavius*, either, not so much because he was unwilling to flatter as because the Queensberrys appear not to have required this particular "Return" on their investment in John Gay. Notwithstanding his nostalgic references to Gay's "neglected Genius," Pope's placement of Gay is quite deliberate: Pope sets up a continuum of patronage in these lines, with *Bavius* at one end and himself at the other. Gay's position in the middle of the continuum is crucial, for it ensures that no matter how nice the distinction between friendship and patronage might appear at any given moment in Pope's career, Pope could always turn to Gay's substantial frame to stand as a buffer between himself and his nemesis, *Bavius*.

Pope's early use of Gay was prescient and constitutes the inaugural gesture in an entire tradition that, from the 1730s to the present, has measured Pope's independence against the figure of Gay, the dependent who was incapable of letting go of a bygone era of literary patronage. For some critics, among them William Empson, Gay's entire career, from the moment he broke his apprenticeship in 1706 to his final illness under the care of the Queensberrys, can be seen as one long exercise in aristocratic "parasitism," compounded by disavowal of his dependent status: "Gay merely escaped to his uncle when apprenticed to a shop, failed to get the political bribes he thought his due (he is always attacking political bribery), but succeeded in living as a parasite on the nobility (his work is full of horror at parasitism)."[23] It is true that almost immediately after breaking his apprenticeship, Gay became part of the entourage of the young earl of Burlington and that throughout the next twenty years he cultivated friendships with the nobility, and particularly with aristocratic women, including Henrietta Howard, Countess of Suffolk, and Catherine (Hyde) Douglas, Duchess of Queensberry.

The form their patronage most frequently took in Gay's early years was less direct support than an ultimately fruitless intervention in the court and the political elites to attempt to gain a court appointment for Gay. Gay not only never received the position, the story goes, but he sullied his reputation for all time through the role he was willing to adopt, in Collins's phrase, as "a pampered favorite of the nobility" (146).

References to Gay's dependence are as common as those to Pope's independence and often come from the same sources. Collins dismisses Gay as "by nature a dependent born to be a protégé" (146). David Nokes, whose biography of Gay, *A Profession of Friendship*, gives the most complete and nuanced assessment to date of Gay's strategies of dependence, writes of his "instinct for dependency" and his lifelong tendency to "affect . . . the style and tone of a dependent."[24] The comparison to Pope has often been made explicit: Collins writes that Gay had "been unable to attain the independence of mind which Pope won" (145). Another biographer, William Henry Irving, employs a more oblique terminology when he laments that "ambition, and its usual accompaniment, the trick of self-advertisement, would have made [Gay] the equal of Pope" had it not been for his "lack" of "energy."[25]

Gay never did exhibit, publicly at least, the independence, the energy, or the ambition, the lack of which seemingly held him back from attaining the "lofty independence" of Pope.[26] Against the enduring image of Pope's "self-advertisement," Gay seems, in the words of Nokes, "self-effacing" (3). Not surprisingly, critics have tended to read the difference between the two poets in distinctly gendered terms. James Sutherland sums up this tradition when he remarks "the habit among critics of patronizing Gay, of not taking him quite seriously *as a man*" (emphasis in original).[27] Gay's dubious masculinity is a direct result of his dependence, his refusal to "advertise" himself, and his adoption of a retiring attitude toward the nobility—qualities that have consistently been seen as unmanly by later critics. In contrast to what Ian Watt—in an odd disavowal of the great poet's diminutive physical status, if not his professional one—calls Pope's "gallant stance," Gay seems limp and servile; his posture is that of the Renaissance courtier, complete with a tinge of effeminacy and a "cringe of deference."[28]

Yet the prevailing cultural image for the dependent author in the early eighteenth century was not the effeminate courtier but the female whore. "Prostituting one's pen" and "pandering to the masses" were common charges leveled at those who wrote for a patron, a faction, or a popular readership. This shift from the image of the dependent author as an effeminate courtier to the vision of him as a prostitute was a direct result of the changing conditions of the literary marketplace. With the development of a broad popular readership and a market economy for books, it became possible for an author to sell his most intimate wares for cash, as the occasion demanded, rather than establishing a long-term relationship with a particular patron.[29] Although Gay seems to fit the older model of the courtier, he also incorporates the new discourse of prostitution and ends up presenting himself as a courtesan, willing to dispense pleasures in exchange for favors. As he coyly bragged in a letter to Henrietta Howard in 1723, "I know something of the Art of pleasing great men" (*Gay Letters*, 46).

This is not the only occasion on which Gay seems content to lay claim to the privileges of a female identity: his feminized role, along with his more general dependence, actually seem to have worked as a lifelong shield against a variety of woes, from penury to legal prosecution. In order to sustain this pose over the course of a lifetime, however, Gay had to be careful not to be too polished in his self-presentation as a woman of pleasure. In the same letter to Mrs. Howard, Gay adopts a slightly different pose, less knowing, more helpless, and more childlike than that of the woman of the world: "What will become of me I know not," Gay writes, "for I have not now and fear never shall have a will of my own" (*Gay Letters*, 47). This *Shamela*-esque rhetoric perfectly captures Gay's appropriation of a mixture of female roles, part ingenue, part fallen woman, part femme fatale.

Gay's contemporaries participated in this simultaneous infantilization and feminization of the poet. As late as 1728, Swift could complain to Pope that their mutual friend possessed "as little foresight of age, sickness, poverty, or loss of admirers, as a girl of fifteen" (16 July 1728; *Swift Letters*, 3:294).[30] Gay certainly did nothing to disabuse his friends of the notion of his helplessness and addressed them in a voice more suited to a "girl of fifteen" than to a fellow "Scriblerian." After the publication of *Polly*, Gay wrote to Swift, in proud but ingratiating, almost pathetic, and now *Pamela*-esque tones, "you see my fortune (as I hope my Virtue will) increases by oppression" (18 March 1729; *Gay Letters*, 80). Nokes remarks upon this pathetic quality of Gay's female posturing, in a reading of what he sees as Gay's self-portrait in his fable "The Hare and Many Friends" (1727): "Here Gay's sense of personal emasculation is made explicit. He not only chooses to characterize himself as a helpless, inoffensive creature, but, more specifically, as a *female* creature. His instinctive sense of social vulnerability finds its most natural expression in the adoption of a female persona" (389). Nokes here identifies crucial features of Gay's female posture: its intentionality, its roots in perceived "social vulnerability," and its dramatic form. Critics have been true to the evidence in their inability to take Gay seriously "*as a man*," for he did not intend to be taken as one. The problem for these critics has been their inability to read Gay's "female persona" as a strategy of self-protection—even of ambition—rather than as what Collins calls one of the "failings of his character" (148).

Gay's alliance with and appropriation of female roles and personae is compounded by the fact that he consistently associated himself with female patrons, including but not limited to Henrietta Howard and the duchess of Queensberry. As his letter to Howard suggests, Gay approaches these female patrons with a very subtle rhetorical familiarity. He writes to them in the voice of another woman rather than that of a man; as Nokes puts it, he is "an honorary female, sharing their sense of dependence on the favors of more powerful men" (340). Gay's alliance with female patrons is strategic on a number of levels: he is able to approach them as an equal, a secret sharer in the cultural system that makes some members of society dependent on others; he mitigates the differential effects of patronage by emphasizing the plight he shares with those very figures on whom he is dependent; in addition, he turns to female patrons in the hopes that they will use their own "Art[s] of pleasing great men" to protect Gay and win favors for him; and finally, as the case of *Polly* demonstrates, he avoids the danger that his patrons will themselves be the ones responsible for passing judgments on the works they are being asked to support. Rather than turning to the men of the court and government, such as Walpole, as subscribers for *Polly*, Gay turns to what a contemporary poem called "The Female Faction, or, The Gay Subscribers" to shield him from reprisals against his play.[31]

Gay's female faction protects him from the consequences of writing satire: "Against the C——rt his Pen he dauntless draws, / And bids the foremost *There*, spouse his Cause" (ll. 15–16). The Gay subscriber "spouses" the poet, that is, presumably, joins herself to him as wife to husband. In the poem's formulation, however, Gay is both husband and wife, bidding his female patron but doing her bidding as well: "Grateful, the generous Patronage repay," the poem warns, "And shew, she errs not, when she smiles on G——" (ll. 33–34). Ultimately, the female faction actually secures for Gay a place even more prestigious than that of Homer (and we might wonder here whether the anonymous poem was making a tongue-in-cheek comparison yet again between the merits of Pope and those of Gay): Homer, the poem contends, was recognized for his greatness only after his death; he is thus "unequal" (l. 106) to Gay, whose monumental status is recognized, by women at least, in the present:

By Nations deify'd be Homer's shade;
He smiles unconscious of the Honours paid:
Thy Works, whilst *Here*, sublimest Columns raise,
From Woman's Bounty, and from Woman's Praise;
The *brightest Sex* Thy Worth in Rev'rence hold,
And load Thee *living* with *Renown* and *Gold*. (ll. 15–20)

The attitude to Gay's "Honours" in these lines is heavy with irony, damning Gay with "Woman's Praise." Gay's ability to win "*Renown*" and "*Gold*" in the present and from only the "*brightest Sex*" is clearly meant to be read as ignoble in comparison with the enduring "Monumental Structures" built in Homer's name (l. 107). Yet beneath the ridicule in the poem there is also an appreciation of the sheer artfulness Gay has exhibited in securing such noble (and wealthy) champions. Gay may not go down in history as a poet of Homer's stature, but he has demonstrated that he knows how to ensure that he is "smile[d] on" in his lifetime.

However dismissive the contemporary response to Gay's cultivation of a "female faction" may have been, he profited extensively from the patronage of women. Moreover, like the female authors of Gallagher's *Nobody's Story*, who "emphasized their femininity to gain financial advantage" (xiii), Gay adopted his own "female persona" to please great men as well as great women. He willingly adopted the posture of submission rejected, rhetorically at least, by other male authors of his generation, in the hopes of advancing himself in the traditional manner, through securing a place at court. In the period immediately preceding the publication of *The Dunciad* and *Polly*, however, Gay is thought to have abandoned his hopes of a court appointment. With the accession of George II in 1727, Gay waited eagerly for the list to appear but found his hopes dashed when he discovered that he had been appointed only gentleman usher to the two-year-old Princess Louisa. One wonders whether, when the list of appointments was being drawn up, those in charge were deliberately making fun of Gay's own infantile and girlish pose.

Outraged, Gay rejected the position and embarked on an exchange of letters with Pope that deals explicitly with the question of dependence. Pope wrote to Gay in solemn tones on 16 October 1727, congratulating him "on this happy Dismission from all Court-Dependence" and promising Gay that "men of worth" will respect him more for his self-sufficiency than they would have, even had he gained the most coveted position: "You will enjoy . . . your own Integrity, and the satisfactory Consciousness of having *not* merited such Graces from them, as they bestow only on the mean, servile, flattering, interested, and undeserving. The only steps to their favour are such complacencies, such compliances, such distant decorums, as delude them in their Vanities, or engage them in their Passions" (*Pope Letters*, 2:453). Pope's language is thick with horror at the emasculating effects of trying to "engage" great men "in their Passions." He took so seriously his own lecture on the necessity of Gay's independence that when, only eighteen months later, Gay resorted to the help of the duchess of Queensberry in selling subscriptions to *Polly*, Pope severed all communication. "I can give you no account of Gay," Pope wrote to Fortescue," since he was raffled for, and won back by his Dutchess, but that he has been in her Vortex ever since" (13 September 1729; *Pope Letters*, 3:52). Pope, it seems, had seen one too many instances of Gay's propensity for dependence and broke off the friendship for a time rather than witness Gay's return to the ranks of the "mean, servile, flattering, interested, and undeserving."

Considering the violent "aversion" to patronage of any kind displayed in Pope's letters between 1727 and 1729, it is somewhat surprising to find that Pope himself did not succeed in throwing off all vestiges of "compliances" and "complacencies" in his publication of the *Dunciad Variorum*. Rather than selling the copyright to the work on the open market, Pope first circulated the amended text, complete with the names of all the Dunces, among his aristocratic "friends," the Lords Burlington, Bathurst, and Oxford. He ultimately signed over the copyright to them in hopes of shielding his bookseller, and presumably himself, from reprisals and protecting his work from piracy.[32] As J. R. Moore concisely sums up the strategy, "Pope chose to protect himself against obscure individuals in Grub Street by sheltering *The Dunciad* under the names of aristocratic patrons."[33] Most significantly, in March of 1729, before Pope actually allowed the work to be sold in the shops, he offered it to Sir Robert Walpole and through Walpole, to George II and the queen. Pope did so, it seems, for much the same reason that he turned to the three noble lords: he hoped, as Collins puts it, that this "higher patronage" would provide "security," or protection, against lawsuits (and perhaps against cruder responses) on the part of the Dunces.[34]

Thus the events of early 1729 mark a moment in the history of authorship replete with ironies. Gay's *Polly* and Pope's *Dunciad* are each understood, albeit in rather different ways, to mark an end to dependence on the part of their respective authors. Gay promised to renounce all "Court-Dependence" after his disappointment in 1727 and resigned himself, as he put it in a letter to Swift, to "depending wholly upon my self, and my own conduct" (22 October 1727; *Gay Letters*, 68). Gay might have been successful in this bid for self-sufficiency if the dependence in question were purely financial, for the next year he made a comfortable fortune through receipts from performances and publications of *The Beggar's Opera.*[35] In Pope's case, the publication of *The Dunciad* signals an end to fifteen years of translating and collaborative publishing. It marks, in Foxon's terms, "Pope's return to original composition" and, more significantly, the moment when the author "takes charge" of the publication of his own works (102).

At this turning point in the history of authorship, however, we actually find Gay still, in his own words, "not free from dependance" (Gay to Pope, 2 August 1728; *Gay Letters*, 77), living in the household of the Queensberrys, relying on the aid of his female faction, and publishing his banned *Polly* through the aid of a range of noble friends. Pope, more astonishingly, requires the assistance of three noble lords, the prime minister, and the king himself—along with, most important, one piratical female bookseller—to bring *The Dunciad* into the world. Arthur Collins's treatment of *The Dunciad* publication seems a fitting way to close this discussion of the problem of dependence in the early eighteenth century for two reasons: first, it betrays the long-standing critical commitment—at the expense even of sense—to maintaining Pope's reputation as an independent against the specter of Gay's dependence; and second, it exposes the extent to which Pope's own vocabulary of "nice" distinctions has endured, setting the terms of any debate about authorial independence and obscuring the persistence of the need to depend: "The affair of *The Dunciad* was the only cause of Pope's having to depend on the assistance of others, and we cannot call the action of the peers patronage, for it was hardly more than an act of friendship. The rest of his life was a continuous manifestation of his independence and power" (132). Whether we call Pope's use of the noble lords friendship, patronage, or dependence ultimately makes no difference: what is clear is that neither financial security nor control of the means of publication was sufficient to reduce the risks of authorship enough to allow the early eighteenth-century author to emerge as an autonomous, financially independent, propertied subject, endowed with the qualities of full personhood. The particular "sufferings" of authorship Pope and Gay faced continued to provoke dependence, a dependence that stemmed directly from those much-vaunted changes in the status of the proprietary author that occurred at the turn of the eighteenth century and that ultimately required recourse to protection female patrons were well positioned to offer.

Owning *The Dunciad*

Whoever publishes, puts himself on his trial by his Country.
—*"A Letter to the Publisher,"* The Dunciad Variorum, *1729*

Declaring *The Dunciad* "Pope's first independent publication," David Foxon concludes that "it was no coincidence that it was also the first lawsuit he became involved in" (242). Taking for granted the relationship between "independence" and legal troubles, Foxon confesses himself unsurprised that the work should have sent Pope's bookseller, Lawton Gilliver, into a court battle. Considering the inflammatory character of *The Dunciad*, however, it is astonishing that Pope managed to keep himself from being put "on his trial" in a more literal sense and almost as surprising that *The Dunciad* litigation entailed only the relatively minor charge of copyright infringement rather than the more obvious and flagrant offense of libel. The lawsuit, *Gilliver v. Snaggs*, technically resulted from an act of literary piracy committed against the expanded 1729 edition of Pope's work, *The Dunciad Variorum*, and from the bookseller's attempt to stop unauthorized editions from appearing. Yet the true cause of the suit was Pope's carefully orchestrated attempt to remain "independent" of mercenary members of the publishing trade while simultaneously guarding himself from the consequences of "owning" his book outright.

Pope predicted that the 1729 *Dunciad* might put him in grave danger of a legal battle, but the trial for which he prepared was not copyright infringement but libel. As he wrote to the earl of Burlington early in 1729, "The whole Question is only this: If there be any thing in these Sheets . . . which an Action may be grounded upon" (*Pope Letters*, 3:4). Not trusting his own ability to predict which components of his work held the potential to provoke legal action, Pope asked Burlington to show the work to the eminent lawyer Nicholas Fazakerley in the hopes that Fazakerley could identify potentially libelous passages and "alter them" as necessary (*Pope Letters*, 3:4). Pope was clearly intent on finding the line between dangerous authorship and authorship that was explicitly criminal identified by Defoe in his *Essay on the Regulation of the Press.* Unlike Defoe, though, Pope seems to have been confident that the logic of the legal system was capable of making such designations legible in advance.

Legal action was not the only punishment to which *The Dunciad* exposed its author, however, as the lesser-known publication history of the 1728 edition makes clear. Although the work was published anonymously, it is fairly clear that Pope feared "physical chastisement" visited upon the authorial body even more than "the good old English method of going to law."[36] There can have been little doubt among the Dunces as to the author's identity: Pope had already published his *Peri Bathous; or, The Art of Sinking in Poetry* in March, in the third volume of the *Miscellanies in Prose and Verse*, thereby alerting his contemporaries to the impending war on literary mediocrity. Letters began appearing in periodicals in May warning the literary world that Pope was about to publish his poem on "Dulness," although nobody could have predicted the detailed ad hominem attacks *The Dunciad* would contain.[37] By the time it was actually published, on 18 May, Pope's responsibility for the work was public knowledge. Physical reprisals would likely have seemed a more serious threat than an action for libel, though, for the simple reason that the Dunces were not, in this earlier edition, identified by name (although their identities were—and were meant to be—as legible as Pope's). Without a sure case against their adversary, and with the benefit of numbers on their side, the Dunces could be expected to find physical reprisals an effective alternative to the vagaries of the legal system.

The potential for menace was not lost on Pope. As Maynard Mack recounts, after the publication of *The Dunciad*, there was a period during which Pope never "sallied forth . . . except in the company of Bounce, his Great Dane, and with pistols in his pocket."[38] Whether Pope actually faced a direct attack at the hands of the Dunces is a matter of some dispute: a contemporary pamphlet, *A Popp upon Pope*, suggests that he suffered the indignity of being whipped in an alley by two "Gentlemen." Although Pope publicly denied the attack, the fact that he bothered to repudiate the story in the *Daily Post* renders it somewhat plausible that an assault did take place, even if it was not the travesty so colorfully detailed in the pamphlet.[39] At the very least, Pope apparently believed that his contemporaries would be sufficiently convinced by the scandalous tale to merit a public rebuttal.

Yet dogs and pistols were not, thankfully, the only protection Pope had on hand to defend himself against the blows he expected were coming his way: his very publishing strategy was designed to divert those blows before they could reach him. The rather convoluted tale starts on 18 May 1728 when, also in the *Daily Post*, the following advertisement appeared: "This Day is Publish'd, The Dunciad. An Heroic Poem. In Three Books. Dublin, Printed, London re-printed for A. Dodd, 1728."[40] This advertisement—like the similar information on the title page of the published work—identified Anne Dodd as the ostensible publisher of this octavo edition and hence, presumably, as both the owner of the copyright and the person "responsible" for the work.

However, an entry in the Stationers' Register on 30 May contradicts any such claims of ownership and responsibility. On that day, the printer James Bettenham deposited nine copies of the three-volume octavo *Dunciad* in Stationers' Hall and ordered the book to be "entered for his copy."[41] Bettenham, it would seem, was the actual holder of the copyright to the three-volume *Dunciad.* Although as a printer, rather than a publisher, it would have been somewhat unlikely that Bettenham would have had the copyright assigned to him by the author, nothing in the Act of Anne prohibited Pope from designating Bettenham his assignee. Apparently no one prevented the printer from making the requisite entry in the register despite the fact that he had never made such an entry before.[42] It seems plausible to conclude, then, that Bettenham was the "true" publisher of *The Dunciad* of 1728 and Dodd merely a shadow figure, the only name—and the only body—to whom the work could be traced by the reading public.

Critics, however, have been unanimous in concluding that Bettenham was never intended to be the ultimate holder of the copyright to *The Dunciad.* The work was not printed "for" Bettenham any more than it was for Dodd. There may have been a "temporary assignment" of copyright to Bettenham for the sake of the entry, as David Foxon argues, but it seems more likely that he simply agreed to make the entry in exchange for the exclusive right to print—if not to profit from—what promised to be a best-seller, running to numerous editions. As Foxon points out, the financial risk to Bettenham under these circumstances would have been minimal, since it is "very likely that Pope (like many authors of controversial pamphlets) paid the printing costs and recovered them, together with the profits, from the pamphlet sellers" (110). The question, though, is why under these circumstances Pope had Bettenham enter the work in his name at all rather than entering it "for the Author," as Gay would do ten months later. Sutherland concludes that Bettenham's entry was "a bluff" designed "to guard against the risk of piracy," although, as the next chapter shows, Gay managed that risk well enough without relinquishing his copyright ("*The Dunciad* of 1729," 347). Pope, unlike Gay, was in fact trying to manage two risks at the same time—the desire to prevent piracies of his work but also and more urgently the desire to prevent his name from being associated with the book. Through his puppet publisher Bettenham, Pope hoped to "own" the book in the sense of maintaining his property in it (and thereby keeping the profits to himself) without "owning" it as his responsibility.

Having established why Pope went to such lengths to involve Bettenham, one is left to wonder why he did not simply put Bettenham's name on the work where Dodd's ultimately would be found. There are two possible readings of this strategy, one rather more charitable toward Pope than the other. On the one hand, Pope may legitimately have wanted to protect his friend and printer from the reprisals of the Dunces. On the other, he may have been afraid that Bettenham's name on the title page would prove too easy a link to the author himself. When pressed by legal authorities or, more likely, threatened by the Dunces, Bettenham would have lost nothing by revealing the name of the author. Pope needed someone loyal to him to make the semipublic gesture of entering the work in the Stationers' Register as insurance against piracy, but he preferred that the name on the title page and the public assumption of responsibility for the work belong to someone unable to redirect any impending punishments onto the author himself—ideally, someone who could claim complete ignorance as to who was actually responsible for the work. That person was Anne Dodd.

Anne Dodd, Patroness

Lest Pope's elaborate precautions seem excessive, and his preparations for full-scale "Warfare" unwarranted, one need only turn to an account by Richard Savage of the reception of *The Dunciad* on 18 May 1728 to see his strategy vindicated: "On the Day the Book was first vended, a Crowd of Authors besieg'd the Shop; Entreaties, Advices, Threats of Law, and Battery, nay Cries of Treason were all employ'd to hinder the coming out of the *Dunciad*: On the other side, the Booksellers and Hawkers made as great efforts to procure it."[43] Already, it is clear, there were more than two sets of interest at stake here. The initial war among authors could not be contained as the booksellers and hawkers—impromptu arms dealers—sought to cash in on the growing antagonism. Since no other bookseller was named in the advertisements preparing for *The Dunciad*, Dodd's must have been the shop "besieg'd" by the authors in Savage's account. Foxon points out that this passage "suggests that there was a single shop involved, and whose but Dodd's?" (109). Just as Pope seems to have predicted, Dodd's premises became the focus of anti-*Dunciad* sentiment, putting the hapless bookseller in considerable danger of loss of property or, worse yet, "Battery" itself. Yet her shop also became a hive of commercial opportunity, attracting merchants intent on cashing in on the market for controversy. By deliberately placing

Dodd as an obstacle on the warpath, Pope also put her in the path of considerable profit if, as seems to have been the case, she had access to copies of Pope's work—a work bearing her own imprint—on the day it was first sold.

In selecting the topic with which to introduce his full-length study of Pope's relations to the book trade, Foxon chose "The Meaning of the Imprint." His choice is a telling one, suggesting the importance of the imprint as a guide, a miniature key, to publishing relations in the era immediately following the Act of Anne. In addition to the requirements for entry in the register set up by that legislation, the Stamp Act of 1712 required that all pamphlets and newspapers bear an imprint in order to be eligible for public sale. Imprints, then, provided the most important means of deciding accountability for a given work in what was still, in the early eighteenth century, a very "rough-and-tumble world" of publishing.[44] Yet imprints could as easily be used to dodge accountability, as the case of the 1728 *Dunciad* shows. In particular, this imprint, through its flagrant act of substitution, succeeded in guaranteeing a measure of anonymity, and hence of immunity, to a number of male figures—Pope foremost among them—seeking to profit from the market for *The Dunciad* and its lucrative spin-offs.

Their immunity, of course, came at the expense of figures like Dodd, newly opened to "penal appropriation" by the public use made of their names. Foxon's introduction addresses head-on the costs entailed by this substitution: "The anonymity conferred by the use of publishers and mercuries was only achieved at the expense of their being frequently arrested and interrogated" (8). Certainly, this was Dodd's lot, as her involvement in the *Dunciad* piracy case amply demonstrates. Yet the very frequency with which authors intent on maintaining anonymity resorted to the use of false or illegal imprints frustrated interrogators bent on putting a stop to the practice. Dodd's name appears in the imprints of literally dozens of books published between 1728 and 1732, to take only the most active four years of her career. Counting exclusively those works advertised in the *Monthly Chronicle*—works, that is, legitimate enough to be promoted openly—Dodd's name appears at least forty-two times, almost always associated with works published anonymously or pseudonymously. Nine of these works are "printed for" Dodd alone, another twelve sold by her exclusively.[45] We can safely assume that there were many more pamphlets, newspapers, and even books published with her imprint that did not meet the qualifications of the Stamp Act or otherwise merit public advertisement. It was simply impossible, considering the sheer volume of works coming off the presses, to tell which imprints were made with the consent of the publisher and which were not.

Moreover, from the standpoint of the trade, as Savage's account of *The Dunciad* release suggests, each imprint bearing the name of a publisher or mercury constituted a kind of free advertising. With or without consent, it was worthwhile for a bookseller to make "great efforts to procure" copies of the work published under his or her name in order to serve the book-hungry public who might come in search of the latest editions. Having one's name used surreptitiously might, in the end, even prove financially preferable to legal publishing, since there was no need to pay for the costs of the copyright or of printing and advertising the work. A sort of mutually profitable exchange seems to be at work here between authors and those publishers unable—or unwilling—to compete in the increasingly litigious marketplace for printed books.[46]

Was Dodd an innocent pawn in a game among authors, her name put on the title page for no other end than Pope's protection and profit? Or, as seems to have been the case, was she at least aware that Pope had appropriated her thus, as the sale of his work at her shop suggests? It is not enough to say, with Griffith, that the use of Dodd's name was nothing more than "a piece of deception" by which no one was deceived ("The *Dunciad* of 1728," 16). While it is certainly the case that she never "owned" *The Dunciad* in the sense of having copyright, as the imprint implies, Dodd's responsibility for the work's dissemination is somewhat more difficult to ascertain. The question of that responsibility is nonetheless important, not only for reconstructing Pope's strategies in publishing *The Dunciad* and *Dunciad Variorum* but also for comprehending the roles women played in the early eighteenth-century book trade. Whether voluntary or involuntary, the appropriation of Dodd's name helps to expose the extent to which authors—especially male authors—solidified their position as independent agents by relying on women to protect, defend, and shield them from the exigencies of that independence.

To suggest how much might be lost by failing to explore Dodd's role fully, it is instructive to turn to David Vander Meulen who, in his edition of the 1728 *Dunciad*, dismisses the question of Dodd's participation thus: "The only book trade member identified, Ann Dodd, probably had no direct responsibility for the publication, and in any event her profession as a 'mercury,' or distributor or seller of newspapers and pamphlets would make her connection with a particular author too vague to be meaningful."[47] There is no discounting the difficulty of trying to ascertain just exactly what Dodd's "connection" to Pope was in the *Dunciad* affair, but the "vagueness" of that connection results not from the fact that it is meaningless but precisely from the fact that it is "meaningful" enough to have required deliberate obfuscation. Even without the deeper understanding of Dodd's responsibility enabled by an analysis of the events of 1729, it seems safe to say that with or without her consent, Dodd did succeed in protecting Pope from the "Battery" the mob of authors was determined to visit upon him when they came clamoring at her shop in May of 1728. It is in this sense that I would define Dodd's relationship to Pope, however provisionally, as one of patronage.

Dodd's role as patron, however, is complicated by the fact that, unlike Bettenham, she seems to have done as much to contribute to Pope's suffering as she did to alleviate it. She was clearly a more effective ally than Bettenham in that she managed to draw the attack off Pope and onto her shop, while Bettenham failed to prevent piracies of *The Dunciad* as the use of his name was supposed to do. Yet throughout 1728, Dodd participated in the sale and perhaps also in the preparation of many of the anti-Pope pamphlets that poured off the presses. In some cases, her participation in these enterprises may well have been involuntary: her name was used, for instance, on the title page of the Curll piracy of the three-volume *Dunciad,* just as it had been used in Pope's own edition, but there is no evidence that she sanctioned Curll to use her name or even that she sold his edition of the work. Evidence does exist, though, to suggest that she was part of Curll's conspiracy to publish the anti-Pope *Key to* The Dunciad that came out on 27 May. This pamphlet was advertised as "Printed for Anne Dodd" and was almost certainly available at her shop. When the second edition of the key appeared, her name had been expunged from the title page and the following, somewhat cryptic message put in its place: "A. Dodd is forbid selling any more Key, on pain of Mr. Pope's displeasure."[48] It is hardly likely that Curll cared about "Mr. Pope's displeasure" with Dodd, considering what Pope must have felt toward Curll himself. The new imprint constitutes yet another appropriation, this one comic, in the service of the warfare among Pope and the members of the book trade. By 12 June, a poem titled *The Progress of Dulness,* ostensibly the work of "Henry Stanhope" (but again attributed to the press of Curll), was "Printed: and sold by A. Dodd without Temple Bar." Yet another Curll production, the *Popiad* of early July, was printed for Dodd, among others. That some or all of these works were "sold by" Dodd suggests that whether or not she agreed to lend her name to Curll's vitriolic productions, she was more than willing to profit from its use.[49]

Like the Dublin imprint on the original work, the continued use of Dodd's name on the ammunition of the pamphlet wars constituted, in Foxon's phrase, "an attempt to misdirect any pursuer" (109). Authors on both sides of the trenches shielded themselves behind her imprint without, apparently, worrying very much about the fact that their misdirections invariably left the finger pointing directly at Dodd. As far as we know, despite being exposed to both violence and legal actions for piracy, Dodd escaped from the *Dunciad* wars of 1728 unscathed, without aligning herself wholeheartedly with any one of the parties. Whether the pursuer led astray by her name was a Dunce, a judge, or the poet himself can have made little difference to the bookseller as long as she managed to escape either beatings or "Actions," while adding to her store of wealth. From Pope's point of view, the strategy of putting Dodd's name on the imprint and giving the work a false origin in Dublin worked: he managed for the rest of his career to maintain that the 1728 edition was "unauthorized" despite what we know of his elaborate machinations regarding entry of the work in the Stationers' Register.[50] The reprisals against the work were, it seems, textual rather than physical, at least in part as a result of these machinations. With the publication of *The Dunciad Variorum*, however, neither Pope nor Dodd would manage quite so effectively to minimize their risks and evade their pursuers. In deciding to identify the Dunces by name and in adding further inflammatory material in the form of notes and other textual apparatus, Pope transformed the primary threat against him from chastisement to legal action, thereby exposing his patrons—those who voluntarily or involuntarily "owned" his work for him—to a fate more dangerous than mere blows.

Three Earls, a Prime Minister, and a King

Public humiliation of named contemporaries in *The Dunciad Variorum* required new protective safeguards and a new publishing strategy to shield the author from his increasing liabilities. For this, Pope turned to the nobility, to the traditional patron class he had hitherto—for the most part, at least—tried to avoid. Pope's first and without a doubt boldest move to this end came on 18 March 1729 when he sent Walpole a copy of the work and asked him to present it to George II. Pope not only exposed his work voluntarily to the head of state but also, in yet another deft use of an intermediary, made the second most powerful man in the land do the job of presenting it for him. Pope thus implicated the prime minister in the distribution of his work even before it had begun to be circulated by means of the market. If *The Dunciad Variorum* proved libelous, Walpole might find himself in the uncomfortable position of having to defend his dissemination of prohibited material.

When the last of the sheets were being removed from the press, Pope engaged the earl of Burlington to look into the legal questions raised by this new version of his work. He required the help of a member of the nobility merely to gain access to a lawyer capable of determining just how dangerous this work really was. "The material point in which your Lordship's friendship" will be necessary, Pope writes, "is to procure me Mr. Fazakerley's opinion" about whether the work is likely to incite legal "Action." Pope complicates the transaction by asking Burlington to keep the identity of the author hidden from the lawyer: "Your Lordship need not even name *me* as any way concern'd in that publication" (*Pope Letters*, 3:4). Once again, *The Dunciad* will be anonymous in "publication," if not in private circulation, and only those counted among Pope's immediate "friends" will be trusted with evidence of the true "owner." In return for the privilege of being a part of this select group, the lords are asked to protect Pope from having his name exposed to the law, a threat far greater, this time, than that of having his person exposed to the Dunces. Pope, then, understood fully the potential for "penal appropriation" hidden behind every exposure of his name. By insisting that Burlington not even name him to a lawyer on his own "side," Pope was not so much keeping up a ridiculous charade of anonymity as refusing to "own his book" in any legally traceable fashion.

Pope was convinced that he had "guarded against" being known as the author of *The Dunciad Variorum* by "the manner in which it is published" (*Pope Letters*, 3:4). Most significantly, rather than hiring a traditional publisher to see the work through the many stages of production, marketing, and sales, Pope made his own arrangements with a printer—the same printer, John Wright, who was simultaneously overseeing the printing of *Polly*.[51] Moreover, he engaged the bookseller Lawton Gilliver to distribute the work once Pope was ready to begin selling it openly and set Gilliver up in the aptly named shop, "Homer's Head," to prepare for that time.[52] Until then, he tells Burlington, his only real worry is "lest if the printer and publisher be found" (*Pope Letters*, 3:4). Once again, Pope's concern for the well-being of his business associates is overshadowed by his desire to ensure that they do not, under duress, "name *me* as any way concern'd," especially in the most delicate initial phases of *The Dunciad* publication of *Variorum*. In order to maintain his legal anonymity, Pope must do his best to hide the names of those responsible for the production of his work. The book cannot be "owned" by any of those directly involved until the threat of an action against them—and thus ultimately against him—has passed. In addition, the more publicity that surrounds the work's coming into the world, the more likely it is that the Dunces will adopt measures to stop its sale. *The Dunciad Variorum*, then, would require even more clandestine means of publication than *The Dunciad* of 1728, making entry in the Stationers' Register, for instance, or advanced advertising in periodicals far more problematic than they had been a year earlier. The new version was best suited, initially at least, to some more intimate form of publication, of which the gift of the work to Walpole and the king, as public an act as it may seem on the surface to have been, was only the inaugural gesture.

Pope's next step was to begin to allow the work to circulate more widely, although as yet he did not want to open himself to the legal domain of publishing covered by the Act of Anne. Turning to a somewhat archaic, coterielike form of dissemination familiar from his own *Odyssey* translation, Pope decided to have the work distributed privately by the so-called three noble lords, the earls of Burlington, Bathurst, and Oxford. Whether they were to charge for the work or not remains unclear: on 13 March, Pope wrote to Oxford, who was in possession of a number of advance copies, "You are now at full liberty to publish all my faults & Enormities; The King & Queen had the book yesterday by the hands of Sir R.W." (*Pope Letters*, 3:25–26). Pope's "publish" is almost jocular: since he cannot ask the lords, by virtue of their rank, to be the "publishers" of his book in any precise sense, they are instead asked to "publish" his "faults." Pope presents himself as the matter to be made public here, the work only as the medium of his publication; here, moreover, the commercial element in the transaction is diminished, presumably out of fear of offending the lords' nobility.

Richard Savage likewise records that after the monarchs had their copy, "the whole Impression was taken and dispersed by several Noblemen."[53] Savage's use of "dispersed" suggests an almost haphazard distribution as though it is the task of the lords to circulate the books as quickly as possible, like seeds, in all directions. Pope himself used the term in a letter to his friend Caryll, dated 8 April, in which he claimed that "the publishers had not then permitted any to be sold, but only dispersed by some Lords" (*Pope Letters*, 3:31). In all of these cases, to "publish" or to "disperse" is specifically held apart from the more vulgar action of selling. Yet it does seem, from a letter to Oxford dated 27 March, that at least some readers did have to pay for the work: Pope asks Oxford to send twenty copies to Cambridge, "but by no means [are they] to be given to any Bookseller, but disposd of as by your own Order at 6*s*. by any honest Gentleman or Head of a House" (*Pope Letters*, 3:26). Pope here maintains a strict boundary beyond which he does not want the work to pass: only persons of property are to have access to his work, which must be kept out of free circulation in the marketplace. Yet in order for the author at the very least to recoup his costs, someone must be willing to "dispose of" his words and deeds for a price. In the unenviable position of trying to secure a profit from his work without exposing himself to further danger, Pope must avoid the booksellers while trying not to make his "friends" look—or feel—like tradesmen.

What did Pope hope to gain through this delicate form of private circulation? On the one hand, the work—exposed as it was by not being entered in the Stationers' Register—was less likely to be pirated if kept out of the hands of the booksellers. On the other, it was less likely to find its way to the Dunces when circulated through a network of noble, or at least propertied, "friends." Yet, Pope's primary aim seems to have been self-protection, as James Sutherland remarks, concisely illustrating the paradoxes of Pope's strategy: "this form of private publication, while not exposing the author to an action for libel, was no doubt providing him with an advance publicity for his poem. Pope, in fact, was sheltering behind his three noble friends, who were unlikely to be brought into court by the [Dunces] whom he had attacked."[54] The lords, as a direct result of their rank, are the best choice to shepherd Pope's dangerous work into the world and to secure its "advance publicity." Since the distributor is held responsible for an anonymous work, they are also the unofficial "owners" of *The Dunciad Variorum*—the only ones, in fact, who can "own" the work with virtual impunity, because, in the words of David Foxon, "no Dunce would dare to bring their Lordships to a court of law" (111). As safe as this strategy must have seemed initially, the potential profits to be gained by private publishing are minimal, and Pope would have to offer the work to more than gentlemen if he expected to secure even modest profits. Moreover, sooner or later competitive editions would be bound to make their way into the marketplace under someone else's aegis, if not under Pope's, most probably in the form of piracies. Thus, Pope's strategy of "private publication," as successful as it had been thus far, would quickly become untenable as an ongoing means of "dispersing" his work.

Revenge of the Straw Woman

Recourse to more usual means of publication seemed inevitable, and by 8 April, Bathurst had been authorized to release the work to the booksellers. Pope could not allow the work to be distributed by members of the trade, however, without some prior establishment of copyright, if he hoped to protect his work from immediate piracy. Whether or not the work went to the booksellers, Pope was in need of someone able to ward off piracies—ideally, a member of the book trade. Yet at the moment of going public with his work, he also needed all those associated with it to continue to exert the sort of influence offered by the three noble lords against the possibility of a libel suit. Pope, it seems, was in a bind with respect to the basic question of "ownership," the problem of copyright: the lords were unable to prevent piracies, while members of the book trade, in addition to siphoning off Pope's profits, were open targets when it came to an action. Here was a publishing challenge even Pope could not solve: who could protect the author as a "legally empowered figure in the marketplace," to return to Mark Rose's optimistic formulation, by "owning" this book, if not his friends, his publisher, or himself?[55]

How Pope finally came to a decision about the assignment of copyright in the case of *The Dunciad Variorum* remains murky, but it is clear that when booksellers began selling the work on 8 April, no one had yet "owned" it to the satisfaction of the law. The work, in fact, still sported the words "Printed for A. Dod, 1729," as, presumably, had all those circulated privately by the lords (fig. 7).[56] Although her name had undergone a slight transformation, Anne Dodd was still acting as the primary "front," the person to whom the Dunces might be expected to turn, rather than take on the lords who were actually responsible for the work's dissemination. By this time, however, Pope's official publisher, Lawton Gilliver, was tired of waiting for his cue to enter the lucrative market for *The Dunciad Variorum* and decided to take matters into his own hands. Two days later, on 10 April, he began advertising his own quarto edition of the work (at a slim profit), claiming that it was "Printed for Lawton Gilliver . . . and A. Dodd without Temple Bar. Price 6s. 6d."[57] On 12 April, he entered the work in the Stationers' Register and deposited nine copies of the quarto edition with officials of the Stationers' Company, as the Act of Anne demanded. Gilliver never actually sold a quarto edition bearing his own name, though, for such an edition was never printed: Gilliver's deposit copies, like all those that had come before, bore the name of Anne Dodd. By 17 April, however, he was selling an octavo edition, the first to advertise on its title page that it was "Printed for L. Gilliver." Even in the case of the octavo edition, Gilliver seems to have taken a title page already bearing the words "Printed for A. Dodd" and, as some of those who later pirated the work put it, "cancelled the Title Page of the said Octavo edition with the said A Dod's name to it and added a new title page to the said Booke to which he put his own name."[58] Hereafter,

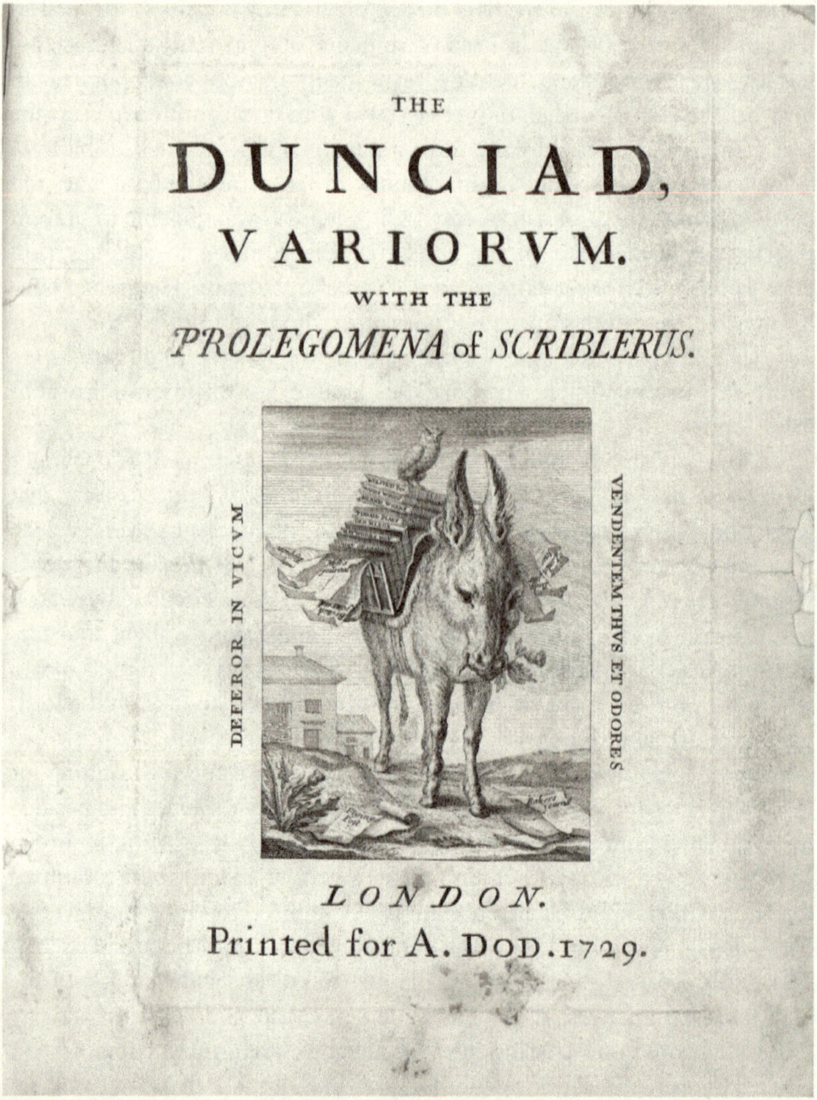
THE

DUNCIAD,

VARIORVM.

WITH THE

PROLEGOMENA of *SCRIBLERUS.*

DEFEROR IN VICVM

VENDENTEM THVS ET ODORES

LONDON.

Printed for A. DOD. 1729.

Figure 7. Title page, *Dunciad Variorum*, by Alexander Pope, Rare Books PR +3625 .A1 .1729i. Courtesy of the Division of Rare Books and Manuscripts, Cornell University Library.

"authorized" editions of the work—editions, that is, that were not, technically speaking, piracies—all announced that they had been "printed for" Gilliver.

Dodd's link to *The Dunciad Variorum* would not be so easy to "cancel," however, and Gilliver's claim to "ownership" of the work would be much more difficult to establish than the preceding details—and the Act of Anne—might have us believe. Taking Gilliver's case first, it seems that despite the entry of the work in the register on 12 April, Pope had not definitively relinquished copyright to Gilliver by that date. If he had, he was not above trying to get it back, should the situation prove dangerous to the author and the new owner insufficient to the task of protecting Pope and his interests. Just as Pope had predicted, within a week of the work's first appearance at the booksellers, the Dunces did indeed prepare to bring an "Action"—a number of actions, in fact—against those responsible for their humiliation. Pope also foresaw accurately that the legal battle would be waged against "the printer or publisher," and not in the first instance against the author. The Dunces were well aware that an anonymous work must be legally considered the responsibility of those who distribute it and thus that Gilliver was their only legitimate target; they may also have hoped that under pressure Gilliver would find it in his best interests to reveal to them, and to the legal system as a whole, the person more fundamentally responsible for the publication of *The Dunciad.*

Within ten days of the initial public sale of *The Dunciad Variorum*, one thing had become quite clear to Pope: legal, copyrighted, "public" publication was simply not suited to the needs of the author of this dangerous work. Pope, as Dustin Griffin puts it, needed to "secure . . . an updated form of 'protection,'"[59] and on 18 April there is evidence in a letter to the earl of Oxford of Pope's ongoing attempts to secure that protection: "the Gentlemen of the Dunciad intend to be vexatious to the Bookseller & threaten to bring an action of I can't tell how many thousands against him. It is judgd by the Learned in Law, that if three or four of those Noblemen who honour me with their friendship would avow it so openly as to suffer their Names to be set to a Certificate of the nature of the inclosed, it would screen the poor man from their Insults" (*Pope Letters*, 3:31–32). The enclosed "Certificate" read, "Whereas a Clamor hath been raisd by certain Persons, and Threats uttered, against the Publisher or Publishers of the Poem calld the *Dunciad* with notes Variorum &c. We whose names are underwritten do declare ourselves to have been the Publishers and Dispersers thereof, and that the same was deliverd out and vended by our Immediate direction" (*Pope Letters*, 3:32). In order to publish safely, this independent author requires "Noblemen" to "avow" his work, to put their names to it, and to "screen" those involved from legal and physical vexations. Although the noblemen are asked to sign their names to a piece of paper claiming only that they have been "the Publishers and Dispersers" of *The Dunciad Variorum*, their security is so necessary to its public existence that without them, it might well have no existence at all.[60] Suddenly, little seems to have changed since the time when, publicly at least, "the true author and only begetter of a work" was the noble patron.[61] If not actually the "begetters" of *The Dunciad Variorum*, these noblemen are still the only ones fully qualified to be its owners under the highly protected terms Pope demands.

Or almost fully qualified. Unfortunately for Pope, the assignment of copyright to the lords eradicated the legitimacy of Gilliver's entry in the Stationers' Register and thus opened the book to piracy just at that vulnerable moment when it was available for sale from the booksellers for the first time. The temptation proved irresistible, and just over a week later, on 26 April, piracies of *The Dunciad Variorum* began to appear. Most notable among these was an octavo edition, "printed for A. Dob," which circulated widely and quickly enough to prompt Gilliver to enter a suit in Chancery on 6 May to try to stop the piracies (fig. 8).[62] Still believing, on the basis of his entry in the register, that he owned the copyright to *The Dunciad Variorum*, Gilliver asked for an injunction to be brought against the four individuals concerned in the "Dob" piracy: James Watson, a printer, and three booksellers, Thomas Astley, John Clarke, and John Stagg.[63] It is from the last of these defendants that the Chancery case takes its muddled name, *Gilliver v. Snaggs*, although we might want to understand the case more generally as one waged between Gilliver and Anne Dodd, or perhaps between Gilliver and all the many uses to which Dodd's name continued, without pause, to be put.[64]

Gilliver's petition offers as evidence of piracy a notice in the *Daily Journal* of 25 April, advertising a "curious and correct edition of the Dunciad . . . printed for A. Dob and sold by the Booksellers of London and Westminster." This is none other than the edition prepared by "Thomas Astley or some or one of his confederates" despite the misleading imprint. "The Name A. Dob," the petition concludes, "is a fictitious one."[65] Gilliver's arguments concerning the "fictitious" A. Dob—however disingenuous, considering his own history of appropriating her name—were sufficient to earn a temporary injunction against the piracies, which went into effect on 8 May.[66] On 3 June, the pirates returned their own response to the charges leveled against them, a response so damaging to Gilliver's case that he must have wished he had never "gone to law" in the first place.

Figure 8. Title page, *Dunciad Variorum*, by Alexander Pope (London: printed for A. Dob, 1729). British Museum 12274.i.11.

The pirates offer up a number of arguments in their defense, all of which are designed to demonstrate not that they did not publish the "Dob" piracy but that they had as much right to publish *The Dunciad Variorum* as Gilliver or any other printer or bookseller who chose to do so. Above all, they quite simply explode Gilliver's claim to hold copyright in *The Dunciad Variorum.*[67] They begin by arguing that the work was "published before the same was so entered"—an irrefutable assertion, based on evidence that Gilliver was advertising a quarto edition of the work on 10 April, two days before he entered it in the register. Further damaging his case, they go on to demonstrate that he "had not in other respects complyd with the said Act of Parliament." The pirates here refer to the fact that Gilliver's entry in the register neither names the author nor attests that he has "purchased the copyright of the author"—that is, that he has gained "the Consent of the Authors or Proprietors," as the act required.[68] The record simply does not show, on the basis of the evidence they have collected, that Gilliver was ever "the sole proprietor" of *The Dunciad Variorum*—a suspicion borne out by his use of Dodd's name on the title page of the first edition of the work he sold. Gilliver, they conclude, never had "any right or title to the Original Copy" of *The Dunciad* of 1729, and as far as they can tell, no one else had such a title either.

In the course of their counterattack, the pirates directly address the problematic Mrs. Anne Dodd, whose name (in some form or other) occupied the place the true publisher ought to have claimed on the title page of virtually every edition of the work. Dodd, they assert, "neither then had nor now hath any right or Title to the said Copy nor any Share whatsoever in the Property thereof." Her name was used "without her Privity Knowledge or Consent" by Gilliver, by Pope, and presumably by themselves too. In this battle among "the Gentlemen of the Dunciad," Dodd is reduced to an empty imprint, a "fictitious" trace who "never sold or disposed of the said Booke" either. Nothing could have been better for the embattled Dodd than this particular line of defense, since she now had four persons vouching for her innocence who might otherwise have had no interest in protecting her from the increasingly hostile effects of her involvement with *The Dunciad.* For the pirates, the plea for Dodd's innocence is purely strategic: they are intent on proving that no one previously held copyright in *The Dunciad Variorum*; asserting Dodd's lack of involvement is merely one step in tidying up their case. By clearing Dodd's name, as it were, from involvement, they may even be said to be acting against their own interests, for had they lost their case and been found guilty of piracy, they would no longer have had the option of passing their own edition off as Dodd's responsibility.

In order to make their case convincing, Astley and his "confederates" had to demonstrate that no one—not even "A. Dodd"—had "owned" the work prior to the "Dob" edition. It was not enough, in the end, for them to claim, against the evidence of all these title pages, that "A. Dodd" was merely "fictitious," a stand-in for a whole series of equally "dispossessed" publishers. The pirates had to produce Dodd in person, to swear that she had no property in or title to the work. This they in fact managed to do, by including as part of their reply a sworn affidavit from the straw woman herself, taken down on 3 June 1729, by the clerk at the Court of Chancery. Should we be surprised, really, to find Dodd once again placing her body between the law and members of the book trade, "capitalizing" on her dispossession to help men secure their property? Even here, her words are in a sense "fictitious," borrowed, provided for her (as is evident by their similarity to the reply itself) by those who sought to capitalize on and with her: "Ann Dodd of the Parish of St. Clement Danes in the County of Middlesex makes Oath that the Quarto Edition of the Book Entitled the Dunciad Variorum with the Prolegomena of Scriblerus about which the said Complainant hath filed his Bill against several persons and which said Book is said to be printed for A. Dod was so printed without the privity knowledge or Consent of this Deft and that this Deft knew nothing of the Printing thereof and hath no right property or interest in the said Book or ever sold or disposed of any of them."[69] Dodd was hardly likely to contradict the testimony already offered concerning her participation in the *Dunciad* affair: she had nothing to lose by her compliance and everything to gain by securing the friendship of those who would doubtless continue to publish the sort of works that required a straw woman to carry them into the world. Sutherland, in a moment of unlikely nostalgia, wishes that Dodd "had not been held so firmly to the point at issue by some ruthless attorney," had, indeed, "been allowed to speak her mind about Alexander Pope and his *Dunciad*."[70] Sutherland's assumptions here—that Dodd had nothing to gain from being in court, that her tongue was all too ready to let loose a torrent of abuse at Pope, that the *Dunciad* affair had brought her only trouble—are characteristic of those explorations of Dodd's role that fail to take into account the full extent of the straw woman's own need to strategize and, finally, to capitalize on her own appropriation.

The pirates' legal maneuvers were immediately successful, and the injunction against them promptly dissolved, as is clear from Arbuthnot's letter of 9 June. Gilliver's loss in the case can be attributed only to one cause, as Arbuthnot well knew: Pope's unwillingness to "own" his book. Dodd, Gilliver, and the three noble lords all fulfilled the role of protector demanded of them, but none of them could ultimately save Pope's work from its own "fate" of appropriation by literary pirates. Pope's refusal to exercise his prerogatives as a property owner, to pay the price of "ownership" by taking responsibility for his work, cost him something, although certainly his "fate" was far less dire than it might have been had he sent his work into the world in a less "protected" manner. Not until 21 November did "the danger of reprisals" seem "remote" enough for Pope to feel safe allowing Gilliver to enter the work in the register, this time with the consent of the author and of his previous assigns, Burlington, Bathurst, and Oxford.[71] Even then, however, Pope was still willing to "own" his work only through a "printer or publisher"; he continued to insist that his associates not "name *me* as any way concernd" with the work. Anonymity, it seems, was a safeguard Pope could not relinquish even now, when demand for his work was waning and the *Dunciad* affair fading into the annals of literary "Warfare."

This, then, was the straw woman's revenge. Insofar as she had been able to profit from her association with the many editions of *The Dunciad*, of course, Dodd could hardly complain of her ill treatment at the hands of Pope and his agents. Yet the very fact that she had been exposed not only to potential "Battery" but once again to the legal authorities would not have inclined her to go out of her way to protect the elusive, mercurial Alexander Pope, or, especially, his rights as an author and owner. Indeed, in part because of Dodd's testimony, Pope and Gilliver ultimately lost their case against the pirates, though they were lucky to suffer no worse fate at the hands of the law. Dodd's testimony proved the imprint unreliable while, in an unusually fitting end to the story, Gilliver's injunction was dissolved based on a technical error in his entry in the register. Gilliver, it seems, failed both to name the author and to state that he had got the "Consent of the Proprietor" before making his claim to the copyright. According to the Act of Anne, as we know, and as Sutherland notes, "Only the author or assignee of the author is entitled to the sole right of printing a book, and it is not sufficient for the publisher to say that he purchased or legally acquired the copy without also saying that he purchased it of the author. It is clear, therefore, that Gilliver's injunction was dissolved partly because Pope refused to admit his authorship, and partly because of the unfortunate complications which he had introduced by assigning the poem to the three noble lords" ("*The Dunciad* of 1729," 353). The very right promised and protected by the Act of Anne—the author's "sole . . . entitlement" to his work until such time as he transfers that title to someone else—depends upon the author's willingness to admit ownership of his work. If an author insists on protecting himself from the consequences of what he has written and published by refusing to appear or to be named, the law will not and cannot protect him in his rights. While Pope could for a time succeed, through the mediation of Anne Dodd and her imprint, in profiting from his work while evading "penal appropriation," he could not, in 1729, exercise the full prerogatives of property while simultaneously refusing to suffer for the sake of *The Dunciad.* A straw woman can only be expected to go so far, we might conclude, in screening the proprietary author from his dangerous fate. At some point, he will be required to shed the protective mantle of dispossession and own his work, if he wants to receive the full benefits, along, of course, with the considerable risks, of proprietary authorship.

The Straw Woman Revisited

It seems fitting to close by offering a few more details about Anne Dodd and those like her who helped shepherd some of the most enduring—if dangerous—works of English literature into the world. While there were many men involved in illegal or quasi-legal publishing ventures in early eighteenth-century London, a surprising number of those involved in the "rough-and-tumble" portion of the trade were women. These were the mercuries, pamphlet sellers, and hawkers who took their name from their "fleet" distribution of important information throughout the streets of London.[72] Some, like Dodd, were the widows of printers, publishers, and booksellers. This fact makes tracing these women in standard histories of printing and publishing both easier and more difficult: on the one hand, we may better be able to identify those women who occupied existing shops and thus know the size, age, and financial success of the businesses they ran; on the other, though, such histories tend to assume that members of the book trade are men, a problem exacerbated by the fact that imprints often contain only the first initial of the publisher's first name. These challenges, combined with the intentionally obfuscatory nature of the traces these women left, make finding out the details of their lives and business dealings virtually impossible. Even R. H. Griffith, one of the greatest of bibliographic sleuths, confessed that he "succeeded in garnering only a few scraps of information" concerning the elusive, mercurial Anne Dodd.[73]

Figures like Dodd are easily lost under these circumstances, their contributions minimized or absorbed into figures concerning the trade as a whole. For a vivid illustration of the process by which Dodd and others like her have been "hidden from history" and then found again, sometimes with surprising results, it is instructive to look to Henry R. Plomer's dictionary of printers and booksellers, a standard reference work in the field. Plomer published one volume of the dictionary, covering the period 1668–1725, in 1922; a decade later, a new work appeared, for the period 1725–1778.[74] The entry under A. Dodd in the 1922 edition reads, "Dodd (A), bookseller in London, Peacock without Temple Bar, 1714–31. In 1714, in partnership with others, he published *The Ladies Tale* and in 1719 a novel, *Charon; or, The Ferry Boat*. . . . He was still publishing in 1731." The preceding entry acknowledges the existence of another family of the name "Dodd (), and Mrs., Printers in London" but fails to connect the Mrs. Dodd of the printing business to the publisher A. Dodd who worked between 1714 and 1731.

By 1932, however, Plomer and his associates had apparently collected more information, including the fact that Dodd was no Mr. at all. These historians do more than alleviate the confusion surrounding Dodd's gender, however: she becomes for them a symbol not only of the inequities of the book trade but of an entire economic system which left women, especially widows, unable to provide for themselves and their families:

> Dod or Dodd (Anne) (Mrs.), book and pamphlet-seller in London (1) without Temple Bar; (2) Peacock, near Temple Bar, 1728; (3) near Essex Street in the Strand, 1726–43. Dealer in newsheets and pamphlets of all kinds. . . She was frequently proceeded against by the authorities. In one of her petitions she said she had been left a widow with a large young family, and was just able to feed them by selling papers. Whenever a public character was satirized or condemned by the press, the unfortunate bookseller, who was probably quite ignorant of the contents of the journals, was fined and imprisoned, as if she or he had been the author of the offending article.

The dictionary's authors are quite capable of identifying the two-hundred-year-old act of substitution by which a bookseller was forced to stand in for the person responsible for a libelous work, "as if she or he had been the author." Notwithstanding the undeniable unfairness of this practice, however, the editors seem surprisingly devoid of skepticism regarding the claims of poverty and ignorance advanced by "unfortunate" booksellers. Nowhere do they suggest that such claims might constitute part of a premeditated strategy designed to keep such booksellers alive and prospering. Taking for granted the "dispossessed" status of Mrs. Anne Dodd and others like her, the dictionary absolves them, perhaps too quickly, of all accountability for the publication and distribution of dangerous works.

The question of women booksellers' "dispossession" is, legally speaking, a highly complex one. Although their names are found on the imprints of books, journals, and pamphlets throughout the period from 1660 to 1750, it is unclear whether these women were ever entitled to be named in an imprint—whether, that is, works could be "printed for" them at all. Indeed, one of the more interesting legal questions pointed up by *The Dunciad* publications concerns whether the work *could* in fact have been "printed for" Dodd, had Pope actually wanted to assign the work to her. Critics have disagreed to an alarming extent, not only about what the words "printed for" mean, but, more strictly, about whether a mercury or pamphlet seller such as Anne Dodd could have had copyright to a work assigned to her or entered a work in the Stationers' Register, or been "responsible" for it under the terms of the Stamp Act. Sutherland is the most straightforward on this issue, arguing that "if she was the publisher of the *Dunciad*, she was entitled to have her copyright secured by entering it, or having it entered in the Stationers' Register."[75] Foxon is less sure: he notes that mercuries "did not as a rule own copyrights" (8). Because some of these same women were the widows of established printers and publishers, however, there may have been some who inherited the company's privileges, along with the actual rights to some works. Yet women were expressly barred from the sales of copyrights periodically held by the members of the company, perhaps in an effort to diminish any claims these widows might make on company stock. "Whether by rule or custom of the Stationers' Company," Foxon concludes, women "lacked the right" to hold copyrights (18).

Margaret Hunt, however, has recently uncovered evidence to suggest that even in the seventeenth century, daughters of printers, as well as widows, could become members of the company. During the 1680s, the company was actually allowing women to purchase membership, for a fee of five pounds, in an effort to cut down on illicit publishing and bookselling efforts on the part of the mercuries, who were chipping away at the profits of company members.[76] We know, too, that the most "radical" innovation enabled by the Act of Anne was that it gave the right to hold copyright "to all persons," regardless of their status or profession, but what about their gender? Could women hold copyright in the 1720s, or could they not? In a sense, the confusion over this question is more important than the answer, indicative as that confusion is of the continuing ability of women in the book trade to claim "dispossession" whenever their accountability for dangerous works was at stake. Moreover, much of the most risky activity undertaken by mercuries was unrelated, ultimately, to the question of ownership. Dissemination, as we know from Stewart, as much as literary property, determined most immediately who "reaped any rewards or punishments" related to a particular work, and mercuries were in the business of dissemination.

Women, as Hunt has shown, seem to have been "disproportionately likely to be involved in radical, illegal, or opposition publishing" in this period (50). Most frequently, they were involved at the level of distribution, either as book- and pamphlet sellers themselves or as agents who dispersed vulnerable materials to other members of what Michael Harris has described as the "buccaneer trade."[77] Booksellers were able to risk openly selling libelous works only because of those shadowy figures who relayed the works from printer to bookseller, and thence to consumer. Both anonymous and invisible, the mercury provided an ideal accomplice for the pirate printer, the Jacobite journalist, the opposition pamphleteer, and the acquisitive bookseller. While men certainly could and did perform clandestine roles in the book trade, women were superior fronts for dangerous works because of their ability to use traditional stereotypes about gender to mitigate the possibility of holding them responsible for their misdeeds. Female printers, booksellers, and mercuries, as much as the authors Gallagher treats, pled ignorance, dispossession, weakness, familial responsibilities, and irreversible financial hardship every time they were picked up and prosecuted for distributing illicit works. It is crucial, though, to understand this emphasis on feminine weakness as a strategy, even when many of its components are true to the condition of these women. Just because the straw woman claims not to understand the contents of the works she sells, we should not necessarily, as so many critics and historians have, fall into the trap of believing her.

These women, in addition to selling books, were responsible for circulating some of the most radical pamphlets and opposition journals of their era. So benighted was their status, and so dangerous were they considered, that special provisions were made for issuing warrants for their arrest. Specifically, unlike printers and publishers, mercuries could be arrested on warrants that had not been signed by one of the secretaries of state; as Laurence Hanson notes, "they might be committed to Bridewell as vagrants for ten days on the orders of a justice of the peace."[78] In addition to actions for piracy, they found themselves dragged into court on charges of sedition with a certain regularity. In 1731, for instance, Anne Dodd, Elizabeth Nutt, and Ann Smith were singled out from all the booksellers of London by a member of the Privy Council as responsible for "*publishing* two false scandalous and seditious Libels." The libelous material turned out to be two issues of the opposition journal, the *Craftsman*, dated 2 and 9 January 1731. The council member,

Thomas Harrington, required that these three women be brought before him "with their papers in safe custody," to be interrogated and "dealt with according to the law."[79] They were captured, according to a note appended to Harrington's warrant, and required to promise to "be of the good Behaviour" until such time as Harrington could examine them. Mercuries, it seems, were not to be trusted to behave even when being held in jail on the charge of sedition.

Such arrests were frequent enough to allow mercuries to develop what Hunt calls "strategies designed to protect themselves and their associates from harassment or prosecution," strategies they learned from their male and female predecessors in the aftermath of the civil war, the Popish Plot, and the Exclusion Crisis.[80] These strategies included claiming ignorance as to the content of the work or denying "knowledge or consent" of the use of one's name in an imprint as Dodd did in the case of *The Dunciad*. Mercuries might also, as we know, appeal to authorities on the basis of their indigence and their need to support their families, defending their crimes as a last resort to ward off hunger or even death. Dodd made use of this tactic on numerous occasions to try to secure her release from prison or to avoid going there in the first place. She shows herself in these appeals a master—or perhaps mistress—of "emphasizing her femininity" to advantage. On 17 October 1728, for instance, she composed a letter to the duke of Newcastle in response to a warrant he had issued for her arrest, apparently on charges of publishing and distributing *Mist's Weekly Journal*.[81] The letter reads,

> To his Grace the Duke of Newcastle, the Humble Petition of Anne Dodd, sheweth,
>
> That your Grace's Petitioner hath been long confined to her Chamber in the Country, thro' a violent & dangerous Indisposition, & still continues in a very ill State of Health.
>
> Yet in Obedience to your Grace's Warrant issued agt. her, She is notwithstanding her Weak Condition, willing to come to Town, hoping upon a Surrender of her Person, your Grace will be pleased to admit her to Bail, without any Confinement, for should she be imprisoned, her Life wd be inevitably endangered.
>
> This Act of your Grace's Clemency she most humbly implores, and as in duty bound will ever Pray &c.

Dodd nowhere denies the charges against her. Her "weak condition," rather than her innocence, demands "Clemency" on the part of the duke of Newcastle. Dodd's willingness to "Surrender . . . her Person" constitutes a confession of her vulnerability as much as an admission of her guilt. Yet, Dodd's confession displays remarkable rhetorical virtuosity; she clearly knows something of the art of persuading great men. Her use of the phrase "violent and dangerous Indisposition," for instance, is calculated to displace the threat she represents, as though her "endangered" status could somehow cancel out the dangerousness of her misdeeds. Grounding her appeal against "Confinement" in the logic that she is already "confined" by her illness, Dodd attempts to convey to the duke the futility of imprisoning a woman already irretrievably incarcerated by circumstance.

There is little doubt that at least some of the suffering conveyed in such documents is genuine: Dodd was a widow, she did have a family to support, and she was subject to repeated and dangerous appropriations of her name and her person committed by figures more powerful than herself, especially those determined to pass her off, if not as the author of their own offending works, then certainly as the person responsible for their distribution. Yet the surviving documents suggest that rather than attempting to reassign blame for her indiscretions onto other, more or less embattled members of the literary world, as she might be expected to do, Dodd resorted again and again to the same, apparently flawless strategy of emphasizing her femininity and capitalizing on her dispossession. Dodd's meticulously composed appeals point out—sometimes ironically, sometimes passionately—the inevitability of turning to crime for those shackled by their dependent, unpropertied status. As evidence of this brilliant and largely successful strategy, we need look no farther than Dodd's greatest masterpiece as an author and a pirate: a letter—again to Newcastle—sent from jail in May of 1731, when she was imprisoned, yet again, for her role in the distribution of the *Craftsman*:[82]

May it Please your Grace

I most humbly beg leave to trouble your Grace with these few lines. I have been left an afflicted widow with a Large Young Family some years, whose only support has been that of selling news papers, which, with as much pains as my own ill state of Health would admit of, has by the assistance of Heaven, just enabled me to Feed my self, and my helpless Children. I need not acquaint your Grace, that this Business sometimes compells me to sell Papers that give Offence, but I must Beg Leave to declare sincerely tis greatly against my Inclination when they are so; and, that what Papers I sell in just Praise of our Happy Government, far exceed the Others in number. Hard Case! that I must either offend where I am shure I would not, or else Starve my Poor Babes. I am to be Tried next Tuesday, for selling a Craftsman, a paper that I neither Read, nor understand; I Beseech you Let my Children plead with your Grace to put a Stop to the Proceedings, which I trust a Line, or two, from your Graces Hand, would effectually do. your Graces known Character is, To Do Good, and To Show Mercy, and where can that Goodness or Mercy, be Better shewn, than by Helping the Fatherless and Widowd. if I have offended, tis an ignorant offence, and as the Distressed have always the surest Title to your Graces Protection, mine will in the strongest Terms plead for

May it Please your Grace
your Graces most Obedient and most Humble Servant
Ann Dodd

London May 26th 1731

Dodd's appeal employs virtually every trope of dispossessed femininity available to her, including her poverty, her physical fragility, and her benighted relation to both politics and literature. By pointing to the fact that she is "Fatherless and Widowd," moreover, she draws attention to her exclusion from the realm of property, a realm to which she would have access, in the dominant paradigm of eighteenth-century gender relations, only as a daughter or as a wife. Dodd even goes so far as to appeal to the duke himself to stand in as her protector, being, as she is, incapable of protecting herself. In moments of greatest urgency, Dodd understands, no matter how heinous the crime, the most expedient strategy for members of the book trade is to insist in any way they can on their own dispossession, their failure of ownership of any kind.

Striking, too, is Dodd's willingness to "Let my Children plead with your Grace" despite the admitted offensiveness which has put those children in danger in the first place. Here, Dodd resorts to a strategy that is by definition confined to women, a strategy called "pleading the belly," by which female prisoners escaped the gallows—ostensibly temporarily but in practice usually permanently—through claiming that they were pregnant.[83] Like the female felon's fetus, Dodd's children become human shields, protecting her from the admittedly justified harassments of the law. Capitalizing on literal as well as metaphorical femaleness, Dodd tries to evade any lasting penalties through confessing her vulnerability as a helpless woman while insisting all the while that it is "Business"—rather than her own personal "Inclination"—that "compells" her to participate in the production of offensive material. Finally, this letter, unlike other, similar productions, does at least acknowledge that the bookseller knows the difference between pro- and antigovernment materials (despite the fact that Dodd takes care to dismiss the *Craftsman* as "a paper that I neither Read, nor understand"). Dodd simultaneously claims total ignorance as to the nature of her offense, justifies whatever wrongs she may have committed through an appeal to her own and her children's most basic needs, and, with a wink, promises her continued allegiance—whenever possible—to the interests of "our Happy Government."

With this elaborate and highly successful strategy, Dodd managed, yet again, to free herself from incarceration so that she could return to take up her indispensable role in the workings of the eighteenth-century book trade. By so doing, I have argued, she also modeled for her male contemporaries, including the authors, a form of strategic self-dispossession designed to protect the embattled subject from the manifold dangers attached to property, independence, and freedom itself, all those other rights and benefits offered up, apparently so generously, by an incipient modernity.

Chapter 5
Hostis Humani Generis: *Owning* Polly

Appropriation I: General Accusations

The publication of *Polly* offers a final meditation on the vexed relationship between property and liability with which much of this book has been concerned. Like Pope, Gay found that literary property was at best a consolation prize—and at worst yet another handicap—in the ongoing "Warfare upon the Earth" called early modern authorship. In particular, Gay discovered that literary property, at least in its earliest form, failed spectacularly to solve the single problem it seemed best designed to alleviate: the problem of the authorized and unauthorized appropriation of literary works—appropriations for which the proprietary author might be held personally responsible, whether or not the author stood to benefit.

This chapter explores three forms of appropriation that proprietary authorship might have been expected to reduce or eliminate: the problem of patronage, the problem of piracy, and the problem of maintaining control over the effects of one's words. In each case, the appropriations continued—may even have increased—as a direct result of the fact that Gay was willing, in unprecedented ways, to "own" his book. Literary property seemed in the first place to promise the end of aristocratic patronage by making it possible for authors to achieve financial independence. Yet as is abundantly clear from the preceding chapter, and as is evident again in the case of *Polly*, literary property was unable to reduce the risks of publication sufficiently to obviate the need for that particular form of appropriation called patronage or, less charitably, dependence. In the second place, the Act of Anne was expressly intended to stem the tide of literary piracy and safeguard authorial copyright by requiring entry in the Stationers' Register and proof of transfer of copyright with full authorial consent. Despite ostensible compliance with the Act of Anne and careful monitoring of the process of publication, however, both Pope and Gay saw their works fall victim to piratical appropriation within days of their initial publication. Literary property, in the third place, seemed to guarantee any author bold enough to claim its full prerogatives the rights of "ownership" and hence a certain measure of control over one's textual production. Yet such ownership, unlike other forms of property, failed to ensure even the most basic protection against appropriation. That which you own may be used against your interests, especially when the possession in question must circulate publicly in order to have meaning or value *as a possession.* Texts in general, and dangerous texts in particular, were subject to—almost seemed to invite—appropriation by readers with their own sometimes hostile or even criminal agendas. More often than not, as Gay would discover in the case of *Polly*, the most immediate result of such an appropriation was the exposure of the author as a criminal agent.

The perils of appropriation were brought home to Gay well before he ever set about publishing *Polly. The Beggar's Opera* had proved offensive to the holders of both political and moral authority, who had waged a consistent campaign against the play from the beginning of its run. Predictably, their public objections had only served to increase the play's popular appeal—a paradox of the marketplace that would be repeated when *Polly* became the focus of ministerial propaganda. According to Gay's own account of the publication of *Polly*, the play was in fact written to excuse the author from the earlier accusations rather than to condemn him further. Thus *Polly* is as much a result as it is a cause of Gay's "dangerous fate" and his consequent need for protection. In particular, *Polly* constitutes a meditation on what David Foxon calls the "danger attached to the enterprise" of printing and publishing, a danger exacerbated by the problem of appropriation Gay addresses head-on in the preface to the play.[1] This preface at once insists upon Gay's authority, lays claim to his property in the work, and articulates his strategies for diminishing his risks when, in late November of 1728, the Lord Chamberlain put a stop to all performances of *Polly.*

As if in fulfillment of Defoe's nightmare scenario of criminal authorship, Gay complains in the preface that his work has been "suppresst . . . without any reason assign'd, or any charge against me of having given any particular offence" (2:70).[2] Gay's preface, which, as he scrupulously points out, he wrote after *Polly* had been inspected and banned by the Lord Chamberlain, is at once the most complete and accurate record of the suppression of his play and at the same time a rather disingenuous attempt to claim complete ignorance as to the reasons for its suppression. In the words of David Nokes, the preface has the "pseudo-authenticity of an alibi" and reads like a "defendant's statement from the dock."[3] Nokes here assumes that Gay has something to defend—that his "alibi" conceals an explicit consciousness that his play was likely to prove controversial. Nokes is almost certainly correct in this assumption. One need only peruse the reception history of *The Beggar's Opera* in the most cursory fashion to understand why Gay might assume that *Polly* would pose a threat to those in power.

Controversy over *The Beggar's Opera* derived from two main camps: those who believed the play satirized specific members of government and was thus libelous or seditious; and those who worried that its anarchic collapsing of high and low, politicians and highwaymen, sanctioned and glamorized criminality and thus encouraged imitation. In the preface to *Polly*, dated 25 March 1729, Gay carefully identifies each of the accusations against the earlier play, only to dismiss them as "absolutely false and without the least grounds" (2:70). Nonetheless, the charges not only are compelling but also pose potentially insurmountable problems for an author intent on defending himself against specific accusations and, more generally, determined to prove his innocence.

The rhetoric of Gay's defense recalls the protestations of virtue and innocence found in the letters to Swift discussed in the previous chapter and shows the same mixture of modesty and worldliness found in all his self-depictions: "Since this prohibition [of *Polly*] I have been told that I am accused, in general terms, of having written many disaffected libels and seditious pamphlets. As it hath ever been my utmost ambition (if that word may be used upon this occasion) to lead a quiet and inoffensive life, I thought my innocence in that regard would never have requir'd a justification" (2:70). Fresh from his success with *The Beggar's Opera*, Gay's claim to have led a "quiet and inoffensive life" rings false. He himself recognizes the dissonance of bringing together "ambition" and "innocence," yet he can find no other language in which to represent the deliberateness of his intention to be "inoffensive." The very choice of the word "inoffensive" is a telling one: to claim one's inoffensiveness implies that the default position, the thing against which one must constantly defend, is the accusation of having given offense. Like Defoe, whose own defense of the author assumes that the author has committed "a Crime," even if the crime "is not known," Gay recognizes that to be an author at all, especially one with the least "ambition," is to risk offending, to endanger one's innocence, and to enter a juridical realm characterized by justifications, pleas, accusations, and defenses. Pope's paranoid vision of authorship in the preface to his *Works*, cited as the epigraph to Part II, begins, in this context, to look somewhat less overstated.

The two foremost accusations leveled against Gay, aside from the apparently fabricated one of having written seditious pamphlets, are the charge of "calumny and slander," and the charge of encouraging imitation by glamorizing immorality. Gay's defense against the first of these charges is signaled by his repetition of the words "general" and "particular," each of which appears at least four times in the course of as many paragraphs of the preface. Their appearance here is more than coincidental, for much of the debate surrounding the dangers of *The Beggar's Opera*, and hence, presumably, of *Polly*, concerned the question of whether Gay had "particular great persons" in mind in his satire or simply wanted to produce a general critique of the corruption of "Great Men" (2:70). The debate was complicated by Gay's repeated claim, echoed in the pages of the opposition journal, the *Craftsman*, that as an author he should not be held responsible if others found "particular" references in his play, as long as his own intentions were "general." In a letter from "Hilarius," printed in the *Craftsman* on 1 February 1729 (no. 135), the paper ridiculed the suppression of *Polly*, using its usual rhetorical technique of ironic reversals: the suppression of the play is applauded not because *Polly* actually has any "*bad intention*" but because regardless of the author's intentions, the audience will "turn every Stroke of *general Satire* into *personal invective*" (4:121).[4] The audience does so either because they have been provided with a "false key" identifying particular statesmen with individual characters (an occurrence, again, over which the author has no control) or, as an earlier *Craftsman* put it during the fracas over *The Beggar's Opera*, in near Swiftian terms, because "a consciousness of guilt" will invariably lead a "particular Man to apply [the satire] to *Himself*" (17 February 1728, no. 85; 2:311). Nokes argues that this possibility of capitalizing on the slippery significations of Gay's satire, regardless of the author's intentions, actually led to condemnation and ultimate suppression of *Polly*: "the danger to the government lay less in the specific content of the opera itself, than in the interpretations that might be placed upon it by opposition forces seeking a focus for their antiministerial campaign" (456). The very generality of the satire—a generality on which Gay's defense is almost entirely based—is precisely what makes it capable of being so particular. The possibilities for appropriation increase in direct proportion to the lack of specificity of the critique, damning to futility every attempt by the author to remain within the domain of inoffensiveness.

Gay's desire to defend his own productions as general and hence inapplicable to individuals (however readers might interpret them) is mirrored uneasily by his own assertion that, in the course of the banning of *Polly*, he has been "accused in general terms" only, without the accusation of having committed "any particular offence." His innocence "in this particular" needs no justification despite and indeed because of the "general aspersions" cast upon him (2:70). The convoluted rhetoric of his defense sets up a strained equivalence: just as the generality of the ministerial critique of *Polly* is insufficient to convict the author of any particular crime, his own "intention" in *Polly* "to lash in general the reigning and fashionable vices" excuses him from any offense he may unintentionally have caused "particular great men." Gay's defense thus depends upon his assenting to two notions: first, that "slander and calumny against particular . . . persons" is an unacceptable, even criminal strategy for an author to adopt; and second, indeed more important, that the appropriation of an author's work is something that the author can neither predict nor control. The author cannot be held responsible for the uncontrollable effects of his or her work, especially when those effects consist of satire misapplied by ignorant viewers, unscrupulous journalists, or guilty great men.[5]

Misapplied satire was not the only danger posed by *Polly*, although it may have been foremost in the Lord Chamberlain's mind when he banned the play. Gay had also, according to the preface to *Polly*, been "charged with writing immoralities" and, in turn, with encouraging vice. The problem for Gay here, as before, is one of appropriation: readers intent upon justifying their own criminal behavior could simply read the play in the most literal fashion, as a meditation on the similarity, indeed the sameness, of highwaymen and "great men." Avowing ignorance as to the play's satiric content, they could claim to have read the play as a textbook on villainy, a how-to manual of robbery, piracy, and fraud. Weighing this accusation against the charge of "slander and calumny," Hilarius, of the *Craftsman*, concludes, with a characteristic jab at the hypocrisy of politicians, "I find some people inclined to believe that the severe Satire contained in that Piece, against *one kind of publick* Robbers, was a more pardonable Offence, than the Encouragement which it was supposed to give to *another*" (4:119).

However sensitive Walpole's supporters may have been regarding the potential exposé of *The Beggar's Opera*, to others the problem of imitation was foremost. The king's chaplain, Dr. Thomas Herring, actually preached a sermon in Lincoln's Inn Chapel against the purported encouragement of immorality in *The Beggar's Opera*, prompting Gay to boast, "I have had a sermon preached against my work by a Court Chaplain, which I look upon as no small addition to my fame."[6] Gay may have been correct to see Herring's sermon as at worst harmless and at best free advertising for his production, but others took the uproar seriously enough to offer a more measured response. Swift, immediately following the Herring sermon, devoted an entire *Intelligencer* to the defense of Gay's satirical methodology, praising him for "plac[ing] vices of all kinds in the strongest and most odious light"; the play not only does not encourage vice but has "done eminent service both to religion and morality." Herring himself, according to Swift, is no better than a "prostitute divine."[7] With this deft phrase, Swift relocates the charge of prostituting oneself for a partisan cause away from Gay and onto Herring himself, making Herring, rather than the author, the party subject to appropriation.

Gay proposed to capitalize on the notoriety of *The Beggar's Opera* by having *Polly* performed at Lincoln's Inn Fields, under the direction of John Rich, who had been responsible for the first production of *The Beggar's Opera*. From the outset, then, Gay sought to secure for the play the widest possible audience and press reception. Once the play had been banned, the author embarked upon his publishing enterprise, complaining bitterly—and publicly—against the work's suppression and his loss of income. His response was to publish *Polly* with his own name on the title page (anonymous publication was presumably no longer an option, since the Lord Chamberlain had seen a copy of the work), to retain his copyright, and to advertise the work widely prior to its appearance. When the work was pirated, Gay, in an almost unprecedented move, entered the suit in Chancery in his own name (*Gay v. Read*), having recourse to neither printer nor publisher to stand in, as they traditionally had, as proxy for the author's property, and hence for his rights. Showing the play to the Lord Chamberlain was thus the first step in a chain of legal appropriations to which Gay exposed himself. Once he had taken that first step, he had little choice but to own, and to keep owning, his play.

Notwithstanding Gay's multiple assertions of both property and responsibility, however, the publication of *Polly* was no triumph of independence. Even before publication, Gay had been sure to secure for himself a cadre of witnesses capable of speaking on behalf of the author. Gay states in the preface, for instance, that he has "several Persons of the greatest distinction and veracity" who are willing to do him "the honour and justice to attest" to the integrity of his text (2:69). Gay predicts that he will be accused of trying to bolster his defense of his own innocence by having softened the satirical content of *Polly* after the ban put on the stage version, but prior to publication. He attempts to block this criticism in advance by applying to outside witnesses. The very fact that he has published the work himself, without the aid of an intermediary publisher, forces Gay to apply to some rather unconventional outside authorities—those unnamed "persons of the greatest distinction" who saw the manuscript prior to its transcription—as material witnesses to each stage of the publication process. Gay demands that his advocates become involved in the mechanics of publication in a manner quite uncharacteristic of literary patronage in the period but somewhat reminiscent of Pope's strategy with relation to *The Dunciad*: patrons might offer the idea for the work or put their name to the finished product in the role of a dedicatee, or even offer their endorsement in the form of a subscription, but it is safe to venture that they had never before been asked to attest to the minutiae of transcription and copyediting.

By offering a history of the work from the "first foul blotted papers," through the stages of copying and transcription, to the work readers hold in their hands, Gay pronounces that he "can, (against all institutions or positive affirmation) prove in the most clear and undeniable manner, if occasion required, what I have here upon my own honour and credit asserted" with relation to the integrity of the text (2:69). Gay here takes absolute responsibility for the authenticity of the printed work, on the basis of his intimate knowledge of the accuracy, singularity, and legibility of the text at each stage of its preparation. His self-presentation as a reliable, credible, and honorable author thus depends as much upon his relation to the material work as to its content. He must maintain this attention to the publication process in order to circumvent charges of tampering with the evidence; yet by vouching for his text in so emphatic a manner, he ensures that any remaining charges against the work cannot be attributed—as those of so many of his predecessors and contemporaries were—to the failure of the printer to reproduce the author's words accurately. By insisting that every word is just as he would want it, by offering his version explicitly as a corrective to passages that have been circulated "which were not in the Play," Gay renders himself responsible for any punishment that the work might bring down upon its maker, even as he definitively maps out his own authority over and property in the work (2:70). This initial care over the question of textual integrity would in fact resurface at a later date when the case of *Gay v. Read* was heard in the Court of Chancery.

Even in this authoritative and exposed moment, Gay is sure to remind his readers of those "Persons of the greatest distinction" willing and ready to spring to his defense. Although he does not identify these advocates by name, he does designate at least one person to whom those with suspicions about the integrity of his text should turn, and his choice is both a surprising and a strategic one: the Lord Chamberlain himself. Starting at the top, Gay enlists the chief prosecutor, the very person who put him in the dock in the first place, as a witness for the defense: "this Edition is a true and faithful Copy as I my-self, in my own hand writing delivered it to Mr. Rich, and afterwards to the Lord Chamberlain, for the truth of which I appeal to his Grace" (2:69). Gay is determined, even in the moment of most flagrantly owning his text, also to gather to him others who will own the work for him, just as Pope had done when he offered *The Dunciad* to the king through the medium of the prime minister. The choice of the Lord Chamberlain is particularly interesting for its ability to turn even the banning of the play to Gay's benefit. Since the Lord Chamberlain has read the original version—he must have done so, as the logic of the preface (if not the evidence of history) indicates, in order to ban it—he surely can best "attest" to the printed version's fidelity to that original. Gay here uses his outlaw status to advantage, making patrons out of those who originally helped to ban his work, and material to increase his credibility and authority out of the stuff of his disgrace.

The banning of *Polly* ultimately worked to Gay's advantage in ways beyond his control as well as within it. As Bertrand Goldgar puts it in *Walpole and the Wits*, "it was perhaps not a wise move on the government's part to turn this dull play into a *cause célèbre*."[8] The very problem of the virtually infinite appropriability of his work, which plagued Gay throughout the *Beggar's Opera* controversy, led him to seek out advocates who would vouch for the inoffensiveness of his work by taking up the cause of *Polly*. Paradoxically, though, at just the moment when Gay was attempting to guard against further bad appropriations of his work, he was forced to open himself to a different kind of appropriation, by patrons and other supporters. His very determination to retain copyright, to put his name on the title page, and to insist upon the authoritative nature of his text, produced a need for protection by a patron that these gestures of independence would seem to have rendered obsolete. As he well knew from his experience with *The Beggar's Opera*, the same patron who ensured Gay's financial independence by supporting the play might contribute to his notoriety by keeping the play in the public eye; the same politician who sprung to action as a defensive shield for Gay might, like Hilarius, threaten to turn him into a puppet of partisan interests. If, as Nokes argues, "Gay's chief motives" in publishing *Polly* "were financial rather than political," he was unable to control the degree to which his financial success might result in political controversy—might, in fact, increase in direct proportion to that controversy (459).

In order to weigh the role of financial need in Gay's decision to publish his dangerous play and to use subscribers to support that publication, it is necessary to know something of his finances at the time *Polly* was written and subsequently banned. According to a contemporary quip recorded by Johnson in his "Life of Gay," *The Beggar's Opera* "had the effect, as was ludicrously said, of making Gay *rich*, and Rich *gay*."[9] The pun must have seemed irresistible when the permanently impoverished Gay suddenly found himself, if not *rich* exactly, then at least out of immediate financial danger. *The Beggar's Opera* ran for sixty-two nights; by halfway through the run, Gay had already estimated that he had cleared almost eight hundred pounds, and Rich upwards of four thousand, leading one to want to respond that however gay Rich may have been by the end of the play's run, he was also richer than Gay at least five times over.[10] Whatever the actual sum of Gay's profits, it seems fair to conclude, with Nokes, that by the end of the play's run, Gay had "more than enough to have secured himself a comfortable independence" (448).

We know, though, that Gay was still lodging with the Queensberrys at the end of the run of the play and that he still considered himself "at the disposal of others" (*Gay Letters*, 74). Nokes seems puzzled by Gay's continuing willingness to "suffer the constraints of a dependent position" (448) despite his ability to support himself—despite, that is, his seeming capacity for independence. Searching for an "objective reason" for Gay's continued submissiveness, Nokes comes up with the hypothesis that "his instinct for dependency was part of a psychological survival strategy which allowed Gay not only to preserve his wealth intact, but also to safeguard a private mental territory which found expression in his satires" (449). Nokes's theory goes some way to banishing the oft-repeated notion that Gay's continual recourse to patrons was nothing but an involuntary and ultimately pathological flaw that chipped away at his authority and detracted from his potential as a writer.[11] Gay's use of his patrons is in fact a key to his success as an author, according to this analysis, because it allows the satirist to take greater risks. Yet, Nokes still assumes that dependency is first an "instinct" and only afterward a "strategy," and that the territory safeguarded by Gay's dependence was predominately "mental." The example of *Polly* allows for a different reading of Gay's relation to his supporters—a reading that explains, perhaps more "objectively" than Nokes's, why an author with a "comfortable independence" might adopt a "survival strategy" designed to keep more than his wealth and his mental health intact.

After the Lord Chamberlain banned production of Gay's play in late November, the impetuous author appears to have wasted no time deciding to bring out a printed version. In his preface, Gay states the reasons for his decisive action: "to justify and vindicate my own character, I thought my-self obliged to print the Opera without delay" (2:70). The choice of the term "obliged" here is interesting: in the language of eighteenth-century literary culture, "obligation" was a key term used to describe the relationship between an author and his patrons.[12] Gay, then, plays on his reputation as an author only too ready to be obliging at the same time that he externalizes the demand for the publication of the work. "I thought my-self obliged" suggests at once that Gay is obligated to himself alone in publishing the play and also that he is obliged to the public whose appropriation of *The Beggar's Opera* has put Gay's "character" into question and caused it to need vindication. Gay thus publishes on his own authority, even as he transfers some of the responsibility for the publication of the work onto his readers.

Gay goes on to insist, however disingenuously, that financial gain is the furthest thing from his mind in publishing his work: "by printing it, I have submitted and given up all present views of profit which might accrue from the stage" (2:70). Gay omits to mention those profits "which might accrue" from publication; in fact, he repeats throughout his correspondence and in advertisements that he published the play "at my own expence," without ever mentioning that it was, as a result, sold exclusively for his benefit (*Gay Letters,* 80). Gay was sure to protect his investment in *Polly* in at least two ways: by retaining copyright and by setting up a subscription list. He engaged the bookseller John Roberts to enter the edition in the Stationers' Register on 3 April, but it was entered "for the Author" rather than for the bookseller or printer.[13] Unfortunately, in the surviving correspondence, Gay makes no mention of why he decided to retain his own copyright, and we can only speculate as to his reasoning: perhaps Gay thought the work too "dangerous" for any publisher to attempt; perhaps he was afraid the work would again be seized and suppressed, and he wanted to guard against the future actions of risk-taking pirates; most probably, though, he was determined not to share the profits from *Polly* with any intermediary as he had shared the receipts from *The Beggar's Opera* with Rich and with the earlier play's publishers, John Watts and Jacob Tonson.[14] When the first edition was announced in the *Whitehall Evening Post* on the day of its entry in the register, the advertisement thus read, "This Day is publish'd, in Quarto POLLY. An Opera. Being the Second Part of the BEGGAR'S OPERA. Written by Mr. Gay. Printed for the Author, and sold by Mr. Heney at Gay's Head."[15] Gay clearly intended to sell many more copies of the book than those destined for subscribers: he had more than ten thousand copies printed by William Bowyer and John

Wright, an extraordinarily large number for a first-print edition, especially one in quarto, priced at six shillings.[16] He could afford to undertake such a large and risky print run, however, because of the help of his subscribers, most notably the duchess of Queensberry, who spearheaded Gay's cause by taking charge of advertising and encouraging—if not actually selling—subscriptions to the work at court.

We do not know whether Gay petitioned the duchess to spring to his aid or whether she did so on her own initiative, but a letter to Swift, dated 18 March 1729, suggests some combination of the two, as well as detailing the consequences of her championing of Gay. "You must undoubtedly have heard," Gay writes, "that the Duchess took up my defence with the King and Queen in the cause of my Play, and that she hath been forbid the Court for interesting herself to increase my fortune for the publication of it without being acted" (*Gay Letters*, 79). Gay's reference to a "cause" to which the duchess has joined herself suggests at first glance that she is merely one participant in a broad effort to help the struggling author. By selling subscriptions, her ostensible goal is to "increase [Gay's] fortune" by securing a readership in advance for the book. A kind of insurance for the author, especially for the author publishing at "own expence," subscriptions relieved some of the risks of the market by ensuring that the work would sell a minimum number of copies. Subscription publishing thus constituted, in the words of Dustin Griffin, "a kind of democratized patronage," in the sense that a large number of subscribers, not all of them members of the traditional, aristocratic, "patronage class," could consider themselves supporters of literary culture "for a relatively small outlay" (267).

Subscription publishing was "democratized" in another sense, too, I would argue, in its radical alteration of the traditionally unequal relationship between author and patrons. The stigma of patronage was reduced by subscription publication in at least three ways. First, because not all of the subscribers were members of the nobility, the class gulf between artist and subscriber was less emphatically demarcated than was the case with other types of patronage. Second, the temporality of the relationship was transformed by the fact that the author's "obligation" to the patron effectively ended once the book was handed over rather than extending indefinitely as a lifelong tie more familial than contractual. Finally, and by extension, subscription publishing signaled an exchange of material goods determined in advance rather than an inchoate "exchange of benefits," to use Griffin's phrase, masquerading as gifts (21). In each case, then, Gay's recourse to subscription publishing seems quite straightforward, a simple answer to a primarily financial problem—that is, the exigencies of publishing a book without the security offered by selling the copyright outright and allowing the publisher and printer to take the financial risks.

This was not, however, an ordinary instance of subscription publishing, as the passage from Gay's letter suggests, and the duchess's role was by no means that of an ordinary subscriber. Not only did the duchess herself take on the task of selling subscriptions to the book—a job usually done either by the publisher or by the author him- or herself—but she took what C. F. Burgess calls the "un-heard of measure" of selling subscriptions at court, in the presence of the king and queen.[17] The duchess thus made public what would essentially have been a relatively private activity—collecting subscriptions—conducted among friends and supporters of the playwright, in a move clearly calculated to draw attention to her participation in the marketing of this dangerous work. Her activities drew so much attention, however, that the duchess was "forbid the Court," at least for a time, for her boldness.

Appropriation II: Solicitous Duchesses

> *All are so ambitious of making their Court to you, that none can be severe to what you are pleas'd to favour.*
>
> *—Dedication to the duchess of York, Sir George Etherege,* The Man of Mode, *1676*

Whether the duchess undertook her scheme out of indignation at the censorship of Gay's play, simple good will toward a beleaguered friend, or some less noble desire to foment discord at court cannot be determined definitively. However, it is clear that some disagreement did already exist between the king and queen and the Queensberrys, as Gay's letter to Swift goes on to suggest. Moreover, the duchess's was not the only exile from court precipitated by the *Polly* controversy. "The Duke too has given up his employment," he writes, "which he would have done, if the Dutchess had not met this treatment, upon account of ill usage from the Ministers; but this hasten'd him in what he had determin'd" (*Gay Letters*, 79). Burgess ventures that "*l'affaire Polly* was not the sole, nor even the fundamental grounds for the Queensberrys' break with the Court" (598). Yet if it was not the "grounds," it was certainly the symbolic occasion for that break. As Burgess puts it, *Polly* was "a token grievance," used by the Queensberrys for "effecting their departure from Court" (598). As devoted as they appear to have been to Gay's well-being, they surely could have found less costly means of endorsing his play than losing the duke's court appointment (he was, among other things, admiral of Scotland) and severing their ties to George II. Their support of *Polly* thus seems to have been at once a statement of their willingness to defend Gay even in the most hostile environment and an opportunity for mutual instrumentalization by which everyone stood to benefit.

The duchess's actions, we should remember, brought risk not only to herself and her husband: by using *Polly* as collateral in an otherwise unrelated dispute with the monarchs, she tempted further royal and ministerial displeasure toward Gay himself. This might lead us to ask why Gay sanctioned the duchess to act so publicly in his defense, and why the duchess, rather than the duke, laid down the challenge at court when, according to Gay's letter, it was the duke who sought to break from the court in the first place. Certainly, the duchess had for many years shown herself an avid supporter of Gay and his work. While Gay was lodging with the Queensberrys following his success with *The Beggar's Opera,* the duchess may even have helped him to compose the tunes for *Polly.*[18] Yet her role as Gay's champion seems attributable neither to some vain personal interest in the success of the play nor to her renowned "redoubtable" nature.[19] The choice of a woman to represent the endangered poet was at once strategic and necessary as contemporary accounts of the controversy amply demonstrate.[20]

In the margins of early accounts of the fracas over *Polly* appear numerous reflections on why a woman might have been the best advocate for a banned play and its author. Mary Pendarves, later Delany, who was present at court during the events, expressed outrage that the response to the duchess had been, in the words of Etherege, so "severe":

> The Duchess of Queensberry, to the great amazement of the admiring world, is forbid the Court only for being solicitous in getting a subscription for Mr. Gay's sequel to *The Beggar's Opera,* which the Court forbid being acted on account that it reflected on the Government. The Duchess is a great friend of Gay's, and has with him much endured, upon which to make him some amends, for he is poor, she promised to get a subscription for his play if he would approve it. She indiscreetly has urged the King and Queen in his behalf and asked subscriptions in the Drawing Room, upon which she is forbid the Court—a thing never heard of before to one of her rank. One might have imagined her beauty would have secured her from such treatment.[21]

However "indiscreet" the duchess's actions may have seemed, her rank, beauty, and, one might extrapolate from the latter, her gender *ought* to have prevented the indignity of being "forbid the Court." While the duke would have had the advantage of rank on his side, one cannot suppose that he would have been considered immune to punishment on the basis of his looks alone. Moreover, Delany speculates that the duchess's support for Gay is an act both virtuous and necessary, "for he is poor." The duchess in this portrait exemplifies, however paradoxically, the peculiarly feminine virtues of pity, charity, and "endurance" in the face of oppression. With such unimpeachable attributes as looks and position, and such irreproachable motives, her fate seems shocking, unjust, and worthy of "amazement."

In John Lord Hervey's remarkably similar (although much less sympathetic) account, the duchess's motives are even more clearly delineated. According to Hervey, when the king demanded to know what the duchess was doing as she huddled with potential subscribers in his drawing room, she replied that "it was an act of charity, and a charity to which she did not despair of bringing his Majesty to contribute."[22] The duchess, according to Hervey, did well to represent herself and her protégé to potential subscribers in these almost religious terms in order to blunt the aura of danger surrounding Gay's cause: "The Duchess of Queensberry set herself at the head of this undertaking and solicited every mortal that came in her way, or in whose way she could put herself, to subscribe. To a woman of her quality, proverbial beauty, and at the top of the polite and fashionable world, people were ashamed to refuse a guinea, though they were afraid to give it."[23] Hervey's memoir is wonderfully graphic in its image of the duchess garnering subscriptions from anyone "in whose way she could put herself." Through this act of physical infiltration, she thrusts Gay's work into the world, bodying forth his text in the most public of locations (and ensuring him, in the process, ever more "guineas"). Yet she also forms a blockage, a "defensive shield" of the type described by Griffin and familiar from Anne Dodd, to protect Gay's reputation from the harm intended it by the ministry (21). As she put it in a letter to the king written in response to her banishment, she has offered "the highest compliment that I could possibly pay the King to endeavour to support truth and innocence in his house."[24] By repeatedly representing Gay as an object of charity, the duchess pressures her acquaintances into a moral obligation to support his work; by insisting on his status as a model of "truth and innocence," though, the duchess takes full responsibility not just for this work but for Gay's authority as a whole. Rather than making herself the possessor of his authority and the beneficiary of his property, she insists that her contemporaries publicly recognize his merits as an author by buying his book. The duchess is protected throughout these events by her "beauty," her status, and the fact that she is, above all, "a woman of quality." Catherine Douglas's position and beauty thus gave her not only an advantage as a fund-raiser but a certain indemnity with relation to punishment.

The final, most compelling proof that a woman was at once the safest and most successful "front" for the embattled author comes from a slightly later period, in an anecdote attributed to Sir Walter Scott. While annotating Swift's letters in preparation for his biography, Scott must have encountered Swift's correspondence concerning the *Polly* affair. In the margins of one of Swift's volumes, Scott scribbled the following: "The Duchess was so vehement in her attempts to have the embargo removed from Gay's play that she offered to read it to his Majesty in his closet that he might be satisfied there was no offence in it. George II escaped from this dilemma by saying that he should be delighted to receive her Grace in his closet, but hoped to amuse her better than by the employment she proposed."[25] The bolder the duchess became in her embodiment of Gay's cause, now even suggesting a private literary audience with the king, the more attention was diverted from the cause as a whole onto her body. She becomes, that is, a kind of monumental distraction, a "substitute" for the "clandestine subject" called John Gay (in Derrida's terms) who can do everything in his power to protect his text (retaining copyright, securing its financial success, managing its integrity) but who is utterly unable to safeguard his own interests.[26] What protects the duchess's exposed, substituted body from punishment is her sex. Although the duchess did ultimately pay a relatively severe penalty for her attempt to aid her friend, that penalty could have been considerably worse had she been prosecuted as an accessory to sedition, a charge some leveled against Gay's play. Instead, in the confrontation between the duchess and the king, Gay's cause is at once enacted and forgotten, publicly dramatized and distorted in such a way as to empty out its urgency. This monumental distraction, this act of charitable shielding, nonetheless benefited the author despite its similarity to other, less salutary acts of appropriation.

In March of 1729, two months before his letter regarding the piracies, Arbuthnot wrote to Swift a lengthy account of "*l'affaire Polly*," which remains one of the most colorful summaries of the events. Arbuthnot's letter is most interesting, though, for its recognition of the way in which, recalling Gallagher's terms, these events forced Gay to "split off" a "disembodied . . . author-self" in order to "keep the physical writer alive."[27] Noting, with some astonishment that Gay "has now become a publick person," Arbuthnot offers Swift the following portrait of Gay's transformation:

> The inoffensive John Gay is now become one of the obstructions to the peace of Europe, the terror of Ministers, the chief author of the Craftsman & all the seditious pamphlets which have been published against the government. he has gott several turnd out of their places, the greatest ornament of the court Banishd from it for his sake, another great Lady in danger of being chasé likewise, about seven or eight duchesses pushing forward like the ancient Circum Celliones in the Church who shall suffer Martyrdome upon his account first, he is the darling of the city; if he should travel about the country, he would have hecatombs of Roasted oxen sacrificd to him. . . . I hope he will gett a good dale of money by printing his play. but I really believe he would gett more by showing his person: and I can assure you that this is the very identical John Gay whom you formerly knew and lodgd with in Whitehall two years ago.[28]

Is Arbuthnot's heroic protagonist indeed "the very identical John Gay" with whom, he insists, Swift formerly lodged? It seems, from Arbuthnot's account, that this John Gay is not "very identical" at all. Arbuthnot's desire for Gay to "show his person" is precisely the mark of his difference from the John Gay they once knew, the John Gay who was emphatically not "a publick person." The price of Gay's publicity is the dissociation of "his play" from "his person" and his willingness to hide the person in order to profit from the play. Most significant for this account, though, is who exactly Gay hides his person behind. Each advocate is, in Arbuthnot's letter, either a "duchess," a "Lady," or an "ornament of the Court," a woman whose rank and physical beauty "push forward" for Gay. Once again, the language suggests a deliberate taking up of space—a paradoxical role for a woman, as the previous chapter suggested, in the context of early eighteenth-century authorship. Gallagher insists that when women writers enacted the self-division of which, I am arguing, Gay's case is also paradigmatic, they undertook "a strategy for capitalizing on their femaleness" by foregrounding the "flickering ontological effect" both of signification and of femaleness itself (xxiv). Gay's strategy also involves "capitalizing on . . . femaleness," as he supplements his own act of disembodiment by allowing a female body to stand in the place of his own. The benefits of this strategy are more than monetary, moreover: through "owning" his play with the help of his female "fronts," Gay achieves "publick" personhood, escapes his "dangerous fate," increases his authority to the point of heroic status, and even, in a final blow to Pope's bleak vision of the personal costs of proprietary authorship, finds someone willing to "suffer Martyrdome upon his account."

Appropration III: Spurious Editions

Gay's triumph might have been short-lived, however, had it not been for the precautions he took to safeguard his property in *Polly* before publication. The "Warfare" must have seemed far from over when, within five days of his entry of the work in the Stationers' Register, piracies of the play began to appear.[29] The very dangerous nature of *Polly* may have contributed to its rapid appropriation by the pirates: its status as a "*cause célèbre*" promised that it would return enormous profits, and the pirates may have predicted that the author of so inflammatory a work would hesitate before bringing it to the attention of the courts by demanding that the pirates be prosecuted, a possibility borne out by the near-disastrous fate of *Burnet v. Chetwood.* Moreover, the fact that the author held copyright might also have been seen as a discouragement to legal action, since in this case the author, rather than a publisher or printer, would be required to pay any legal fees incurred. Works printed for the author were, as the price of six shillings for *Polly* demonstrates, often more costly than trade editions, increasing demand for cheaper versions. Literary pirates, in the words of Foxon, "clearly found controversial works printed for the author an irresistible temptation" (242).

On 10 April, a week after Gay's edition was first advertised, an announcement appeared in the *Evening Post* deploring piracies of *Polly*, which were already selling widely and bringing their producers immediate and substantial financial success. The advertisement is remarkably deliberate in its references to the Act of Anne, which it does not even bother to name, suggesting how widespread was the cultural familiarity with the consequences of the act:

> Yesterday two illegal, false, and spurious editions of *Polly, an Opera; being the second part of the Beggar's Opera* were published; the one in octavo, without the music, printed for Jeffery Walker in the Strand, the other in octavo with music at the end, printed for J. Thomson. This is to advertise all booksellers, printers, publishers, hawkers, etc. not to sell or cause to be sold any of the said editions, the sole property of the said book being, according to the Act of Parliament, vested in the author, for whom the book is printed with the music on copper plates in quarto. Prosecutions with the utmost severity will be put in execution against anyone who shall presume to sell any of the aforesaid illegal, spurious editions.[30]

Each of the editions mentioned here is an octavo; according to Sutherland, the "Thomson" piracy (actually prepared by Thomas Astley and James Watson, the *Dunciad* pirates) sold for "One Shilling and Six-Pence" and the

Walker version for no more than that. Two days later, another octavo, published by "T. Read" and selling for one shilling, was available. Within a week of the appearance of Gay's quarto, three octavo editions at a quarter of the price of his edition had appeared. "Warfare" indeed. Considering how well guarded the manuscript must have been, it seems safe to assume that these editions were, in Sutherland's phrase, "set up, worked, stitched, and published in a matter of three or four days" ("*Polly*," 293) after Gay's own volume appeared in print.

Sometime during that week, Gay submitted a Bill of Complaint to the Court of Chancery, in his own name, to try to stop the piracies. *Gay v. Read* constitutes the first "author's case" since the Act of Anne—the first one ever, in fact—in which an author recorded his own name as plaintiff in a suit concerned with literary property. Mark Rose, in *Authors and Owners*, points out that "what was novel about the Statute was that it constituted the author as well as the bookseller as a person with legal standing."[31] The first case heard on the basis of the statute, *Burnet v. Chetwood* (1720), was also an author's case in the sense that Burnet was indeed the name of an authorial plaintiff. But in this case, the suit, as Chapter 3 made clear, was brought by George Burnet, the son of the author Dr. Thomas Burnet, to try to stop booksellers from printing what he considered unauthorized translations of his father's work. Gay's case has the distinction of being the first case brought by an author in his own name during his lifetime and thus constitutes the first instance in which an author would actively participate in—and pay for—the defense of his legal rights under the statute of Anne.

Although the bill itself is lost, it is clear that by 11 April the proceedings had begun, as is evident from yet another advertisement, this one in the *Daily Post*. As this advertisement attests, however, the Bill of Complaint was only one of a number of measures to which Gay resorted that week as he tried to salvage what he could of the proceeds from *Polly*:

> Several spurious and incorrect Editions of POLLY, an OPERA, having been publish'd and dispers'd, for which the Booksellers and Vendors are now under Prosecution, and an underhand Sale of the same still continuing, the PROPRIETOR of the true genuine and correct Copy finds himself necessarily obliged to dispose of his Impression at a great Loss; so that the only true correct and genuine Edition of Polly, an OPERA, being the Second Part of the BEGGARS OPERA, with the Airs and Basses curiously engraven on Copper, and printed in Quarto, written by Mr. GAY, is now to be sold at TWO SHILLINGS and SIX PENCE, by Robert Gosling in Fleet-Street, John Stagg in Westminster Hall, John Clark at the Royal Exchange, Daniel Browne without Temple Bar, and Tho. Astley in St Paul's Churchyard.[32]

John Stagg, whose name should be familiar from the *Dunciad* piracies of the previous chapter, had apparently decided to do the right thing in this case by selling the authorized version of the work (albeit at a diminished rate). Yet the last name in this list should also sound familiar, and not only because of his association with *The Dunciad*: Thomas Astley, one of those who now contracted to sell Gay's cut-rate quarto *Polly*, was one of the very pirates who had caused him to undertake this extreme measure in the first place. Even as the author-owner was prosecuting Astley in court, he was dealing with him in the marketplace. Proceedings in Chancery being a notoriously slow process, Gay knew that to wait for an injunction would ensure that the pirates sold far more editions than he himself ever could, and so to salvage what he could of his profits, he more than halved the price of his quarto and went, in Sutherland's words, "straight to those booksellers who were most actively pushing the sale" of the pirated editions ("*Polly*," 299).

When a temporary injunction did finally appear, on 12 June 1729, the list of booksellers and publishers prohibited from selling unauthorized editions of *Polly* was long enough to suggest that the injunction could not reasonably have any effect, since the pirated editions had been so liberally distributed across London. Among those named in this and other documents, in addition to Walker, Astley, and Read (though interestingly, not Stagg) were many of the eras best-known publishing figures, including Edmund Curll, Francis Jeffreys, and the printer Samuel Aris. One other name on the list stands out: the name of Anne Dodd. According to one of the affidavits left in the case, Dodd was one of the booksellers Gay visited back in April when he was trying to stem the tide of unauthorized editions.[33] When examined regarding the piracies, Dodd had admitted openly to Gay that she had been selling the Jeffery Walker edition since its original appearance. Sutherland suggests that Gay "had presumably walked into her pamphlet shop at the Peacock without Temple Bar and challenged her with it" ("*Polly*," 300). After making his challenge, though, Gay apparently turned to a now familiar strategy, convincing Dodd to join the ranks of those selling his cut-price quarto edition. Her name appears in advertisements similar to the one in the *Daily Post* as one of the exclusive purveyors of this authorized edition.[34] Dodd thus once again shows herself, as much as Gay, an able strategist in the market for dangerous works. Not only did Gay supply her with free advertising by adding her name to the list of those allowed to sell his *Polly*, but he promised that in return for this deed, she, along with the rest of his agents, would be excused from any damages as a result of having sold the piracies in the first place. Dodd is willingly appropriated by Gay as an advocate for his cause, at least in part as a strategy for minimizing her own risk while maximizing her profits. It is this ability to strategize her way out of a potentially dangerous situation, by turning her appropriation to advantage, which makes her not only, as I have argued on the basis of *The Dunciad*, a patron of eighteenth-century authorship but also a compelling, if unlikely, substitute or agent for the eighteenth-century author, above all in those cases when the author himself was constrained from appearing.

Dodd was not the only bookseller who showed a knack for strategizing in this case, however. Considering the significance of *Gay v. Read* as a foundational moment in the assertion of authorial property rights, it is interesting to note, however briefly, some of the defenses offered by the pirates in their responses to the charges brought against them. In each case, the pirates showed themselves to be intimately aware of the exact terms of authorial property rights laid out in the statute of Anne and determined both to exploit and to challenge those rights at every turn. Most damningly, the pirates repeatedly accused Gay of "publishing before Entrance," which is to say, of having circulated copies of his book prior to entering it in the Stationers' Register.[35] As a result, as one defendant, Thomas Read, put it, he had "no manner of notice to forbid him from printing the said book." Read went on to offer one of the most brilliant defenses of all, a theory, albeit a convoluted one, of why Gay ought not to have been expected to enter his dangerous work in the register in the first place. On the basis of the notoriety of *Polly*, Read claimed, he had speculated that "the Complainant might be unwilling to take Advantage of the Act of Parliament in the Bill mentioned and leave it to the world to Publish his works."[36] Watson echoed this sentiment in his defense when he argued that he had assumed Gay "had no regard to Establish his sole right to the said Book under the said Act of Parliament."[37] The pirates here call into doubt whether Gay could possibly have wanted to retain his full prerogatives as an author when publishing such a risky work. Their statements corroborate and simultaneously illustrate the thesis of this book as a whole, that retaining copyright in a work, asserting one's full rights as an author, was a particularly dangerous approach to publication, especially when the work in question was one for which the author might not want to have been seen as fully responsible. However contrived the pirates' statements may seem to us now, at the time—the entire case makes clear—their pleas were far from implausible.

Further statements submitted by the pirates in their defense bring home other, more theoretical difficulties entailed in safeguarding authorial property rights. These statements vividly illustrate the instability of literary property and its supposed corollary—copyright—and suggest, too, why appropriation should have been such an irresistible temptation in the decades following the passage of the act that was supposed to abolish literary piracy for all time. When the drafters of the Act of Anne proclaimed that entry in the Stationers' Register was sufficient to determine who had the right to copy a given "book or books," they omitted to define, legally or philosophically, what exactly constituted a "book."[38] Robert Walker, brother to Jeffery Walker, who was accused of selling his brother's pirated edition of *Polly*, admitted in his defense only that he sold "a Book of the Same Name mentioned in the Complainant's said Bill."[39] Jeffery Walker himself, in an advertisement in the *St. James's Evening Post*, referred to Gay as "the Author of the Quarto Edition" as if to suggest that he was involved with another work altogether—that is, the (authorless?) octavo edition of *Polly*.[40] Sutherland points out two more quite fascinating attempts by the pirates to escape prosecution, each of which further calls into question whether Gay had secured anything whatsoever for himself when he entered the work in the register on 3 April. In the case of the "T. Thomson" edition, the various printers each submitted that they had been responsible only for preparing a portion of the work. "After all," Sutherland writes, "neither Watson nor Aris had printed Gay's *Polly*. Each man, it is true, had printed a part of the play, but the Act of Anne said nothing about the unauthorized printing of *parts* of an author's work" ("*Polly*," 296). Read could apparently not resist this line of reasoning, since he capped off the list of creative responses to the charge of piracy by claiming that since "there were alterations on every page, the title-page was different, and the music and preface had been omitted," he ought to be excused from all charges. Once again, Sutherland concludes, the logic of the argument was meant to demonstrate that "whatever Read had published it was not Gay's *Polly*" ("*Polly*," 296).

Gay's case, perhaps on the basis of these canny arguments, stretched on for another eight years after the granting of the original injunction in June of 1729 and was not settled finally until 6 December 1737.[41] Unfortunately, in fact, the case outlived even its own complainant, who died in December of 1732 without seeing a perpetual injunction granted. Gay did ultimately win his case in Chancery, a victory that would never have occurred had he refused, like Pope, fully to "own" his book. Astonishingly, in this, the first case entered in an author's name in defense of his right to copy his own work, in an era when proceedings against pirates were almost never successful, even for publishers skilled in protecting their rights, Gay managed to prevail. Maintaining property in one's own work, *l'affaire Polly* thus suggests, no matter how inconvenient and ultimately dangerous, could, given the right combination of circumstances (including engaging the most effective patrons for one's work), result in considerable benefits for the author—benefits inconceivable in the era prior to the Act of Anne.

Conclusion

Gay engaged in a series of battles in the course of publishing *Polly* that may teach us more about early eighteenth-century authorship—in all its haphazard, unstable, chaotic incarnations—than his posthumous triumph over a group of pirates who had long since abandoned the terrain of *Polly* for other, more marketable commodities. We might want to notice, for instance, Gay's ongoing battles with the seemingly inescapable problem of appropriation, a characteristic of the printed word with which authors—and lawyers—were only just beginning to battle and which has gained urgency only in the three hundred intervening years. We have, too, the image of Gay, the "publick person," split off from his own body through the act of publication—indeed, resorting to elaborate and often fruitless methods to create as much space as possible between his authorial person and his "private" self in an attempt to evade or limit "penal appropriation." Gay's case demands our attention, too, because of its exposure of proprietary authorship's vexed relation to gender, its insistent "capitalizing . . . on femaleness" as a means of buttressing authorship's masculine prerogatives. Above all, though, in the publication of *Polly*, we begin to see just how dangerous the fate of authors could turn out to be, when they attempted to exercise the very rights of proprietorship ostensibly designed to mitigate those dangers. Eighteenth-century authors misunderstood the relationship between literary property and liability at their peril, as the cases of Pope and Gay amply demonstrate. Whether or not authorial property rights were conceived and designed primarily as a means of attributing liability for literary works, as Defoe's contributions to the debates suggest they were, they ended up performing that function, and they continue to do so to this day. The author function has not, as Foucault suggests it might have done, succeeded in limiting "the cancerous and dangerous proliferation of significations," but it has, at least, provided someone who can be held responsible for that proliferation.[42]

In the Lockean universe of the late seventeenth and early eighteenth centuries, property and the independence it brings were considered essential to full personhood. As C. B. Macpherson puts it, in his influential elaboration of the role of property in the liberal-democratic theory of subject formation, "the individual . . . is free inasmuch as he is proprietor of his person and his capacities. The human essence is freedom from dependence on the will of others, and freedom is a function of possession."[43] To qualify as a free individual—a legal person—thus requires not only property but also "freedom from dependence."

The importance of both of these elements to the history of the author-subject should have become clearer in the account of the careers of Gay and Pope, neither of whom achieved the independence necessary, according to Macpherson, to achieving full personhood. More generally, though, Macpherson makes it possible to see the veritable equation between property and full personhood, and the ways in which property under liberalism is considered synonymous with freedom. What the study of literary property elucidates, however, is that such freedom does not come without a price. To be a person, and in particular to be a person endowed with proprietary rights, is also to be a subject under the law. Put otherwise, to be endowed with rights is also to assume certain forms of liability. Proprietary rights, including authorial property rights, make one visible or legible to the law in a manner that may ultimately render the subject anything but free.[44]

The story of Gay and the duchess of Queensberry, like the story of Anne Dodd and her entanglement with Pope's authorial career, serves to remind us that "freedom from dependence" is never more than a fantasy for the liberal subject and that, were we ever to approach it, the dangers associated with independence would unquestionably outweigh its benefits. We might do better, in our historical researches and beyond, to recognize and understand the risks associated with such a rights-based mode of individualism, notwithstanding its powerful promise of freedom. We might do better, that is, to identify the elaborate networks of dependence that make the possessive individual's vaunted "freedom" possible and the troubling role played by women in both securing and undermining that promise of "freedom."

Notes

Unpublished government documents cited in the notes are held either at the City of London Record Office (CLRO) or at the Public Record Office (PRO). The PRO documents listed in the notes are classed according to the following abbreviations:

C 11 Chancery. Various Six Clerks. Series 1. 1714–58
C 33 Chancery. Entry Books of Orders and Decrees. 1544–1875
C 41 Chancery. Register of Affidavits. 1615–1747
PC Privy Council
SP State Papers Domestic

Wherever possible, references to court proceedings are given in two forms: to versions published independently in the seventeenth and eighteenth centuries, and to *State Trials.* The full citation for the latter is *Cobbett's Complete Collection of State Trials and Proceedings for High Treason and Other Crimes and Misdemeanors: From the Earliest Period to the Present Time,* 34 vols. (London: published by R. Bagshaw, 1809–28).

Introduction

1. Mark Rose, *Authors and Owners: The Invention of Copyright* (Cambridge: Harvard University Press, 1993), 1.

2. David Saunders and Iain Hunter, "Lessons from the 'Literatory': How to Historicise Authorship," *Critical Inquiry* 17 (1991): 479–509, 499. See also Saunders, *Authorship and Copyright* (London: Routledge, 1992), for a fuller elaboration of this argument. While I concur with Saunders and Hunter on the question of the contingency of the Act of Anne, I would question their desire to draw a firm line between two sorts of authorial personality made possible at the start of the eighteenth century: the proprietary author of the Act of Anne and the "obscene libeler" whose criminal liability for his works is elaborated in the case of *Rex v. Curll* in 1727 (*English Reports* [Edinburgh: William Green and Sons, 1904] 93:849–51). For a related discussion of the ways in which the Act of Anne was addressed to the concerns of the trade more than to those of authors, see the introduction to Martha Woodmansee and Peter Jaszi, eds., *The Construction of Authorship: Textual Appropriation in Law and Literature* (Durham, N.C.: Duke University Press, 1994), 1–13.

3. 8 Anne c. 21 (1709/10), reprinted in *Statutes of the Realm* (London: printed by command of King George III, 1822), 9:256–58. As the author notes, the statute is recorded in other editions as 8 Anne c. 19; because of the old-style calendar, the statute, which was introduced during the legislative session of 1709, is classed under

the earlier year. Although the statute is most frequently referred to as the Copyright Act of 1710, this is something of a misnomer, since the term *copyright* was virtually unknown when the act came into being. For a history of the term's usage, see Rose, *Authors and Owners*, 58 n.4.

4. The very fact that exclusive property in the work reverted to the original owner after fourteen years (or twenty-one years, in the case of books printed before 10 April 1710) suggests that literary property operates somewhat differently from other forms of property. Transfer of copyright is in fact closer to a lease than it is to a sale, and literary property remains, in some fundamental sense, inalienable property—property that always reverts to the author in the end. For a fuller discussion of the specificity of literary property, see Blackstone's *Commentaries on the Laws of England*, Vol. 2, *Of the Rights of Things* (1766; reprint, Chicago: University of Chicago Press, 1979), 405.

5. Lyman Ray Patterson, *Copyright in Historical Perspective* (Nashville: Vanderbilt University Press, 1968), 145. For further information concerning the implications of the Act of Anne for the organization of the book trade, see David, *Authorship and Copyright*, 35–74; Ian Watt, "Publishers and Sinners: The Augustan View," *Studies in Bibliography* 12 (1959): 5–6; John Feather, "The Book Trade in Politics: The Making of the Copyright Act of 1710," *Publishing History* 8 (1980): 19–44; and Terry Belanger, "Publishers and Writers in Eighteenth-Century England," in *Books and Their Readers in Eighteenth-Century England*, ed. Isabel Rivers (New York: St. Martin's Press, 1982), 5–25.

6. For an indispensable and comprehensive analysis of the effectiveness of the licensing system after the Restoration, see Philip Hamburger, "The Development of the Law of Seditious Libel and the Control of the Press," *Stanford Law Review* 37 (1985): 661–765, especially 674–91. For the last years of licensing and the logic behind the act's demise, see Raymond Astbury, "The Renewal of the Licensing Act in 1693 and Its Lapse in 1695," *Library*, 5th series, 33.4 (1978): 296–322. A more general survey of the wide variety of press controls in place in the period covered by this book is Fredrick Seaton Siebert, *Freedom of the Press in England, 1476–1776: The Rise and Decline of Government Controls* (Urbana: University of Illinois Press, 1952). See especially Siebert's chapter, "The Regulation of Printing Acts, 1662–1694" (237–63) and the final chapter, "Responsibility Under the Law" (364–92).

7. For the history of newspapers in this period, see Laurence Hanson, *Government and the Press, 1695–1763* (1936; reprint, Oxford: Clarendon Press, 1967); James Sutherland, *The Restoration Newspaper and Its Development* (Cambridge: Cambridge University Press, 1986); and Joad Raymond, ed., *News, Newspapers, and Society in Early Modern Britain* (London: Frank Cass, 1999).

8. On the use of the false imprint after the Restoration and through the first era of literary property, see Michael Treadwell, "On False and Misleading Imprints in the London Book Trade, 1660–1750," in *Fakes and Frauds: Varieties of Deception in Print and Manuscript*, ed. Robin Myers and Michael Harris (Winchester: St. Paul's Bibliographies, 1989), 29–46.

9. The only full-length study of L'Estrange's career is George Kitchin, *Sir Roger L'Estrange: A Contribution to the History of the Press in the Seventeenth Century* (London: Kegan Paul, 1913). For more recent discussions of L'Estrange and his chequered

career, see Harold M. Weber, *Paper Bullets: Print and Kingship under Charles II* (Lexington: University Press of Kentucky, 1996), 153–71, 205–8; and Adrian Johns, *The Nature of the Book: Print and Knowledge in the Making* (Chicago: University of Chicago Press, 1998), 122–36, 230–48, and passim.

10. Siebert, *Freedom of the Press*, 249.

11. Daniel Defoe, *An Essay on the Regulation of the Press* (London: n.p., 1704), 21.

12. John Feather, *Publishing, Piracy, and Politics: An Historical Study of Copyright in Britain* (London: Mansell, 1994), 62. For a recent reconsideration of the origins of the act, and in particular of the role of the stationers in securing its passage, see Joseph Loewenstein, *The Author's Due: Printing and the Prehistory of Copyright* (Chicago: University of Chicago Press, 2002).

13. *Statutes of the Realm*, 9:256. According to the act, consent of the author as proprietor was required for all books first printed after 10 April 1710. Authorial consent was required to republish works that had appeared prior to this date unless rights had already been transferred to "the Bookseller or Booksellers, Printer or Printers, or other Person or Persons, who hath or have purchased or acquired the Copy or Copies of any Book or Books, in order to print or reprint the same." In such cases, consent had to be obtained from the person who now possessed the "sole Right and Liberty of printing" such a work.

14. Roger L'Estrange, *Considerations and Proposals in Order to the Regulation of the Press* (London: printed for A. C., 1663), 2.

15. *The Triall of Henry Carr, Gent. . . . Also the Tryal of Elizabeth Cellier* (London: printed by I. G. for R[andal] Taylor, 1681), 7.

16. Paula McDowell, *The Women of Grub Street: Press, Politics, and Gender in the London Literary Marketplace, 1678–1730* (Oxford: Clarendon Press, 1998); Marcus Nevitt, "Women in the Business of Revolutionary News: Elizabeth Atkin, 'Parliament Joan,' and the Commonwealth Newsbook," in Raymond, ed., *News, Newspapers, and Society*, 84–108. Perhaps the most influential work in this field was done by D. F. McKenzie—work that has recently been collected in *Bibliography and the Sociology of Texts* (Cambridge: Cambridge University Press, 1999), and *Making Meaning: "Printers of the Mind" and Other Essays*, ed. Peter D. McDonald and Michael F. Suarez (Amherst: University of Massachusetts Press, 2002). For the latest and most influential attempt to unseat the author from the center of book history, in the service of a better understanding of "the culture and credibility of the printed book" as a whole, see Johns, *Nature of the Book*, 58–186 and passim.

17. Nevitt's essay addresses itself primarily to newsbooks and other forms of printed news, in which authorship was almost always unattributed and the roles of editor, publisher, author, and printer were so overlapping as to be indistinguishable much of the time. Nonetheless, his arguments about collective production as well as those about dispersed liability hold just as true for other forms of publication in this period, as the trials discussed below and in the next chapter make clear. For more on questions of attribution and liability as they relate to the newspaper in particular, see Sutherland, *Restoration Newspaper and Its Development*.

18. I intentionally set off "censorship" in quotation marks here because the term seems to me both inadequate and imprecise for describing those who might have been in the business of prosecuting the producers of printed works. At the

most basic level, to describe someone as a "censor" suggests that his or her primary interest lies in controlling texts or the ideas that circulate in those texts. The secretary of state charged with investigating either seditious libel or, in the most extreme cases, treason, did so not in the name of censorship—keeping control over what ideas circulated in textual form—but rather as part of a much larger project of keeping the public peace and protecting the government from attacks of all kinds. For early modern English histories that retain the term but, in some cases, attempt to refine its definition, see Christopher Hill, "Censorship and English Literature," in Hill, ed. *Collected Essays of Christopher Hill* (Amherst: University of Massachusetts Press, 1985), 1:32–71; Annabel Patterson, *Censorship and Interpretation: The Conditions of Writing and Reading in Early Modern England* (1984; reprint, with a new introduction, Madison: University of Wisconsin Press, 1990), 3–31; and "Introduction: Censorship versus Slander," in M. Lindsay Kaplan, *The Culture of Slander in Early Modern England* (Cambridge: Cambridge University Press, 1997), 1–11.

19. Rosemary J. Coombe, *The Cultural Life of Intellectual Properties: Authorship, Appropriation, and the Law* (Durham, N.C.: Duke University Press, 1998), 255.

20. Michel Foucault, "Qu'est ce qu'un auteur?" *Bulletin de la Société française de Philosophie* 64 (1969): 73–104. The English translation of the American version of the lecture, which adds important concluding remarks on the "ideological" dimensions of the "author-function," can be found in Josué V. Harari, ed., *Textual Strategies: Perspectives in Post-Structuralist Criticism* (Ithaca, N.Y.: Cornell University Press, 1979), 141–60.

21. Jacques Derrida, "Signature Event Context," trans. Samuel Weber and Jeffrey Mehlman; and "Limited Inc a b c," trans. Samuel Weber, in *Limited Inc* (Evanston: Northwestern University Press, 1988). "Signature Event Context" was originally published in *Glyph* 1 (1977), along with Searle's reply, "Reiterating the Differences." "Limited Inc a b c" was published in *Glyph* 2 (1978).

22. To understand the distinctions between and among these trials, as well as the portmanteau offense known as "seditious libel," see Hamburger, "Development of the Law of Seditious Libel."

23. Catherine Gallagher, *Nobody's Story: The Vanishing Acts of Women Writers in the Marketplace, 1670–1820* (Berkeley and Los Angeles: University of California Press, 1994), xiii.

24. For a summary of the events surrounding the publication of *Polly*, see David Nokes, *John Gay: A Profession of Friendship* (Oxford: Oxford University Press, 1995), 453–69.

25. Derrida, "Limited Inc a b c . . . ," 37.

26. Alexander Pope, Preface to *The Works of Mr. Alexander Pope* (London: printed by W. Bowyer for Bernard Lintot, 1717), A2v.

27. Defoe, *Essay on the Regulation of the Press*, 21.

Chapter 1. Authorship and the Regulation of the Press

1. Proclamation "Prohibiting Unlicensed Printing of Scripture, Exiling Anabaptists, Depriving Married Clergy, Removing St. Thomas à Becket from Calendar," 16

November 1538, 30 Henry 8. Reprinted in *Tudor Royal Proclamations,* ed. Paul L. Hughes and James F. Larkin (New Haven and London: Yale University Press, 1969), 1:270. Hereafter cited as *TRP.* In the text, unless otherwise noted, all quotations from proclamations are from this work and are cited only by volume and page number after the first reference.

2. Proclamation "Prohibiting Erroneous Books and Bible Translations," 22 June 1530, 22 Henry 8. *TRP,* 1:194.

3. The most concise discussion of the variant meanings of "publisher" is in Harold Love, *The Culture and Commerce of Texts: Scribal Publication in Seventeenth-Century England* (Amherst: University of Massachusetts Press, 1998), 36–38.

4. *Oxford English Dictionary,* s.v. "Liable."

5. Under "Accountability," the *Oxford English Dictionary* lists "responsibility" as one of the primary definitions; under "Responsibility," one of the primary definitions reads, "answerable, accountable (to another for something); liable to be called to account." In this latter definition, the tendency for slippage among the terms is most visible, notwithstanding my attempts to keep them distinct.

6. 14 Car. 2, c.33 (1662). Roger L'Estrange, *Considerations and Proposals in Order to the Regulation of the Press: Together with Diverse Instances of Treasonous, and Seditious Pamphlets, Proving the Necessity Thereof* (London: printed by A. C., 1663). The quotation, which is also the epigraph to this chapter, appears on p. 32.

7. Roger L'Estrange, *A Memento Treating of the Rise, Progress, and Remedies of Seditions: With some Historical Reflections upon the Series of our Late Troubles* (London: printed in the year 1642, and now reprinted for Joanna Brome, 1682), 6. For a summary of L'Estrange's political views, see the *Dictionary of National Biography,* s.v. L'Estrange; and, for a fuller account, George Kitchin's biography, *Sir Roger L'Estrange: A Contribution to the History of the Press in the Seventeenth Century* (London: Kegan Paul, 1913).

8. L'Estrange, *Interest Mistaken* (London: printed for Henry Brome, 1661), 128.

9. L'Estrange, *Truth and Loyalty Vindicated, from the Reproches and Clamours of Mr. Edward Bagshaw: Together with a Further Discovery of the Libeller Himself, and His Seditious Confederates* (London: printed for H. Brome and A. Seile, 1662), Epistle Dedicatory.

10. L'Estrange, *L'Estrange His Appeal* (London: printed for Henry Brome, 1681), 1.

11. L'Estrange, *A Short Answer to a Whole Litter of Libels* (London: printed by J. B. for Henry Brome, 1680), 1–2. L'Estrange here seems, perhaps unconsciously, to be citing a speech made on the topic of libels by Lord Chief Justice Scroggs, in 1679. The speech was printed under the title *The Lord Chief Justice Scroggs His Speech in the Kings-Bench . . . Occasion'd by the many Libellous Pamphlets Which Are Publisht against Law, to the Scandal of Government, and Publick Justice* (London: printed for Robert Pawlet, 1679). Scroggs here draws on the language of authors as vermin and notes their ability to keep themselves outside of the reach of the law when he writes, "they are onely safe whilst they can be secret; but so are Vermine; so long onely as they can hide themselves" (4). Scroggs here seems somewhat more sanguine than L'Estrange about the possibility of ultimately finding the author, but he, too, has a backup plan involving other members of the book trade: "And let their Brokers, those Printers and Booksellers . . . look to it; some will be found, and they shall

know, that the Law wants not power to punish a Libellous and Licentious Press" (4). Like L'Estrange, then, Scroggs would prefer to punish the author, but in the event that he is unable to locate that originary figure, will settle for any available, locatable accomplices. For a fuller discussion of this speech and Scroggs's role in the regulation of the press, see the next chapter.

12. L'Estrange, "The Epistle Dedicatory to the Right Honourable the Lords and, to the Honourable the Commons Assembled in Parliament" in the *Considerations*, a4r. The letters are unpaginated, and I will refer to them according to the folio leaves, A1r–A4v, followed by a1r–a4v. Pagination begins at the start of the essay proper, which corresponds to folio B.

13. In the tradition of Milton's *Areopagitica*—and frequently liberally borrowing from their precursor—one can find any number of defenses of press liberty, including a pair of tracts by Charles Blount, *A Just Vindication of Learning; or, An Humble Address to the High Court of Parliament in Behalf of the Liberty of the Press* (London: n.p., 1679); and *Reasons Humbly Offered for the Liberty of Unlicens'd Printing* (London: n.p., 1693), both published in the period under discussion in this book. Essays in this tradition, however, precisely because they are dedicated to eliminating restrictions on press freedom, do not discuss in detail how to go about the regulation of the press and thus fall outside the scope of this chapter.

14. The most detailed account of the formulation and enforcement of the 1662 Press Act comes in Fredrick Seaton Siebert, *Freedom of the Press in England, 1476–1776: The Rise and Decline of Government Controls* (Urbana: University of Illinois Press, 1952), 237–60.

15. Richard Atkyns, *Original and Growth of Printing: Collected out of History, and the Records of this Kingdome* (London: printed by John Streater for the author, 1664). For more on Atkyns, see the introduction to Carey S. Bliss, *A Pair on Printing* (North Hills, Pa: Bird and Bull Press, 1982).

16. Love, *Culture and Commerce*, offers a fuller discussion of the particular issues associated with regulating materials that circulated in manuscript, especially the section "Censorship and the Scribal Text," 184–91. See also Sheila Lambert, "State Control of the Press in Theory and Practice: The Role of the Stationers' Company before 1640," in *Censorship and Control of the Press in England and France, 1600–1910*, ed. Robin Myers and Michael Harris (Winchester: Saint Paul's Bibliographies, 1992), 5–6.

17. Marcus Nevitt, "Women in the Business of Revolutionary News: Elizabeth Atkin, 'Parliament Joan,' and the Commonwealth Newsbook," in Raymond, ed., *News, Newspapers, and Society*, 86.

18. In *Paper Bullets: Print and Kingship under Charles II* (Lexington: University of Kentucky Press, 1991), Harold M. Weber offers a similar reading of the centrality of the author to L'Estrange's regulatory scheme in *Considerations* (153–56). While my account of the place of the author in Restoration press regulation agrees with Weber's and is in many places indebted to his analysis, part of the function of the present chapter is to show that this focus on the author is not new in the period following the Restoration. Rather than inventing a system of regulation that privileges the author as the primary site of responsibility and liability, L'Estrange rationalizes and systematizes a discourse about authorial liability that had been developing in English writing on the press for as long as the English had had presses.

19. As Love, in particular, has shown, throughout the seventeenth and into the eighteenth century, there was not only a practice of private or "coterie" publication but also a market for manuscripts and other "scribally published" materials—as his subtitle puts it. There were booksellers who specialized in the sale of these materials and authors who preferred for a wide variety of reasons to distribute their work in this way. See Love, *Culture and Commerce*, 35–89 and passim, as well as, more generally, Arthur F. Marotti, *John Donne: Coterie Poet* (Madison: University of Wisconsin Press, 1986).

20. "Mr Lestraings Proposition concerning Libells, &c," 11 November 1675, quoted from the original in the House of Lords Record Office by Love, *Culture and Commerce*, 74.

21. Harry Ransom, *The First Copyright Statute: An Essay on* An Act for the Encouragement of Learning, *1710* (Austin: University of Texas Press, 1956), 23.

22. Representative cases of authors on trial in the period covered by the present chapter include those of John Stubbes in 1579; Sir John Hayward in 1599; Alexander Leighton in 1630; and Wiliam Prynne in 1634 and 1637, the last of which I touch on at the opening of the next chapter. All of these trials are discussed in Annabel Patterson, *Censorship and Interpretation: The Conditions of Reading and Writing in Early Modern England* (1984; reprinted with a new introduction, Madison: University of Wisconsin Press, 1990), 52–58.

23. Adrian Johns, *The Nature of the Book: Print and Knowledge in the Making* (Chicago: University of Chicago Press, 1998), 189.

24. While Siebert, *Freedom of the Press*, remains the standard reference for these matters, the most detailed analysis to date of Tudor and early Stuart censorship practices can be found in a pair of works by Cyndia Clegg: *Press Censorship in Elizabethan England* (Cambridge: Cambridge University Press, 1997); and *Press Censorship in Jacobean England* (Cambridge: Cambridge University Press, 2001). Clegg also concludes, with Johns, that numerous obstacles existed under both Elizabeth and James that made nearly impossible the actual enforcement of regulations such as those I study in the remainder of this chapter.

25. Early specialists on copyright who looked to these proclamations for evidence of the ancestry of copyright include Augustine Birrel, *Seven Lectures on the Law and History of Copyright in Books* (London: Cassell, 1899), 41–68; and Ransom, *First Copyright Statute*, 17–93. Most recently, this terrain has been carefully covered by Joseph Loewenstein in *The Author's Due: Printing and the Prehistory of Copyright* (Chicago: University of Chicago Press, 2002), 27–51.

26. Loewenstein, *Author's Due*, 55.

27. Proclamation "Enforcing Statutes against Heresy; Prohibiting Unlicensed Preaching, Heretical Books," 6 March 1529, 20 Henry 8. *TRP*, 1:181–85.

28. For a detailed discussion of early Tudor printing regulation, see David M. Loades, "The Press under the Early Tudors," *Transactions of the Cambridge Bibliographic Society* 4.1 (1964): 29–50. This essay is reprinted along with other, more recent considerations by Loades of the same topic in *Politics, Censorship, and the English Reformation* (London and New York: Printer Publishers, 1991). Information on even earlier attempts at the regulation of books, including before the advent of printing, can be found in Howard W. Winger, "Regulations Relating to the Book Trade in London from 1357–1586," *Library Quarterly* 26 (1956): 157–95; and William M. Clyde,

The Struggle for the Freedom of the Press from Caxton to Cromwell (London: Oxford University Press, 1934).

29. Proclamation "Prohibiting Erroneous Books and Bible Translations," 22 June 1530, 22 Henry 8. *TRP*, 1:193–97.

30. Although the 1530 proclamation represents Henry's first public statement on the topic of what would later become the attempt to license all books before publication, his was not the first attempt to institute such a system in the history of English books. As Siebert notes, as early as 1408 the church in England began insisting that translations of the Bible into the vernacular should be submitted to ecclesiastical authorities for examination. In addition, throughout the 1520s, as Siebert documents, the English clergy were engaged in the maintenance and enforcement of prepublication examination for all English books on religious subjects. Henry's pronouncement thus constitutes an attempt to transfer such enforcement from ecclesiastical to royal prerogative and, in later proclamations, to extend the system of examination beyond religious books, to all printed materials. See Siebert, *Freedom of the Press*, 41–44.

31. Proclamation "Prohibiting Unlicensed Printing," *TRP*, 1:270–76.

32. For an extended discussion of the significance of this formulation, see Loewenstein, *The Author's Due*, 7–10, 265 nn. 16–20. Loewenstein rehearses and gives commentary on an early twentieth-century debate over the phrase *Ad imprimendum solum*, carried on in a series of journal articles: Alfred W. Pollard, "The Regulation of the Book Trade in the Sixteenth Century," *Library*, 3rd series, 7 (1916): 18–43; Evelyn M. Albright, "*Ad Imprimendum Solum*," *Modern Language Notes* 34 (1919): 97–104; Pollard, "*Ad Imprimendum Solum*," *Library*, 3rd series, 10 (1919): 57–63; Albright, "*Ad Imprimendum Solum* Once More," *MLN* 38 (1923): 129–40; and Walter Greg, "*Ad Imprimendum Solum*," *Library*, 5th series, (1954): 242–47.

33. In *The Author's Due*, Loewenstein also takes notice of this habit of substitution in materials related to the regulation of the press—in particular, the ability of other members of the trade to substitute for the author—although he traces the phenomenon only to 1642 (160, 229).

34. Proclamation "Prohibiting Heretical Books; Requiring Printer to Identify Himself, Author of the Book, and Date of Publication," 8 July 1546, 38 Henry 8. *TRP*, 1:373–76, 374.

35. Proclamation "Enforcing Statute against Heresy; Prohibiting Seditious and Heretical Books," 13 June 1555, 1 & 2 Philip and Mary. *TRP*, 2:57–60, 59.

36. Proclamation "Suppressing Seditious Rumours," 28 July 1553, I Mary I. *TRP*, 2:4.

37. Proclamation "Ordering Arrest for Circulating Seditious Books and Bulls," 1 July 1570, 12 Elizabeth 1. *TRP*, 2:341–43.

38. Proclamation "Ordering Discovery of Person Bringing in Seditious Books and Writings," 14 November 1570, 12 Elizabeth 1. *TRP*, 2:347–48; 347, 348.

39. Proclamation "Offering Rewards for Information on Libels against the Queen," 26 March 1576, 18 Elizabeth 1. *TRP*, 2:400–401, 400. This document is also reprinted in Edward Arber, ed., *A Transcript of the Registers of the Company of Stationers of London, 1554–1640* A.D. (London: privately printed, 1875–94; reprint, New York: Peter Smith, 1950), 2:474. Arber writes, "We are quite unable at present to ascertain the occasion of this Proclamation."

40. Proclamation "Declaring Books by Robert Browne and Robert Harrison Seditious and Schismatic," 30 June 1583, 25 Elizabeth 1. *TRP*, 2:501–2.

41. On occasion, the authorities did actually manage to track down the offending author, as occurred in the case of Philip Stubbes. A 1579 proclamation "Denouncing Stubbs' Book, *The Discovery of a Gaping Gulf*" (27 September 1579, 21 Elizabeth 1), rails against "such a seditious author" and "the crooked nature of the seditious libeler" (*TRP*, 2:447, 449). Nonetheless, in laying out expedients for remedying the situation, the decree makes no mention of the author, only demanding that the offending books should "be destroyed in open sight of some public officer" (2:449). Despite this silence concerning the author, however, Stubbes lost his hand for his part in the composition of the *Gaping Gulf*, as Patterson recounts in *Censorship and Interpretation*, 33–34.

42. David M. Loades, "Illicit Presses and Clandestine Printing in England, 1520–1590," in A. C. Duke and C. A. Tamse, eds., *Too Mighty to Be Free: Censorship and the Press in Britain and the Netherlands* (Zutphen, Netherlands: de Walburg Press, 1987), 9–27. See also Loades, "Press under the Early Tudors," 29–31.

43. Loades, "Illicit Presses," 15.

44. Weber, *Paper Bullets*, 140.

45. Donald Thomas, *A Long Time Burning: The History of Literary Censorship in England* (New York: Frederick A. Praeger, 1969), 9. For alternative, more skeptical views of the stationers' part in the licensing system, see Lambert, "State Control of the Press," and Johns, *Nature of the Book*, 230–48.

46. Siebert, *Freedom of the Press*, 64. On the notion of stationers' copyright, see Siebert, 74–82; Ransom, *First Copyright Statute*, 33–40; John Feather, *Publishing, Piracy, and Politics: An Historical Study of Copyright in Britain* (London: Mansell, 1994), 10–63; and Lyman Ray Patterson, *Copyright in Historical Perspective* (Nashville: Vanderbilt University Press, 1968), 42–77.

47. The 1586 Star Chamber decree concerning printers is reprinted in *The Tudor Constitution: Documents and Commentary*, 2nd ed., ed. G. R. Elton (Cambridge: Cambridge University Press, 1982), 183–87. The 1637 Star Chamber decree can be found in Arber, *Transcript*, 4:528–36.

48. Walter Greg, "Entrance, Licence, and Publication," *Library*, 4th series, 25 (1944): 1–22. On the significance of the register, see also Ransom, *First Copyright Statute*, 38–41; and Johns, *Nature of the Book*, 213–30.

49. Joseph Loewenstein has argued, on the basis of this provision that the author be named, that "authorship was not made part of the structure of press censorship until the Star Chamber Decree of 1637" ("Legal Proofs and Corrected Readings: Press-Agency and the New Bibliography," in *The Production of English Renaissance Culture*, ed. David Lee Miller, Sharon O'Hair, and Harold Weber [Ithaca, N.Y.: Cornell University Press, 1994], 95 n. 7). While Loewenstein's point about the revolutionary nature of the provision concerning authorial naming is well taken, the first portion of this chapter suggests that if authorship was not part of the "structure" of press regulation until this time, finding, punishing, and silencing the author had been a key regulatory ambition from the start.

50. According to Christopher Hill, despite its elaborate provisions, the 1637 decree was no more successful than its predecessors in increasing the proportion

of material perused by the authorities before it reached the printing press or the reading public. By Hill's estimate, "65% of books published in 1640 were unlicensed" ("Censorship and English Literature," in Hill, ed. *Collected Essays of Christopher Hill*, volume 1 [Amherst: University of Massachusetts Press, 1985], 49). In preparing this calculation, Hill relies on F. B. Williams, *Index of Dedications and Commendatory Verses in English Books before 1641* (London: Bibliographical Society, 1962), 237–40.

51. On the abolition of Star Chamber and its immediate consequences for the press, see Weber, *Paper Bullets*, 140–42; and Siebert, "Chaos in the Printing Trade," in *Freedom of the Press*, 165–78. Despite the undeniable threat of chaos documented by Siebert, Loewenstein notes that even before the abolition of Star Chamber, in May 1641, Commons had already established a Committee on Printing to begin drafting new parliamentary orders for press regulation, in order to fill the vacuum left by the abolition of royal privilege (*Author's Due*, 161–62).

52. David Cressy, *Literacy and the Social Order: Reading and Writing in Tudor and Stuart England* (Cambridge: Cambridge University Press, 1980), 47. This often cited statistic is repeated by, among others, Weber, in *Paper Bullets*, 5. Christopher Hill notes the "explosion" of newspapers in the same period, from four in 1641 to 722 in 1645 ("Censorship," 39).

53. For series of petitions emanating from the stationers after 1641, see Loewenstein, *Author's Due*, 160–70; Arber, *Transcript*, 1:583–88; and Siebert, *Freedom of the Press*, 173–78.

54. The parts of the order I cite are reprinted in Loewenstein, *Author's Due*, 162–64. The document is cited as BME 207 (2) and reprinted, as Siebert notes (171 n. 11), in the *House of Commons Journal* (29 January 1641–42) 2:402.

55. Francis Barker, *The Tremulous Private Body: Essays in Subjection* (Ann Arbor: University of Michigan Press, 1995), 45.

56. Closest to my reading of the order is that of Feather, who writes, in *Publishing, Piracy, and Politics*, "the real purpose was, of course, to enable easy identification of the authors of unacceptable books and pamphlets and we should certainly not ascribe any motive beyond that to the framers of this Order. Even so, they show a clear recognition that *it is the author who is ultimately responsible for the book*" (40, emphasis added).

57. "An Ordinance for the Regulation of Printing," 14 June 1643. Reprinted in *Acts and Ordinances of the Interregnum, 1642–1660*, ed. C. H. Firth and R. S. Rait (London, 1911), 1:184–86. In notes and in the text, this work will be cited as *A&O*.

58. "An Act for the Reviving of a Former Act [the 1643 Act], etc.," 7 January 1653. *A&O* 2:696–99, 697.

59. "An Ordinance against Unlicensed or Scandalous Pamphlets, and for the Better Regulating of Printing," 30 September 1647. *A&O* 1:1021–23.

60. "An Act against Unlicensed and Scandalous Books and Pamphlets, and for Better Regulating of Printing," 20 September 1649. *A&O* 2:245–54.

61. Siebert, *Freedom of the Press*, 239.

62. *By the King, a Proclamation for the Suppressing of Seditious and Treasonable Books and Pamphlets* (London: printed by John Bill, Thomas Newcomb, and Henry Hills, 1679), [1].

Chapter 2. The Trials of Ownership

1. On Prynne's career and legal difficulties, see Ethyn Williams Kirby, *William Prynne: A Study in Puritanism* (Cambridge: Harvard University Press, 1931); William Lamont, *Marginal Prynne, 1600–1669* (London: Routledge and Kegan Paul, 1963); and William Lamont, *Puritanism and Historical Controversy* (London: University College London Press, 1996), 15–25 and passim.

2. Annabel Patterson, *Censorship and Interpretation: The Conditions of Writing and Reading in Early Modern England* (1982; reprint, Madison: University of Wisconsin Press, 1990). Patterson's main point about the Prynne case is that it constitutes something of an anomaly in the history of early modern press regulation. For Patterson, literary language and practice developed in the Renaissance as a means of circumventing laws that put limits on expression. Indirection, allusiveness, susceptibility to multiple interpretations: these features of literary language, which Patterson terms literature's "functional ambiguity," were specifically designed to make it possible to test the limits of allowable expression without transgressing existing prohibitions (18). At the same time, a "hermeneutics of censorship" developed that allowed the early modern state to keep pace with its enemies (18). The Prynne case is for Patterson an example of a moment at which these "strategies of indirection" have failed, and the "codes governing sociopolitical communication [have] broken down" (53).

3. Samuel Rawson Gardiner, ed., *Documents Relating to the Proceedings against William Prynne, in 1634 and 1637* (London: Camden Society, 1877), 16.

4. Michel Foucault, "What Is an Author?," in Josué V. Harari, ed., *Textual Strategies: Perspectives in Post-Structuralist Criticism* (Ithaca, N.Y.: Cornell University Press, 1979), 148. It is perhaps worth noting that later in life, during the Commonwealth and afterward, Prynne himself became active in the cause of press regulation. He was, in a particularly odd twist, responsible after the Restoration for chairing the committee in Parliament that was charged with coming up with new measures for the regulation of printing. See Harry Ransom, *The First Copyright Statute: An Essay on* An Act for the Encouragement of Learning, *1710* (Austin: University of Texas Press, 1956), 74, 77.

5. William Prynne, *Histriomastix: The Players Scourge; or, Actors Tragedie* (London: printed by E. A. and W. I. for Michael Sparke, 1633).

6. Gardiner, *Documents*, 2, 3. For Prynne's later complaint that he had been accused of writing "by combinacion"—i.e., as part of a Puritan cabal—see 34–35.

7. Edward Arber, ed., *A Transcript of the Registers of the Company of Stationers of London, 1554–1640 A.D.* (London: privately printed, 1875–94; reprint, New York: Peter Smith, 1950), 4:241. The entry was crossed out in the original register by order of the court of Star Chamber on 1 December 1634 but remains legible nonetheless. For evidence of the date of original licensing, see Gardiner, *Documents*, 52.

8. Roger L'Estrange, *Considerations and Proposals in Order to the Regulation of the Press* (London: printed by A. C., 1663), 2.

9. The single best account of the volatility of the press after the Restoration can be found in Harold M. Weber, *Paper Bullets: Print and Kingship under Charles II* (Lexington: University Press of Kentucky, 1996). An excellent study of one particular case, that of Henry Carr (or Care), which sets Carr's case in the context of

broader trends in print cultures, can be found in Lois G. Schwoerer, *The Ingenious Mr. Henry Care, Restoration Publicist* (Baltimore: Johns Hopkins University Press, 2001). The classic study of printed news in the period remains James Sutherland, *The Restoration Newspaper and Its Development* (Cambridge: Cambridge University Press, 1986).

10. 14 Car. 2, c.33 (1662).

11. Joseph Loewenstein, "Legal Proofs and Corrected Readings: Press-Agency and the New Bibliography," in *The Production of English Renaissance Culture*, ed. David Lee Miller, Sharon O'Dair, and Harold Weber (Ithaca, N.Y.: Cornell University Press, 1994), 93–122, 122. Harold Weber similarly notes a new emphasis on the author in the reign of Charles II but dates the change to the late 1670s, with the lapse of the Licensing Act in 1679. Weber, however, is not as interested in the instability of the term—its sheer mobility—earlier in the century and thus finds the emergence of interest in the author in the 1670s to be more sudden than it actually was. See *Paper Bullets*, 174–208.

12. L'Estrange, *Considerations*, 2.

13. Francis Smith, *An Account of the Injurious Proceedings . . . against Francis Smith, Bookseller . . . Sept. 16. 1680* (London: printed for Francis Smith, [1681]), 17 [second page so numbered].

14. My account of the trial in this chapter is similar to the one given by Loewenstein in "Legal Proofs," focusing as they both do on the court's preoccupation with the nature of proof correction as a form of authorship. For Loewenstein, in addition, the Twyn case offers a lesson for contemporary historians of authorship and bibliography about the dispersed and unstable character of authorial work, its inescapably collaborative nature. While I am entirely in agreement with Loewenstein's analysis here, the case is equally important for what it has to say about the role played by liability in the emergence of the modern author. "The legal constitution of authorship," as he calls it, especially in its proprietary form, is less "a reaction to the proliferation and dispersal of authorial functions" than it is a response to the needs of Restoration judges to locate responsibility for dangerous texts in a single individual (122).

15. *An Exact Narrative of the Tryal and Condemnation of John Twyn, for Printing and Dispersing of a Treasonable Book, with the Tryals of Thomas Brewster, Bookseller, Simon Dover, Printer, and Nathan Brookes, Bookbinder, for Printing, Publishing, and Uttering of Seditious, Scandalous, and Malitious Pamphlets* (London: printed by Thomas Mabb for Henry Brome, 1664), 27. All references to Twyn's trial proceedings in the text are taken from this pamphlet, which is also reprinted in *State Trials* 6: cols. 514–39. Note that Thomas Mabb was one of L'Estrange's assistants in his capacity as surveyor of the imprimery and that Henry Brome was L'Estrange's own publisher, as indicated by the imprints on the pamphlets cited in the previous chapter. Given that Twyn's was one of the first cases tried after L'Estrange assumed his new public role, and that he was a witness in the case, it is clear that he had a hand in the production of this pamphlet. Indeed, printed with Twyn's case was the trial of three other members of the opposition press, Thomas Brewster, a publisher; Simon Dover, a printer; and Nathan Brookes, a bookbinder. Clearly, L'Estrange wanted to put the members of the trade on notice that a new regime of press regulation was

in force. With the exception of Loewenstein's "Legal Proofs," however, historians of the book trade in this period have failed to attend in much detail to Twyn's trial. For passing references to the proceedings, see Richard L. Greaves, *Deliver Us from Evil: The Radical Underground in Britain, 1660–1663* (New York: Oxford University Press, 1986), 222–25; George Kitchin, *Sir Roger L'Estrange: A Contribution to the History of the Press in the Seventeenth Century* (London: Kegan Paul, 1913), 117; Fredrick Seaton Siebert, *Freedom of the Press in England, 1476–1776: The Rise and Decline of Government Controls* (Urbana: University Press of Illinois, 1952), 267; J. Walker, "The Censorship of the Press during the Reign of Charles II," *History* 35 (1950): 233–35; and Weber, *Paper Bullets*, 156.

16. The printer, William Carter, had been tried for treason in 1579 and acquitted. The next time, in 1584, he was not so lucky, and after being convicted at the Old Bailey, he was put to death. Siebert, *Freedom of the Press*, 90.

17. 25 Edw. 3 St. 5, c.2 (1352). On the early history of treason, the standard reference is John Bellamy, *The Tudor Law of Treason: An Introduction* (London: Routledge, 1979). For the specific relationship between treason law and the regulation of the press, see Roger B. Manning, "The Origins of the Doctrine of Sedition," *Albion* 12 (1980): 103–5; Philip Hamburger, "The Development of the Law of Seditious Libel and the Control of the Press," *Stanford Law Review* 37 (1985): 666–68; and Siebert, *Freedom of the Press*, 265–69.

18. 28 Henry 8, c.13 (1534).

19. Treason Acts, 14 May 1649 and 17 July 1649, reprinted in *Acts and Ordinances of the Interregnum, 1642–1660*, ed. C. H. Firth and R. S. Rait (London: Her Majesty's Stationery Office, 1911), 2:120–21; 193–94; 13 Car. 2, c.1 (1661).

20. In 1693, another printer, William Anderton, was brought up on treason charges for printing two Jacobite pamphlets. In his defense, Anderton argued that "bare printing" was not enough to constitute an overt act. He lost and was executed, based not on the 1661 statute but on the rationale that if writing was an overt act, as it had been determined to be in 1534, printing surely was as well. See Hamburger, "Seditious Libel," 717–18; and Siebert, *Freedom of the Press*, 267–68. Anderton's trial is reprinted in *State Trials* 12: cols. 1245–63.

21. One of the major pieces of evidence leveled against Twyn in the trial was his purported comment to L'Estrange on the night of 7 October that the *Treatise* contained "mettlesome stuff" (13 and passim). For the prosecution, this comment gave the lie to Twyn's claim that he had no idea what was contained in the book but had simply agreed to print it as a means of earning money, without regard to its content. The comment, the prosecution claimed, confirmed that he had read, absorbed, and passed critical judgment on the work.

22. Loewenstein, "Legal Proofs," 121.

23. For the composition of the jury, see the *Exact Narrative*, 9. Perhaps the court was also alarmed by Twyn's defense because the printer was being tried at the same sessions as Brewster, Dover, and Brookes. These other members of the trade were on trial for the common-law crime of seditious libel, for their part in the publication of other, Puritan-leaning pamphlets. Clearly, observers considered these cases to be in dialogue with each other, since the trial of Brewster, Dover, and Brookes was published, along with the Twyn trial, as a single narrative. In the case

of the seditious libelers, however, Hyde insisted that "printing alone is not enough, for if a man print a book to make a fire on, that's no offence, it is the *publishing* of it which is the Crime" (*Exact Narrative*, 70). The need to prove publication in this case was a result of the fact that seditious libel had its roots in the law of defamation, which had since the Middle Ages required the making public of the defamatory comments. See Hamburger, "Seditious Libel," for the most comprehensive account of the development of this offense, as well as John March, *Actions for Slander, Parts One and Two* (London: printed for Matthew Walbanck and Richard Bell, 1655); William Sheppard, *Actions upon the Case for Slander* (London: printed for Charles Adams, J. Starkey, and T. Baffet, 1662); R. H. Helmholz and Thomas A. Green, *Juries, Libel, and Justice: The Role of English Juries in Seventeenth- and Eighteenth-Century Trials for Libel and Slander* (Los Angeles: William Andrews Clark Memorial Library, 1984); and M. Lindsay Kaplan, *The Culture of Slander in Early Modern England* (Cambridge: Cambridge University Press, 1997).

24. The claim that L'Estrange was responsible for the *Exact Narrative* is made by Greaves, *Deliver Us from Evil*, 225. The claim seems plausible, given L'Estrange's intimate involvement with the cases detailed in the pamphlet, along with the style of the prefatory material and the postscript to the case, both of which seem unabashed in their desire to deliver public pronouncements about the proper measures to be taken for regulating the press. In addition, although certainly not proof in itself, the extraordinarily liberal use of italics in both the "Letter to the Reader" and the postscript is distinctly L'Estrangean.

25. In sentencing Twyn to death, Hyde offered his own uncanny version of a plea of trade when he stated, "I am heartily sorry that your carriages and grievous offences should draw me to give that Judgment upon you that I must. It is the Law pronounces it, God knows it is full sore against my inclination to do it" (33–34). In this odd echo of Twyn's own defense, Hyde claims also to be acting without intention (or "inclination"), solely out of a sense of duty to his profession. For a reprise of the plea of trade, see the 1680 trial of bookseller Benjamin Harris: *A Short but Just Account of the Tryal of Benjamin Harris* (London: n.p., 1679 [actually 1680]). Reprint, *State Trials* 7: cols. 925–32.

26. "For the *Authors*, nothing can be too severe" (L'Estrange, *Considerations*, 32).

27. *The Triall of Henry Carr, Gent.* (London: printed by I. G. for R[andal] Taylor, 1681), 7. Reprint, *State Trials* 7: cols. 1111–30. All references to Carr's trial proceedings in the text are taken from this pamphlet.

28. For the lapse and its immediate aftermath, see Hamburger, "Seditious Libel," 682–87; Schwoerer, *Henry Care*, 83–90; Siebert, *Freedom of the Press*, 295–301; and Sutherland, *Restoration Newspaper*, 186–90.

29. For information on Scroggs, and especially on his role during the Popish Plot crisis and its aftermath, see John Kenyon, *The Popish Plot* (London: Heinemann, 1972).

30. PRO PC 2/68, at 60 (28 May 1679). Quoted in Hamburger, "Seditious Libel," 684. In Hamburger (684 n. 69), the source is misprinted as PC 3/68, at 60, though the document in question is in the second set of Privy Council records. My account of what occurred between the king, the judges, and the Privy Council from May 1679 to May 1680 is indebted to Hamburger, "Seditious Libel," 684–87; and to Schwoerer, *Henry Care*, 90–111.

31. PRO PC 2/68, at 212 (24 September 1679). Quoted in Hamburger, "Seditious Libel," 684.

32. William Scroggs, *The Lord Chief Justice Scroggs his Speech in the Kings-Bench the first day of this present Michaelmas Term* (London: n.p., 1679). Reprint *State Trials* 7: cols. 701–8.

33. On the Wakeman trial, see Schwoerer, *Henry Care*, 76–103; and Kenyon, *Popish Plot*, 166–76, and passim.

34. PRO PC 2/68, at 236 (17 October 1679). Quoted in Hamburger, "Seditious Libel," 684–85.

35. PRO PC 2/68, at 256–57 (27 October 1679). Quoted in Hamburger, "Seditious Libel," 685.

36. *By the King, a Proclamation for the Suppressing of Seditious and Treasonable Books and Pamphlets* (London: printed by John Bill, Thomas Newcomb, and Henry Hills, 1679).

37. Hamburger, "Seditious Libel," 685. The request for a second decision can be found at PRO 2/68, at 369 (20 January 1680).

38. Schwoerer, *Henry Care*, 103.

39. PRO PC 2/68, at 496 (4 May 1680). At the end of the reading of the decision, Charles ordered the attorney general, Sir Creswell Levinz, to prepare a royal proclamation announcing the king's newly restored powers of licensing. The proclamation appeared 12 May 1680 under the title *A Proclamation for Suppressing the Printing and Publishing Unlicensed News-Books and Pamphlets of News* (London: n.p., 1680).

40. For the history of the *Weekly Pacquet*, see Schwoerer, *Henry Care*, 49–75.

41. *The Weekly Pacquet of Advice from Rome* 1.1 (3 December 1678).

42. One example of an anti-Scroggs pamphlet can be found in *Some Observations upon the Late Tryals of Sir George Wakeman* (London: printed for A. Brewster, 1679), in which Scroggs is ridiculed as Justice Clod-Pate. See also the *Weekly Pacquet* 2.4 (1 August 1679). Scroggs's initial prosecution of Carr is described in Schwoerer, *Henry Care*, 90–93.

43. The trials immediately preceding Carr's include those of Benjamin Harris, bookseller, *State Trials* 7: cols. 925–32; Francis Smith, bookseller, *State Trials* 7: cols. 931–60; and Jane Curtis [wife of Langley Curtis], publisher, *State Trials* 7: cols. 959–60. Contemporary pamphlet versions of these trials appear in *A Short, but Just Account of the Tryal of Benjamin Harris* (London: n.p., [1680]); and *An Impartial Account of the Trial of Francis Smith . . . As Also of the Tryal of Jane Curtis* (London: n.p., 1680).

44. *Triall of Henry Carr*, 2.

45. I have been unable to determine the identity of this printer, who is referred to only by his last name in the trial proceedings. It is possible that he was simply an apprentice or assistant to Langley Curtis, the primary printer of the work. What is clear is that this is not Robert Stevens, or Stephens, messenger of the press, also known as Robin Hog, who was active with L'Estrange in suppressing antigovernmental pamphlets in this period, including in the Benjamin Harris and Francis Smith trials. For Stevens, see Sutherland, *Restoration Newspaper*, 190–91; and Schwoerer, *Henry Care*, 248 n. 57.

46. Schwoerer, *Henry Care*, 125.

47. *Articles of High Misdemeanors . . . against William Scroggs, Knight* (London: n.p. 1680); *The Answer of Sir William Scroggs, Kt., Lord Chief Justice of the King's Bench, to the Articles of Dr. Titus Oates and Mr. William Bedloe* (London: n.p., 1680); Scroggs's impeachment proceedings in *State Trials* 8: cols. 163–223; and, for an overview, Lois Schwoerer, "The Attempted Impeachment of Sir William Scroggs, Lord Chief Justice of the Court of King's Bench, November 1680–March 1681," *Historical Journal* 38 (1995): 843–73.

48. *The Triall of Henry Carr, Gent. . . . Also the Tryal of Elizabeth Cellier, at the Kings-Bench Bar, July the 11th. 1680.* (London: printed by I. G. for R[andal] Taylor, 1681).

49. *The Triall of Elizabeth Cellier, at the Kings-Bench-Barr, On Friday June the 11th. 1680.* (London: printed for Randal Taylor, 1680). Reprint, *State Trials* 7: cols. 1043–68. In what follows, I will refer to this as the *Triall of Elizabeth Cellier* [for treason], in order to avoid any confusion with the later case surrounding *Malice Defeated.*

50. *The Tryal and Sentence of Elizabeth Cellier; for Writing, Printing, and Publishing, a Scandalous Libel, Called* Malice Defeated (London: printed for Thomas Collins, 1680), 16. Rpt. *State Trials* 7: cols. 1183–1218. For the purposes of clarity, I will refer to this in what follows as *Tryal of Elizabeth Cellier* [for *MD*].

51. For the Popish and other plots in this period, see Kenyon, *Popish Plot*; John Miller, *Popery and Politics in England, 1660–88* (Cambridge: Cambridge University Press, 1973), 154–88; and Mark Knights, *Politics and Opinion in Crisis, 1678–1681* (Cambridge: Cambridge University Press, 1994). An exploration of the changing historiographic conventions surrounding the plot can be found in Jonathan Scott, "England's Troubles: Exhuming the Popish Plot," in *The Politics of Religion in Restoration England*, ed. Tim Harris, Paul Seaward, and Mark Goldie (Oxford: Basil Blackwell, 1990), 107–31.

52. One obviously partial account of these events can be found in *Malice Defeated*, the tract for which she was later imprisoned, tried, and pilloried. [Elizabeth Cellier], *Malice Defeated; or, A Brief Relation of the Accusation and Deliverance of Elizabeth Cellier* (London: printed for Elizabeth Cellier, 1680). The pamphlet has been reprinted, with an introduction offering some background on Cellier's life and legal troubles, in Elizabeth Cellier, Malice Defeated *and* The Matchless Rogue, *1680*, with an introduction by Anne Barbeau Gardiner (Los Angeles: William Andrews Clark Memorial Library, 1988; Augustan Reprint Society, nos. 249–50). Other overviews of the events of the Meal Tub Plot and Cellier's legal proceedings can be found in two chapters: Frances E. Dolan, "'The Wretched Subject the Whole Town Talks of': Representing Elizabeth Cellier (London, 1680)," in *Catholicism and Anti-Catholicism in Early Modern English Texts*, ed. Arthur F. Marotti (London: Macmillan, 1999), 218–58; and Rachel Weil, "'If I Did Say So, I Lyed': Elizabeth Cellier and the Construction of Credibility in the Popish Plot Crisis," in *Political Culture and Cultural Politics in Early Modern England*, ed. Susan D. Asmussen and Mark A. Kishlansky (Manchester: Manchester University Press, 1995), 189–209. A brief but influential summary of Cellier's biography appears in Antonia Fraser, *The Weaker Vessel: Woman's Lot in Seventeenth-Century England* (London: Weidenfeld and Nicolson, 1984), 454–62. Fraser concludes her widely read book by arguing that we may find the wily, scrappy, resourceful Cellier a "more engaging" and "more admirable" representative of seventeenth-century womanhood than the "submissive" and

aristocratic female figures who have historically received more attention than such middling women (470).

53. All three images in this chapter are taken from *The Popish Damnable Plot against Our Religion and Liberties, Lively Delineated in Several of its Branches* (London: printed for Richard Baldwin, 1681). While it is possible to identify many of the key figures in the illustrations by referring to the "Explanation" that accompanies the broadside, I am conjecturing that the image in figure 1 represents Cellier with Dangerfield. The explanation reads, "VI. In the Sixth, the Manner of Mrs. *Cellier's* (one of the Pope's *Amazons*) going to do that Great Work her *self* (Mr. *Dangerfield* having fail'd in the Attempt) and of her turning down Stairs." Whether she is pictured going down the stairs of the prison where she visited Dangerfield, or into the cellar where the Meal Tub was found, remains unclear.

54. For another version of the same events, see [Thomas Dangerfield], *Thomas Dangerfield's Answer to a Certain Scandalous Lying Pamphlet entituled* Malice Defeated (London: printed for the Author, 1680), in which Dangerfield gives his own, equally partial history of the Meal Tub debacle.

55. Dolan, "'Wretched Subject,'" 220.

56. *Triall of Elizabeth Cellier* [for treason], 4.

57. In *Malice Defeated,* Cellier reports that she applied for bail to the justices of the court of King's Bench after her original arrest on treason charges but was refused on the grounds that those accused of treason could not be bailed. She claims to have replied, not a little pedantically, that she "had as yet no Accuser; *And by the Law, no person ought to be committed for Treason, till accused by two honest, sufficient, lawful, and credible Witnesses, witnessing one and the same Individual Fact*" (18). Her knowledge of the law, it turns out, was absolutely correct, according to Bellamy, *Tudor Law of Treason,* 152–62.

58. *Triall of Elizabeth Cellier* [for treason], 16.

59. [Dangerfield], *Thomas Dangerfield's Answer,* 5.

60. *Triall of Elizabeth Cellier* [for treason], 14.

61. *Triall of Elizabeth Cellier* [for treason], 16–17. Cellier's success in disqualifying Dangerfield as a witness is only one in a number of examples of her legal acumen. As she notes in *Malice Defeated,* when she was brought before a committee of lords in January of 1680, as the Meal Tub Plot was beginning to unfold, she refused to answer their questions, on the grounds that she should be tried not by a jury of peers but by a jury of her peers. She petitioned the king himself in January and February to be released from Newgate, insisting that her French husband and her children were facing dire financial and legal difficulties from which they could not extricate themselves without her aid (*Malice Defeated,* 30–31). According to her own "Abstract" of her treason trial, printed as part of *Malice Defeated,* she demanded to know whether she was "Indicted at Common Law, or upon any Statute, and what Statute" (33). Finally, she asked that all Dissenters be prevented from sitting on her jury, because "it is they *against whom the fact* is said to be *committed*" (31). If even some of these anecdotes are true—and competing accounts bear them out—Cellier clearly knew the law better than most men of her era not trained in that discipline, and perhaps as well as some that were.

62. *Triall of Elizabeth Cellier* [for treason], 17.

63. *To the Praise of Mrs. Cellier the Popish Midwife: On her Incomparable Book* (London: printed for Walter Davis, 1680).

64. The speed at which she composed the pamphlet is attested by the fact that at the close of the "Abstract" portion of *Malice Defeated*, the following words appear: "Finished, Fryday, July the 2d. By *Elizabeth Cellier*" (42). Thus, although the work was not brought out until late August, she seems to have composed the bulk of *Malice Defeated* in the three weeks following her trial.

65. [Elizabeth Cellier], *The Matchless Rogue; or, A Brief Account of the Life of Don Thomazo the Unfortunate Son, Together with . . . Some Reflections on Madam Cellier's Case* (London: printed for Elizabeth Cellier, 1680), 6.

66. [Cellier], *Malice Defeated*, 43–44. The actual date of the raid on William Downing's shop is unclear: Cellier claims in her postscript to *Malice Defeated* that it took place Monday, 16 August (43). The postscript itself is dated 12 August. However, Downing claimed in the trial that Cellier did not even contact him to print the work until "about the 22d of *August*" (*Tryal of Elizabeth Cellier* [for *MD*], 18).

67. It is probable that the second printer of *Malice Defeated* was Nathaniel Thompson, Royalist and Catholic sympathizer. His name is associated with Cellier's on the basis of a broadside, *A True Copy of a Letter of Consolation Sent to Nat the Printer* (London: printed for W. Johnson, 1681). The broadside, which ridicules Thompson's Romish predilections, is primarily composed of a letter "signed" by Cellier, offering Thompson sympathy in his own legal troubles. Thompson was himself ultimately arrested in 1682 for violating the judges' third opinion concerning the licensing of news. See *State Trials* 8: cols. 1359–98.

68. Gardiner, introduction to *Malice Defeated*, viii. Fraser, in *The Weaker Vessel*, states that Cellier was tried, "this time for libel" (459); Weil, "'If I did say so,'" speaks of her "conviction for libel" (202); and Dolan, "'Wretched Subject,'" leaves her "tried and convicted for libel" (221).

69. Hamburger, "Seditious Libel," 689.

70. There are two printed versions of the *Malice Defeated* trial, the first of which, *The Tryal and Sentence of Elizabeth Cellier*, is the official one. A note at the beginning of the text, dated 13 September, the day Cellier was sentenced, reads, "I Do appoint *Thomas Collins* Stationer to Print the Tryal of Mrs. *Cellier* at the Sessions, and that no other do presume to Print the same. Robert Clayton Mayor." All references to this *Malice Defeated* trial in the text refer to this version. The other account, comical and irreverent, is titled *The Tryal of Elizabeth Cellier, the Popish Midwife: At the Old Baily Septemb. 11. 1680.* (London: printed by A. Godbid for L. C., 1680).

71. The indictment charges Cellier with "falsly and maliciously endeavouring and intending our Soveraign Lord King Charles the Second that now is, and the Government of this Kingdom of *England*; as also the true Protestant Religion within this Kingdom of *England* by Law Established to bring to hatred and contempt; And also to bring Scandal and Infamy upon divers Persons produced as Witnesses" in her treason trial (10). Her crimes thus encompassed libel of private persons, *Scandalum Magnatum*, and seditious libel. For the distinctions among these, see Hamburger, "Seditious Libel."

72. To take just one example, *The Tryal of . . . the Popish Midwife* is seemingly obsessed with Cellier's impudence: she is called "this prodigy of impudence" (1),

scorned for her "lying Impudence" (2), and said to have acted "with an Impudence peculiar to her self and her *Cause*" (2).

73. *Tryal of . . . the Popish Midwife*, 1. Another pamphlet speaks of "the contrivers of *Celliers* Libel" (*Mr. Prance's Answer to Mrs. Cellier's Libel . . . to Which is Added the Adventure of the Bloody Bladder* [London: printed for L. Curtis, 1680], 13). In *The Matchless Rogue*, Cellier interestingly throws back the charge of hiring ghostwriters on Dangerfield himself: when reading Dangerfield's *Answer* to *Malice Defeated*, Cellier writes, she found "so much wit and ingenuity" in the text that "sometimes I was apt to think its Author's Name must be *Legion*" (5).

74. For the notion of literary paternity, see Sandra Gilbert, "Literary Paternity," in *Contemporary Literary Criticism: Modernism through Poststructuralism*, ed. Robert Con Davis (New York: Longman, 1986), 188–200.

75. *Tryal of . . . the Popish Midwife*, 1.

76. Cellier's tribulations on the pillory are described in *Mistriss Celiers Lamentation for the Loss of Her Liberty* (London: printed for S. F., 1681); and in *The Adventure of the Bloody Bladder*, the tract appended to *Mr. Prance's Answer*. A series of anti-Catholic engravings published in 1681 included the famous image of Cellier on the pillory with her shield reproduced in this chapter and on the cover; see *The Popish Damnable Plot*. Finally, a series of playing cards was produced associated with the Meal Tub Plot and the Popish Plot; reproductions of the sketches used to prepare these cards—include a number that feature Cellier—can be found in Virginia and Harold Wayland, *Francis Barlow's Sketches for the Meal Tub Plot Playing Cards* (Pasadena, Calif.: H. & V. Wayland, 1971). As the Waylands note, the Popish Plot cards were all published by Randal Taylor, publisher of the proceedings of Carr's trial and of both of Cellier's trials.

77. My account of Cellier's strategies as an author here closely parallels—and is indebted to—the account of female authorship given by Catherine Gallagher in *Nobody's Story: The Vanishing Acts of Women Writers in the Marketplace, 1670–1820* (Berkeley and Los Angeles: University of California Press, 1994).

Chapter 3. Daniel Defoe, the Act of Anne, and the Obligations of Ownership

1. Daniel Defoe, *A Vindication of the Press* (London: printed for T. Warner, 1718), 36.

2. How's edition appeared under the title *A Collection of the Writings of the Author of the True-Born English-Man* (London: n.p., 1703).

3. Alexander Pope, preface to *The Works of Mr. Alexander Pope* (London: printed by W. Bowyer for Jacob Tonson and Bernard Lintot, 1717), A2v.

4. Daniel Defoe, *An Essay on the Regulation of the Press* (London: n.p., 1704), 3.

5. Mark Rose, *Authors and Owners: The Invention of Copyright* (Cambridge: Harvard University Press, 1993), 35. John Feather argues more forcefully that "Defoe's ideas [in the *Essay*] were implanted in the minds of some moderate Tories," but he also makes the somewhat shaky claim that Defoe's ideas on the topic were influenced by the Tory speaker of the house, Robert Harley. If anything, the events

detailed in this chapter suggest that the line of influence moved in the opposite direction (Feather, *Publishing, Piracy, and Politics: An Historical Study of Copyright in Britain* [London: Mansell, 1994], 56).

6. For a similar, though more cautious, understanding of the consequences of the act for the relationship between copyright and censorship, see Joseph Loewenstein, *The Author's Due: Printing and the Prehistory of Copyright* (Chicago: University of Chicago Press, 2002), 53.

7. Paula Backscheider, "No Defense: Defoe in 1703," *PMLA* 103 (1988): 274–84, 274.

8. John Robert Moore, "Defoe in the Pillory," in *Defoe in the Pillory and Other Studies* (Bloomington: Indiana University Publications, 1939), 3–32, 3.

9. The most influential early account on which later critics have drawn, and the one to identify many of the key documents in the case, is Moore, "Defoe in the Pillory." Moore later revisited the topic in *Daniel Defoe: Citizen of the Modern World* (Chicago: University of Chicago Press, 1958), 107–42. Backscheider supplements and elaborates on the details given in "No Defense" in her biographical study, *Daniel Defoe: His Life* (Baltimore: Johns Hopkins University Press, 1989), 95–135. In the tradition of Defoe biographers, it seems, Maximillian E. Novak has also written on Defoe's experiences in the pillory on at least two occasions, in "Defoe's *Shortest Way with the Dissenters*: Hoax, Parody, Paradox, Fiction, Irony, and Satire," *Modern Language Quarterly* 27 (1966): 402–17; and, more recently, in *Daniel Defoe, Master of Fictions: His Life and Ideas* (Oxford: Oxford University Press, 2001), 173–94. Works from which I have garnered additional details include F. Bastian, *Defoe's Early Life* (London: Macmillan Press, 1981), 275–301; James Sutherland, *Daniel Defoe: A Critical Study* (Cambridge: Harvard University Press, 1971), 43–48; J. A. Downie, "Defoe's *Shortest Way with the Dissenters*: Irony, Intention, and Reader-Response," *Prose Studies* 9.2 (1986): 120–39 (a response to Novak's 1966 piece); and Miriam Lerenbaum, "'An Irony Not Unusual': Defoe's *Shortest Way with the Dissenters*," *Huntington Library Quarterly* 37 (1974): 227–50.

10. Daniel Defoe, *An Enquiry into the Occasional Conformity of Dissenters, in Cases of Preferment, with a Preface to the Lord Mayor, Occasioned by His Carrying the Sword to a Conventicle* (London: n.p., 1697 [for 1698]). Quotations in the text are taken from the Dublin edition, published, presumably illicitly, the following year: *An Enquiry into the Occasional Conformity of Dissenters, in Cases of Preferment* (Dublin: printed by J. B. and S. P. for Jacob Milner, 1698).

11. *The Shortest Way with the Dissenters; or, Proposals for the Establishment of the Church* (London: n.p., 1702). This satirical tract was not Defoe's only response to the Occasional Conformity Bill. Even before he published this work, he had prepared *An Enquiry into Occasional Conformity, Shewing that the Dissenters are No Way Concern'd in It* (London: n.p., 1702). For the publication histories of these works, see P. N. Furbank and W. R. Owens, *A Critical Bibliography of Daniel Defoe* (London: Pickering and Chatto, 1998), 35–39. As to the date of publication of *The Shortest Way*, Defoe seems to have had the work ready for sale in early December, and the date of publication has traditionally been given as 1 December. Bastian points out, however, that the court records note that the work was for sale only on 22 December (*Defoe's Early Life*, 278). Furbank and Owens give the date as "the first half of December, 1702" (37).

12. Henry Sacheverell, *The Political Union: A Discourse Showing the Dependence of Government on Religion in General, and of the English Monarchy on the Church of England in Particular* (Oxford: printed by Leonard Lichfield for George West and Henry Clements, 1702), 61. Quoted in Backscheider, "No Defense," 275.

13. Quotations in the text are taken from the 1703 edition, *The Shortest Way with the Dissenters: [Taken from Dr. Sach—ll's Sermon, and Others]; or, Proposals for the Establishment of the Church, by the Author of the True-Born English-Man* (London: n.p., [1703]), 13.

14. The list is taken from the title of Novak, "Defoe's *Shortest Way*."

15. Ian Watt, *The Rise of the Novel: Studies in Defoe, Fielding, and Richardson* (Berkeley and Los Angeles: University of California Press, 1959), 126.

16. Sutherland, *Daniel Defoe*, 11.

17. Daniel Defoe, *The Present State of the Parties in Great Britain* (London: printed by J. Baker, 1712), 24. Quoted in Novak, *Daniel Defoe*, 173.

18. George Harris Healey, ed. *The Letters of Daniel Defoe* (Oxford: Clarendon Press, 1955), 5 n. 3. The letter itself can be found in the British Museum, Add. Mss. 29, 589 f. 400. The Healey volume is cited in the text as *Defoe Letters*.

19. For a detailed description of the role the secretaries came to play in press regulation after 1695, see Laurence Hanson, *Government and the Press, 1695–1763* (1936; reprint, Oxford: Clarendon Press, 1967), 36–46.

20. *By the King and Queen, A Proclamation, for the Better Discovery of Seditious Libellers* (London: printed by Charles Bill, 1691 [for 1692]); *By the Queen, A Proclamation for Restraining the Spreading False News, and Printing and Publishing of Irreligious and Seditious Papers and Libels* (London: printed by Charles Bill, 1702). Unusually, a scathing response to the 1692 proclamation was printed and distributed, which complained that "the last Resort [of weak rulers] is to Gag the Mouth, Tye up the Hand, Imprison the Body, to prevent and hinder all going forth of such True and right Words" (*Animadversions upon That Proclamation of September 13, 1692, Entituled, for the Better Discovery of Seditious Libellers* [n.p., 1692], 1).

21. Backscheider, *Daniel Defoe*, 102.

22. Most of the text of the indictment is reprinted in Backscheider, *Daniel Defoe*, 104. The original is in the City of London Record Office, CLRO SF 472.

23. Novak, *Daniel Defoe*, 180.

24. Moore, "Defoe in the Pillory," 6.

25. According to Moore, there was an account of the trial, or rather, of the sentencing hearing, which included speeches made by judges, lawyers, and members of the government, as they sought to have Defoe punished as harshly as possible. The account, which was destroyed in the Second World War, was titled *The Proceedings on the Queen's Commission of the Law . . . Held . . . in the Old Bailey . . . 7th, 8th, 9th of July 1703* (*Daniel Defoe*, 130).

26. *A Brief Explanation of a Late Pamphlet, Entitul'd,* The Shortest Way with the Dissenters was appended to the 1703 edition of *The Shortest Way with the Dissenters* (publication details supra).

27. Backscheider, *Daniel Defoe*, 110; Moore, "Defoe in the Pillory," 5.

28. *Poetry and Prose of Alexander Pope*, ed. Aubrey Williams (Boston: Houghton Mifflin, 1969).

29. Michel Foucault, "What Is an Author?," in Josué V. Harari, ed., *Textual Strategies: Perspectives in Post-Structuralist Criticism* (Ithaca, N.Y.: Cornell University Press, 1979), 141.

30. I discuss the use of the pillory and the problem of the sympathetic crowd in more detail in "Public Secrets: Sodomy and the Pillory in the Eighteenth Century, and Beyond," *The Eighteenth Century: Theory and Interpretation* 44.2–3 (summer–fall 2003): 203–32.

31. Moore, "Defoe in the Pillory," 5–6.

32. Daniel Defoe, *A Hymn to the Pillory* (London: n.p., 1703).

33. Charles Leslie, *The Wolf Stript of his Shepard's Clothing*, 3rd ed. (London: n.p., 1704), 59. Quoted in Novak, *Daniel Defoe*, 191.

34. Moore, "Defoe in the Pillory," 6.

35. The most extensive treatment of the publication of this volume can be found in Moore, "Defoe's First Collected Works," in *Defoe in the Pillory*, 51–67. While full of fascinating bibliographical and biographical details, Moore's piece makes the ultimately unconvincing contention that Defoe knew about and sanctioned How's *Collection*, a claim that is poorly substantiated and that is properly rejected by all later critics. For further details, see Furbank and Owens, *Critical Bibliography*, 3–6; Bastian, *Defoe's Early Life*, 291; Novak, *Daniel Defoe*, 199–200; and Backscheider, *Daniel Defoe*, 127–28.

36. *A True Collection of the Writings of the Author of the True Born English-Man* (London: n.p., 1703).

37. Defoe, *The Little Review* (20 June 1705), printed at the end of volume 2 of the *Review*, 18. All quotations from Defoe's *Review* and *Little Review* are taken from the facsimile edition, *Defoe's* Review, edited by Arthur Wellesley Secord (New York: Columbia University Press, 1948). Citations are by date, volume number, and page.

38. Feather, *Publishing, Piracy, and Politics*, 56.

39. Loewenstein, *Author's Due*, 214–15.

40. Raymond Astbury, "The Renewal of the Licensing Act in 1693 and Its Lapse in 1695," *Library*, 5th series, 33 (1978): 291–322, 301. It is important to note that there is another John Howe who figures in Defoe's biography in these years, who should not be confused with the piratical printer. This Howe was a Presbyterian minister with whom Defoe sparred in print in 1701 on the topic of occasional conformity. Howe, like other prominent Dissenters, questioned Defoe's uncompromising stance on the practice and wrote an essay titled *Some Consideration of a Preface to an Enquiry, Concerning the Ocassional Conformity of Dissenters* (London: printed for Thomas Parkhurst, 1701). Defoe responded with *A Letter to Mr. How* (London: n.p., 1701), a work addressed, alas, not to the printer but to the priest. I am grateful to Maximillian Novak for clearing up my confusion on this point.

41. Just months before passage of the Act of Anne, in November 1709, How was still harping on the topic he had proposed to address in Parliament, this time in print, in a tract called *Some Thoughts on the Present State of Printing and Bookselling.* He argues in that work "that when-ever Parliament shall think fit to secure *Property* in *Books* by a Law, then, and not 'till then, will every Man of that Trade be upon an equal Footing." (John How, *Some Thoughts on the Present State of Printing and Bookselling* [London: n.p. n.d., but presumably 1709], 3). The statute, How believes, should

require registration of all copies in order to provide legal recourse in the event of infringement. Despite their differences, then, How and Defoe have at least two things in common: each believes that a new statute is required in order to guarantee the protection of property, and each believes that universal registration is the key to securing copyright.

42. Hanson, *Government and the Press*, 36.

43. By far the most comprehensive treatment of the events of 1693 to 1695 is Astbury, "Renewal of the Licensing Act."

44. Lord [Peter] King, *The Life and Letters of John Locke* (London: George Bell, 1884; reprint, New York: Garland Publishing, 1984), 202.

45. Quoted in King, *Life and Letters of John Locke*, 203.

46. Roger L'Estrange, *Considerations and Proposals in Order to the Regulation of the Press* (London: printed by A. C., 1663), 2. The resemblance is also remarked by Loewenstein, *Author's Due*, 209.

47. John Milton, *Areopagitica* (1644), in *John Milton: Complete Poems and Major Prose*, ed. Merritt Y. Hughes (New York: Macmillan, 1985), 749.

48. Rose, *Authors and Owners*, 38.

49. Astbury, "Renewal of the Licensing Act," 311. A copy of the bill appears in the Locke archives examined by Astbury, *Locke MSS.*, b.4, f.77.

50. For an overview of these measures, see Fredrick Seaton Siebert, *Freedom of the Press in England, 1476–1776: The Rise and Decline of Government Controls* (Urbana: University of Illinois Press, 1952), 260–304; Harry Ransom, *The First Copyright Statute: An Essay on* An Act for the Encouragement of Learning, *1710* (Austin: University of Texas Press, 1956), 76–93; Lyman Ray Patterson, *Copyright in Historical Perspective* (Nashville: Vanderbilt University Press, 1968), 114–42; Feather, *Publishing, Piracy, and Politics*, 51–63; and Hanson, *Government and the Press*, 8–10.

51. *The Manuscripts of the House of Lords* (London: Her Majesty's Stationery Office, 1965), 3:271–76, 274.

52. Loewenstein, *Author's Due*, 231.

53. [Matthew Tindal], *Reasons against Restraining the Press* (London: n.p., 1704); Hanson, *Government and the Press*, 8.

54. Rose, *Authors and Owners*, 34–40; Loewenstein, *The Author's Due*, 214–16, 229–31; Feather, *Publishing, Piracy, and Politics*, 52–55.

55. *To the Honourable the C—s of England Assembled in P—t: The Humble Petition and Representation of the True Loyal and Always Obedient Church of England, Relating to the Bill for Restraining the Press* [London: n.p., 1704]. The only copy, according to Furbank and Owens, is in Robert Harley's papers in the British Museum, Add. MS 70267 (*Critical Bibliography*, 50–51). The work is reprinted in full, along with a thoroughly convincing case for Defoe's authorship, in J. A. Downie, "An Unknown Defoe Broadsheet on the Regulation of the Press?," *Library*, 5th series, 33 (1978): 51–58. All page references to the broadsheet refer to the Downie article.

56. Feather, *Publishing, Piracy, and Politics*, 56–57. For the petition, see *Journal of the House of Commons*, 15:313–16.

57. For the sequence of bills and amendments that led to the final passage of the act, and for the act itself, see Ransom, *First Copyright Statute*, 94–117 (including the text of the act), and Patterson, *Copyright in Historical Perspective*, 143–50.

58. 8 Anne c. 21 (1709/10), reprinted in *Statutes of the Realm* (London: printed by command of King George III, 1822), 9:256–58.

59. The consequences of "vesting" authorial property rights rather than "securing" them constitute the main topic of Rose, *Authors and Owners*, 67–112.

60. Rose, *Authors and Owners*, 48; Siebert, *Freedom of the Press*, 249; Patterson, *Copyright in Historical Perspective*, 141.

61. Feather, *Publishing, Piracy, and Politics*, 62.

62. Patterson, *Copyright in Historical Perspective*, 145. A similar point is made in Augustine Birrell, *Seven Lectures on the Law and History of Copyright in Books* (London: Cassell, 1899), 95.

63. Ransom notes that few proprietors took advantage of the invitation to enter new works in the register, which "reveals a meager result for registration" in the years after 1710 (*First Copyright Statute*, 101).

64. Siebert, *Freedom of the Press*, 306–18. See also Hanson, *Government and the Press*, 10–14.

65. Quoted in Siebert, *Freedom of the Press*, 309.

66. John Asgill, *An Essay for the Press* (London: printed for A. Baldwin, 1712), 7.

67. *Arguments Relating to a Restraint upon the Press, Fully and Fairly Handled in a Letter to a Bencher from a Young Gentleman of the Temple, with Proposals Humbly Offer'd to the Considerations of Both Houses of Parliament* (London: printed for R. and J. Bonwicke, 1712), 27.

68. [Joseph Addison], *The Thoughts of a Tory Author, Concerning the Press* (London: printed for A. Baldwin, 1712). Note that this work was published by the same printer as Asgill's pamphlet, which made the diametrically opposed argument.

69. In *The Author's Due*, Loewenstein points out that Swift, too, spoke out in his *Tale of a Tub* (1708) against what Loewenstein calls the "climate of compulsory authorship" (229).

70. *The Printers Case with Their Proposals for Regulating the Press* [London, 1711?]. The suggestion of the date in the *Short Title Catalogue* presumably arises from its coincidence with numerous other tracts addressing the topic of the author's name.

71. The phrase was coined in 1951 in J. W. Saunders, "The Stigma of Print: A Note on the Social Bases of Tudor Poetry," *Essays in Criticism* 1 (1951): 139–64.

72. *Burnet v. Chetwood*, in *English Reports* (Edinburgh: William Green and Sons, 1904), 35:1008–10. Page references in the text are to this version. The case is discussed in Rose, *Authors and Owners*, 49–51; and in Benjamin Kaplan, *An Unhurried View of Copyright* (New York: Columbia University Press, 1967), 9–10.

73. Kaplan, *Unhurried View of Copyright*, 9–10.

Chapter 4. Revenge of the Straw Woman

1. For the text of the letter, see *The Correspondence of Jonathan Swift*, ed. Harold Williams (Oxford: Clarendon Press, 1963–65), 3:338. Hereafter cited in the text as "*Swift Letters.*" The best accounts of the publication of *The Dunciad* can be found

in R. H. Griffith, "*The Dunciad* of 1728," *Modern Philology* 13 (1915): 1–18; James Sutherland, "*The Dunciad* of 1729," *Modern Language Review* 31 (1936): 347–53; and David Foxon, *Pope and the Early Eighteenth-Century Book Trade*, rev. and ed. James McLaverty (Oxford: Clarendon Press, 1991), 102–16, 242. The most complete account of the publication and piracy of *Polly* can be found in another James Sutherland essay, "*Polly* among the Pirates," *Modern Language Review* 42 (1942): 291–303.

2. Catherine Gallagher, *Nobody's Story: The Vanishing Acts of Women Writers in the Marketplace, 1670–1820* (Berkeley and Los Angeles: University of California Press, 1994), xx.

3. This is Michel Foucault's foundational insight in "What Is an Author?," in *Textual Strategies: Perspectives in Post-Structuralist Criticism*, ed. Josué V. Harari (Ithaca, N.Y.: Cornell University Press, 1979), 141–60. The most comprehensive recent treatment of the relationship between property, authorship, and punishment is Susan Stewart's *Crimes of Writing: Problems in the Containment of Representation* (Durham, N.C.: Duke University Press, 1994), 3–30 and passim.

4. Gay to Swift, 2 December 1728, in *The Letters of John Gay*, ed. C. F. Burgess (Oxford: Clarendon Press, 1966), 78. This volume will hereafter be cited as *Gay Letters.*

5. The first-edition title page reads, "Polly: An Opera, being the Second Part of the Beggar's Opera. Written by Mr. Gay. London: Printed for the Author, [1729]."

6. For the concept of appropriation and its relationship to proprietary authorship, see especially, Rosemary J. Coombe, *The Cultural Life of Intellectual Properties: Authorship, Appropriation, and the Law* (Durham, N.C.: Duke University Press, 1998).

7. I borrow the notion of the "front" from Jacques Derrida's essay, "Limited Inc a b c . . . ," in *Limited Inc*, trans. Sam Weber (Evanston, Ill.: Northwestern University Press, 1988), 37.

8. Alexander Pope, *The Dunciad* ([Dublin, Printed] London: reprinted for Anne Dodd, 1728).

9. Alexander Pope, *The Works of Mr. Alexander Pope* (London: printed by W. Bowyer for Jacob Tonson and Bernard Lintot, 1717), A2v.

10. David Saunders and Ian Hunter, "Lessons from the 'Literatory': How to Historicise Authorship," *Critical Inquiry* 17 (1991): 485. See also Saunders, *Authorship and Copyright* (London: Routledge, 1992), for a fuller elaboration of the argument.

11. Stewart, *Crimes of Writing*, 12.

12. R. H. Griffith, *Alexander Pope: A Bibliography* (Austin: University of Texas Press, 1927), 2:xlvii.

13. Arthur S. Collins, *Authorship in the Days of Johnson* (London: Robert Holden, 1927), 123.

14. Laura Brown, *Alexander Pope* (Oxford: Blackwell, 1985), 130; Foxon, *Pope and the Book Trade*, 102–52; Maynard Mack, *Alexander Pope: A Life* (New York: Norton, 1985), 298, 270.

15. For a recent treatment of Pope's "independence" and the question of dependence more generally, see Dustin Griffin, *Literary Patronage in England, 1650–1800* (Cambridge: Cambridge University Press, 1996).

16. James Winn, "On Pope, Printers, and Publishers," *Eighteenth-Century Life* 6 (1981): 94; for more-extended discussions of early eighteenth-century patronage, see Bertrand A. Goldgar, *Walpole and the Wits: The Relation of Politics to Literature,*

1722–1742 (Lincoln: University of Nebraska Press, 1976); and Collins, *Authorship*, 114–212.

17. Ian Watt, "Publishers and Sinners: The Augustan View," *Studies in Bibliography* 12 (1959): 19.

18. Foxon, *Pope and the Book Trade*, 39. I have drawn extensively on Foxon's account of Pope's use of subscription publishing (51–63).

19. Foxon prints a list of the thirty-five patrons, almost all titled, who subscribed for five or more copies of the *Odyssey* (*Pope and the Book Trade*, 100).

20. *The Correspondence of Alexander Pope*, ed. George Sherburn (Oxford: Clarendon Press, 1956), 2:160 n. Hereafter cited as *Pope Letters*.

21. Pope, "Epistle to Dr. Arbuthnot," in *Poetry and Prose of Alexander Pope*, ed. Aubrey Williams (Boston: Houghton Mifflin, 1969), 197–211.

22. Pope, *Poetry and Prose of Alexander Pope*, 206 n.

23. William Empson, "*The Beggar's Opera*: Mock-Pastoral As the Cult of Independence," in *Some Versions of Pastoral* (New York: New Directions, 1974), 204–5. As his title suggests, Empson reads *The Beggar's Opera* as a defense of just that brand of independence that Gay himself never succeeded in attaining.

24. David Nokes, *John Gay: A Profession of Friendship* (Oxford: Oxford University Press, 1995), 449.

25. William Henry Irving, *John Gay: Favorite of the Wits* (Durham, N.C.: Duke University Press, 1940), 316. For another, even more extended comparison between the two men, see Mack, *Alexander Pope*, 187–88.

26. Nokes, *John Gay*, 449.

27. James Sutherland, "John Gay," in *Eighteenth-Century English Literature: Modern Essays in Criticism*, ed. James L. Clifford (New York: Oxford University Press, 1959), 133.

28. Watt, "Publishers and Sinners," 20; Nokes, *John Gay*, 457.

29. See Gallagher's first chapter, "The Prostitute and the Playwright in the Works of Aphra Behn," in *Nobody's Story*, 1–48, for a discussion of the image of the female author as prostitute.

30. Swift did not direct his musings on Gay's financial management only to Pope: in a letter of 28 March 1728, he advises Gay himself to "prepare against age and dulness and Sickness and coldness or death of friends. A whore has a ressource left that She can turn Bawd: but an old decayd Poet is a creature abandond and at mercy when he can find none" (Swift, *Letters*, 3:277). Was Swift's suggestion that Gay should act more like a whore and less like a poet?

31. "The Female Faction; or, The Gay Subscribers" (London: printed for J. Roberts, 1729).

32. Watt, "Publishers and Sinners," 19; Collins, *Authorship*, 129; Foxon, *Pope and the Book Trade*, 111.

33. John Robert Moore, *Defoe in the Pillory and Other Studies* (Bloomington: Indiana University Publications, 1939), 31.

34. Collins, *Authorship*, 129–30.

35. For an account of Gay's earnings from *The Beggar's Opera*, see Nokes, *John Gay*, 420–23.

36. Sutherland, "*The Dunciad* of 1729," 348.

37. Griffith quotes an anonymous letter from the *Daily Journal* of 11 May, attributed to John Dennis, which warns that "this *Animalculum* of an Author," Pope, is "at this very Juncture, writing the *Progress of Dulness*." See Griffith, "*The Dunciad* of 1728," 5–6.

38. Mack, *Alexander Pope*, 490.

39. *A Popp upon Pope; or A True and Faithful Account of a Late Horrid and Barbarous Whipping, Committed on the Body of A. Pope, a Poet* (London: printed for A. Moore, 1728). Quoted in Mack, *Alexander Pope*, 490. I am grateful to Jennifer Snead for pointing out to me that Bounce, Pope's great dane, was a bitch, providing yet another example of a female intermediary standing between Pope and his adversaries in literary warfare.

40. *Daily Post*, 18 May 1728. Quoted in Griffith, "*The Dunciad* of 1728," 6.

41. "Notes on Editions of 'The Dunciad,'" *Notes and Queries*, no. 270 (1854): 519.

42. Foxon, *Pope and the Book Trade*, 109.

43. Richard Savage, *A Collection of Pieces in Verse and Prose, Which Have Been Publish'd on Occasion of* The Dunciad, *by Mr. Savage* (London: printed for L. Gilliver, 1732), vi.

44. For a description of the "rough-and-tumble world" of the Restoration, and the consequent need for new forms of literary patronage, see Griffin, *Literary Patronage*, 21ff.

45. David Foxon, ed., *A Register of Books, 1728–1732, Extracted from* The Monthly Chronicle (London: Gregg—Archive, 1964).

46. Griffin defines patronage as "a systematic economic arrangement, a complex exchange of benefit to both patron and client" (*Literary Patronage*, 12). Griffin, like other commentators on the history of patronage, is here drawing on the anthropological literature on gift giving as a means of understanding the complexity of patron-client relations. See, for instance, Marcel Mauss, *The Gift: The Form and Reason for Exchange in Archaic Societies*, trans. W. D. Halls (New York: Norton, 1990); Lewis Hyde, *The Gift: Imagination and the Erotic Life of Property* (New York: Vintage, 1983); and Jacques Derrida, *Counterfeit Money*, vol. 1 of *Given Time*, trans. Peggy Kamuf (Chicago: University of Chicago Press, 1992).

47. David L. Vander Meulen, *Pope's Dunciad of 1728: A History and Facsimile* (Charlottesville: University Press of Virginia, 1991), 17.

48. "Pope and the Pirates," *Notes and Queries*, no. 254 (1854): 198.

49. See Griffith, "*The Dunciad* of 1728," 9–10, for the announcements of each of these works reprinted from the *Daily Journal*.

50. Sutherland, "*The Dunciad* of 1729," 347; see also Griffith, "*The Dunciad* of 1728," 16.

51. Foxon, *Pope and the Book Trade*, 242; Winn, "On Pope," 96.

52. For information about Gilliver's relationship with Pope, see James McLaverty. "Lawton Gilliver: Pope's Bookseller," *Studies in Bibliography* 32 (1979): 101–24.

53. Savage, *Collection of Pieces*, quoted in *Pope Letters*, 3:26 n. 1.

54. James Sutherland, introduction to *The Dunciad*, vol. 5 of *The Twickenham Edition of the Poems of Alexander Pope* (London: Methuen, 1943), xxviii.

55. Mark Rose, *Authors and Owners: The Invention of Copyright* (Cambridge: Harvard University Press, 1993), 1.

56. Alexander Pope, *The Dunciad Variorum* (London: printed for A. Dod, 1729).

57. *Daily Post*, 10 April 1729. Quoted in Sutherland, "*The Dunciad* of 1729," 349.

58. PRO C 11/2581/36(2).

59. Griffin, *Literary Patronage*, 126–27.

60. Foxon argues that it is "likely" that the three noble lords did not in fact sign the certificate, as Pope requested, but "instead bought the copyright—thus achieving the same end without exposing themselves to publicity" (*Pope and the Book Trade*, 112). This is conjecture on Foxon's part, and for once his conjecture seems to me unwarranted. Nothing in the correspondence, in the Stationers' Register from November 1729 (when copyright was reassigned to Gilliver by the lords), nor in the materials from *Gilliver v. Snaggs* anywhere suggests that the lords paid for the copyright, and they would have gained nothing by doing so. Their names were already publicly associated with the work to a high degree, and none of them seem to express any reservations in the surviving letters about the extent of that publicity.

61. Griffin, *Literary Patronage*, 30.

62. Alexander Pope, *The Dunciad Variorum* (London: printed for A. Dob, 1729). In his *Seven Lectures on the Law and History of Copyright in Books* (London: Cassell, 1899), Augusine Birrell notes that while the Act of Anne had given authors and members of the trade access to common-law remedies for copyright infringement, most of these figures in fact preferred to use the Court of Chancery to settle their disputes: "One of the grievances the Statute of Anne was meant to alleviate was the absence from our common law of pains and penalties [for invasion of proprietary rights], and these the statute inflicted. But the booksellers did not in practice make much use of such penalties. They suddenly fell in love with the High Court of Chancery, and sought injunctions to restrain the publication of the book of which they alleged themselves to be the proprietors" (101).

63. See Sutherland, "*The Dunciad* of 1729," for details of the piracies and the Chancery suit. I have had an opportunity to examine most of the documents in this case. Quotations are taken from my transcriptions of these primarily handwritten documents.

64. According to Sutherland, the outcome of the case is not recorded in any of the books of decrees and orders of the Court of Chancery. The only surviving reference—which turns Stagg to "Snaggs"—is in Charles Viner's *General Abridgement of Law and Equity* (London: printed for the author, 1742). See Sutherland, "*The Dunciad* of 1729," 353 n. 1.

65. PRO C 11/2581/36(1).

66. PRO C 33/351, f 284. Sutherland, in "*The Dunciad* of 1729," puts the date of the injunction at 19 May, but the entry in the Chancery records is dated "Jovis 8 May."

67. PRO C 11/2581/36(2).

68. Sutherland, "*The Dunciad* of 1729," 353; 8 Anne c. 21 (1710), reprinted in *Statutes of the Realm* (London: printed by command of King George III, 1822), 9:256–58.

69. PRO C 41/44, no 570. Sutherland cites this document as PRO C 41/43, no. 570, which, again, puts the case in the wrong year. Interestingly, he does not quote from Dodd's testimony at all. Fortunately, the book of depositions in Chancery from 1729 (unlike that from 1728) is actually legible, making it possible to read the entry in question, which is, I believe, here reproduced for the first time.

70. Sutherland, "*The Dunciad* of 1729," 352.

71. Sutherland, "*The Dunciad* of 1729," 350. The text of the entry in the Stationers' Register is reprinted in "Notes on Editions of 'The Dunciad,'" 519–20.

72. The only extended discussion of these women can be found in Paula McDowell, *The Women of Grub Street: Press, Politics, and Gender in the Literary Marketplace, 1678–1730* (Oxford: Clarendon Press, 1998); and in Margaret Hunt, "Hawkers, Bawlers, and Mercuries: Women and the London Press in the Early Enlightenment," in *Women and the Enlightenment*, a special issue of *Women and History*, ed. Margaret Hunt, Margaret Jacob, Phyllis Mack, and Ruth Perry (London: Institute for Research in History and Haworth Press, 1984), 41–68.

73. Griffith, "*The Dunciad* of 1728," 17.

74. Henry R. Plomer, *Dictionary of the Printers and Booksellers Who Were at Work in England, Scotland, and Ireland, from 1668–1725* (Oxford: Oxford University Press, 1922); Henry R. Plomer, G. H. Bushnell, and E. R. McC. Dix, *Dictionary of the Printers and Booksellers Who Were at Work in England, Scotland, and Ireland, from 1726–1775* (Oxford: Oxford University Press, 1932).

75. Sutherland, introduction to *The Dunciad: The Twickenham Edition*, 5:xviii.

76. Hunt, "Hawkers, Bawlers, and Mercuries," 46.

77. Michael Harris, "Paper Pirates: The Alternative Book Trade in Mid-Eighteenth Century London," in *Fakes and Frauds: Varieties of Deception in Print and Manuscript*, ed. Robin Myers and Michael Harris (Winchester: St. Paul's Bibliographies, 1989), 47–69.

78. Hanson, *Government and the Press*, 50.

79. Harrington's letter is preserved in the Public Record Office, in State Papers Domestic (hereafter SP) 36/22, f 12. The letter is dated 9 January 1731—the date the second offending issue of the *Craftsman* appeared—which only serves to prove that the authorities wasted no time in prosecuting mercuries for distributing these works. This document, along with others cited in this chapter related to the participation of mercuries in opposition journalism, is quoted in Hunt, "Hawkers, Bawlers, and Mercuries," 42–58. Many of the same documents are also cited in McDowell, *Women of Grub Street*. For the purposes of this chapter, I have consulted all of the documents from which I quote, and the transcriptions are my own. My purpose in returning to these same documents is to extend the analysis offered by Hunt and McDowell by taking the documents out of what might be seen as a minoritizing history of women mercuries and placing them in the context of the workings of the trade as a whole. In addition, my account seeks to bridge the gap between histories of canonical literary figures like Pope and new feminist histories of women in the book trade—models of literary historiography that have rarely seemed to connect in these recent studies. This lack of connection between these different sorts of history has allowed canonical literary histories to ignore precisely the messy relations among authors and members of the book trades that this essay attempts to expose.

80. Hunt, "Hawkers, Bawlers, and Mercuries," 52.

81. PRO SP 36/8, f 244. Also quoted in Hunt, "Hawkers, Bawlers, and Mercuries," 53.

82. PRO SP 36/23, f 134. Also quoted in Hunt, "Hawkers, Bawlers, and Mercuries," 57–8.

83. On the topic of pleading the belly, see James Oldham, "On Pleading the Belly: A History of the Jury of Matrons," *Criminal Justice History* 6 (1985): 1–64.

Chapter 5. Hostis Humani Generis

1. David Foxon, *Pope and the Early Eighteenth-Century Book Trade*, rev. and ed. James McLaverty (Oxford: Clarendon Press, 1991), 242.

2. All page references to *Polly* are taken from John Fuller's edition of Gay's *Dramatic Works* (Oxford: Clarendon Press, 1983), 2:67–146.

3. David Nokes, *John Gay: A Profession of Friendship* (Oxford: Oxford University Press, 1995), 454.

4. Page and volume references are to the fourteen-volume edition of the first decade of the *Craftsman* (nos. 1–511), printed for R. Francklin between 1726 and 1736. For the best introduction to the role played by the *Craftsman* in the political life of the second quarter of the eighteenth century, see Bertrand A. Goldgar, *Walpole and the Wits: The Relation of Politics to Literature, 1722–1742* (Lincoln: University of Nebraska Press, 1976). Also useful is Simon Varey's short piece on the *Craftsman* in *Telling People What to Think: Early Eighteenth-Century Periodicals from the* Review *to the* Rambler, ed. J. A. Downie and Thomas N. Corns (London: Frank Cass, 1993), 58–77.

5. Gay was by no means the first English author to become embroiled in a debate about the "construccions" put on his work by malevolent readers; as the third chapter above suggests, the problem had been plaguing English authors at least since the time of William Prynne. In the early decades of the eighteenth century, some effort was made to specify exactly what an author's legal responsibilities ought to be, if particular readers of his or her work rendered seditious what had originally (ostensibly) been innocently put forward. Richard Steele himself had suggested, in *Mr. Steele's Apology for Himself and His Writings* (London: printed by R. Burleigh, 1714), that "if an author's words in the obvious and natural interpretation of them, have a meaning which is innocent, they cannot without great injustice be condemned of another meaning which is criminal" (quoted in Laurence Hanson, *Government and the Press, 1695–1763* [Oxford: Clarendon Press, 1936], 24). Hanson notes that in 1729, in the case of *Rex v. Clarke*, the attorney general offered the somewhat unhelpful suggestion that a work should be judged according to the meaning "the generality of readers must take it in, according to the obvious and natural sense of it"—a requirement that gave prosecutors and judges the widest possible latitude in judging seditious intention (24).

6. Gay to Swift, 6 July 1728, in *The Letters of John Gay*, ed. C. F. Burgess (Oxford: Clarendon Press, 1966), 75. This volume will hereafter be cited as *Gay Letters.*

7. Swift, *Intelligencer* 3 (25 May 1728).

8. Goldgar, *Walpole and the Wits*, 82.

9. Samuel Johnson, *Lives of the English Poets*, ed. George Birkbeck Hill (Oxford: Clarendon Press, 1905), 2:275.

10. Gay wrote to Swift on 20 March 1728 that after thirty-six performances, he has "got by all this success between seven and eight hundred pounds" (*Gay Letters,*

72). For other estimations of Gay's profits, see *The Correspondence of Alexander Pope*, ed. George Sherburn (Oxford: Clarendon Press, 1956), 2:480, 482, 484. See also J. V. Guerinot and Rodney D. Jilg, *The Beggar's Opera* (Hamden, Conn.: Shoestring Press, 1976), 160–64; and Frank Kidson, The Beggar's Opera*: Its Predecessors and Successors* (Cambridge: Cambridge University Press, 1922), 86.

11. Dustin Griffin points out, for instance, that Gay constitutes Johnson's primary "example of the moral lassitude brought on by patronage." See Griffin's *Literary Patronage in England, 1650–1800* (Cambridge: Cambridge University Press, 1996), 239.

12. Perhaps this is why, as Griffin points out, eighteenth-century Britain was "a society in which men were very sensitive about 'obliging' and being 'obliged' to each other" (*Literary Patronage*, 107).

13. Sutherland, "*Polly*," 293.

14. For the lump sum of £94 10s., John Watts and Jacob Tonson purchased the copyright to *The Beggar's Opera* and Gay's *Fables* on 6 February 1728. Although little information remains about the profits made by Watts and Tonson, we can speculate that their profits on these works and on the numerous spin-offs—ballads, musical scores, later editions—from *The Beggar's Opera* repaid the initial investment many times over. See Kidson, *The Beggar's Opera*, 86–87.

15. *Whitehall Evening Post*, 3–5 April 1729. Quoted in James Sutherland, "*Polly* among the Pirates," *Modern Language Review* 42 (1942): 293.

16. Nokes estimates the usual number of a first edition at one thousand, making Gay's a "huge print-run" (*John Gay*, 458).

17. C. F. Burgess, "John Gay and *Polly* and a Letter to the King," *Philological Quarterly* 47 (1968): 596. See also John Lord Hervey, *Some Materials towards Memoirs of the Reign of George II*, ed. Romney Sedgwick (London, 1931), 98. Quoted in Nokes, *John Gay*, 464.

18. Nokes, *John Gay*, 464; L. W. Conolly, "Anna Margaretta Larpent, The Duchess of Queensberry, and Gay's *Polly* in 1777," *Philological Quarterly* 51 (1972): 955–56. For Gay's relationship with the Queensberrys, see Johnson's "Life of Gay," in which he describes "the affectionate attention" given to Gay by the pair, "into whose house he was taken, and with whom he passed the remaining years of his life" (*Lives of the English Poets*, 2:280).

19. Burgess, "John Gay and *Polly*," 596.

20. These accounts are collected in Charles E. Pearce, *Polly Peachum: The Story of Lavinia Fenton and* The Beggar's Opera (New York: Benjamin Blom, 1968). Pearce's chapter titled "A Great Lady's Championship" (245–54) is the only location where many of these early accounts of the *Polly* affair are available, although his documentation is extremely sketchy. For more precise bibliographical information, I have referred to Nokes, *John Gay*, 464.

21. Mrs. Mary Delany, *The Autobiography and Correspondence of Mary Granville, Mrs. Delany* (London: R. Bentley, 1862). Quoted in Pearce, *Polly Peachum*, 247.

22. Hervey, *Memoirs*, 98. Quoted in Pearce, *Polly Peachum*, 249.

23. Quoted in Pearce, *Polly Peachum*, 248.

24. An autograph copy of the letter is available in the British Museum, MS 15599. It is quoted in its entirety in Burgess, "John Gay and *Polly*," 597, and misquoted in Pearce, *Polly Peachum*, 247.

25. Quoted in Pearce, *Polly Peachum*, 247–48.

26. Jacques Derrida, "Limited Inc a b c," trans. Samuel Weber, in *Limited Inc* (Evanston: Northwestern University Press, 1988), 37.

27. Catherine Gallagher, *Nobody's Story: The Vanishing Acts of Women Writers in the Marketplace, 1670–1820* (Berkeley and Los Angeles: University of California Press, 1994), xix.

28. *The Correspondence of Jonathan Swift*, ed. Harold Williams (Oxford: Clarendon Press, 1963–65), 3:326.

29. Unless otherwise noted, the major details of the *Polly* piracies are taken from Sutherland's article, "*Polly* among the Pirates." Sutherland found most of the documents in the case, which are housed in the Public Record Office, although he was unable to locate Gay's original Bill of Complaint. When quoting from the original documents in Gay's Chancery case, I am using my own transcriptions of the documents.

30. Arthur Collins says that William Bowyer, one of the printers of *Polly*, placed the announcement (*Authorship in the Days of Johnson* [London: Robert Holden, 1927], 57). Why Bowyer rather than Gay would have done so is unclear: Bowyer did not immediately stand to lose money as a result of the piracies, since he had been paid in advance for printing *Polly*. Perhaps it was thought that a member of the trade would have more influence to stop the piracies than a "mere" author.

31. Mark Rose, *Authors and Owners: The Invention of Copyright* (Cambridge: Harvard University Press, 1993), 49.

32. Quoted in Sutherland, "*Polly*," 299.

33. Sutherland cites this document as PRO C 41/43, no 47. In fact, the document PRO C 41/43 contains Chancery records for 1728; the actual citation for the document is PRO C 41/44, no. 47.

34. Sutherland, "*Polly*," 299.

35. PRO C 11/1272/7(2), "The Farther Answer of James Watson," 5 November 1730. See also PRO C 11/1272/18, "The Further Answer of Th. Read: One of the Defts in the Bill of Complaint of John Gay Esq. the Complaint," 26 June 1730, in which the same charge is leveled against Gay.

36. PRO C 11/1272/18.

37. PRO C 11/1272/7(2).

38. For the specific wording of the Act of Anne, see *Statutes of the Realm* (London: Printed by command of King George III, 1822), 9:256–58.

39. PRO C 11/1739/34.

40. Sutherland, "*Polly*," 301.

41. Foxon, *Pope and the Book Trade*, 242; Sutherland, "*Polly*," 303.

42. Michel Foucault, "What Is an Author?," in Josué V. Harari, ed., *Textual Strategies: Perspectives in Post-Structuralist Criticism* (Ithaca, N.Y.: Cornell University Press, 1979), 158.

43. C. B. Macpherson, *The Political Theory of Possessive Individualism: Hobbes to Locke* (1962; reprint, Oxford: Oxford University Press, 1990), 3.

44. For an extended critique of the ways in which liberal historiography has obscured elements of the history of authorship and its relation to copyright, see David Saunders, *Authorship and Copyright* (London and New York: Routledge, 1992).

Bibliography

Many of the primary sources related to book history are collected in *The English Book Trade, 1660–1853: 156 Titles Relating to the Early History of Publishing, Bookselling, and the Struggle for Copyright and Freedom of the Press*, 38 vols., ed. Stephen Parks (New York: Garland Publishing, 1974). In the bibliography, these works are indicated by EBT, followed by the volume and work number.

Primary Sources

Acts and Ordinances of the Interregnum, 1642–1660. 3 vols. Edited by C. H. Firth and R. S. Rait. London: Her Majesty's Stationery Office, 1911.

[Addison, Joseph]. *The Thoughts of a Tory Author, Concerning the Press*. London: printed for A. Baldwin, 1712. *EBT* 7B.

Animadversions upon that Proclamation of September 13, 1692, Entituled, for the better discovery of Seditious Libellers. [N.p., 1692].

The Answer of Sir William Scroggs, Kt., Lord Chief Justice of the King's Bench, to the Articles of Dr. Titus Oates and Mr. William Bedloe. London: n.p., 1680.

Arguments Relating to a Restraint upon the Press, Fully and Fairly Handled in a Letter to a Bencher from a Young Gentleman of the Temple, with Proposals Humbly Offer'd to the Considerations of Both Houses of Parliament. London: printed for R. and J. Bonwicke, 1712. *EBT* 7A.

Articles of High Misdemeanors . . . against William Scroggs, Knight. London: n.p., 1680.

Asgill, John. *An Essay for the Press*. London: printed for A. Baldwin, 1712. *EBT* 7C.

Atkyns, Richard. *Original and Growth of Printing: Collected out of History, and the Records of this Kingdome*. London: printed by John Streater for the author, 1664. *EBT* 2E.

Blackstone, William. *Commentaries on the Laws of England*. 1766. Reprint, Chicago: University of Chicago Press, 1979.

Blount, Charles. *A Just Vindication of Learning; or, An Humble Address to the High Court of Parliament in Behalf of the Liberty of the Press*. London: n.p., 1679. *EBT* 3B.

———. *Reasons Humbly Offered for the Liberty of Unlicens'd Printing*. London: n.p., 1693. *EBT* 3C.

By the King and Queen, A Proclamation, for the Better Discovery of Seditious Libellers. London: printed by Charles Bill, 1691 [for 1692].

By the King, a Proclamation for the Suppressing of Seditious and Treasonable Books and Pamphlets. London: printed by John Bill, Thomas Newcomb, and Henry Hills, 1679.

By the Queen, a Proclamation for Restraining the Spreading False News, and Printing and Publishing of Irreligious and Seditious Papers and Libels. London: printed by Charles Bill, 1702.

[Cellier, Elizabeth.] *Malice Defeated; or, A Brief Relation of the Accusation and Deliverance of Elizabeth Cellier.* London: printed for Elizabeth Cellier, 1680.

———. Malice Defeated *and* The Matchless Rogue. 1680. Introduction by Anne Barbeau Gardiner. Los Angeles: William Andrews Clark Memorial Library, 1988; Augustan Reprint Society, nos. 249–50.

———. *The Matchless Rogue; or, A Brief Account of the Life of Don Thomazo the Unfortunate Son, Together with . . . Some Reflections on Madam Cellier's Case.* London: printed for Elizabeth Cellier, 1680.

The Craftsman. 14 vols. London: printed for R. Francklin, 1726–36.

[Dangerfield, Thomas]. *Thomas Dangerfield's Answer to a Certain Scandalous Lying Pamphlet Entituled* Malice Defeated. London: printed for the author, 1680.

[Daniel Defoe.] *A Collection of the Writings of the Author of the True-Born English-Man.* [Edited by John How]. London: n.p., 1703.

———. *An Enquiry into Occasional Conformity, Shewing That the Dissenters Are No Way Concern'd in It.* London: n.p., 1702.

———. *An Enquiry into the Occasional Conformity of Dissenters, in Cases of Preferment.* Dublin: printed by J. B. and S. P. for Jacob Milner, 1698.

———. *An Enquiry into the Occasional Conformity of Dissenters, in Cases of Preferment, with a Preface to the Lord Mayor, Occasioned by His Carrying the Sword to a Conventicle.* London: n.p., 1697 [for 1698].

———. *An Essay on the Regulation of the Press.* London: n.p., 1704. *EBT* 4E.

———. *To the Honourable the C—s of England Assembled in P—t: The Humble Petition and Representation of the True Loyal and Always Obedient Church of England, Relating to the Bill for Restraining the Press.* London: n.p., 1704. British Library, Add. MS 70267.

———. *A Hymn to the Pillory.* London: n.p., 1703.

———. *A Letter to Mr. How.* London: n.p., 1701.

———. *The Letters of Daniel Defoe.* Edited by George Harris Healey. Oxford: Clarendon Press, 1955.

———. *The Present State of the Parties in Great Britain.* London: printed by J. Baker, 1712.

———. *Review.* Edited by Arthur Wellesley Secord. New York: Columbia University Press, 1948.

———. *The Shortest Way with the Dissenters; or, Proposals for the Establishment of the Church.* London: n.p., 1702.

———. *The Shortest Way with the Dissenters: [Taken from Dr. Sach—ll's Sermon, and Others:]; or, Proposals for the Establishment of the Church, by the Author of the True-Born English-Man.* London: n.p., [1703].

———. *A True Collection of the Writings of the Author of the True Born English-Man.* London: n.p., 1703.

———. *A Vindication of the Press.* London: printed for T. Warner, 1718.

English Reports. 176 vols. Edinburgh: William Green and Sons, 1900–1930.

*An Exact Narrative of the Tryal and Condemnation of John Twyn, for Printing and

Dispersing of a Treasonable Book, with the Tryals of Thomas Brewster, Bookseller, Simon Dover, Printer, and Nathan Brookes, Bookbinder, for Printing, Publishing, and Uttering of Seditious, Scandalous, and Malitious Pamphlets. London: printed by Thomas Mabb for Henry Brome, 1664. *EBT* 3A.

"The Female Faction; or, The Gay Subscribers." London: printed for J. Roberts, 1729.

Gay, John. *Dramatic Works.* Edited by John Fuller. Oxford: Clarendon Press, 1983.

———. *The Letters of John Gay.* Edited by C. F. Burgess. Oxford: Clarendon Press, 1966.

———. *Polly.* London: printed for the author, [1729].

Hervey, John Lord. *Some Materials towards Memoirs of the Reign of George II.* Edited by Romney Sedgwick. London: Eyre and Spottiswoode, 1931.

How, John. *Some Thoughts on the Present State of Printing and Bookselling.* [London: n.p., 1709]. *EBT* 4F.

How, John, ed. *A Collection of the Writings of the Author of the True-Born English-Man.* London: n.p., 1703.

Howe, John. *Some Consideration of a Preface to an Enquiry, Concerning the Ocassional Conformity of Dissenters.* London: printed for Thomas Parkhurst, 1701.

An Impartial Account of the Trial of Francis Smith . . . As Also of the Tryal of Jane Curtis. London: n.p., 1680. *EBT* 1C.

Johnson, Samuel. *Lives of the English Poets.* Edited by George Birkbeck Hill. Oxford: Clarendon Press, 1905.

Leslie, Charles. *The Wolf Stript of his Shepard's Clothing,* 3rd ed. London: n.p., 1704.

L'Estrange, Roger. *Considerations and Proposals in Order to the Regulation of the Press: Together with Diverse Instances of Treasonous, and Seditious Pamphlets, Proving the Necessity Thereof.* London: printed by A. C., 1663. *EBT* 2C.

———. *Interest Mistaken.* London: printed for Henry Brome, 1661.

———. *L'Estrange: His Appeal.* London: printed for Henry Brome, 1681.

———. *A Memento Treating of the Rise, Progress, and Remedies of Seditions: With Some Historical Reflections upon the Series of Our Late Troubles.* London: 1642. Reprinted for Joanna Brome, 1682.

———. *A Short Answer to a Whole Litter of Libels.* London: printed by J. B. for Henry Brome, 1680.

———. *Truth and Loyalty Vindicated, from the Reproches and Clamours of Mr. Edward Bagshaw: Together with a further Discovery of the Libeller Himself, and his Seditious Confederates.* London: printed for H. Brome and A. Seile, 1662. *EBT* 2B.

The Manuscripts of the House of Lords. London: Her Majesty's Stationery Office, 1965.

March, John. *Actions for Slander: Parts One and Two.* London: printed for Matthew Walbanck and Richard Bell, 1655.

Milton, John. *Areopagitica.* 1644. In *John Milton: Complete Poems and Major Prose.* Edited by Merritt Y. Hughes. New York: Macmillan, 1985.

Mistriss Celiers Lamentation for the Loss of Her Liberty. London: printed for S. F., 1681.

Mr. Prance's Answer to Mrs. Cellier's Libel . . . to which Is Added the Adventure of the Bloody Bladder. London: printed for L. Curtis, 1680.

Pope, Alexander. *The Correspondence of Alexander Pope.* Edited by George Sherburn. Oxford: Clarendon Press, 1956.

———. *The Dunciad.* [Dublin, printed] London: reprinted for Anne Dodd, 1728.

———. *The Dunciad Variorum.* London: printed for A. Dob, 1729.

———. *The Dunciad Variorum.* London: printed for A. Dod, 1729.

———. *Poetry and Prose of Alexander Pope.* Edited by Aubrey Williams. Boston: Houghton Mifflin, 1969.

———. *The Works of Mr. Alexander Pope.* London: printed by W. Bowyer for Jacob Tonson and Bernard Lintot, 1717.

The Popish Damnable Plot against Our Religion and Liberties, Lively Delineated in Several of its Branches. London: printed for Richard Baldwin, 1681.

A Popp upon Pope; or, a True and Faithful Account of a Late Horrid and Barbarous Whipping, Committed on the Body of A. Pope, a Poet. London: printed for A. Moore, 1728.

To the Praise of Mrs. Cellier the Popish Midwife: On Her Incomparable Book. London: printed for Walter Davis, 1680.

The Printers Case with Their Proposals for Regulating the Press. London: [1711?]. *EBT* 1E.

A Proclamation for Suppressing the Printing and Publishing of Unlicensed News-Books and Pamphlets of News. London: n.p., 1680.

Prynne, William. *Histriomastix: The Players Scourge; or, Actors Tragedie.* London: printed by E. A. and W. I. for Michael Sparke, 1633.

Sacheverell, Henry. *The Political Union: A Discourse Showing the Dependence of Government on Religion in General, and of the English Monarchy on the Church of England in Particular.* Oxford: printed by Leonard Lichfield for George West and Henry Clements, 1702.

Savage, Richard. *A Collection of Pieces in Verse and Prose, Which Have Been Publish'd on Occasion of the Dunciad.* London: printed for L. Gilliver, 1732.

Scroggs, William. *The Lord Chief Justice Scroggs: His Speech in the Kings-Bench the First Day of This Present Michaelmas Term.* London: n.p., 1679.

———. *The Lord Chief Justice Scroggs: His Speech in the Kings-Bench . . . Occasion'd by the Many Libellous Pamphlets Which Are Publisht against Law, to the Scandal of Government, and Publick Justice.* London: printed for Robert Pawlet, 1679.

Sheppard, William. *Actions upon the Case for Slander.* London: printed for Charles Adams, J. Starkey, and T. Baffet, 1662.

A Short, but Just Account of the Tryal of Benjamin Harris. London: n.p., 1679 [1680].

Smith, Francis. *An Account of the Injurious Proceedings . . . against Francis Smith, Bookseller . . . Sept. 16, 1680.* London: printed for Francis Smith, [1681]. *EBT* 1B.

Some Observations upon the Late Tryals of Sir George Wakeman. London: printed for A. Brewster, 1679.

Statutes of the Realm. London: printed by Command of King George III, 1822.

Steele, Richard. *Mr. Steele's Apology for Himself and His Writings.* London: printed by R. Burleigh, 1714.

———. *The Correspondence of Jonathan Swift.* Edited by Harold Williams. Oxford: Clarendon Press, 1963–65.

Swift, Jonathan. *The Intelligencer.* [London]: Printed at Dublin, London reprinted, and sold by A. Moor, 1729.

[Tindal, Matthew]. *Reasons against Restraining the Press.* London: n.p., 1704. *EBT* 4D.

The Triall of Elizabeth Cellier, at the Kings-Bench Barr, on Friday June the 11th. 1680. London: printed for Randal Taylor, 1680.

The Triall of Henry Carr, Gent. London: printed by I. G. for R[andal] Taylor, 1681.

The Triall of Henry Carr, Gent. . . . Also the Tryal of Elizabeth Cellier, at the Kings-Bench Bar, July the 11th. 1680. London: printed by I. G. for R[andal] Taylor.

A True Copy of a Letter of Consolation Sent to Nat the Printer. London: printed for W. Johnson, 1681.

The Tryal and Sentence of Elizabeth Cellier, for Writing, Printing, and Publishing, a Scandalous Libel, Called Malice Defeated. London: printed for Thomas Collins, 1680.

The Tryal of Elizabeth Cellier, the Popish Midwife: At the Old Baily Septemb. 11. 1680. London: printed by A. Godbid for L. C., 1680.

The Tudor Constitution: Documents and Commentary, 2nd ed. Edited by G. R. Elton. Cambridge: Cambridge University Press, 1982.

Tudor Royal Proclamations. 3 vols. Edited by Paul L. Hughes and James F. Larkin. New Haven and London: Yale University Press, 1969.

Viner, Charles. *General Abridgement of Law and Equity.* London: printed for the author, 1742.

The Weekly Pacquet of Advice from Rome; or, The History of Popery. 4 vols. London: printed by Langley Curtis, 1679–82.

Secondary Sources

Albright, Evelyn M. "*Ad Imprimendum Solum.*" *Modern Language Notes* 34 (1919): 97–104.

———. "*Ad Imprimendum Solum* Once More." *Modern Language Notes* 38 (1923): 129–40.

Arber, Edward, ed. *A Transcript of the Registers of the Company of Stationers of London, 1554–1640 A.D.* London: privately printed, 1875–94. Reprint, New York: Peter Smith, 1950.

Astbury, Raymond. "The Renewal of the Licensing Act in 1693 and Its Lapse in 1695." *Library,* 5th series, 33 (1978): 291–322.

Backscheider, Paula. *Daniel Defoe: His Life.* Baltimore: Johns Hopkins University Press, 1989.

———. "No Defense: Defoe in 1703." *PMLA* 103 (1988): 274–84.

Barker, Francis. *The Tremulous Private Body: Essays in Subjection.* Ann Arbor: University of Michigan Press, 1995.

Bastian, F. *Defoe's Early Life.* London: Macmillan Press, 1981.

Belanger, Terry. "Publishers and Writers in Eighteenth-Century England." In *Books and Their Readers in Eighteenth-Century England,* edited by Isabel Rivers, 5–25. New York: St. Martin's Press, 1982.

Bellamy, John. *The Tudor Law of Treason: An Introduction.* London: Routledge, 1979.

Birrel, Augustine. *Seven Lectures on the Law and History of Copyright in Books.* London: Cassell, 1899.

Bliss, Carey S. *A Pair on Printing.* North Hills, Pa.: Bird and Bull Press, 1982.

Brown, Laura. *Alexander Pope.* Oxford: Blackwell, 1985.

Burgess, C. F. "John Gay and *Polly* and a Letter to the King." *Philological Quarterly* 47 (1968): 596–98.

Clegg, Cyndia. *Press Censorship in Elizabethan England.* Cambridge: Cambridge University Press, 1997.

———. *Press Censorship in Jacobean England.* Cambridge: Cambridge University Press, 2001.

Clyde, William M. *The Struggle for the Freedom of the Press from Caxton to Cromwell.* London: Oxford University Press, 1934.

Collins, Arthur S. *Authorship in the Days of Johnson.* London: Robert Holden, 1927.

Conolly, L. W. "Anna Margaretta Larpent, the Duchess of Queensberry, and Gay's *Polly* in 1777." *Philological Quarterly* 51 (1972): 955–57.

Coombe, Rosemary J. *The Cultural Life of Intellectual Properties: Authorship, Appropriation, and the Law.* Durham, N.C.: Duke University Press, 1998.

Cressy, David. *Literacy and the Social Order: Reading and Writing in Tudor and Stuart England.* Cambridge: Cambridge University Press, 1980.

Delany, Mary. *The Autobiography and Correspondence of Mary Granville, Mrs. Delany.* London: R. Bentley, 1862.

Derrida, Jacques. *Given Time. Vol. 1* of *Counterfeit Money.* Translated by Peggy Kamuf. Chicago: University of Chicago Press, 1992.

———. *Limited Inc.* Translated by Sam Weber. Evanston: Northwestern University Press, 1988.

Dolan, Frances E. "'The Wretched Subject the Whole Town Talks of': Representing Elizabeth Cellier (London, 1680)." In *Catholicism and Anti-Catholicism in Early Modern English Texts,* edited by Arthur Marotti, 218–58. London: Macmillan, 1999.

Downie, J. A. "Defoe's *Shortest Way with the Dissenters*: Irony, Intention, and Reader-Response." *Prose Studies* 9.2 (1986): 120–39.

———. "An Unknown Defoe Broadsheet on the Regulation of the Press?" *Library,* 5th series, 33 (1978): 51–58.

Empson, William. *Some Versions of Pastoral.* New York: New Directions, 1974.

Feather, John. "The Book Trade in Politics: The Making of the Copyright Act of 1710." *Publishing History* 8 (1980): 19–44.

———. *Publishing, Piracy, and Politics: An Historical Study of Copyright in Britain.* London: Mansell, 1994.

Foucault, Michel. "Qu'est ce qu'un auteur?" *Bulletin de la Société française de Philosophie* 64 (1969): 73–104.

———. "What Is an Author?" In *Textual Strategies: Perspectives in Post-Structuralist Criticism,* edited by Josué V. Harari, 141–60. Ithaca, N.Y.: Cornell University Press, 1979.

Foxon, David. *Pope and the Early Eighteenth-Century Book Trade.* Revised and edited by James McLaverty. Oxford: Clarendon Press, 1991.

———. ed. *A Register of Books, 1728–1732, Extracted from* The Monthly Chronicle. London: Gregg–Archive, 1964.

Fraser, Antonia. *The Weaker Vessel: Woman's Lot in Seventeenth-Century England.* London: Weidenfeld and Nicolson, 1984.

Furbank, P. N., and W. R. Owens. *A Critical Bibliography of Daniel Defoe.* London: Pickering and Chatto, 1998.

Gallagher, Catherine. *Nobody's Story: The Vanishing Acts of Women Writers in the Marketplace, 1670–1820*. Berkeley and Los Angeles: University of California Press, 1994.

Gardiner, Samuel Rawson, ed. *Documents Relating to the Proceedings against William Prynne, in 1634 and 1637*. London: Camden Society, 1877.

Gilbert, Sandra. "Literary Paternity." In *Contemporary Literary Criticism: Modernism through Poststructuralism*, edited by Robert Con Davis, 188–200. New York: Longman, 1986.

Goldgar, Bertrand A. *Walpole and the Wits: The Relation of Politics to Literature, 1722–1742*. Lincoln: University of Nebraska Press, 1976.

Greaves, Richard. *Deliver Us from Evil: The Radical Underground in Britain, 1660–1663*. New York: Oxford University Press, 1986.

Greene, Jody. "Public Secrets: Sodomy and the Pillory in the Eighteenth Century, and Beyond." *The Eighteenth Century: Theory and Interpretation* 44.2–3 (summer–fall 2003): 203–32.

Greg, W. W. "*Ad Imprimendum Solum*." *Library*, 5th series, 9 (1954): 242–47.

———. "Entrance, Licence, and Publication." *Library*, 4th series, 25 (1944): 1–22.

Griffin, Dustin. *Literary Patronage in England, 1650–1800*. Cambridge: Cambridge University Press, 1996.

Griffith, R. H. *Alexander Pope: A Bibliography*. Austin: University of Texas Press, 1927.

———. "The *Dunciad* of 1728." *Modern Philology* 13 (1915): 1–18.

Guerinot, J. V., and Rodney D. Jilg. *The Beggar's Opera*. Hamden, Conn.: Shoestring Press, 1976.

Hamburger, Philip. "The Development of the Law of Seditious Libel and the Control of the Press." *Stanford Law Review* 37 (1985): 661–765.

Hanson, Laurence. *Government and the Press, 1695–1763*. 1936. Reprint, Oxford: Clarendon Press, 1967.

Harris, Michael. "Paper Pirates: The Alternative Book Trade in Mid-Eighteenth Century London." In Myers and Harris, *Fakes and Frauds*, 47–69.

Hemholz, R. H., and Thomas A. Green. *Juries, Libel, and Justice: The Role of English Juries in Seventeenth- and Eighteenth-Century Trials for Libel and Slander*. Los Angeles: William Andrews Clark Memorial Library, 1984.

Hill, Christopher. "Censorship and English Literature." In *Collected Essays of Christopher Hill*, Vol. 1, edited by Christopher Hill, 32–71. Amherst: University of Massachusetts Press, 1985.

Hunt, Margaret. "Hawkers, Bawlers, and Mercuries: Women and the London Press in the Early Enlightenment." In *Women and the Enlightenment*. Special issue of *Women and History*, edited by Margaret Hunt, Margaret Jacob, Phyllis Mack, and Ruth Perry, 41–68. London: Institute for Research in History and Haworth Press, 1984.

Hyde, Lewis. *The Gift: Imagination and the Erotic Life of Property*. New York: Vintage, 1983.

Irving, William Henry. *John Gay: Favorite of the Wits*. Durham, N.C.: Duke University Press, 1940.

Johns, Adrian. *The Nature of the Book: Print and Knowledge in the Making*. Chicago: University of Chicago Press, 1998.

Kaplan, Benjamin. *An Unhurried View of Copyright.* New York: Columbia University Press, 1967.

Kaplan, M. Lindsay. *The Culture of Slander in Early Modern England.* Cambridge: Cambridge University Press, 1997.

Kenyon, John. *The Popish Plot.* London: Heinemann, 1972.

Kidson, Frank. The Beggar's Opera*: Its Predecessors and Successors.* Cambridge: Cambridge University Press, 1922.

King, [Peter]. *The Life and Letters of John Locke.* London: George Bell, 1884. Reprint, New York: Garland Publishing, 1984.

Kirby, Ethyn Williams. *William Prynne: A Study in Puritanism.* Cambridge: Harvard University Press, 1931.

Kitchin, George. *Sir Roger L'Estrange: A Contribution to the History of the Press in the Seventeenth Century.* London: Kegan Paul, 1913.

Knight, Mark. *Politics and Opinion in Crisis, 1678–81.* Cambridge: Cambridge University Press, 1994.

Lambert, Sheila. "State Control of the Press in Theory and Practice: The Role of the Stationers' Company before 1640." In Myers and Harris, *Censorship and Control of the Press,* 1–32.

Lamont, William. *Marginal Prynne, 1600–1699.* London: Routledge and Kegan Paul, 1963.

———. *Puritanism and Historical Controversy.* London: University College London Press, 1996.

Lerenbaum, Miriam. "'An Irony Not Unusual': Defoe's *Shortest Way with the Dissenters." Huntington Library Quarterly* 37 (1974): 227–50.

Loades, David M. "Illicit Presses and Clandestine Printing in England, 1520–1590." In *Too Mighty to Be Free: Censorship and the Press in Britain and the Netherlands,* edited by A. C. Duke and C. A. Tamse, 9–27. Zutphen, Netherlands: de Walburg Press, 1987.

———. *Politics, Censorship, and the English Reformation.* London and New York: Printer Publishers, 1991.

———. "The Press under the Early Tudors." *Transactions of the Cambridge Bibliographic Society* 4.1 (1964): 29–50.

Loewenstein, Joseph. *The Author's Due: Printing and the Prehistory of Copyright.* Chicago: University of Chicago Press, 2002.

———. "Legal Proofs and Corrected Readings: Press-Agency and the New Bibliography." In *The Production of English Renaissance Culture,* edited by David Lee Miller, Sharon O'Hair, and Harold Weber, 93–122. Ithaca, N.Y.: Cornell University Press, 1994.

Love, Harold. *The Culture and Commerce of Texts: Scribal Publication in Seventeenth-Century England.* Amherst: University of Massachusetts Press, 1998.

Mack, Maynard. *Alexander Pope: A Life.* New York: Norton, 1985.

Macpherson, C. B. *The Political Theory of Possessive Individualism: Hobbes to Locke.* 1962. Reprint, Oxford: Oxford University Press, 1990.

Manning, Roger B. "The Origins of the Doctrine of Sedition." *Albion* 12 (1980): 103–5.

Marotti, Arthur. *John Donne: Coterie Poet.* Madison: University of Wisconsin Press, 1986.

———. *Manuscript, Print, and the English Renaissance Lyric.* Ithaca, N.Y.: Cornell University Press, 1995.

Mauss, Marcel. *The Gift: The Form and Reason for Exchange in Archaic Societies.* Translated by W. D. Halls. New York: Norton, 1990.

McDowell, Paula. *The Women of Grub Street: Press, Politics, and Gender in the London Literary Marketplace, 1678–1730.* Oxford: Clarendon Press, 1998.

McKenzie, D. F. *Bibliography and the Sociology of Texts.* Cambridge: Cambridge University Press, 1999.

———. *Making Meaning: "Printers of the Mind" and Other Essays.* Edited by Peter D. McDonald and Michael F. Suarez. Amherst: University of Massachusetts Press, 2002.

McLaverty, James. "Lawton Gilliver: Pope's Bookseller." *Studies in Bibliography* 32 (1979): 101–24.

Miller, John. *Popery and Politics in England, 1660–88.* Cambridge: Cambridge University Press, 1973.

Moore, John Robert. *Daniel Defoe: Citizen of the Modern World.* Chicago: University of Chicago Press, 1958.

———. *Defoe in the Pillory and Other Studies.* Bloomington: Indiana University Publications, 1939.

Myers, Robin, and Michael Harris, eds. *Censorship and Control of the Press in England and France, 1600–1910.* Winchester: Saint Paul's Bibliographies, 1992.

———, eds. *Fakes and Frauds: Varieties of Deception in Print and Manuscript.* Winchester: St. Paul's Bibliographies, 1989.

Nevitt, Marcus. "Women in the Business of Revolutionary News: Elizabeth Atkin, 'Parliament Joan,' and the Commonwealth Newsbook." In Raymond, *News, Newspapers, and Society,* 84–108.

Nokes, David. *John Gay: A Profession of Friendship.* Oxford: Oxford University Press, 1995.

"Notes on Editions of 'The Dunciad.'" *Notes and Queries,* nos. 268–70 (1854): 477–78, 497–98, 517–20.

Novak, Maximillian E. *Daniel Defoe, Master of Fictions: His Life and Ideas.* Oxford: Oxford University Press, 2001.

———. "Defoe's *Shortest Way with the Dissenters*: Hoax, Parody, Paradox, Fiction, Irony, and Satire." *Modern Language Quarterly* 27 (1966): 402–17.

Oldham, James. "On Pleading the Belly: A History of the Jury of Matrons." *Criminal Justice History* 6 (1985): 1–64.

Patterson, Annabel. *Censorship and Interpretation: The Conditions of Writing and Reading in Early Modern England.* 1984. Reprinted with a new introduction, Madison: University of Wisconsin Press, 1990.

Patterson, Lyman Ray. *Copyright in Historical Perspective.* Nashville: Vanderbilt University Press, 1968.

Pearce, Charles E. *Polly Peachum: The Story of Lavinia Fenton and* The Beggar's Opera. New York: Benjamin Blom, 1968.

Plomer, Henry R. *Dictionary of the Printers and Booksellers Who Were at Work in England, Scotland, and Ireland from 1668–1725.* Oxford: Oxford University Press, 1922.

Plomer, Henry R., G. H. Bushnell, and E. R. McC. Dix. *Dictionary of the Printers and Booksellers Who Were at Work in England, Scotland, and Ireland from 1726–1775*. Oxford: Oxford University Press, 1932.

Pollard, Alfred W. "*Ad Imprimendum Solum*." *Library*, 3rd series, 10 (1919): 57–63.

———. "The Regulation of the Book Trade in the Sixteenth Century." *Library*, 3rd series, 7 (1916): 18–43.

"Pope and the Pirates." *Notes and Queries*, no. 254 (1854): 197–200.

Ransom, Harry. *The First Copyright Statute: An Essay on* An Act for the Encouragement of Learning, *1710*. Austin: University of Texas Press, 1956.

Raymond, Joad, ed. *News, Newspapers, and Society in Early Modern Britain*. London: Frank Cass, 1999.

Roberts, David. *The Ladies: Female Patronage of Restoration Drama, 1660–1700*. Oxford: Clarendon Press, 1989.

Rose, Mark. *Authors and Owners: The Invention of Copyright*. Cambridge: Harvard University Press, 1993.

Saunders, David. *Authorship and Copyright*. London: Routledge, 1992.

Saunders, David, and Ian Hunter. "Lessons from the 'Literatory': How to Historicise Authorship." *Critical Inquiry* 17 (1991): 479–509.

Saunders, J. W. "The Stigma of Print: A Note on the Social Bases of Tudor Poetry." *Essays in Criticism* 1 (1951): 139–64.

Schwoerer, Lois G. "The Attempted Impeachment of Sir William Scroggs, Lord Chief Justice of the Court of King's Bench, November 1680-March 1681." *Historical Journal* 38 (1995): 843–73.

———. *The Ingenious Mr. Henry Care, Restoration Publicist*. Baltimore: Johns Hopkins University Press, 2001.

Scott, Jonathan. "England's Troubles: Exhuming the Popish Plot." In *The Politics of Religion in Restoration England*, edited by Tim Harris, Paul Seaward, and Mark Goldie, 107–31. Oxford: Basil Blackwell, 1990.

Siebert, Fredrick Seaton. *Freedom of the Press in England, 1476–1776: The Rise and Decline of Government Controls*. Urbana: University of Illinois Press, 1952.

Stallybrass, Peter, and Allon White. *The Politics and Poetics of Transgression*. Ithaca, N.Y.: Cornell University Press, 1986.

Stewart, Susan. *Crimes of Writing: Problems in the Containment of Representation*. Durham, N.C.: Duke University Press, 1994.

Sutherland, James. *Daniel Defoe: A Critical Study*. Cambridge: Harvard University Press, 1971.

———. "*The Dunciad* of 1729." *Modern Language Review* 31 (1936): 347–53.

———. Introduction to *The Dunciad*. Vol. 5 of *The Twickenham Edition of the Poems of Alexander Pope*. London: Methuen, 1943.

———. "John Gay." In *Eighteenth-Century English Literature: Modern Essays in Criticism*, edited by James L. Clifford, 130–43. New York: Oxford University Press, 1959.

———. "*Polly* among the Pirates." *Modern Language Review* 42 (1942): 291–303.

———. *The Restoration Newspaper and Its Development*. Cambridge: Cambridge University Press, 1986.

Thomas, Donald. *A Long Time Burning: The History of Literary Censorship in England*. New York: Frederick A. Praeger, 1969.

Treadwell, Michael. "On False and Misleading Imprints in the London Book Trade, 1660–1750." In Myers and Harris, *Fakes and Frauds,* 29–46.

Vander Meulen, David L. *Pope's Dunciad of 1728: A History and Facsimile.* Charlottesville: University Press of Virginia, 1991.

Varey, Simon. "*The Craftsman.*" In *Telling People What to Think: Early Eighteenth-Century Periodicals from* The Review *to* The Rambler, edited by J. A. Downie and Thomas N. Corns, 58–77. London: Frank Cass, 1993.

Walker, J. "The Censorship of the Press during the Reign of Charles II." *History* 35 (1950): 219–38.

Watt, Ian. "Publishers and Sinners: The Augustan View." *Studies in Bibliography* 12 (1959): 3–20.

———. *The Rise of the Novel: Studies in Defoe, Fielding, and Richardson.* Berkeley and Los Angeles: University of California Press, 1959.

Wayland, Virginia, and Harold Wayland. *Francis Barlow's Sketches for the Meal Tub Plot Playing Cards.* Pasadena: H. & V. Wayland, 1971.

Weber, Harold M. *Paper Bullets: Print and Kingship under Charles II.* Lexington: University of Kentucky Press, 1996.

Weil, Rachel. "'If I Did Say So, I Lyed': Elizabeth Cellier and the Construction of Credibility in the Popish Plot Crisis." In *Political Culture and Cultural Politics in Early Modern England,* edited by Susan D. Asmussen and Mark. A. Kishlansky, 185–209. Manchester: Manchester University Press, 1995.

Williams, F. B. *Index of Dedications and Commendatory Verses in English Books before 1641.* London: Bibliographical Society, 1962.

Winger, Howard W. "Regulations Relating to the Book Trade in London from 1357–1586." *Library Quarterly* 26 (1956): 157–95.

Winn, James. "On Pope, Printers, and Publishers." *Eighteenth-Century Life* 6 (1981): 93–102.

Woodmansee, Martha, and Peter Jaszi, eds. *The Construction of Authorship: Textual Appropriation in Law and Literature.* Durham, N.C.: Duke University Press, 1994.

Index

Acknowledgments

This is a book, at least in part, about the strategies authors use to avoid responsibility for their works. Certainly, one of those strategies is and always has been to find others to bear the responsibility for your work in your place. While trying not to succumb to that temptation, I wish to thank the following people for their help, support, and advice over the time it took to write this book. Whatever is good in it belongs to them.

In the early stages of this project, Neil Saccamano, Laura Brown, Rick Bogel, Walter Cohen, Peggy Phelan, David Halperin, Anna Neill, and especially Roxi Hamilton discussed the work at length with me, offering invaluable assistance in beginning to shape an inchoate mass into something somewhat more coherent. That task was continued at Santa Cruz by Helene Moglen, who read the work at numerous stages and each time offered suggestions that made it better than it had been before. Other colleagues and friends at the University of California, Santa Cruz who nudged the manuscript along in a variety of ways include Bettina Aptheker, Jonathan Beller, Jim Clifford, Susan Gillman, Hugh Raffles, Sharon Simpson, Neferti Tadiar, and Dick Terdiman. To each of them, a special thanks.

The completion of the book was helped along by the advice and friendship of colleagues in the field of eighteenth-century studies—above all, by George Haggerty, the most gentle and generous friend and advisor a scholar could hope to have. Other comrades in the field (and conference coconspirators) to whom I wish to express my gratitude include Srinivas Aravamudan, Katherine Binhammer, Lisa Freeman, and Robert Markley.

Audiences at the Modern Language Association, the American Society for Eighteenth-Century Studies, the Group for Early Modern Cultural Studies, the University of Kansas, Duke University, and the University of Pennsylvania made helpful comments on parts of the manuscript. I am especially grateful to the Stanford Seminar on Enlightenment and Revolution and the Stanford Mellon Seminar on the History of the Book, along with conveners Jennifer Summit, John Bender, Leah Price, and Seth Lerer, for offering me a place to keep up with developments and share work in both fields. I am quite sure many things said in all of these settings have been incorporated into these pages without sufficient acknowledgment.

Financial support during the writing of this book was provided by the Spencer T. and Ann W. Olin Foundation, the Andrew W. Mellon Foundation, the Cornell University English Department, the UCSC Committee on Research, and the UCSC Institute for Humanities Research. Funding for completion of the book was provided by a University of California President's Research Fellowship in the Humanities and—three times—by the UCSC Humanities Dean's Office. My thanks to Dean Wlad Godzich for his assistance and support and for providing a model of committed scholarship at the highest level.

Without the patient work of the UCSC McHenry Library Interlibrary Loan staff, this book would not have been finished. Invaluable help in the preparation of the manuscript was provided by research assistants Becky Woomer, Ian Wallace, Steve Carter, Tallie Ben Daniel, and Scott Thompson. Equally essential help was provided along the way by UCSC graduate students Maria Frangos, Sherri Helvie, and Katharine Norwood. My gratitude goes out to all of them for the care they took with the manuscript and with its occasionally harried author.

The most precious debts are those to friends and loved ones, and these are the ones hardest to reckon with in a site such as this. To my twin brother, James, who lived to see the book finished but not published and who sustained me in countless quiet ways—including providing advice on legal matters—through the many years of its preparation; to my mother and sister, Fayal and Lou, for their unflinching support, general good humor, and devotion to words; to the entire Freccero clan, for welcoming me and giving me a second home; to Chris, for holding me to the highest standards and teaching me why the work is important; to Dana, for always being right there; to the magnificent birthday club—Gail, Grace, Emily, Wendy, and Judy—dearest friends, fiercest advocates, and, dare I say it, role models in both work and life: my love to you all.

This book is for Carla, who named the trouble with ownership, both here and elsewhere. Thank you for giving me the heart to do this, for the divine Biko and Maji (who offer their own resistance to ownership), and for so much else too precious to mention here.

www.ingramcontent.com/pod-product-compliance
Lightning Source LLC
LaVergne TN
LVHW091516200926
848483LV00005B/434/J
9780812238624